THE INDUSTRIAL MUSE

CROOM HELM SOCIAL HISTORY SERIES

General Editors:
Professor J.F.C. Harrison and Stephen Yeo
University of Sussex

CHRISTIAN SOCIALISM AND CO-OPERATION IN
VICTORIAN ENGLAND
Philip N. Backstrom

CLASS AND RELIGION IN THE LATE VICTORIAN CITY
Hugh McLeod

THE INDUSTRIAL MUSE

A Study of Nineteenth Century British Working-Class Literature

MARTHA VICINUS

CROOM HELM LONDON

Z
1029.3
V5
1974

First published 1974
©1974 by Martha Vicinus

Croom Helm 2–10 St. John's Road, London, SW11

ISBN 0–85664–131–6

Printed by Biddles of Guildford

CONTENTS

PLATES

In memory of
my mother

PREFACE

I have incurred many debts during the years of research and writing of this book. The first stage of my research was made possible by the Graduate School and the Department of English of the University of Wisconsin, Madison, and the Ford Foundation. During the years 1966–68 I was provided with funds for a year of research in England and was relieved of a heavy teaching load. In the years 1969–70 I received timely grants from Indiana University, Bloomington, for summer research and grants-in-aid for photocopying, microfilming and other essential material. In the final stages of the research I was aided in countless ways by the staff of the Indiana University Library, particularly the inter-library loan department. I am grateful for their assistance. Evelyn Cramer, who typed the final typescript amidst her duties as Executive Secretary of *Victorian Studies*, has given me unfailing help, cheerfully winding her way through not only my messy copy, but also the vagaries of dialect spelling and punctuation. Her work both on this book and for *Victorian Studies* during the time I have been associated with the journal has been invaluable in countless ways.

My thanks also go to the many local history librarians of northern England who, though they might have thought it bizarre that a midwestern American should be interested in such remote aspects of local history, were unfailingly helpful in searching for rarely examined material. The chief part of my research was done at the following libraries: The British Museum, Manchester Central Reference Library, Newcastle Central Reference Library, the Enthoven Library, Victoria and Albert Museum, the Harris Public Library, Preston, Wigan Central Library, Barnsley Public Library, the Widener and Houghton Libraries, Harvard University, the Memorial Library, University of Wisconsin, and the Indiana University Memorial Library: I have also found material at the Nottingham Central Reference Library, Bolton Public Library, the John Johnson Collection, the Bodleian Library, Oxford, Leeds Public Library, the Goldsmiths' Library, University of London, Sheffield Central Reference Library, Brown, Picton and Hornby Libraries, Liverpool, Halifax Public Library, Cecil Sharp House, London, the Methodist Archives, London, the North of England Institute of Mining and Mechanical Engineers, Newcastle, and the State Historical Society, Madison, Wisconsin.

I would like to thank Robert Wood of West Hartlepool for permitting me to examine his collection of the papers of John Procter, printer. He also kindly took me around the Hartlepool area, showing me nineteenth-century sites of music halls, tent theatres and circuses. A. L. Lloyd and Dan Ross generously sent me material from their collections of industrial folk song and music-hall songs respectively. My thanks to George Falkners and Sons, Ltd of Manchester, for permission to examine and quote from their original account book, 1843–47, and to Ronald Marshall, the Stone Gallery, Newcastle, for permission to quote from the letters of Joseph Skipsey in his possession.

The manuscript of this book was read in whole or in part by the following friends, to whom I am grateful for comments and suggestions: Donald Gray, John Harrison, Louis James, Thomas Milton Kemnitz, Charles Kleinhans, Margaret Myers, Colin J. Partridge, and Marilyn Zilli. Donald Gray and Marilyn Zilli frequently set aside their own work to re-read yet another version of each chapter; their careful criticism has been invaluable and inspiring. I am particularly indebted to Thomas Milton Kemnitz for his assistance in preparing the final copy. His scrupulous reading and incisive questioning helped me to rewrite this book with fewer unexamined assumptions and a clearer organization.

Portions of this book have appeared previously in 'The Study of Nineteenth-Century Working-Class Poetry', in *College English* (February, 1971) and later in *The Politics of Literature*, eds. Louis Kampf and Paul Lauter. My thanks to the National Council of Teachers of English and to Pantheon Books, a Division of Random House, Inc. for permission to reprint this material, held under their copyright.

I would like to thank the Indiana University Photography Laboratory for their preparation of Plates 1, 3, 5, 7, 8, 10, 11, 12, 21, 24 and 29. Plate 2 is printed courtesy of the Sheffield Public Library. Plates 6 and 22, courtesy of the Newcastle Central Library. Plate 9 is courtesy of the Library of Congress. Plates 15, 16 and 18 are courtesy the Manchester Central Reference Library. Plate 19 is courtesy the Leeds Central Library. Plate 20 is courtesy the Bolton Public Library. Plates 23 and 28 are courtesy the Enthoven Library, Victoria and Albert Museum. Plates 25, 27, 30, 31 and 32 are courtesy the Harvard Theatre Collection, Harvard University. Plate 26 is courtesy the British Museum.

INTRODUCTION

It now becomes a matter of the highest necessity, that you all join hands and head to create a literature of your own. Your own prose, your own poetry . . . would put you all more fully in possession of each other's thoughts and thus give you a higher respect for each other, and a clearer perception of what you can do when united.

THOMAS COOPER   "To the Young Men of the Working Classes"

The literature of the working class has been little explored. Although studies of the literature written for the poor and the poorly educated have been written,[1] it has been tacitly assumed that the working class had no literature beyond the vaguely defined perimeters of popular culture. Those who have noticed the poetry columns of working-class newspapers and periodicals have dismissed the verse as 'thin and feeble'.[2] There appears to be almost unanimous agreement with T. H. Lister in the *Edinburgh Review* that 'Experience does not authorize us to regard it as probable, that the world will be favoured with any poetry of very exalted merit from persons in humble life and of defective education.'[3] The overwhelming condescension of scholars toward the literature written by working people arises out of a long tradition of judging art from a position of educational superiority. What we call literature, and what we teach, is what the middle class — and not the working class — produced. Our definition of literature and our canons of taste are class bound; we currently exclude street literature, songs, hymns, dialect and oral story telling, but they were the most popular forms used by the working class. This book is a study of the literary achievements of the working class. The focus is upon the cultural environment and assumptions of self-educated writers, their literary preoccupations and careers, and the content, form and structure of their writings.

This literature must first be considered from the perspective of the working people who read and wrote it, for it functioned in their lives in a number of important ways. Its character was due largely to the conscious efforts of educated workers who wished to gain cultural recognition along with social and economic justice. It helped to shape individual and class consciousness by clarifying working men's relationships with those who held cultural and political power. It also imbued a sense of class solidarity that encouraged working people to fight for social and political equality. Working-class literature, however, both

1

mirrored and negated the literary values of the dominant culture. Some writers were ambiguous about their relationship to their own class and to their 'betters' and alternately attacked and reinforced the values inculcated by the powerful. A central issue in the making of working-class culture was the struggle to create and sustain a distinctive literature in the face of bourgeois economic and cultural control.

Since working-class writers believed that literature could influence people's behaviour, they wrote to persuade readers to adopt particular beliefs. Some hoped to convince them to change the social and political status quo; others to embrace the values of the middle class and its literature; and still others reassured their readers of the value of their own culture within a class-based society.

The politically aware wished to create a literature favourable to working people to counteract the effect of popular literature written for the poor, which glorified the wealthy and aristocratic and treated working people as comic. As the *English Chartist Circular* declared,

> . . . But whenever sketches are given of the poor in any literary periodical, it is generally the composition of some clever, irresistible humorist, seeking to raise, it may be, a good natured smile, or even a broad grin at provincialisms; the peculiar habits and usage of trade, the eccentricities of individuals remarkable in some other mode than their poverty, but how rarely do we hear of the benevolence, the active sympathy, or charities of the poor.[4]

The writers who answered the *Circular's* call emphasized both the virtues of the working class, and described the injustices of society that prevented the full development and recognition of the positive qualities of working people. They wrote to arouse and focus social tension in order to channel it toward specific political actions. Their literature was an assertion of new class values.

Not all working-class writers were involved in politics. Many saw writing as a means of escaping their class roots, or of creating a small haven within a world they disliked and could not leave. They embraced the culture they had learned in school or in books as superior to that surrounding them, and wrote imitations of the masterpieces of the past. Their literature defused their own, and their readers, social frustrations and asserted the necessity if not validity of the status quo.

The most common function of working-class literature was re-assurance: writers described and defined working-class strengths and difficulties to reaffirm the merit of their class in the face of the cultural domination of the upper classes. Writers – and readers – accepted a class-ordered society and their place in it. They provided both entertainment and consolation within the sphere of the familiar. By mirroring the best qualities ofpub life, courting or the home, these writers and performers were particularly popular among the many working people who enjoyed reading, or attending a dialect reading or the music hall. A great many songs protested against existing conditions, but offered only consolation and confirmation of traditional values. They were an effective outlet for social tensions among those who believed they could not change the conditions that had brought about their present situation. This literature asserted the autonomy of the working class, but did not posit a new world view, lest the gains of class solidarity be lost irretrievably.

Self-educated writers struggled against severe adversity in their efforts to write a literature they and their readers could respect. As Gerald Massey said, 'Poverty is a poor place to write poetry in.' He also mentioned the added difficulties of overwork, a lack of privacy or leisure, inadequate education and a lack of intellectual encouragement.[5] This backdrop of personal struggle cast a shadow over many writers' lives and works. But since reading had changed them, they were convinced that others would be equally affected by their work, if it were sufficiently inspiring. Their hopes saw fruition in sales, reviews and general acclaim; for the less successful, authorship was its own reward, providing satisfactions worthy of sacrifice.

The extraordinary strength of bourgeois culture in the nineteenth century affected working-class culture in many ways. Self-educated men read deeply in its literary tradition and admired its achievements; they incorporated many of its suppositions into their own work. Although efforts were made to strengthen an alternative, radical tradition, based upon Milton, Burns, Shelley and Byron, they were countered by greater forces. Many writers judged themselves and their peers by the standards of the literary establishment; the closer they came to their favourite writers, the better they fulfilled their own expectations. Those who drew upon their heritage of traditional songs and such writers as Burns felt limited to writing humorous or sentimental songs; for their highest efforts they imitated the most regarded authors. Outside of the Chartist movement – which made political demands upon writers – those who did not adhere to bourgeois aesthetics had few guides and little encouragement.

Every ambitious working-class writer had to deal with the literary market place. The middle class controlled the major publishing houses, distribution and reviews. Those who published locally or with a small radical firm could avoid complying with middle-class presuppositions but profits probably would also elude them. Successful journalists or performers were forced to write too much or to adopt a style that would appeal to the maximum number of people. They were tempted to sacrifice their class base for a mass base to avoid controversy and gain greater popularity. The result of these economic influences was an uneven literature. Many writers hesitated to break away from the familiar; those who most strenuously supported their own class could become bombastic and sensational. Nevertheless, good working-class literature was produced which spoke with a clear and confident voice about and for the people; it should not be forgotten.

The best way to approach this literature is not through a general description or survey, but through detailed studies of specific areas, people and problems. Much working-class literature is repetitious, and too many unfamiliar names blend into an indistinguishable composite figure. I have concentrated on the foundations of working-class literature where so many themes, approaches and attitudes were formed. However, in the second half of the century, the music hall and dialect literature were of great importance, and are studied in detail as the fruition of nineteenth-century working-class literature. I have drawn most of my evidence from those areas most intensely affected by the Industrial Revolution — Lancashire, the West Riding of Yorkshire and the coal mining districts of the Northeast. These areas also had the longest traditions of folk songs and lore, upon which the new industrial culture was built. I have also considered the national Chartist movement and the London-based music hall. With the exception of the Chartist Ernest Jones, I am concerned with working-class writers who began their adult lives as working men. The best educated and most talented often became teachers, lecturers, journalists and performers, but few began with the expectation of such success.

Although a great deal of ground is covered in this book, much has also been left out. I have not examined improving literature or religious material, nor have I considered the tunes that often accompanied the works I discuss. I have not attempted to include Ireland or Scotland where folk traditions were richer in many ways than in England, and have proven stronger against the onslaught of the mass media. Since I have chosen to study a few areas in depth, other equally interesting areas have been slighted — Birmingham, Nottingham and many other towns had active working-class literary groups. I have not included a study of the literature of the socialist movements of the late nineteenth and early twentieth centuries; a study of it would make a valuable comparison with Chartist literature. Although women wrote verses for political movements, including their own separatist organizations, and they were often responsible for reading aloud to their husbands, fathers or brothers, very few published regularly. In the three areas I have studied intensively I found only some half-dozen volumes, published by working-class women. Here as in so many other cases, we know little of the riches of working-class literature. This book is an initial foray. This study is organized around the major types of working-class literature in the nineteenth century. There is no clear line of development in this literature, nor any developing 'great tradition'. The appropriate model for working-class creativity isperhaps best drawn from sociology; it varies as much as the workers' response to industrialization and urbanization. I have chosen the most dominant forms during their strongest periods in order to establish the variety and strength of working-class literature. The major areas are street literature, political writing, dialect and the music hall. I have also included a chapter on literature imitative of the mainstream of English literature since the largest quantity of poems belongs to this category.

Chapter 1 is a discussion of street literature, the roots of nineteenth-century working-class literature. As literacy became a cornerstone of industrial society, reading matter had a powerful effect upon the traditional culture of the labouring poor. The shift from a predominantly oral to a largely written culture went hand in hand with the development of an industrialized working class. This chapter traces the changes in the literature written by working people – largely broadsides and ballads – during the years of greatest economic and social change, 1780–1830.

Chapter 2 is a case study in the use of literature as propaganda. All organized groups seeking social change in the nineteenth century used literature to disseminate their beliefs; leaders of the working class were not slow to recognize the importance of literature in teaching both their followers and the general public about their cause. The mining unions of the North-east built a new literature upon the rich folk, religious and political traditions of the miners, and therefore are a particularly good example of a phenomenon to be found throughout England. Writers wrote to inculcate the virtues of sobriety, self-discipline and solidarity; they created a new specifically working-class culture to replace the traditional folk culture.

The aims of the Chartists, discussed in chapter 3, were much more complete; they desired no less than the creation of a people's literature.

They wrote about the role literature should play in workers' lives, about the kind of literature that should be written and about the culture that would exist after Chartist goals had been achieved. They drew from the poetic and fictional conventions of both popular and established English literature in order to create a new class-based literature. Although not always successful by their own terms, they wrote a remarkable variety of works, establishing the primacy of political literature.

Chapter 4 is a discussion of working men who imitated the major writers of English literature. These men wrote to escape an uncongenial environment, to enrich their own lives and to offer a better culture to their readers. Psychologically and financially dependent upon their middle-class patrons, their works are largely inoffensive portrayals of established values.

Chapter 5 considers the dialect writers of northern England. The efforts of the Chartists to found a class-based literature culminated in the dialect literature of 1860–85. The main subject matter of dialect writers was the daily life of workers; they attempted to recreate actual events and conversations. The values of family contentment, sturdy liberalism and class solidarity gave both strength and unity to workers who shared the idyllic world of these writers, reciters and singers.

The final chapter is a discussion of the musical hall. It was a vital form of entertainment for working people seeking an escape from their ordered, disciplined working days. It began as a regional class-based entertainment, but with the development of a national network of halls, the star system, booking agents and national financing, it became a London-based mass entertainment. Performers at first shared a communal art with their fellow workers, but by the end of the century they sold a commodity to purchasers. With this shift to a cash-nexus entertainment, working-class literature merged into a mass popular culture or into the literature of the dominant middle class.

My sources have been drawn largely from local history collections in the libraries of northern England. A great deal of material is available on individual authors in obituary columns, local histories and newspapers; when available, personal papers, diaries and letters were most helpful. Local newspapers, magazines, Mechanics' Institutes and other organizations published the writings of working people regularly. Memoirs and reminiscences have provided insight into the lives of writers. Since this is a ground-breaking study I have included a full bibliography of sources.

Notes

1. See Richard D. Altick, *The English Common Reader: A Social History of the Mass Reading Public 1800–1900* (Chicago: University of Chicago Press, 1957); Margaret Dalziel, *Popular Fiction 100 Years Ago* (London: Cohen and West, 1957); and Louis James, *Fiction for the Working Man 1830–1850* (London: Oxford University Press, 1963).
2. See, for example, John W. Osborne, *The Silent Revolution* (New York: Scribner's, 1970), pp.162–3.
3. 'Review of *Attempts at Verse, by John Jones, an old servant; with some account of the Writer by himself; and an Introductory Essay on the Lives and Works of Uneducated Poets*, by Robert Southey', *Edinburgh Review*, 54(1831), p.81 [Authorship per Wellesley Index].
4. 'A Simple Story', *English Chartist Circular*, I (1841), p.162.
5. Gerald Massey, *Poems and Ballads* (New York: J. C. Derby [based on 3rd London ed.], 1854), pp.xx–xxi.

CHAPTER 1 Street Ballads and Broadsides: The Foundations of a Class Culture

Ye muses who mount on Parnassian towers,
Come trooping to Sheffield, and help me to sing
The time when our sons have all got their sours,
And relate all the joys that our Saturdays bring.

This study of the literature of the British working class will begin with an examination of street ballads and broadsides, the foundation for a more diverse and sophisticated literature. During the late eighteenth and early nineteenth centuries the labouring poor were coming to look upon themselves as a separate class, with separate interests, political demands and culture from their 'betters', be they the middle class or the aristocracy. Street literature flourished with few influences from above, and was the most natural outlet for literary feeling, protest and public comment. Throughout the nineteenth century its main purpose was to amuse and inform its readers, but unlike the music hall, it was never taken up by the wealthy and made into a mass entertainment. It was also important in socializing and politicizing those who found their old habits and customs inappropriate, but who had not yet internalized the new patterns of behaviour and attitudes of an urban and industrial society. As the educational level of the people rose, individual writers sought more sophisticated forms to communicate their thoughts, and broadsides appealed to a narrower audience. But even in decline they were an introduction to literature for the very poor who had little access to other light reading matter.

I will discuss in Part I the major characteristics of broadsides at the beginning of the Industrial Revolution, and how they reflected traditional customs. Part II is a description of those who published, wrote and sold street literature – the men who sustained the old traditions and conveyed the new. Part III is a discussion of how this literature reflected the needs and aspirations of the urban poor during the years 1780–1830 and a discussion of the transition from a predominantly oral culture to a literate culture. Part IV is an analysis of those Lancashire weaving songs that reflect the attitudes of people to the early Industrial Revolution.

I

Broadsides and Traditional Customs

Broadly defined street literature encompasses any printed matter sold on the streets, but far and away the most important was the broadside, a ballad or tale printed on one side of flimsy paper, and sold for a penny or halfpenny.[1] They were the most widely available reading matter among the urban poor until the rise of penny dreadfuls in the 1820s and '30s. Working-class housing was overcrowded, poorly heated and lit, so people spent a great deal of time on the streets and in pubs. Hawkers and singers had a ready-made audience in these crowds, particularly since broadsides had a reputation for topicality. Sung or read aloud, broadsides gave a very large number of people access to current events, trade customs, local legends and the cultural life around them.

The street ballad had been printed from the sixteenth century, but in the eighteenth century it took on characteristics that carried over into an industrializing society. Increasingly people wished to hear about themselves – the common man as hero. 'The Golden Vanity', where the cabin boy is betrayed by the captain after sinking the enemy's ships, is a good example of the new attitudes grafted upon an old form. In 'Gil Morice', a Glasgow ballad first published in 1755, alterations appear to have been made so that the page boy is the voice of moral right. Willie refuses to carry a message to a lady for his master, and when forced to do so, he betrays her by speaking in front of her husband.[2] In 'The Sheffield Apprentice', a perennial broadside favourite, the hero is faithful to the chamber maid, Polly, and refuses his mistress's overtures. Rebuffed, she has him hanged for thievery; as he goes to the gallows he swears, 'May God forgive my mistress, for she has wronged me.' Pages and messenger boys in earlier ballads were rarely the heroes.

Another side of the increased interest in the common man was the development of a feminine point of view in many ballads. By the eighteenth century women had become the main repositories of traditional songs, and the major purchasers of romantic broadsides. Part of the popularity of 'The Sheffield Apprentice' was clearly due to the number of readers, or listeners, who identified with Polly and admired her lover's fidelity. Despite the predominantly humorous treatment of love and sex in street ballads, romanticism thrived. New stanzas were added to old songs explaining the woman's point of view. Many ballads began with a woman out walking on a May morning (adventures never occur at home); she soon meets her true love and after a brief courtship is happily married, or is betrayed. These women frequently did the wooing, aggressively volunteering their sexual charms. In both 'The Mower' and 'Buxom Young Lass' the maid invites the mower to enter 'her little meadow' 'that ne'er has been trampled down.' 'Lady Jane' in 'The Pretty Factory Boy' foils her father's attempt to send her lover off with a press gang. She pleads her case before the captain, 'who refused to take her golden store/But quickly did discharge and set her factory lad at large.' This combination of forthright independence and romantic love can be seen in the nineteenth-century 'The Collier Lass (see Appendix). Polly Parker from Worsley thinks of a collier lad that 'strangely runs into my mind,' but she also adds 'should he prove surly and will not befriend me,/Perhaps a better chance will come to pass.'

From their origins broadsides had catered to a demand for sensation and scandal. Violence remained one of the most popular subjects throughout their history; in 1850 a street patterer told Henry Mayhew, 'There's nothing beats a stunning good murder, after all.' The more traditional broadsides played upon the superstitions of readers, evoking fears of hell and the return of the devil to punish transgressors. By the late eighteenth century murders, rapes and arson were most commonly narrated in the first person, emphasizing the wrongdoer's guilt and repentance. They concluded with general admonishments against wrong and prayers for forgiveness. A major change at this time was toward a combination of sexuality and violence. In agricultural areas long-winded ballads about desperate murders and rapes became unusually widespread. 'The Miller's Apprentice', about an apprentice who murdered his beloved, circulated from the beginning of the eighteenth century, and then became extraordinarily popular during the years 1780–1850.[3]

Broadsides along with the unstamped press were the poor man s newspaper until the rise of the popular press in the 1850s.[4] The unstamped contained more news, political analysis and factual information, but did not reach as wide an audience as broadsides, which printed headline news without too much concern for factual accuracy. They covered every conceivable event from the supposed rows between members of the royal family, pecadilloes of MPs, fashions, and various battles fought by the British overseas. The treatment of subjects was dramatic – grandiose gestures of patriotism, moral indignation or comic dismay invariably found favour amongst buyers. At every public hanging hawkers sold the last dying confession of the culprit and the details of the hanging itself – all printed before the event, and therefore available before any newspaper. Occasionally a printer was caught out;

the broadside 'Execution of J. Rutterford' has a note added to it, 'This man was to have been hung; but they let him off because they thought it would hurt him.'[5]

The foundations of nineteenth-century working-class culture were laid in the eighteenth century with the consolidation of trade customs and traditions. Old processes which had governed the work of artisans were clung to as a defence against machinery in some trades and a new capitalist spirit of wage cutting in other trades. For hundreds of years colliers had kept all the Christian holidays, plus 'collier Monday' and paydays. They celebrated these days by wearing 'posey jackets' (waistcoats with embroidered designs) and silver buckles on their shoes, and by going dancing and singing.[6] In time heavy fines checked absenteeism, and religion and social mores stopped the colourful clothing, but well into the nineteenth century miners enjoyed a broadside ballad describing their holidays. Samuel Bamford, from Lancashire, described in his autobiography the numerous local customs and superstitions practiced in his youth at the end of the eighteenth century. He particularly relished the rush-bearing ceremonies, dancing and singing. In Sheffield until the 1840s cutlers celebrated a 'Lozin', when an apprentice came of age. Early in the morning the cutlers at his workplace announced the day by striking suspended ingots of steel with their hammers. At night a supper was provided and the young man was toasted with the song,

> This young man's health, an it shall gooa rahnd,
> It shall gooa rahnd, it shall gooa rahnd;
> This young man's health, an it shall gooa rahnd,
> It shall gooa rahnd, hoi o!

The following verses were then sung, each man enacting the words:

> Houd yer likker a boon yer chin, &c.
> Oppen yer mahth, an let likker run in, &c.
> O'l houd ya a crahn it's all gone dahn, &c.

Culminating in,

> Here's a health to he, that is nah set free,
> Which once was a prentice bahnd;
> It is for his sake, this holiday we make,
> An sooa let his health gooa rahnd[7]

It was a wonderfully rousing ceremony, particularly since the life expectancy of cutlers was about thirty-five years; breathing metal dust

quickly brought on lung diseases. And they refused safety devices for
fear of making their vocation too attractive, and thereby glutting the
market with workers.[8]

Most of these trade ceremonies and customs were linked to specific
privileges and honours. Their demise before the demands of punctuality
and orderliness in the industrial world represents a defeat for the
artisan. The last procession and ceremony for Bishop Blaize, the
woolcombers' patron saint, was in 1825 in Bradford. The woolcombers
staged an elaborate ceremony involving hundreds of workmen; there
were several bands, shepherds and shepherdesses, 'royalty', and the
members of the various friendly societies dressed in the colours of their
trade. The procession began at ten in the morning and continued until
five. This show of strength, however, proved hollow. Six months later
the woolcombers, some 20,000 strong, were defeated in a strike that
broke their union and effectively ended their prestige and power.[9] The
new trade unions and the Chartists created similar ceremonies at their
mass meetings. Individual lodges were encouraged to march to open-air
meetings carrying banners and playing instruments, and the speakers'
stands were decked with bunting. The banners, and the meetings
themselves, were a symbol of the workers' strength, and an emotionally
satisfying link with past customs.

Verses were especially composed for these important ceremonial
events. In addition, many songs were written in the eighteenth century
celebrating particular trades. These were usually a raucous declaration
of the superiority of a particular shop, pit or skill; the dominant tone
was self-confidence and pride. These songs survived long after the
particular skills they celebrate had been superseded. In 'The Collier's
Rant' the miner skilfully knocks off the devil's horns and club feet with
one swing of his pick. Despite the loss of some verses and phrases this
song remains very popular; it was sung at the nationalization ceremonies of the National Coal Board in 1947. The private language and
lore of an occupation were always used, making some songs almost
incomprehensible to outsiders. The rousing 'Cum all yo Cutlin Heroes'
is a call to the flat-back knife makers of Sheffield to hurry and finish
their work in order to go to a 'penny-hop', a dance in a local hall in
which the cutlers and their girl friends each paid a penny for the cost of
the band and the room. Before they go the singer brags about his skill,
showing off 'won at o've just fooaged uppa Jeffra's bran new
stidda;/Look at it well, it duz excel all'd flat backs e ahr smitha.'*

*"One that I've just forged upon Jeffrey's anvil; Look at it well, it does excel all
other flat-backs I ever forged."

A number of songs praised particular characters, real or mythical, who were capable of great prodigies of work. Various occupations were popular metaphors for sexual intercourse. The ploughman had long been a familiar figure, sowing his seed, and leaving the woman to reap a 'bonny bairn'. Urban variations included shoemakers, builders, grocers and cutlers. Many of these songs show great ingenuity and humour, and not a few are naturally delicate, such as 'The Mower', about a mower whose scythe is too dull to mow a young woman's field.

The great bulk of broadsides were about romance, sensation and topical events, but they also included local commentaries, trade songs and political statements, making them one of the most complete sources for studying the development of working-class culture. Their range of both subject matter and attitudes was greater than the unstamped press or other more specifically political working-class publications. They were by far the most widely available reading matter. Moreover, they reflected and rarely led or manipulated popular attitudes. Broadsides heightened the awareness of new readers, and encouraged literary creativity. In time working-class culture came to encompass not only ballads, but also poetry, essays, fiction and autobiographies. But this new culture did not arrive one day at the railway station; it had to be fought for and gained individually and collectively by literate working men and women. The broadside was one of their major weapons in this struggle.

II
The Printers, Sellers and Singers of Street Literature

Broadsides were an important source of profit for many publishers, singers and sellers. By the beginning of the nineteenth century hundreds of printers (seventy-five in London alone) sold broadsides and chap-books, achieving enormous sales throughout the country. H. P. Such, one of the largest and longest lasting firms (1849–1917) had over 5,000 titles available for wholesale purchase, including both broadsides and music-hall songbooks. In 1859 W. S. Fortey advertised 4,000 ballad titles alone. Circulation figures, however, are difficult to estimate accurately. One informant told Mayhew that 10,000 copies of his song 'Husband's Dream' were sold. By working day and night for eight days with four presses, Catnach printed 250,000 copies of 'The Full, True and Particular Account of the Murder of Mr Weare by John Thurtell and His Companions.' It has been claimed that 2½ million copies describing the murders of Rush and Manning were sold.[10] The only rivals in circulation were the Religious Tract Society and the Society for Promoting Christian Knowledge, but they gave away most of their publications. In the year 1820 the S.P.C.K. published 700,000 tracts. Like Catnach, it found executions a good site for disseminating broadsides. At one, 42,575 were distributed; at another, 40,850.[11]

The publishers' expenses were minimal and profits could be enormous, though the business was highly speculative. Song writers were invariably paid a shilling a song, no matter how many copies were later sold. The flimsy paper cost 1s. per gross for quarter-size sheets, 2s. per gross for half-sheets and 3s.6d. per gross for whole or broadsheets suitable for execution speeches. (An even cheaper blue-grey stock had been used until competition from Catnach in the 1820s forced publishers to buy a thin white paper.) Second-hand type and wood-cuts were bought cheaply from printers going out of business or replacing their stock. The printed broadsides were sold to sellers for 3d. or 5d. per dozen, yielding them a profit of 7d. to 9d. if each sheet brought a penny.[12] The printers might be paid in script, or unsold broadsides. After this became illegal some publishers paid workmen with the pennies they had received from sellers; Catnach, notorious for his parsimony, is said to have made £500 on the murder of Rush, and up to £10,000 during his career, from 1813 to 1838.[13]

Little information has survived about individual entrepreneurs other than Catnach; often the only available facts are legal notices. John Marshall of Newcastle was in business from 1801 until 1831, when he declared bankruptcy. The auction advertisement for his stock speaks of 'upwards of 300 superior Wood-Cuts, of Great Beauty and Variety, by the celebrated Mr. Bewick', and a circulating library 'of upwards of 6,000 volumes'. During his prime Marshall was one of the largest publishers outside London; he published almost every variety of chapbook and broadside, but specialized in 24-page songbooks.[14] He was also the only printer in Newcastle willing to print the pamphlets of the miners' union in 1825 and 1826. Aside from these facts and the date of his father's death, nothing is known about him. Equally little is known about John Harkness of Preston, who apparently published from 1838 until 1875 or 1880. He reprinted most of Catnach's works, in addition to his own repertoire of local songs; his numbered broadside collection goes as high as 1,200, but no complete set exists. In addition to broadsides, he briefly printed and published *The Preston Illustrated Times*. After his death his collection of blocks, print and stock were taken to Blackburn and sold for waste material.[15] The leading London printer before Catnach was John Pitts (1765–1844), the son of a Norwich baker, who set up business in Seven Dials in 1802. Pitts revived many traditional ballads; he also found it profitable to bring old country songs to London, and to send copies of the latest hits from the pleasure gardens and supper clubs out to the rural villages.[16]

'Jemmy' Catnach (1792–1841) was the son of an Alnwick printer, James Catnach (1769–1813). The older Catnach left his family in poverty, with little more than a wooden press with which they started business in London. Jemmy, however, quickly built up a trade through ruthless and enterprising business methods. He bought whatever cocks – false stories – he thought would sell, including a thinly disguised story of a Drury Lane butcher who made sausages from human meat. This landed him a six-month sentence for criminal libel in 1818. While he was in jail two of his chaunters were arrested for tooting their horns and circulating information about a nonexistent murder.[17] Catnach continued to sell a series of traditional chapbooks and song books printed from the stock he had brought from the North, but his remarkable success lay in picking up fads. He lost no time in publishing several verse episodes about Tom and Jerry during the *Life in London* craze of the early 1820s. The Jim Crow songs of the 1830s brought forth an endless stream of imitations, including such titles as 'Jim Crow's description of the London Lasses', which has nothing to do with Negro minstrels, or even London lasses. Catnach's financial success, however, was guaranteed by his popular pieces on murders and last dying confessions. Yet here again he used ingenuity – and illegal methods. His most famous hoax was after the hanging of John Thurtell, the murderer of William Weare, when he published a ballad with the headline 'We are alive again'. The first two words were printed so closely together that persons were tricked into believing Weare had miraculously returned.

For all of the entrepreneurship of Catnach and his rivals, they followed rather than led public opinion. Cocks, last dying confessions and mysterious foretellings answered a need within the poor themselves. Critics have seen the lurid descriptions of murders and hangings as pandering to the more unfortunate side of common life, and have taken at face value Mayhew's patterer who claimed, 'I find a foolish nonsensical thing will sell twice as fast as a good moral sentimental one, and while it lasts, a good murder will cut out the whole of them' (vol.I, p.251). Obviously a murder was exciting and gave the ordinary buyer a taste for vicarious excitement. But such a simple judgment does not take into consideration conditions in the slums. Near murders, brutal beatings and physical mutilation were common events on many streets. This closeness to violence and brutality produced two reactions: a total denial, built upon the ethic of respectability, or an embracing of the inevitable. The respectable turned inward to their homes, and separated themselves from street life. (Much of the literature to be discussed in Chapters 4 and 5 was aimed specifically at such working-class families.) Others recognized the facts of violence — wife beatings, pub brawls union quarrels and the like — and found some means of coping with these facts. The most obvious outlet for many was drink. Another less recognized way was literature. The melodramatic situations and striking descriptions of penny novels and broadsides provided forms and language for understanding the daily violence of one's own life. Despite the undeniable fact that Catnach, G. W. M. Reynolds and Edward Lloyd concocted recipes of robbery, rape and murder which sold in large quantities, they also provided readers with a means of interpreting and managing violence. The lives of many working men and women were all but melodramatic in their oscillation between over-work and no work, deaths and births, individual injuries and diseases, and other occurrences bringing unforeseen and unwanted 'adventure'. The litera-ture of escapism was rooted in a reader's daily concerns.

The 'Confession of the Murderess' on the broadside 'The Esher Tragedy: Six Children Murdered by their Mother' portrays a state of mind which many readers must have recognized — overcrowded housing, excessive hours of work and poor health were common enough to working mothers.

On Friday last, I was bad all day; I wanted to see Mr. Izod, and waited all day. I wanted him to give me some medicine. In the evening I walked about, and afterwards put the children to bed and wanted to go to sleep in a chair. — About nine o'clock, Georgy (meaning Georgianna) kept calling me to bed. I came to bed, nearly 12 o'clock. I had one candle lit on the chair — I went and got another, but could not see, there was something like a cloud, and I thought I would go down and get a knife and cut my throat, but could not see. I groped about in master's room for a razor — I went up to Georgy, and cut her first; I did not look at her. I then came to Carry, and cut her. Then to Harry — he said, 'don't mother.' I said, 'I must,' and did cut him. Then I went to Bill. He was fast asleep. I turned him over. He never awoke, and I served him the same. I nearly tumbled into this room. The two children here, Harriet and George were awake. They made no resistance at all. I then lay down myself.[18]

Most cheap fiction or narrative poetry was florid and redundant, filled with clichés, inaccurate metaphors and other stylistic errors. In contrast, conversations or confessions could be terse, realistic and moving. Both 'The Rent Day' (p.31) and 'The Esher Tragedy' are written in this more natural style. The accompanying verses on this broadside tell the reader 'She nursed the blooming Prince of Wales'. This information does not lift Mary Ann Brough into a romantic world; rather, it reinforces the anguish of her unnatural deed. No one, not even a wetnurse for royalty, is safe from the cloud of despair. The accumulation of factual information conveys an atmosphere of relentless terror. Facts do not dispel the irrational, but intensify its pathos. Art here defines – and makes intelligible – life.

Despite the moving pathos of 'The Esher Tragedy' and other similar confessions, the accusations of sensationalism hurled at Catnach and other broadside printers were not totally invalid. It is difficult to separate class-oriented street literature from other forms of cheap literature; both were criticized indiscriminately. Broadsides were certainly influenced by penny dreadfuls, political pamphlets and scandal sheets. If exciting accounts of seduction and thievery were wanted, they were provided; popularity was the main criterion of publication. Yet, broadsides were never as scurrilous as the 'criminal-conversation' journals, such as *The Town* (1840), *Crim-Con Gazette* (1838–40) and *Paul Pry* (1826), with their delight in aristocratic adultery and innuendo. One ballad writer indignantly told Mayhew that all the indecent songs were written by 'lords and gentlemen, and city swells, and young men up from college' who frequented the Cyder-cellars and night-houses (vol.I, p.278). In comparison urban broadsides were often simply crude and silly in their treatment of sex. Street literature had always been irreverent toward love, and often but a short step from coarse farce. The influence of the scandal sheets and cheap fiction was sufficient to push many nineteenth-century broadsides into a bawdy self-consciousness.

A good example of this kind of broadside is 'The Old Woman of Rumford',

> There was an old woman of Rumford,
>   And she was a gay old lass.
> And many an honest penny got,
>   By selling asparagrass.

As through the streets she goes,
  With her barrow as she'd pass,
Soliciting her customers
  To buy her precious Ar --
    (Chorus) tichokes an' Colliflowers,
    Come buy, come buy of me,
    They are the finest of the sort,
    That ever you did see.

This old woman had a daughter,
  And the girl her name was Ciss,
And she went into the garden
  Every morning for to pick
Some parsley, time, and sage,
  Likewise some asparagrass,
To decorate her barrow,
  When she cried come buy my Ar -- tichokes, etc.

This old woman had a lodger too,
  Who used to bed and board,
She resolved one morn to treat him with
  A good brown roast tur-key.
She boiled some colliflowers,
  Likewise some asparagrass,
For she had made a lucky hit,
  And sold her precious Ar-tichokes.[19]

The lodger, instead of being pleased, threatens to 'kick your precious Ar-'. But the old woman offers him £500 if he marries Ciss, and the offer is closed. The young man ends by attending parties,and everywhere drinking to the success of 'the old woman's Ar-'. The agricultural metaphors of sex, from traditional ballads, have been debased; as costermonger's vegetables they lose much of their resonance. This coy and crude treatment of sex and money was quite popular in the larger cities. Yet, if reading last dying confessions provided solace for those facing intolerable conditions, so might such songs as this provide amusement and relief at a time when sexual roles were confused and changing.

    One of the most popular subjects of the mid-century was the comic bachelor. He is made to look foolish by aggressive mothers and daughters or is trapped into marriage. Often enough he deserves his fate. In 'Slap-up Lodgings' the young man is arrested for lodging in a bawdy house, and 'Six months upon the mill, with ups & downs & dodgings,/I serv'd against my will, thro' being in slap-up lodgings.' The bawdy songs sung at all-male parties are a continuation of a long-established outlet for sexuality that cannot otherwise be expressed in an industrialized society. This argument, however, does not deny the fundamental purpose of both dying confessions and bawdy songs for Catnach and other publishers – to make money. When other products sold better, broadsides were gradually dropped. By the 1860s twopenny and threepenny songbooks with the latest music-hall hits were more popular, and few new titles were added that did not have their origins in the halls.

The gradual shift to songbooks obviously hurt broadside writers, but even during their prime most were anonymous hacks. Since they were usually paid only a shilling a song, many had to hawk their own works. Mayhew estimated their number to be only six in London, and their weekly wages to average ten shillings; this estimate is probably too low, but it is difficult to prove otherwise. A Catnach favourite, John Morgan, was interviewed by both Mayhew in 1851 and Charles Hindley in 1870 and 1876. Morgan appears to have turned to writing songs because it was neither laborious nor difficult. He started at eighteen, when Catnach first took over his father's business; he wrote songs, assisted in setting type, buying paper and doing other hand work. Morgan lived into his seventies, long after his verse-writing skills had become obsolete. He is the only known London song writer, and it is impossible to distinguish his work from others.[20]

The character of broadsides was revealed in the selling. The chaunter brought to life the story or song, portraying it dramatically to catch the eye of potential buyers. As a skilled performer he considered himself above the ordinary costermonger or vendor, but his income was as precarious as theirs. It varied markedly with the weather (rain and snow emptied the streets) and the topicality of the broadsides offered (a murder was soon old news). Many chaunters relied on a few houses where they knew they could receive donations, either to leave the neighbourhood or because a wealthy gentleman collected broadsides. Mayhew calculated that chaunters who sang, numbering about 200 in London in 1851, averaged 3s. a day, while sellers earned 7s.6d. to 10s.6d. a week (vol.I, pp.306–9).

The proper presentation of a song was essential to attract a buyer. A chaunter, as the name indicates, sang in a monotonous flat twang to conserve his voice and to be heard above the other street noises. He began with a spoken patter, directed toward the audience gathering around, including some local gossip and commentary, while recommending the purchase of the new song about to be rendered. He would then launch into selected verses, calling upon the audience to join in the choruses, pausing to make sales, while keeping an eye out for the police or possible trouble-makers. The audience was left in suspense about the conclusion of the tale to encourage buying the broadside. Those who performed in pubs provided convivial entertainment to increase the sale of beer, and were therefore dependent upon the largesse of the publican. They had their faithful clientele and earned a smaller but possibly steadier living. Their singing style was similar to the outdoor chaunter, with more emphasis on group singing and on songs about the pleasures of drink.

In the larger cities broadside sellers specialized in their selling methods and material. A 'running patterer' worked with other persons, who ran about shouting out the latest catch phrases, such as 'Horrible', 'Frightening', or 'Recent Events'. Amid the clamour they pointed to the seller, who would sell as many copies as he could without revealing the contents. These broadsides were frequently cocks, describing nonexistent murders or fires. The Houses of Parliament burned several times for the benefit of running patterers. However, they could not work the same neighbourhood frequently. During the time of the unstamped press standing patterers would sell straws and give away such periodicals as Carlile's *Republican*; by the 1850s pornography was occasionally sold in this manner, but most standing patterers specialized in ballads on a subject – love, battles or hard times. In the rural areas ballad sellers also sold small household necessities, such as thread, needles, etc. Groups of sellers known as 'death hunters' walked from village to village selling last dying speeches and execution scenes. They carried a long pole with a canvas suspended between two horizontal cross-bars; on one side was a vivid scene of the murder, and on the other that of the execution.[21] The broadsides purported to carry an authentic picture of the villain, who invariably confessed his guilt and begged pardon of man and God just before his death.

The nineteenth-century broadside seller was very different from the traditional singer. The former sold his songs, whereas the latter performed his regardless of the size or importance of his audience. The traditional singer was as impersonal in his presentation as his ballards; he saw himself as a conduit passing on the words to the listener, who would naturally understand and appreciate them. One singer stopped in the middle of her song to exclaim to Cecil Sharp, 'Isn't it beautiful?' – not her singing, but the song itself.[22] Such performers were equally indifferent to the authorship of a song. On occasion they would claim to have written a well-known ballad, or would say a neighbour had written it since her life history resembled the heroine of the song. Patterers, on the other hand, heightened the excitement and mystery of a work by claiming it was written by an underpaid curate or a sister of mercy or a popular poetess, but seldom by one of the people. Because the streets were crowded and noisy, the vendors had to shout or dance to attract attention. The Irish Come-all-ye's, sung with many gestures, may have been another source of the chaunter's style. Street ballads were sold to passers-by, and were not part of a shared, communal art, as were the songs of an oral tradition.[23] Chaunters were forerunners of music-hall artistes in their style and salesmanship. Although broadsides were an integral part of popular culture, they contained the seeds of a commodity-based mass entertainment.

Buyers were usually young people, interested in romance and adventure, though occasionally the singing of a traditional ballad might attract an old country woman. An inability to read did not stop buyers, since they could either piece together a few choruses or they could find a sweetheart, fellow servant or the seller himself to spell out the words. Servant girls out running errands were a favourite audience. They had virtually no free time except what they could steal from under the eye of their mistress. Shopping for the household was one of the few ways a young girl might meet her suitor, or loiter on the way home to listen to the latest gossip or a song. She might be able to purchase a broadside with her grocery money without being caught. On quieter streets bored or curious housewives could be lured from their homes to listen to a song or an interesting bit of news. Young men wishing to keep abreast with the latest songs would buy a copy of the words from a seller. Sunday was usually the best day for chaunters because working people were out on the streets or in their doorways looking for diversion. The bane of many a seller's life was the ubiquitous street urchin, who was looking for pennies that might escape the seller, or for pockets to pick, or simply for excitement. They never had money to buy broadsides, but they attracted the attention of policemen and kept away the cautious and more respectable.

The noisy street hawker had been a target for persecution since the sixteenth century. The pressing demands for order and respectability in the nineteenth century led to increased agitation against him. Even Henry Mayhew, normally sympathetic to street sellers, considered chaunters to be a species of mountebank, gulling the less educated. As early as 1819 the residents of Oldham Street, Manchester, presented a petition to the magistrates, complaining,

> We the undersigned inhabitants of Oldham Street, Manchester, respectivelly [sic] present this memorial to your worship; -- That we are everyday (except Sundays) troubled with the pestilent and grievous nuisance of profane and debauched ballad singing by men and women, to the corrupting of the minds and morals of the public in general, and our children and servants in particular. We therefore most humbly request, that you will use the power committed to you, in removing this evil immediately; and we will ever acknowledge of the benefit.[24]

Law and order forced the hawker out of the more respectable neighbourhoods, and working conditions curtailed the time in which people could listen to him. As the century progressed leisure and work became increasingly separated into distinct and different times. In the cities entertainment was at night and inside; chaunters who could not adapt by finding a friendly pub usually went into the country. There men and women could still stop their work without penalty to listen to a song or tale.

Most sellers and chaunters were anonymous characters who lived by their verbal skill and wit. However, in many towns and in specific parts of London, a few song writers who sang and sold their works were well-known favourites among the working people. As eccentrics who satirized local persons and issues, they were midway between the traditional singer from the country and the noisy hawker. Unwilling or unable to hold a regular job (in coal-mining towns singers were almost invariably ex-miners injured in a pit accident), they still identified with working men. Since they were not dependent upon the good will of a master or the 'better' classes, they could tread close to personal libel. Their songs had a wit and daring lacking in the more laboured tracts and songs of organized groups. They usually had favourite pubs or streets where they could be found, ready to write a song for a drink or a few pence.

One of the most colourful ballad writers of the early days of industrialism was Joseph Mather (1737–1804) from Sheffield. He sometimes sold his songs riding through town sitting backwards on a donkey, from which he would sing, cajole and sell. One rainy day he rode straight into his favourite public house. He attended all the fairs and races, singing and hawking with success, but his greatest influence was among the cutlers. Brought up a Methodist, he frequently used biblical allusions and stories to emphasize the injustice of those who oppressed the workers. A frequent metaphor, which recurs throughout the nineteenth century in trade-union struggles, was Pharaoh's tyrannical treatment of the children of Israel and God's wrath against those who mistreated His people. Mather's most famous song was 'W   's Thirteens', an attack on the Master-Cutler Watkinson who tried to enforce thirteen knives to the dozen when paying workmen in the 1780s (see Plate 2):

> That monster oppression behold how he stalks
> Keeps picking the bones of the poor as he walks
> There's not a mechanic throughout this whole land,
> But what more or less feels the weight of his hand
> That offspring of tyranny, baseness and pride,
> Our rights hath invaded and almost destroy'd,
> May that man be banish'd who villainy screens,
> Or sides with big W   with his thirteens.
>
> And may the odd knife his great carcase dissect,
> Lay open his vitals for men to inspect,
> A heart full as black as the infernal gulph,
> In that greedy blood-sucking bone scraping wolf.[25]

For years afterwards many master-cutlers quaked when they heard these words, and an apprentice was reportedly jailed for singing them under his breath.[26]

'Blind Willie' Purvis (1752–1832) was Newcastle's most famous town eccentric (see Plate 3). He could usually be found at a popular public house singing traditional songs and his own works. He also had a regular round of houses where he would run errands for refreshment or a gratuity. Blind Willie, without a hat and in the traditional buckled shoes of a keelman, was known throughout Newcastle for his strange appearance and unfailing memory. One morning he was satirizing a local dignitary, when to tease him someone called out that the man was approaching. Willie immediately recognized the impostor's voice and proceeded to torment him with his verses and jibes. His favourite song was 'Buy Broom Busoms', which he rendered as a mixture of traditional verses and his own comments about local people. To have Willie sing

'Call at Mr. Loggie's/He does sell good wine' was excellent publicity.[27]
In Blind Willie's day much of Newcastle was crowded along the Tyne.
The closely packed streets and chares made it easy to slip in and out of
different pubs, listening to gossip and singing. Men from every class
dropped by Willie's pub to mingle with the crowd. In later days he was
remembered nostalgically as an example of a freer, happier time.[28]

Bradford's Reuben Holder (1797–?) was a licensed hawker who had
started life as a trapper boy at five years, later became a brickmaker,
and finally a seller of fish and poetry. As a strong teetotaller before the
temperance movement, he wrote many poems against drink. He also
wrote appropriate verses for all important events in Bradford, including
such newsworthy items as 'A correct account of the fire at Bradford,
which took place on Sunday morning, the 13th of July, 1838', various
verses 'on the distressed state of the country', and both the traditional
and the new celebrations of the West Riding. He supported Oastler's
factory movement, but attacked the local Owenites as godless 'poor
silly men . . . those cowards and shufflers', for their refusal to debate
with the Rev. Joseph Barker.[29] One of his most popular broadsides was
'The New Starvation Law Examined – on the New British Bastiles
[sic]', against the regimentation of the New Poor Law workhouses.
Some lines have the zest of Mather: the men who passed the Law are
described as 'Like the fox in the farm-yard they slyly do creep;/These
hard-hearted wretches, O how dare they sleep.' He also accurately
mirrored his readers' anger:

> There's many poor children go ragged and torn,
> While they and their horses are pamper'd with corn;
> Now is not this world quite unequally dealt?
> The Starvation Law by some few is felt.
>
> When a man and his wife for sixty long years
> Have toiled together through troubles and fears,
> And brought up a family with prudence and care,
> To be sent to the Bastile it's very unfair.[30]

Holder, like Blind Willie, was fiercely loyal to the crown. He composed
verses on the coronation, the christening of the Prince of Wales and
other royal events, proclaiming the loyalty of the residents of Bradford.

Town commentators such as these three could be found until the
middle of the nineteenth century. But increasingly public readings, the
free-and-easies, and other indoor entertainments caught the working

man's pennies. When the town eccentric died, no one replaced him. The tradition of commemorating local events with a broadside however, continued throughout the century. Manchester was large enough to support at least five versifiers all of them with nicknames such as 'the Bard of Colour', which applied to a West Indian writer. Typical of this generation is Barnsley's George Hanby (1817–1904), known as 'Peter Pledge' because of his ardent espousal of temperance. He worked as a surfaceman at a colliery near Barnsley and supplemented his income by writing verse. Much of his doggerel was written for charitable causes. One with a self-explanatory title was 'Verses on the Temperance and Sunday School Tea Meeting, held on the 11th of November, 1864, in Miss Pilkington's Reading Room, Newmillerdam, near Wakefield, convened for the purpose of presenting a testimonial to Mr. William Gates of Rotherham, late of Barnsley, for his unwearied zeal in the Church Sunday School at Walton.' 'The viands were luscious and told on each face,/For the sign of a cloud was not seen in the place' is a sad decline from 'The New Starvation Law Examined'. The specifically educational function of the town rhymer had dropped away, and his work had become purely celebratory. Holder or Mather voiced the complaints of the people, and explained various new laws or regulations and their possible effects. Hanby, on the other hand, merely offered commemorative verse that described an event interesting only to those who attended.

However, by the time Hanby came to write, social divisions were channeled into many different institutions. Within the trade unions, the tradition of public debate, exhortation and song continued throughout the century. The union's bard was expected to turn out a song for every occasion, educating members and the public. Tommy Armstrong (1848–1919) (see Plate 22), from Durham County, explained his responsibilities to the community, 'When you're the Pitman's Poet, they say: What's wi' Tommy Armstrong? Has someone druv a spigot in him an' let oot all the inspiration?'[31] And so Tommy wrote songs about the union, drinking and community gossip. But the majority of talented singers and writers who wished to escape the discipline of the pit or factory went into the music hall, journalism or teaching. An established dialect reader could earn thirty shillings for an evening's entertainment, while a successful music-hall artiste earned fabulous sums. Better paid and educated workers demanded a higher level of entertainment and could support full-time professionals — and it was more comfortable inside a warm hall. Marginal town characters could not join such an ordered society.

III
Broadsides as an Introduction to a New Life

The town eccentrics provided songs for every class of person, but they also sold printed copies for their listeners to take home. They were among the many social pressures that encouraged people to learn to read. From 1760 to 1840 literacy rates rose steadily but slowly to about 66 per cent for men and 50 per cent for women in 1840, increasing to nearly 100 per cent for both sexes by 1900. Some evidence suggests however, that literacy may have fallen in the larger cities during the early years of the nineteenth century. Moreover, estimates of literacy — based on marriage licenses — may be exaggerated because many of the very poor never married.[32] But the level of literacy needed for reading a broadside was low; many who could not sign the marriage license, or did not read a newspaper with ease, might be able to piece together a song. Even when there were relatively few economic incentives to learn to read, many social incentives existed in the rapidly growing towns. Pressures to keep up with the times, or to read about the latest murder or romance were stronger than they had been in the country. Obviously by 1840 considerable social distinctions separated the respectable working people who needed reading skills in their daily work from the very poor whocould not read and worked irregularly. The continuation of broadsides beyond the 1840s provided a popular and cheap means of learning to read. Throughout the century broadsides were instrumental in helping the poor to make the transition from an oral to a written culture.

Broadsides included many pre-literate devices, such as rhymes, repetitions and proverbs. Woodcuts, fanciful allusions, attractive type and secret information all lured the new reader. Old tales, known from oral circulation, were often published in a new manner. 'The Far Famed Tale of Fenella' is a tongue-twisting updated version of the eighteenth-century French tale 'Beauty and the Beast.' Conundrums, riddles, and textual mysteries, popular as parlour games, were also enjoyed by the newly literate. Writing was often treated comically, perhaps because it was less frequently taught. Readers could enjoy reading mistakes they might actually commit themselves. In 'Pretty Maidens Beware!' Sarah writes her 'lovin der Charls', swearing 'I will be yowr der vartus wife til deth', and 'A Poetical Version of the foregoing', properly spelled, was added. These comic and dramatic visual devices encouraged new readers to buy street literature.

The curiosity of the literate could be captured by that common broadside topic, the hidden love letter or speech, which was usually written in a simple code or a mirror image. 'Extraordinary and Funny Doings in the Neighbourhood' has four verses at the top of the page describing the interesting peccadilloes of neighbours, with the mocking refrain 'Mind your/their/my own business.' The gossip is general enough to be applicable to any neighbourhood, giving the seller the opportunity to pretend that he has the latest information about an area. The verses are followed with two mystery letters whose humour could only be understood by the literate. The gentleman addresses his love:

Madam,
    The love and tenderness I have hitherto expressed to you is false, and I now feel that my indifference towards you increases every day, and the more I see you the more you appear ridiculous in my eyes, and contemptible — I feel inclined and in every respect disposed and determined to hate you. Believe me I never had any inclination to offer you my hand. Our last conversation I assure you left a tedious and wretched inspidity which has not possessed me with an exalted opinion of your character, your inconstant temper would make me miserable, and if ever we are united, I shall experience nothing but the hatred of my parents, added to the everlasting, pleasure in living with you, I have a true heart to bestow, but however I do not wish you for a moment to think it is in your service, as I could not give it to one more inconstant and capricious than yourself, and one less capable to do honour to my choice, and my family. You, Madam, I beg and desire you'll be persuaded that I think seriously, and you will do me a great favour to avoid me. I shall excuse you taking the trouble to give me an answer to this, as your letters are full of nonsense and impertinence, and have not a shadow of wit and good sense. Adieu, and believe me truly, I am so averse to you, that it is impossible I should ever be, Madam, your Affectionate Servant and Lover. R. G.[33]

The truth is easily found out — at the bottom is a warning, 'By reading every other line of the above letters the true meaning will be found out.'

    A mixture of oral elements with those that must be written characterized the broadside throughout the nineteenth century. Later

in the century readers came more exclusively from the poorest sections
of the city or countryside, but it is precisely these persons, who, like
the many members of the new working class a generation earlier, were
in transition between an oral culture and literacy. Remarkably little
changed in the form of street literature during the century. However, it
changed in tone, becoming more satiric and self-mocking, as literacy
became widespread and essential for daily use. An amused and detached
view of 'progress' became a common attitude. Skilled workers were
increasingly successful in pushing their political and economic demands;
their educational and social needs were met by a different, more
'useful' class of literature. In contrast, the marginal, unskilled worker
found little improvement in his lot, and therefore took a sceptical view
of 'progress' and 'self-help'.

Many of the labouring poor felt that they would have to pay, one
way or another, for every improvement made, and doubted if their own
lot would ever be fundamentally altered, except for the worse. 'The
March of Intellect in the Butchering Line' is typical of this ironic view
of progress. The phrase 'the march of intellect' had been popularized in
the 1820s by Lord Brougham, the head of the Society for the
Diffusion of Universal Knowledge, as a sign of the inevitability of
human progress.

> I keep a snug shop, which once had a good stock in,
>   But the life I now lead is indeed very shocking;
> I contrive to get money by industry's plan,
>   My family spend it as fast as they can,
> My spouse, who once work'd hard as any wife going,
>   By this 'march of intellect's' so genteel growing.
> She dresses herself and her daughters up fine,
>   Although I am but in the butchering line.

> Spoken — She takes in all the penny publications, though
> she can't read without spelling the hard words — makes
> poetry though she can't write, and as to blank verse,
> makes nothing of it — she had made herself a HALBUM
> out of an old day book, and my eldest daughter write
> down all the good things they can scrape together — if
> she goes into the shop to serve a quarter of a pound
> of suet, or a pennyworth of lights, she puts on a
> pair of white kid gloves, with the fingers cut off —
> and its all through the march of intellect.[34]

The butcher goes on to complain about the new fashion of learning French, drinking Madeira wine, and wearing the latest feminine apparel. His family's social pretensions drive him into bankruptcy. Although written from the butcher's point of view, the mocking tone undercuts any sympathy for his plight. The broadside is a comic attack on the social distance 'the march of intellect' has created between the poor and the 'shopocracy.' Broadside readers felt that so-called progress had brought only greater social divisions, and the butcher's bankruptcy was a perfectly just fate. 'The New Times' and 'The Hand-Loom Weavers' Lament'(see Appendix) are serious treatments of this same theme.

Yet the march of intellect clearly had an impact upon the common people. Literacy was obviously no guarantee of a better job, nor of more common sense, but it did lead to a different attitude toward oneself and others. Psychologically literacy separates one from others, intensifying a sense of individualism and of differences among individuals.[35] Oral transmission becomes suspect in comparison with the finished and seemingly complete printed explanation of events. Printed matter also alters a person's sense of time. Events can be frozen in print, where they can be re-examined. As print becomes a normal means of communication, those who cannot read are barred from vital contacts. Those who can are given new powers; they can accept, reject and select information from a variety of sources.[36] Before the nineteenth century partial literacy among the people had already begun altering individual and group perspectives. Laissez-faire capitalism, pitting worker against worker in a scramble forjobs, accentuated this heightened individualism. Literature as a means of communication and of binding persons together came only as the second stage of the march of intellect. The first stage was individualism and self-awareness.

The conservative and religious hoped that literacy would make the poor humble, obedient and Bible-reading; the radical hoped it would give order and unity to inchoate struggles. But the effects of literacy proved more complicated. Certainly it was the foundation of learning, but it became above all else a cheap form of entertainment. Street literature, penny dreadfuls and tracts provided wonderful and astounding adventures. Reading matter, however, also aided working people in adjusting to and understanding the urban experience. Comic explanations about renting a room, buying and cooking food and travelling in the city recreated experiences readers had undergone, giving order and humorous distance to them. Many city dwellers knew they were being cheated, but their only weapons were humour and guile — two lessons broadsides taught easily and cheaply.

The newcomer to the city was obviously fair game, and many broadsides mock the country boy following the first pretty girl to come up to him. But equally popular was 'the biter bitten', a familiar theme in pre-literate tales, about the shrewish wife silenced, the flirt seduced, the Don Juan ditched or the country bumpkin who defeats the wiley city lass. In 'Quite Politely' the canny Yorkshireman foils a beautiful pickpocket by putting fish hooks in his pockets; the hooks catch her diamond ring. A more bawdy version finds 'Country John' offering a crown to the 'pretty young damsal',

> O where shall we go for to find a bed,
> That I may enjoy your sweet maidenhead,
> Why dang it says she there's no head to be found
> But I'll show you fine sport as I lie on the ground.[37]

Several verses later everyone in town has the 'p   '. Broadsides such as these offered the protection of humour to young men who might feel uncertain about themselves and life in the city.

Comic broadsides drew attention to injustices and focused anger against tradesmen, landlords and others who seemed to profit from the poor. 'New Intended Act of Parliament, agreed to by Sir John Fairplay, and seconded by Mr. Steady, for the public good', is a humorous attack on shopkeepers who adulterated food. Since the poor could not afford to buy the very best quality goods, they often received watered milk, flour with bone dust and tea with sloe leaves. The 'act' goes on to admonish women who drink gin, men who beat their wives and foolish bachelors and old maids. A frequently reprinted 'quarrel poem' is 'Fifteen Shillings a Week', with versions for eight, eighteen and twenty-five (for tradesmen). The wife details how she spends every farthing her husband earns, down to a penny for poison for fleas, twopence for 'the chamber pot you broke', and a penny for him to read a newspaper at the local coffee-house. An interesting variation on this is 'A Humorous and Interesting Dialogue' between a master and one of his men who earns twelve shillings a week. The master accuses the workman of being drunk the night before. When the man defends himself, explaining that his weekly expenditures leave him no money to get drunk, the master declares meat is unnecessary for the poor. Just as the workman drives home his best arguments, the conversation is cut short by the master fining him a quarter of a day's wages for wasting his time talking. The dialogue ends leaving the reader to draw the obvious conclusion: workers must organize to prevent such tyranny.

A good example of an entertaining and educational broadside is 'The Rent Day, or Black Monday Morning', exposing a landlord who cheats his good tenants, but has difficulty squeezing anything out of everyone else:

Well, Mrs. Paywell, have you got any rent for me? – Yes, sir. – You are the best tenant I have got; let me see, 20s., here's your receipt. – Stop, sir, before I pay you this money, you must send a bricklayer and a carpenter; there's the top of the house wants repairing, the stairs are all to pieces, and the privy door is off, and I am desired by my husband not to pay you a farthing till you have put the whole in complete repair. – No. I won't repair it at all, so if you don't like it leave it. – Yes, but I am not a going to give you 20s. When it rained the othernight we were obliged to get up, and move the children into the middle of the room, and my husband and I were compelled to keep up all night with an umbrella over our heads to keep the rain off. I think if landlords were as fond of sending carpenters and bricklayers as they are of sending bailiffs, it would be more to their advantage, – But, Mrs. Paywell, where's your husband, I must speak to him about it. – Why, he's at work, and he can't afford to lose a day to wait on you, so as soon as you get the repairs done here's your money.

> Away then he goes, for he's quite in the dumps,
> And at the next door he gives some hard thumps;
> But on looking up you'd have thought he'd have swooned,
> For his tenants were gone by the light of the moon.

Now, I'll call on Mother Lushy, Well, my little girl, is your mother at home? – No, sir, she popped out as you popped in. – Has she left any rent for me? – Yes, sir, she left 9d. in the teacup on the mantlepiece. – What, 9d. out of two months. Why your mother must think I'm a fool. – No, sir, mother says you're an old rogue. – Well, tell her I shall send the broker. – She says you have broke her of the last 9d. she had. – Has your mother left any money in the teapot? – No, sir, there's only a quartern of gin in it that mother was going to drink, but she went out in a hurry. – Ah, I suppose she knew I was coming. – Yes, Mrs. Longface told her the old rogue of a landlord was coming.

> You see how the tenants the landlords abuse,
> If you ask for your rent you're sure to get abuse;
> They'll pester your brains about lots of repairs,
> But who pays the rent, there is nobody cares.[38]

Lest the reader feel too much sympathy for the landlord, Mrs. Meek reveals in the next episode that he has illegally gained control over property rightfully belonging to Mr Neasy's son, but she is bribed into silence by free rent. 'The Rent Day' is a vivid recreation of probable events ina conversational style similar to a fable from Bunyan. Short direct sentences, witty puns and colloquialisms add to the humour and realism. The reader or listener need only transfer the characters with allegorical names to her own courtyard. She mighthink her landlord a crook, and suspect her neighbours; the pleasure of reading about such goings-on would give her confidence in her understanding or another perspective on her situation.

All of these broadsides treated serious subjects with a humour that protected and encouraged the reader in her or his daily struggle. However, a great many songs were filled with zest and vitality for the customs and holidays growing up in the new cities, created under changed circumstances. For young people the city meant many more opportunities to meet each other and to seek out a whole range of recreations beyond the control of parents, local squire or minister. The very anonymity of the city was part of its excitement, attracting them to the streets, where so much took place. The density, richness and variety of popular entertainment can be seen from the number of broadsides about the theatre, fairs, horse races, boat races, music halls and, of course, the Crystal Palace. Saturday night was the most popular time of the week, with work done and a free day ahead. The Sheffield song 'Saturday Night' describes the various activities, or 'stirrings', of the cutlers and their girls, including the comment 'some ballad singers so slowly are walking/And warbling so sweetly their lays in the street.' 'Victoria Bridge on Saturday Night' describes similar stirrings in Manchester. It was a hard time for shop clerks, but everyone else went out buying, courting and generally enjoying themselves.

Seven Dials, the home of all the main London printers, was close to Drury Lane and the theatre district; every evening the aggressive hawkers and chaunters would 'busk' for the waiting crowds. Important theatrical events were sure to yield a crop of new broadsides. The O.P. (Old Price) riots in the autumn of 1809, protesting the introduction of higher prices at Covent Garden, were zealously discussed by men and women who probably could not afford even the cheapest of the old prices, but felt involved with an issue that had political ramifications. 'Snip in the Gallery; or Play up Nosy' is about typical broadside buyers at the theatre. Snip the tailor takes his girl to the shilling gallery and is attacked by a barber and a cobbler. The woodcut accompanying the song shows the cobbler kissing the girl and the crowd yelling at the disturbance.[39]

Almost every event had its broadside – a boat race, a visiting dignitary, the opening of a new public house, and the many traditional holidays. Local pride was particularly strong in the growing industrial towns. 'Manchester's Improving Daily' (see Appendix) shows no doubts about the advantages of living in the town, 'a rare fine place', where 'country folk' cry out 'Laws! Pickle and presarve us!' A more ambiguous song is 'Preston's Alterations', in which the anonymous author declares 'When Bess did reign on England's throne, the houses were built of clay,/But now they are built of stone and brick, and a brass knocker takes the sway.' The coming of the factories is a less pleasant change:

So now to conclude and make an end if I am not mistaken,
Where roast beef once was eat, now is eaten American peas and
    bacon;
Potatoes now are grown so bad, and so are people's wages,
For the world is now all going by steam – it can't last many days.[40]

Newcastle was one of the liveliest and most prosperous towns of the early nineteenth century. It was a traditional trading centre, where the annual races and fair drew pleasure-seekers from the entire region. The local pitmen often went to Newcastle to celebrate their payday. Since the town was also a printing centre for the North, it was easy to get works published; many Northumbrian songsters sold out quickly, even at 6s. and 10s. a copy. Songs usually went through a winnowing process in the local theatres and pubs; only the best appeared in books or chapbooks.[41] Three men led in song writing at the turn of the nineteenth century: Tommy Thompson, a timber-merchant, John Selkirk, a merchant, and John Shields, a clerk. All three wrote most of their songs while they were young and still enjoyed visiting the quay-side; as early as 1807 parodies of their work appeared, along with satires on 'The Bards of the Tyne'.

The most famous character of the time was the miner 'Bob Cranky', the subject of many songs that were sung everywhere in the Newcastle area. 'Bob Cranky's 'Size Sunday' (1806), the first and most famous version, celebrates Assize Sunday when 'the Judges went to St Nicholas Church, [and] the cavalcade was an imposing sight, with Sheriff boys and trumpeters dressed in their gorgeous liveries.'[42] All the miners in the area, dressed in their posey jackets, went to Newcastle to see the famous parade. John Selkirk (1783–1843), who died mysteriously in poverty, was the original creator of Bob. Selkirk and the other Newcastle song writers were not miners, and an air of condescension creeps into many of their songs, but the miners took to Bob as one of their own. The celebration of holidays, and the accompanying joys of dancing, drinking and wooing mattered more than Bob's rough, 'od smash' behaviour. Indeed, such boisterous behaviour was considered appropriate on special occasions in the Newcastle area around the turn of the nineteenth century, and was celebrated in 'Wreckenton Hiring', 'XYZ at Newcastle Races' and other Bob Cranky style songs.

Bob prepares for the big day by putting on his special holiday clothes, and calling together his mates and girl friend to walk with him into Newcastle. They engage in friendly jostling and sparring about who is the best hewer and who Nancy loves best, but they see all the fine people, and have a happy dance in the ale house before staggering home.

When aw pat on my blue coat that shines se,
My jacket wi' posies se fine se,
  My sark* sic sma† threed, man,
  My pig-tail se greet, man!
Od smash! what a buck was Bob Cranky.

Blue stockings, white clocks+, and reed garters,
Yellow bre&ks○, and my shoon wi' lang quarters,
  Aw myed wour bairns⊕ cry,

*sark: shirt †sic sma: such small, i.e., fine +clocks: ornamental figure on the ankle ○breeks: trousers ⊕wour bairns: our children. In northern England 'our' is often used to refer to members of the family. For example, instead of 'my sister Jane', they say 'our Jane'. Thus, Bob refers to his younger brothers and sisters.

Eh! sarties!* ni! ni!
Sic verra fine things had Bob Cranky.

Aw went to awd Tom's and fand Nancy;
Kiv aw, lass, thou's myed to my fancy!
    Aw like thou as weel
    As a stannin-pye heel†,
Ho'way to the toon wi' Bob Cranky.

    . . . . . .

'So, Geordy, od smash my pit sarik+,
Thou'd best haud thee whist about warik,
    Or aw'll sobble thee body○,
    And myek thee nose bloody,
If thou sets up thy gob to Bob Cranky.'

Nan laugh'd — t'church we gat without 'im;
The greet crowd, becrike, how aw hew'd 'em!
    Smasht a keel bully roar'd,
    'Clear the road! whilk's my Lord?'
Owse⊕ se high as the noble Bob Cranky.

Aw lup up, an' catch'd just a short gliff□
O' Lord Trial, the Trumpets, and Sheriff,
    Wi' the little bit mannies☆
    Se fine and se canny,
Ods heft! what a seet for Bob Cranky!

Then away we off te the yell-hoose,
Wiv a few hearty lasses an' fellows:
    Aw tell'd ower the wig,
    Se curled and se big,
For nyen saw'd se weel as Bob Cranky.

*sarties!: certies! †stannin-pye heel: remains of a roast +sarik: pit shirt
○ sobble thee body: thrash you in a stand up fight ⊕ owse: ought, anything
□ gliff: glimpse ☆ mannies: little men, i.e., boys

Aw gat drunk fit, and kick'd up a racket,
Rove my breeks and spil'd aw my fine jacket;
   Nan cry'd and she cuddled.
   My hinny*, thou's fuddled!†
Ho'way hyem now, my bonny Bob Cranky!

Se we stagger'd alang fra the toon, mun,
Whiles gannin', whiles byeth fairly doon, mun;
   Smasht a banksman or hewer,
   No, not a fine viewer+,
Durst jaw to the noble Bob Cranky.[43]

The subjective first person distinguishes the song from earlier folk songs, but the lack of sentimentalism distinguishes it from later descriptions of a pitman's holiday. By mid-century the relationship between Nan and her two rivals would have been the centre of action rather than Bob. The bullying braggart who drank and danced fell into disfavour, but Bob's pride in his work carried over into very different times, and both trade unionists and Newcastle writers refer to him for many years.

The folk hero who smashes all the bullies, drinks gallons of ale, dances longer than anyone else, and yet hews more coal, could exist only in a tightly-knit community that shared long hours of work and bursts of holiday-making. In the alienated world of the city, frequently the only thing a worker shared with his neighbours was hardship. Urban broadsides mocking outsiders became more common. Mining, cutlery and weaving communities had long had a series of initiation rites for newcomers, complete with songs; now in the new factories and city neighbourhoods teasing a recent arrival was a favourite sport. While still insecure about city ways, confidence could be gained at the price of mocking someone more uncertain. For every 'biter bitten' tale there was one about 'country John' or 'the Yorkshire lad in London' who is defeated by the London lasses. Individuals who had not kept up with the times or were ignorant of local customs were always fair game. In the 1840s the Irishman became a common figure in broadsides; Pat, Paddy or Mike were usually treated with sardonic humour as barely civilized creatures.

---

*hinny: honey, the most common term of affection in the North-east
†fuddled: drunk   +viewer: chief manager of a colliery

Those who had moved to an industrial town or city came to feel as great a love for a grimy, smoky corner as they might have felt for a small country village. Such songs as 'Saturday Night' and 'Bob Cranky's 'Size Sunday' and others like them show the happy side of this love; the emigrant and transportation ballads show the misery of those forced to leave England. The convict songs emphasize the horror of going so far and the hideous conditions in Australia, rather than the crime committed. The felon is almost invariably passive and repentent. 'The Female Transport' has a large woodcut with a woman in irons standing on a small palm-covered island with her arms outstretched toward a departing ship in full sail. Sara Collins (Collings in some versions) was 'enticed by bad company' and so is transported for fourteen years. The trip is described in detail, and so too the conditions in Van Dieman's land, where chained 'two by two, and whip'd and lash'd along,'

We labour hard from morn to night, until our bones do ache,
Then every one they must obey, their mouldy beds must make,
We often wish, when we lay down, we ne'er may rise no more,
To meet our savage governors upon Van Diemen's shore.[44]

The dreary pace, the failure to describe any of Sarah's faults, and the solemn exhortation to the reader to be careful are all characteristics of this genre of broadside. Poaching ballads have more life to them, possibly because most readers did not consider poaching a crime.[45]

Emigrant societies, usually founded by the bourgeoisie or the more prestigious trade unions, distributed broadsides depicting the joys of Canada and Australia, where opportunity met the unemployed worker at the dock. The poor were unconvinced; no street broadside portrays the emigrant as happy; indeed, the most solemn metre and language were always used. The funereal tone captures the resignation and misery of those who felt they had to leave home. A frequently reprinted song was 'The Emigrant's Farewell',

Farewell my love, my Mary true,
Adieu! my native land, adieu!
And now admidst the billows roar,
Good bye! to all my friends on shore.[46]

The emotions are highly generalized, but broadsides were rarely able to rise to an emotional occasion; writers were apt to run to cliché. The natural sequel to 'Adieu!' was 'The Emigrant's Child', telling of a fever on board ship that kills the child, leaving the parents facing 'a foreign shore' 'all in dark despair.' Once on shore, cannibals, heat and more fever were generally expected. To counter this dreariness a few comic songs were written, some with a political edge, such as 'National Emigration', recommending 'Malt-a' to brewers, Guinea to misers, and finally commenting in terse prose, 'A speedy exportation of all knaves, and may a change of country change their habits.' In the 1840s and '50s many songs were written about 'poor Paddy', reflecting the massive emigration of Irishmen to England and the new world. The emotional hold of emigrant songs continued well into the nineteenth century, and many an up and coming music-hall artiste made his career by singing sad Irish songs of emigration.

The fragility of the new customs and order created by working people, rather than that imposed upon them from above, took its toll upon broadsides. The sententious and hackneyed treatment of serious subjects contrasts poorly with the comic works – and yet the ironic pose so many authors took was also debilitating. The topical nature of material encouraged writers to churn out familiar phrases and sentiments. At a shilling a song writers were not paid to take care with their language. Yet the strongest single quality of broadsides persists to the very end – the vitality of the best is far superior to all but a handful of the verses written by better-educated men who were anxious to show off their correct sentiments. Ironic distance, moreover, acted as self-protection; life was often desperate enough, but few survived on complaints, and humour proved to be the backbone of a developing class consciousness.

IV
The Weavers' Response to Industrialization

Broadsides contain a wealth of commentary on industrialization. Many works praise various inventions and improvements, such as 'Steam Boots', about a 'Hollander bold' who wears steam boots to rocket about Europe. But far more common was anger and resistance to change. The intensification of work in the mines and cottages and the development of the factory system meant the death of an older, more varied life. With these changes songs became more critical of the present and nostalgic for the past. The deepest reactions to change came in those areas or occupations that were long established, with their own songs and lore. In contrast, the railways did not yield many songs until after the first two waves of building. (In the United States and Canada the industry was one of the richest in tales and songs; it was the American missionaries who first brought to England the familiar metaphor of the railway to heaven or hell.)[47] The situation was even bleaker in entirely new industries, such as chemistry, or in new towns, such as Middlesbrough. A full generation of an industry was necessary before customs grew up. A new culture, albeit unsettled and fragmented, only came out of settled living patterns.

Cotton was the first major commercial enterprise to alter radically through industrialization; the change from self-sufficient families weaving and spinning at home to the employment of hundreds under one roof to run the new power-driven machinery caused severe cultural and economic dislocation.[48] Stories about those suffering in the 'dark Satanic mills' were all set in Lancashire and the adjoining West Riding — and yet the county's long and respected weaving traditions continued in spite of these enormous changes. The poems and songs dating from the sixteenth century about hand-loom weavers and their lasses were replaced by factory songs, and writing and singing continued unabated. The first and most severe process of industrialization existed side by side with the continuation of a rich and powerful literature and customs.

In eighteenth-century songs the weaver is presented as the backbone of the economy. As one 'Weaver's Garland' declared, 'If weaving and spinning should totally stop,/I am sure the whole nation will instantly drop.' In 'The Weaver' (1769) the young man falls in love with a servant girl. His father is scornful that he should so lower himself, 'When there is ladies fine and gay/Dressed like the Queen of May.' It is a love song, so the young man successfully wins his love, and she spins for him, but clearly the independent weaver was superior to any servant. At times the weaver was made the hero of tales unrelated to his occupation. In 'Will Weaver' a husband who suspects his wife is unfaithful returns home to find Will hiding in the chimney. He builds an enormous fire, sending Will running, with the warning 'Come no more to stop my smoak.' 'Will Weaver' was a favourite in the nineteenth century and was frequently reprinted by Harkness and the Manchester printers.

The tradition of boldness in the face of adversity and comic self-awareness flourished during the golden age of handloom weaving, the years 1790–1810 of the French Wars. Anyone connected with the weaving trade was a natural hero or heroine. At this time the new Dobbie looms, permitting the weaving of elaborate patterns, were widespread in Lancashire. They needed frequent and skilful attention,

so an itinerant joiner was usually called upon to 'square' or fix these
looms. Like so many earlier picaresque figures he was soon
characterized as a free-and-easy blade who attracted the village women.
One of the most popular poems celebrating the life of a joiner was 'The
Bury New Loom', first published as a broadside in 1804:

As I walked between Bolton and Bury, 'twas on a moonshiny night,
I met with a buxom young weaver whose company gave me delight.
She says: Young fellow, come tell me if your level and rule are in
    tune.
Come, give me an answer correct, can you get up and square my new
    loom?

I said: My dear lassie, believe me, I am a good joiner by trade,
And many a good loom and shuttle before me in my time I have
    made.
Your short lams and jacks and long lams I quickly can put in tune.*
My rule is in good order to get up and square a new loom.

She took me and showed me her loom, the down on her warp did
    appear.
The lams, jacks and healds put in motion, I levelled her loom to a
    hair.†
My shuttle run well in her lathe, my treadle it worked up and
    down,+
My level stood close to her breast-bone, the time I was reiving her
    loom.○

The cords of my lams, jacks and treadles at length they began to give
    way.
The bobbin I had in my shuttle, the weft in it no longer would stay.
Her lathe it went bang to and fro, my main treadle still kept in tune,
My pickers went nicketty-nack all the time I was squaring her
    loom.⊕

*lams: foot treadles that operate the jacks. Jacks: levers on the Dobbie
machine that raise the harness controlling the warp thread.   †healds: a loop of
cord or wire through which the warp threads pass; a number of these make up a
harness.   +lathe: supporting stand on the loom ○reiving: to rob or raid
⊕pickers: attachments to the upper end of the picking stick which impels the
shuttle through the warp threads during the weaving.

My shuttle it still keptin motion, her lams she worked well up and
down.
The weights in her rods they did tremble; she said she would weave a
new gown.
My strength now began for to fail me. I said: It's now right to a hair.
She turned up her eyes and said: Tommy, my loom you have got
pretty square.

But when her foreloom-post she let go, it flew out of order amain.*
She cried: Bring your rule andyour level and help me to square it
again.
I said: My dear lassie, I'm sorry, at Bolton I must be by noon,
But when that I come back this way, I will square up your jerry
hand-loom.[4][9]

The familiar form of sexualizing the implements of one's craft has here
a new emphasis on its technicalities. The special knowledge needed to
understand the poem must have been relished by the Lancashire
weaving community. The vocabulary is an amusing combination of
technical terms with overtly sexual images, such as 'reiving her loom,'
'the down on her warp', and 'nicketty-nack', which is not only
onomatopoeic for the motion of the loom but also was slang for the
female sexual organs.

'The Bury New Loom' combines highly specific details with
complete impersonality, partially because it deals with sexual intercourse and not individuals, but also because the writer speaks in
complete confidence that his audience will understand the world he
describes, and the nature of the symbols used. There is no distance
between them and the poem since it is based ontheir own knowledge of
the harmonious movement of an intricate machine as representative of
the most important human actions. The richness of the weaving
community life can be seen in its contribution to the creative
imagination of both poet and reader; only a deeply felt and understood
vocation can become symbolic of basic needs and desires – and be
within the good humour and comedy implicit in this poem. The weaver
and joiner are part of a society in which their identity and actions are
furnished by the machinery that is central to their respective vocations.
Their energy does not go into acquiring each other or material goods,
but into enjoying each other. The competitive pace of power-loom

*foreloom post: the front overhanging portion of a loom.

weaving and factory work was reflected in later poems by the
acquisitive, materially-oriented nature of the verse, but this poem is
based on mutual harmony and good will. It is both a celebration of
sexual pleasure and a reflection of the cultural strength of a vital
community.

The close identification of the couple with the implements of their
craft would not be possible at a later date when factory work left the
operative with less knowledge of the machinery he worked, and
responsibility for only one part of the process of production. Although
a good bit of skill and understanding were needed to work such
imperfect machinery as power looms, the weaver worked under
conditions that divided him or her from the family and from a close
association with all parts of the cloth-making trade. Inevitably the
meaningfulness of a vocation as the symbol of human life was lost; few
persons could feel the necessary intimacy with their work and its tools
to identify with them.

Separate processes during work rather than the work itself became
topics for working-class verse. Factories were rarely described in songs
or poems, other than political works, after about 1830. The work place
became an accepted part of the background, with the emphasis instead
upon plot and characterization. Among the skilled craftsmanship still
flourished, but for the majority of cotton operatives work was a
monotonous routine. They were most interested in whatever might
interrupt this work, be it gossip, courtship or an accident. Illicit
courtship during working hours was a popular subject for many factory
broadsides during the 1830s and '40s. 'Sam Shuttle and Betty
Reedhook' describes the overlooker s love for a steam-loom weaver; he
courts her by coming 'oft her loom to fettle' [fix]. Betty, however,
prefers the cut looker, Billy Crape, who never bates [fines] her for
faults in her cuts of cloth. Billy and Sam fight on Lacky Moor, and:

> When Betty yeard that Sam had lost,
>   On him no notice took, sir,
> But went walkin' out on Sunday last,
>   With that sly old Cut Looker.
> Sam swore he could not stand it,
>   And on 'em no more he'd look,
> He'd blow his brains out wi' his Shuttle
> Or stab him wi' his Reedhook.
>   Tow, row, row, etc.[50]

The jaunty rhythms, realistic details and humorous names make this an amusing and attractive song, but there has been a loss in comparison with 'The Bury New Loom'. The richness and subtlety of the earlier song have been reduced to a simple use of vocational names. The commonplace is defined in and of itself.

'The Bury New Loom' was frequently reprinted as a broadside; in a later version, 'The Steam Loom Weaver', the joiner becomes an engine driver and the woman a power-loom weaver (see Appendix). Poems of a similar type about faithless soldiers, handsome rakes and aristocratic strangers remained popular throughout the century. The old tale of the prince marrying the beautiful and virtuous peasant maid became the tale of the factory girl marrying a rich stranger (see Plate 4). In this sort of song the language is usually more elevated, as if references to Venus and Cupid were necessary to confirm the authenticity of the story. Unlike the handsome young gentlemen factory girls may have met coming home from work, this stranger proves his honorable intentions:

> I said lovely maid if you'll not be my bride,
> My life I will waste in some foreign land.
> What pleasure in treasure where love it is wanting.
> Your beauty upon me has now cast a spell,
> I'll marry you speedy and make you a lady,
> If you'll be mine dear factory girl.[51]

The reverse story of a wealthy damsel in love with a factory boy also existed. In this case the angry father has the boy impressed, but the lady buys his freedom; they marry and live happily ever after. These broadsides seemed within the realm of the probable because they were built upon realistic details, even when the action was improbable. But narratives about 'the fortunate factory girl' and the like were purely escapist. They were most appealing to those many operatives who found their lives uneventful and unnoticed – in contrast to the more tumultuous lives of the very poor discussed earlier.

The general message of this type of broadside is that inexplicable fate rules the characters' lives. In songs that end unhappily for the lovers, such as 'Old Weaver's Daughter' about a girl who turns down a rich courter to remain with her father or 'Factory Girl' about Betsey Gray who proves unfaithful and dies on the streets, events move forward in an inexorable pattern beyond the control of the lovers. Chance guides personal virtue, good fortune or the probable future; it appeared to be the prime mover of life, just as it had appeared to a much earlier peasantry. Only through chance could the monotony of the factory be broken and excitement, happiness or adventure be found. But chance was also the cause of inexplicable periods of unemployment, a poor marriage or personal unhappiness. The theme of virtue rewarded – particularly active, earned virtue – is quite rare, and as a theme would appear to be prominent only in the literature of a more upwardly mobile class or among the religious.

'The Bury New Loom' came out of a well-established community in the midst of prosperity. Although conditions were changing Saint Monday and other holidays could still be celebrated as an escape from work, with the assurance of a well-earned rest. But even then, times of sharp and sudden unemployment could bring a family to the edge of starvation. As industrialization brought a temporarily-improved standard of living, it also meant a change in traditional ways that many older men and women were unwilling to accept. The transitional years of 1780–1830 fell harshly on those in traditional trades, and protest songs were widespread. Many of these songs have survived only in fragments. Those that urged violent actions against factory owners or the putter-out (a middleman who gave out the warps and yarn, and paid for the finished weaving) often circulated orally, lest the printer or seller be arrested. A far more common style of song is the 'consolatory verse', lamenting changes brought about by forces beyond any single person's control. Usually written under the impact of cultural change or economic distress, the best examples rise above the limitations of a specific occasion; they were frequently reprinted later in the century during hard times. These songs and poems were a remarkably powerful form of consolation because they were true to the conditions and attitudes of those who read them both for solace and as an explanation of their plight. Generally few solutions were offered, as in most cases none was available, except the passage of time.

Reactions to the new factories could be swift and bitter. In 1790 Robert Grimshaw attempted to introduce power-loom weaving to the town of Gorton, near Manchester. No sooner was the mill completed and the looms working than the place was burned down. A man named Lucas who could not write and could barely read composed a song in commemoration of the fire; it was very popular at the time but now survives only in a fragment. One verse runs,

> For coal to work his factory
> He sent unto Duke*, sir;
> He thought that all the town
> Should be stifled with smoke, sir;
> But the Duke sent him an answer,
> Which came so speedily,
> That the poor should have the coal,
> If the Devil took th' machinery.[52]

When the Devil did not take the machinery, poor men took matters into their own hands. The underlying justification for fighting the factory system was God and nature – it was against natural laws for men to work such devilish machinery. Weavers were particularly bitter about those who became so extraordinarily wealthy from the new methods of weaving. 'The Hand-Loom Weavers' Lament' has a chorus declaring 'You tyrants of England, your race may soon be run,/You may be brought unto account for what you've sorely done.' (see Appendix). All the time they are growing rich from the labour of the poor, they claim that hard times are the fault of the wars, but the author, John Grimshaw (no relation to Robert), bitterly comments,

> If there be a place in heaven, as there is in the Exchange,
> Our poor souls must not come near there; like lost sheep they must
> range.[53]

Poor men, of course, were not to wander like lost sheep, but to go like sheep into the new factories. Violent protest against factories went hand in hand with a sense of doom. In 'Hand-Loom v. Power-Loom' John Grimshaw recommended capitulation to the inevitable:

> Come all you cotton-weavers, your looms you may pull down;
> You must get employ'd in factories, in country or in town,
> For our cotton-masters have found out a wonderful new scheme,
> These calico goods now wove by hand they're going to weave by
> steam.

---

*Duke: the Duke of Bridgewater, a great coal owner.

In comes the gruff o'erlooker, or the master will attend;
It's 'You must find another shop, or quickly you must mend;
For such work as this will never do; so now I'll tell you plain,
We must have good pincop-spinning*, or we ne'er can weave by
    steam.'

      . . . . . .

The weavers' turn will next come on, for they must not escape,
To enlarge the master's fortunes they are fined in every shape.
For thin places, or bad edges, a go†, or else a float+,
They'll daub you down, and you must pay three pence, or else a
    groat.

If you go into a loom-shop where there's three or four pair of looms,
They all are standing empty, incumbrances of the rooms;
And if you ask the reason why, the old mother will tell you plain,
My daughters have forsaken them, and gone to weave by steam.

So, come all you cotton-weavers, you must rise up very soon,
For you must work in factories from morning until noon:
You mustn't walk in your garden for two or three hours a-day
For you must stand at their command, and keep your shuttles at
    play.[54]

A song such as this opposes the factory system because it destroys a
traditional way of life, even when it brings prosperity. The young
women left their handlooms because they made more money in the
factories, and were willing to accept the harsh regulations and orders
from 'the gruff o'erlooker.' (A generation later Betty Reedhook flirts
with the overlooker Sam Shuttle.) But in the eyes of many cotton
weavers the factories were humiliating places for pauper children.
Others were fearful for the character of their daughters; the masters or
the overlooker might threaten blacklisting if a woman refused their
sexual overtures. The hand-loom weaver was a proud maker of cloth
who controlled his own working hours and could look upon his finished
product with pride; to enter the factory meant becoming a 'hand',

    *pincop-spinning: a pincop is a pear shaped cop or roll used for the weft in a
power loom.
    †a go: break or tear.
    +a float: the passing of weft threads over a portion of the warp without
being interwoven into it.

controlled by a machine. One hand-loom weaver declared in 1834, 'I am determined for my part, that if they will invent machines to supersede manual labour, they must find iron boys to mind them.'[55]

A later poem, 'The Factory Bell,' dating from before 1840 protests against the factory system because it forced men to compete against each other for jobs, and because of the lack of good will within the factory. While just as fatalistic as Grimshaw's song, the author recommends 'man to man do what is right', and then 'Each would enjoy his little store,/And die in peace when life is o'er.'

> Oh, happy man, oh happy thou
> While toiling at thy spade and plough,
> While thou amidst thy pleasures roll,
> All at thy labour uncontroll'd
> While at the mills in pressing crowds
> Where high build chimneys puff black clouds
> And all around the slaves do dwell,
> Who are called to labour by a Bell.
>
> You have just got time to eat & sleep
> A man is set your time to keep;
> And if you chance to come too late,
> You'r mark'd on paper or on slate
> No matter e'er what be the cause,
> You must abide by their own laws,
> All the time you draw your wage
> For coming late there's so much charged.
>
> And if a word chance to be spoke,
> Some catches it that wears a cloak
> Be it right or wrong, be it truth or lies,
> It quickly to the master flies.
> But Masters, they are not to blame,
> The men are worst, you know the same,
> For man to make himself a king,
> Cares not who sink if he but swim
>
> Some wheedling foreman every hour
> Makes big himself with stolen powers;
> He hectoring goes in every place,
> Few know his heart who see his face

But a time will come that will forsooth,
And show that man that wears a cloak;
Altho' well clothed long time ere past
He must be naked stript at last[56]

The poem, published anonymously and with no publisher's name, appears to refer to a specific factory where 'unknown spies/For envy long sits forging lies.' It contains a veiled threat to the foreman in the metaphor of naked at death. Starting with a familiar lament for the freer life outside factories, and criticizing the discipline within, it soon becomes an attack upon the nastiness engendered by a group of men working closely together in competition. Petty lies, gossip and general ill-will further undermine the already unhappy worker. Although these tensions must have been common in factories few broadsides commented upon them except for politics or vengeance.

This eerie poem contrasts with the most famous figure of protest in Lancashire during the nineteenth century – Jone o' Grinfilt. In the 1790s, during the first patriotic enthusiasm for the French Wars, a poem was written by a schoolmaster, Joseph Lees, about John of Greenfield, a small village near Oldham. One story goes that Lees and a friend were on their way home from Manchester without any money and wanted to stop for a drink; during a rain storm they composed the song under a hedge. They intended to sing a few verses at all the inns as they walked home. It was three days before they had the song printed, but it soon became a best seller among Lancashire broadsides.[57] The theme was simple and appropriate to the times. Since the weaving trade was temporarily depressed Jone decides to enlist in the army and help his country 'ha'e a battle wi'th' French.' This first publication soon led to dozens of imitations throughout the North. A discontented weaver who leaves poor conditions at home to find redress or a better life was a loose enough narrative to fit almost any occasion. In the best folk tradition Jone was soon capable of prodigies of sight-seeing, bravery and political insight. Queen Caroline's trial, the Reform Bill of 1832, the New Poor Law and the Crimean War were all reasons for Jone to leave Greenfield. Like Bob Cranky, Jone was a comic, pugnacious character who took on every foe. All of the Jone poems contain a good deal of sardonic conversation between the hero and others, exaggerating his prowess, and sometimes that of the enemy. But Jone, unlike the pitman, was less tied to particular customs and became the proverbial wise common man.[58]

The version of Jone's adventures that became best known was

written during the post-war period of 1815–19 when economic and political repression were at their greatest. 'The Oldham Weaver', or 'Jone o' Grinfilt, Jr.' is a magnificently laconic description of the hand-loom weaver's situation at the time. In many ways this song is the summation of all protest against the new conditions brought by industrialization. Although no mention is made of power-loom weaving, clearly Jone's poverty is a direct result of his inability to compete with factory woven goods. By the end of the French Wars the hand-loom weaver had become a symbol of all that was valued from the past and was disappearing. Throughout the century working men referred to the hand-loom weaver as a symbol of their own cultural and economic losses. Versions of 'Jone o' Grinfilt, Jr.' were still being sold in the 1860s, and a few years ago Ewen McColl discovered an old power-loom weaver from Delph, a small village in the Pennines, who sang a starker and harsher version than any printed in the nineteenth century.[59]

The following version comes from a broadside published in Manchester in the early 1860s. The American Civil War had brought the Lancashire cotton mills to a virtual standstill, and so the song was reprinted as a statement of current conditions. The dialect is clearer than earlier versions and a few words have been altered, but otherwise it is unchanged from the earliest version:

> I'm a poor cotton weaver as many one knows,
> I've nowt to eat i'th house an I've worn out my cloas,
> You'd hardly give sixpence for all I have on,
> My clogs they are brossen* and stockings I've none,
> You'd think it wur hard to be sent into th' world,
>   To clem† and do th' best ot you con.
>
> Our church parson kept telling us long,
> We should have better times if we'd hold our tongues,
> I've houden my tongue till I can hardly draw breath,
> I think i' my heart he means to clem me to death;
> I know he lives weel by backbiting the de'il+,
>   But he never picked o'er○ in his life.
>
> I tarried six week an thought every day wur t' last,
> I tarried and shifted till now I'm quite fast;

*brossen: broken   †clem: starve   +de'il: devil   ○picked o'er: woven

I lived on nettles while nettles were good,
An Waterloo porridge* were best of my food;
I'm telling you true I can find folks enew,
That are living no better than me.

Old Bill o' Dan's sent bailiffs one day,
For a shop score I owed him that I could not pay,
But he wur too late for old Bill o' Bent,
Had sent tit† and cart and taen goods for rent,
We had nou bur a stoo+, that wur a seat for two,
And on it cowered Margit and me.

The bailiffs looked round asslyº as a mouse,
When they saw aw things were taen out ot house,
Says one to the other all's gone thou may see,
Aw sed lads never fret you're welcome to me;
They made no more ado, but nipp'd up th' owd stoo,
And we both went wack upoth flags.

I geet howd of Margit for hoo wur strucken sick,
Hoo sed hoo ne'er had such a bang sin hoo wur wick⊕
The bailiffs scoured off with owd stoo on their backs,
They would not have cared had they brook our necks,
They're mad at owd Bent cos he's taen goods for rent,
And wur ready to flee□ us alive.

I sed to our Margit as we lay upoth floor,
We shall never be lower in this world I'm sure,
But if we alter I'm sure we mun amend,
For I think in my heart we are both at far end,
For meat we have none nor looms to weave on,
Egad they're as weel lost as found.

Then I geet up my piece and I took it em back
I scarcely dare speak mester looked so black,
He said you wur o'erpaid last time you coom,

---

*waterloo porridge: porridge made with water, according to *Wright's Dialect Dictionary*. More probably stale bread with hot water poured over it.   †tit: horse +nou bur a stoo: nought but a stool º assly: sly ⊕wick: born □flee: beat

> I said if I wur 'twas for weaving bout loom*,
> In a mind as I am in I'll ne'er pick o' er again,
>   For I've woven myself thoth' fur end.
>
> Then aw coom out and left him to chew that,
> When aw thought again aw wur vext till aw sweat,
> To think that we mun work to keep them and awth set†,
> All the day o' my life and still be in their debt;
> So I'll give o'er trade an work with a spade,
>   Or go and break stones upoth road.
>
> Our Margit declared if hoo'd cloas to put on,
> Hoo'd go up to Lundun an see the big mon+
> An if things didn't alter when hoo had been,
> Hoo swears hoo'd feight blood up toth e'enO,
> Hoo's nought again th' Queen but likes a fair thing,
>   An hoo says hoo can tell when hoo's hurt.[60]

Much protest verse, indeed verse by working men, was awkward in phrasing and veered between a stilted literary language and the vernacular, giving the work an odd tone and inconsistent form. This poem, on the other hand, is taut and flexible in its conversational tone and easy use of the weaver's dialect. A clear narrative of events is presented and the available consolation honestly recorded.[61]

A dominant characteristic of this poem is its insistence on the rights and personal dignity of the individual; the weaver knows his position in the world and has no desire to overturn its hierarchic order, but oppression he will not tolerate. The poem combines a highly specific attack on those in power – the church parson, the putter-out, the shopkeeper and the houseowner – with a general acceptance of economic instability as an uncontrollable factor in life. Thus, the main threat of the poem inthe final stanza is based on an if-clause which negates the possibility of ever visiting the King (or Queen, as this updated version reads). This stanza comes out of a long tradition of appealing to justice at its source, the crown, and of struggling as individuals. The political unity of the workers was an ideal that only slowly became an integral part of working-class consciousness, although its appeal was always present. The poem conveys no sense of the larger

*bout loom: without a loom   †awth set: all their set   +the big mon: The King. Altered to read 'The Queen' two lines later, to fit the date of publication O e'en: eyes

economic forces at work, nor of any revolutionary possibilities for
change; rather, it emphasizes the continuation of self-respect – and a
willingness to fight for it – in spite of social and economic repression.
Both the limits and the strengths of this view partially explain why the
English weavers did not rise up violently against their 'mesters', but
sought redress through appeals to justice and to Parliament, or simply
waited for a turn of fate.[62]

This sardonic song of protest did not yield any imitations; its
continuation almost unchanged through the nineteenth century is a
mark of its power within folk memory, and of the hold a printed
broadside held in comparison with oral transmission. But the comic
Jone lived on in many different forms. By 1840 he had become Johnny
Green in the songs of Alexander Wilson. For some twenty years, along
with his father and brother, Wilson wrote occasional verse in
Manchester. The family, who entertained in the local pubs, came from
an old hand-loom weaving family, but had adapted to the new age; they
all made a good living as small-ware manufacturers. They took many
traditional songs and altered them to fit the most recent events in the
city. The father wrote 'Jone's Ramble fro Owdem to Karsey Moor
Races'. Alexander used Johnny Green as a visitor to the sights of
modern Manchester, including a balloon ascent, Tinker's Gardens
(Manchester's pleasure gardens), and the new railway to Liverpool. The
charm of these songs rests entirely on the familiarity of both places and
characters.

> We seed sich lots o' jerry shops,
> Boh we'd na stay to drink their slops,
> Eend-way we went an' made no stops,
>   An' just i' toime we nick'd um;
> For helter-skelter sich a crew,
> Wur comink in fro' Liverpoo;
> Aw'm shure they could no faster goo,
>   If th' devil i' hell had kick'd um.[63]

So goes a descriptionof a visit to see the first train. Obviously the comic
Jone could be used by song writers as a handy commentator for almost
any event. His very popularity meant that Wilson and others did not
have to supply much comedy in their songs, but could depend upon a
built-in response from their audience. This technique was commonly
used by the next generation of local writers, who created a single comic
hero for their sketches and stories.

Jone was again revived in the 1880s by Ben Brierley, a Lancashire dialect writer, in 'The Wayver of Wellbrook'. Brierley imitated the sounds of an old hand-loom in his poem, a nostalgic lyric of contentment. Jone praises his lot with Margit at his side, working the spinning wheel. He is happy with 'a quiet heawse nook, – a good wife an' a book,' forgetting the reality of 'I've nowt to eat i'th house and I've worn out my cloas.' Brierley's distortion of the traditional Jone, both comic and serious, illustrates well the decline of the broadside. Conditions had changed by the 1880s – life was still hard enough, but new traditions, including greater literacy, union activities, and a warm family life, had replaced the harsh subsistence level endured by the original Jone. Relative stability in the present cast a glow of warm nostalgia across the past, strengthening the myth of the golden age.

The broadside celebrated many positive attributes of factory life before it died. Betty Reedhook and Sam Shuttle knew no other life but working in a factory; by their time hand-loom weavers were usually the poorest of the Irish. By the 1840s, in spite of the undeniably bad conditions during certain years, factory life was increasingly accepted. Songs were written praising the liveliness and vitality of factory towns. 'Oldham Workshops' and 'Owdam Streets at Dinner Time' both describe the many factories in Oldham and the pleasures of the workers freed for an hour,

> Till half-past one they're never still –
> It's like a fair at Lousey Banks.
> The lasses then, who think they're fair,
> Blackball their heels and curl their hair,
> Sayin', 'Put up my hair nicely Nelly,
> For to day at noon I'st meet my felly.'[64]

Another song speaks triumphantly of 'The Fair maids of Manchester, the factory belles'. The acceptance of the factory system and the changed conditions of life meant a change in the type of literature working people wrote and read. Although they might return to 'Jone o' Grinfilt, Jr.' in hard times, increasingly they turned to creating new songs that defined the new issues. But these early industrial songs served the people well when they came to forge a new literature and language for propaganda, pleasure and education. The works discussed in the next five chapters all owe a cultural debt to street literature.

Notes

1. For a discussion of street literature, see Leslie Shepard, *The Broadside Ballad* (London: Herbert Jenkins, 1962); John Holloway, 'Cherry Girls and Crafty Maidens', 'Broadside Verse Traditions', 'The Irish Ballads', *The Listener*, 83 (21 May, 28 May, 4 June 1970), pp.680–5, 710–14, 744–8; Robert Collinson, *The Story of Street Literature, Forerunner of the Popular Press* (London: Dent, 1973); Victor E. Neuburg, 'The Literature of the Street', *The Victorian City*, eds. H. J. Dyos and Michael Wolff (London: Routledge and Kegan Paul, 1973), I, pp.191–209; and Leslie Shepard, *The History of Street Literature* (Newton Abbot: David and Charles, 1973).
2. David C. Fowler, *A Literary History of the Popular Ballad* (Durham, N. C.: Duke University Press, 1968), p.240.
3. A. L. Lloyd, *Folk Song in England* (London: Lawrence and Wishart, 1967), pp.234–5.
4. The exception to this is the immensely popular Chartist newspaper, the *Northern Star* (1837–52). For a discussion of the unstamped, see Patricia Hollis, *The Pauper Press: A Study of Working-Class Radicalism in the 1830s* (London: Oxford University Press, 1970).
5. Reprinted in Charles Hindley, *Curiosities of Street Literature* (London: Redwood Press, 1970 [1871]), p.237.
6. For a description of early coal mining life, see Edward Chicken, *The Collier's Wedding* (Newcastle: T. and J. Hodgson, 1829). The poem was originally published in 1729.
7. Abel Bywater, *The Sheffield Dialect* (Sheffield: G. Chaloner, 1839), pp.v–vi. Bywater adds at the end of his description of a Lozin', 'We are happy to inform our readers that this custom is now but seldom practiced.'
8. The average life expectancy of a dry grinder was 35 years, of a wet grinder, 45 years. See Friedrich Engels, *The Condition of the Working Class in England*, eds. W. O. Henderson and W. H. Chaloner (London: Basil Blackwood, 1958), pp.229–32.
9. John James, *The History and Topography of Bradford* (London: Longmans, Brown, Green and Longman, 1867), pp.163–8; John James, *History of the Worsted Manufacture in England* (London: Longman, Brown, Green, Longmans and Roberts, 1857), pp.400–8; and James Burnley, *The History of Wool and Woolcombing* (London: Sampson, Low, Marston, Searle and Rivington, 1889), pp.186–210.
10. Charles Hindley, *The History of the Catnach Press, at Bewick-upon-Tweed Alnwick and Newcastle-upon-Tyne in Northumberland and Seven Dials, London* (London: Charles Hindley, 1887), pp.69–71, 92.
11. R. K. Webb, *The British Working Class Reader, 1790–1848* (London: George Allen and Unwin, 1955), p.27.
12. Henry Mayhew, *London Labour and the London Poor* (New York: Dover Publications, 1968 [1861–2]), I, p.220.

13. Charles Hindley, *The Life and Times of James Catnach* (*Late of Seven Dials*), *Ballad Monger* (London: Reeves and Turner, 1878), pp.142, 412; and see Mayhew, I, p.220. Hindley feels that rumour has exaggerated Catnach's earnings,and that he probably did not earn more than £5,000 to £6,000 in his lifetime – a large enough sum from the sale of penny and halfpenny broadsides.
14. Quoted by Frances M. Thomson, *Newcastle Chapbooks in Newcastle-upon-Tyne University Library* (Newcastle: Oriel Press, 1969), p.12.
15. J. H. Spencer, 'A Preston Chap Book and Its Printer , *Preston Herald*, 2 January 1948. I am indebted to Victor E. Neuburg for drawing my attention to this newspaper article. Catnach's vast collection of type and wood-cuts met a better end. Leslie Shepard speculates that the Wilson Collection at the Printing Library of the St Bride Foundation contains many of his woodcuts, type and copies of his broadsides. See *John Pitts, Ballad Printer of Seven Dials, 1765–1844* (London: Private Libraries Association 1969), p.93.
16. Shepard, *John Pitts*, pp.35–47.
17. Hindley, *The Life and Times of James Catnach*, pp.84–8.
18. (Preston: J. Harkness, n.d.), Hindley, *Curiosities* p.199.
19. (London: J. Catnach, n.d.), Broadside Collection, British Museum.
20. Hindley, *History of the Catnach Press*, pp.xvii–xxx. He is also mentioned by the author of 'Street Ballads', *National Review*, 13 (1861), pp.409–10.
21. Fred Leary, 'Manchester Ballads', unpub. ms. collection, *c.* 1893. Manchester Central Reference Library.
22. Cecil J. Sharp, *English Folk Songs: Some Conclusions*, 4th rev. ed. prepared by Maud Karpeles (Belmont, California: Wadsworth, 1965), p.134.
23. Willa Muir discusses her first impressions of the two different singing styles in *Living With Ballads* (London: The Hogarth Press, 1965), pp.35–41. A. L. Lloyd in *Folk Song in England*, pp.228–32, discusses the relationship between social change in the eighteenth century and the music of folk songs. He suggests that the increase in a wavering melodic line, found particularly in Irish songs, echoes the loss of traditional more and social standards. Walter Tomlinson, 'A Bunch of Street Ballads', *Papers of the Manchester Literary Club*, 12 (1886), pp.305–16, also discusses the older style of singing. (In spite of its title Tomlinson discusses country singing more than the modern street ballad.) He particularly comments upon the 'low, monotonous and lugubrious tone' of songs of 'perfectly fearful' length and duration. He is also surprised at how often women did the courting in these songs, commenting, '[it] would seem to intimate the prevalence of a different code of social ethics from that which we are fain to believe obtains at the present day' (p.311). For a discussion of the differences between the street ballad and folk ballad, see V. de Sola Pinto and. A. E. Rodway, *The Common Muse: Popular British*

Ballad Poetry from the 15th to the 20th Century (Harmondsworth: Penguin, 1965), pp.19–21.

24. Quoted by Fred Leary, unpub. ms. collection, from *Imperial Magazine*, May, 1819. Evidently in this neighbourhood chaunters found it most profitable to work on week days.
25. Broadside Collection, Sheffield Central Reference Library.
26. John Wilson, 'Memoir of Mather', *The Songs of Joseph Mather*, ed. John Wilson (Sheffield: Pawson and Brailsford, 1862), pp.vii–xxiv.
27. *Allan's Illustrated Edition of Tyneside Songs and Readings*, rev. edn. (Newcastle: T. and G. Allan, 1891), pp.235–55, 54–7; and David Harker, 'John Bell, The Great Collector', in John Bell, *Rhymes of Northern Bards* (Newcastle: Frank Graham, 1971 [1812]), pp.xxxvi–li.
28. For a description of Blind Willie's Newcastle, see David Harker, 'Thomas Allan and "Tyneside Song" ' in *Allan's Illustrated Edition of Tyneside Songs and Readings*, rev. ed. (Newcastle: Frank Graham, 1972 [1891]), pp.ix–xii.
29. William Scruton, *Pen and Pencil Pictures of Old Bradford* (Bradford: T. Brear, 1889), pp.247–8; and broadsides and notes in the Scruton Papers, no.4₁, Box 3, Bradford Central Reference Library.
30. Scruton Papers, no.4₁, Box 3, Bradford Central Reference Library.
31. Quoted by A. L. Lloyd, *Folk Song in England*, p.378.
32. Lawrence Stone, 'Literacy and Education in England, 1640–1900', *Past and Present*, 42 (1969), pp.118–26. See also R. K. Webb, 'Literacy Among the Working Classes in Nineteenth Century Scotland', *Scottish Historical Review*, 33 (1954), pp.100–14; and Michael Sanderson, 'Literacy and Social Mobility in the Industrial Revolution', *Past and Present*, 56 (1972), pp.75–104.
33. Hindley, *Curiosities*, p.13.
34. Broadside Collection, Harris Public Library, Preston. See Richard D. Altick, *The English Common Reader: 1800–1900* (Chicago: University of Chicago Press, 1957), pp.269–77 for a discussion of Brougham's work. Also, see R. K. Webb, *The British Working Class Reader, 1790–1848*, passim.
35. David Reisman, *The Oral Tradition, The Written Word, and the Screen Image* (Yellow Springs, Ohio: Antioch Press, 1955), p.12.
36. For a discussion of the impact of literacy on totally pre-literature societies and on early European cultures, see Jack Goody and Ian Watt, 'The Consequences of Literacy', *Literacy in Traditional Societies*, ed. Jack Goody (Cambridge: Cambridge University Press, 1968), pp.27–68.
37. 'Country John', Broadside Collection, Harris Public Library, Preston.
38. (Spitalfields: Taylor, n.d.). Hindley, *Curiosities*, p.46. Also printed by W. Fordyce, Newcastle, and H. P. Such, London.
39. For a discussion of broadsides about theatre life, see J. W. Robinson, *Theatrical Street Ballads* (London: The Society for Theatre Research, 1971).

40. (Preston: Harkness n.d.). Harris Public Library, Preston.
41. David Harker, 'John Bell, The Great Collector', p.xli.
42. *Allan's Tyneside Songs*, p.88.
43. *Allan's Tyneside Songs*, pp.88—90. For the same version with slightly different spelling and punctuation, see John Bell, *Rhymes of Northern Bards*, pp.25—7. According to Allan, pp.84—5, a broadside version of 'Bob Cranky's 'Size Sunday' can be found among Bell's 'Cuttings' without a date but amongst othermaterial from 1803. The song, therefore, may date from as early as 1803; it probably circulated for at least several months before it was in print.
44. There are many versions of this poem. See Broadside Collection, British Museum; and *Victorian Street Ballads*, ed. W. Henderson (London: Country Life, 1938), pp.36—7.
45. For a full discussion of poaching and transportation songs, see A. L. Lloyd, *Folk Song in England*, pp.236—50.
46. Almost every major broadside printer appears to have reprinted this song. See Harkness no.123 in Broadside Collection, Harris Public Library, Preston, for a copy of the song accompanied by a striking woodcut of Indians with spears.
47. For a discussion of the lack of railway navvy songs, see Terry Coleman, *The Railway Navvies* (London: Hutchinson, 1965), pp.139—43. After the railways were a flourishing and established form of transportation, a number of railway poets arose. The most famous was Alexander Anderson. He wrote, among other volumes, *A Song of Labour and other Poems* (Dundee: Advertiser Officer 1873) and *Songs of the Rail* (London: Simpkin and Marshall, 1878). His works are very like those discussed in chapter 4.
48. The most detailed examination of industrial dislocation and its impact upon individual workers and their families is Neil J. Smelser's *Social Change in the Industrial Revolution: An Application of Theory to the British Cotton Industry* (Chicago: University Press, 1959). See also R. S. Fitton, and A. P. Wadsworth, *The Strutts and the Arkwrights 1785—1830* (Manchester: University Press, 1958); William Radcliffe, *The Origin of Power Loom Weaving* (Stockport, 1828); and Andrew Ure, *The Cotton Manufacture of Great Britain*, 2 vols. (London: H. G. Bohn, 1861).
49. Broadside Collection, John Johnson Collection, Bodleian Library, Oxford. It should be noted that the weaver is a woman in a trade traditionally associated with men. See Duncan Bythell, *The Handloom Weavers: A Study in the English Cotton Industry during the Industrial Revolution* (Cambridge: University Press, 1969), pp.60—1, for an analysis of the number of women in the trade. See also Ivy Pinchbeck, *Women Workers and the Industrial Revolution 1750—1850* (London: George Routledge & Sons, 1930).
50. (Preston: Harkness, n.d.). Harris Public Library, Preston.
51. (Manchester: G. Jacques, n.d.). Harris Public Library, Preston. Catnach also published this under the title 'The Factory Girl'.

52. John Harland and T. T. Wilkinson, *Ballads and Songs of Lancashire, Ancient and Modern*, 3rd ed. (Manchester: John Heywood, 1882), pp.202−4.
53. Harland and Wilkinson, pp.193−5.
54. ibid., pp.188−9.
55. *Select Committee on Hand-Loom Weavers' Petitions* (1834). Quoted by E. P. Thompson, *The Making of the English Working Class* (London: Gollancz, 1963), p.307.
56. Since this poem is undated and has no publisher or place of publication it is difficult to date or to give a place of origin. It is accompanied by a poem called 'The Ashes of Napoleon', describing the return of Napoleon's ashes to Paris in 1840. 'The Factory Bell', however, probably dates from an earlier time. This particular version comes from the Leeds Public Library.
57. The authorship of the original 'Jone o' Grinfilt' is under some dispute. For the best known account, see Harland and Wilkinson, pp.162−75. For a correction, see Charles Higson, ' "Jone o' Grinfilt, Jr." and "Oldham Rushbearing" ', *Oldham Standard*, 1 May 1926.
58. John of Greenfield appears frequently in political anecdotes. The Chartist leader Feargus O'Connor in a speech given at Carlisle said, ' . . . he thought it unnecessary that those who were to choose the persons who were to make the laws should be educated; it was sufficient for them to possess plain common sense. This reminded him of a story told of John of Greenfield, who said that all the stuff in the world was made for all the people in the world. Some one told John that he knew nothing about making laws, to which he replied, 'No and I know nothing about making a shoe, and yet I can tell when the shoe pinches − (A laugh) − and so I would be d   d fool to go a second time to a man who made a shoe to pinch me, so I would be a d   d fool to go a second time to the man who made a bad law.' *Carlisle Patriot*, 19 January 1839. I am indebted to Thomas Milton Kemnitz for drawing my attention to this reference.
59. Ewen McColl, *The Shuttle and the Cage* (London: Workers' Music Association, 1954), p.3. One hundred and fifty years of oral circulation changed 'Jone o' Grinfilt, Jr.' into a song much closer in form and emotion to a traditional ballad.
60. (Manchester: Bebbington, n.d.), Broadside collection, Chetham's Library, Manchester. Mrs. Gaskell in *Mary Barton* (1848) changes the lines attacking the parson. 'Our church parson' is changed to 'Owd Dicky o' Billy's', and 'I know he lives weel by backbiting the de'il' is changed to 'Owd Dicky's weel crammed, he never wur clemmed.' The final threat of Margit is softened. 'Hoo swears hoo'd feight blood up toth e'en' is changed to 'Hoo's fully resolved t' sew up meawth an' eend.'
61. There seems, however, to be a break between the seventh and eighth stanzas; whether by intention or because all surviving versions read this way is unclear. The weaver declares that things

are at 'fur end', using a weaving term that means the end of a piece of woven cloth, to describe the plight of himself and his wife. There seems to be no way out of their dilemma of no looms, no furniture and no money, except to argue as he does, that since they have nothing left, things must improve. Then, the next two stanzas describe an event one would have supposed occurred previous to the confiscation of the furniture. Since he says that he was weaving 'bout loom' the previous week where does the final piece of cloth come from? It may be that these verses come after his comment to Margaret inorder to indicate that he could indeed he made lower in the world by means of his master's degrading attitude. Or, his declaration to 'ne'er pick o'er again' may be a defiant recognition of the inevitable; accepting poor relief and its required labour of stone breaking or spadework is made to seem a choice by his refusal to work any longer for the putter-out (who has no work for him anyway). Given the combination of melancholy tone and sardonic comment, it seems that the weaver accepts poor relief and all it entails, but as the final stanza indicates, demands justice; indeed, the final three lines became proverbial in Lancashire as a comment on hard times.

62. The exceptions to this generalization are such movements as the early nineteenth-century Luddite and Captain Swing movements that largely attacked machinery and not men. See Frank Peel. *The Risings of the Luddites, Chartists and Plug-Drawers* 4th ed. (London: Frank Cass, 1968); and E. J. Hobsbawm and George Rudé, *Captain Swing* (London: Lawrence and Wishart, 1968).

63. *The Songs of the Wilsons,* ed. John Harland (Manchester: John Heywood, n.d. [1842]), p.62.

64. Broadside Collection, Manchester Central Reference Library.

CHAPTER 2 Literature as Propaganda: The Coal Miners' Unions, 1825–1845

Mother wept, and father sighed;
    With delight a-glow
Cried the lad, 'To-morrow,' cried,
    'To pit I go.'

Up and down the place he sped, –
    Greeted old and young,
Far and wide the tidings spread, –
    Clapt his hands and sung.

Came his cronies some to gaze
    Wrapt in wonder; some
Free with counsel; some with praise;
    Some with envy dumb.

'May he,' many a gossip cried,
    'Be from peril kept;'
Father hid his face and sighed,
    Mother turned and wept.

When Joseph Skipsey, a collier poet, published this poem in 1878 Dante Rossetti found it 'very striking'.[1] All England knew why Mother wept. Skipsey did not have to explain the dangers of a pitman's life – pit disasters during the previous twenty years and the good public relations of the miners' unions had made the general public respect the life of the pitman. He was no longer looked upon as a lawless barbarian. Just as reading Tennyson assumed a familiarity with classical myths, reading Skipsey implied a recognition of the English working man and his place in society. His poem was the culmination of half a century of educating the miners and the public by trade unions and their literary spokesmen.

The distance between 'Mother Wept' and 'Jone o' Grinfilt, Jr.' provides a measure of the changes working-class literature underwent during the nineteenth century. The development of a class-based ideology was reflected in a new literature. Trade unions used both songs and printed material as propaganda in their campaign to dispel the Bob Cranky image of the working man. The gullible, carousing braggart had to be transformed both in actuality and in the public's mind, to the sober, self-disciplined, literate union man. The straight-forward broadsides discussed in Chapter 1 were increasingly replaced by educational and literary works. As one trade unionist declared, 'Literary pursuits . . . tend to diminish and remove the coarseness and violence which are characteristic of ignorance, and to substitute in their stead politeness and civility. They open the mind to perceive the real condition and relations of man, and convey to it a deep conviction of the propriety of discharging the social duties.'[2] In this chapter I shall discuss how the early coal-mining unions developed literature as propaganda.[3] In the next chapter I shall discuss the broader uses of literature by the Chartists; under the political aegis of Chartism we find the development of a working-class literary aesthetic and the first efforts to create a revolutionary fiction.

Although one could study the literature of many different unions that rose and fell during the first half of the nineteenth century by concentrating on a particular time and place, it is possible to trace in detail the use of literature during a period of developing class consciousness. The coal miners of the North-east have a complete and continuous literary tradition; the composing of songs, poems and dialogues had been an integral part of pit communities from the seventeenth century. Isolated in small villages and subject to particularly arduous and dangerous working conditions, miners had long seen themselves and had been seen as a race apart. They were highly work-conscious; class consciousness and union solidarity were built upon this sense during the growth of trade unionism in theperiods 1825–32 and 1842–5. The changes, however, were not easy. The very characteristics that united the miners isolated them from the general public, who feared and distrusted demands for better wages and working conditions. It was necessary, on the one hand, to educate the public to the similarity between the hopes and ideals of the miners and other men, and on the other, to instruct miners to behave more like other men and less like 'terrible and savage pitmen'.[4] The literature written during this time, therefore, had the combined function of building union solidarity and self-discipline, and of appealing to shared values among all men. Many songs came out of the traditional lore and songs of pitmen, but many more were based on hymns, patriotic verse and other literary sources.

Two sources particularly important for the propaganda of the miners' unions were Methodism and Radicalism. The Primitive Methodists gave a number of union leaders organizational experience and the values they tried to impress upon the rank and file, such as sobriety and self-discipline. Their union dedication and high seriousness rose from the same emotional source as their religious fervour.[5] Methodist hymns with union words were used at nearly every meeting and rally. Biblical tales and characters appear repeatedly as symbols of injustice and righteousness. The image of working people as Israelites oppressed by Pharoah, used by Sheffield's Joseph Mather and many others, appears in much union material. As members of an oppressed class, the miners found satisfaction in identifying with a higher cause. God's justice, as embodied in this Old Testament story, gave them comfort and hope in their struggles against man's injustice. Radical ideas of equality, natural rights and liberty provided an ideological framework for building the self-respect and unity of members, and gave men courage to pursue social justice in the face of powerful opponents. Radical heroes such as Tom Paine, Henry Hunt and William Cobbett provided the language and imagery of class struggle.

The unions used traditional methods for distributing and propagating their literature. They relied heavily upon broadsides, which were either given away by organizers or sold to raise funds. Broadsides, pamphlets and newspapers could be easily distributed among both the miners and the general public by union members. New material was constantly being printed in order to keep miners and their sympathizers up to date. Most miners, however, were not accustomed to reading regularly. Since the mining culture was basically oral, most of the literature printed by the union was meant to be sung or read aloud. Works were written for specific occasions and died with the event. Some were revived under similar circumstances a generation later, and others lived on in oral tradition. Every working-class struggle brought forth such literature, and methods of distribution, which satisfied the emotional and organizational needs of the cause.

I
The 1831 Strike: The Struggle for Justice

Although miners' organizations date from the seventeenth century, the first union activity in the nineteenth century was apparent in 1810, when the miners of the North-east struck against proposed changes in their annual bond (contract). They were successful, and little evidence of association surfaces until 1825 with the publication of *A Voice from the Coal Mine*.[6] This work spoke in terms that were to appear again and again — the coal owners and overviewers (managers) are attacked for their tyranny and the men warned against becoming slaves:

> On whatever side the pitman looks, he sees nothing but horror
> darkness, ɑ and oppression — *scripture* – *reason* – *humanity*, all
> violated in his person. The word of God, which recommends a spirit
> of universal charity; to even the brute part of the creation, is
> overlooked with regard to him: the solemn precept, 'wrong not the
> hireling of his wages' is a dead letter to his callous employers.[7]

The demands for higher wages and better conditions were described in
the language of eighteenth-century rationalism and the natural order of
the Christian world. The repressive political climate of the 'twenties
scarcely encouraged reason and justice, but the early union leaders
counselled patience. The men, on the other hand, frequently took
matters into their own hands and served rough justice upon the most
hated overviewers and non-union members. The miners' publications of
the 1820s and '30s show these two tendencies — order and revenge

'Unjust actions' continued through the 'twenties, and in 1831, under
the leadership of Thomas Hepburn, the first major pitmen's strike was
held. In March 1831 the men refused to be bound until their demands
were met, principally the limitation of boys' hours to twelve and
payment in cash, to eliminate Tommy shops (company stores). The
union's propaganda followed the general lines laid out in 1825.
Economic and social justice both found their ultimate source in God's
justice over all men.

One dirge-like hymn published by Hepburn's union is a mixture of
passive appeals to those in power and of startling images of
degradation:

> O Lord hear the poor pitmen's cry
> Look down on us with pitying eye;
> With heavy bondage are opprest,
> And all our families are distrest.
>
> Thou heard the Israelites of old,
> And led them to a blessed fold;
> Deliver us from slavery
> And set the Sons of Britain free.
>
> In the dark pit where we are bound,
> The iron hand of oppression's found;
> Our labour's hard, our wages small
> Some days we work for nought at all.

As lions greedy for their prey,
They take our rights from us away;
To starvation we are driven,
Pale and wan we are ill thriven.

Our masters pinch us very sore,
We never felt such smart before,
They have us so completely bet,
Not one in fifty's out of debt.

The Indian slaves for freedom groan,
We have a greater cause to moan,
You often pity slaves abroad,
But we have now a greater load.

Come, O ye rulers of our land,
Pray take our cause into your hand,
Then let us have fair Britain's law,
And save us from proud Pharoah's paw.

Beneath the harrow we are crush'd,
Our blood lies mangled with the dust;
Regardless of our cries and groans,
They suck the marrow of our bones.

As cannibals they have eat our flesh,
Their bellies swell to great excess,
To quench their thirst have drunk our blood,
And left us wallowing in the mud.

Does not the trumpet sound reform,
And are we not free Britons born;
We want to have a jubilee,
The slavish pitmen now set free.

Our flesh pots now are stained with rust,
Our cup-boards now without a crust,
The tears run from the mother's eyes,
They can not bear their children's cries.

> Arise my brethren from the dust,
> And in the Lord let's put our trust,
> Then all our foes he will confound,
> And in the sea proud Pharoah dround.[8]

The alternating stanzas of description and command suggest a very clear idea of injustice, but a less clear conception of how men could actively change their lives. Change is asserted by means of imperative verbs, requesting outsiders to intervene. In spite of the broadside's title, little in the verses indicates that this is specifically 'a pitman's complaint'. Rather, familiar Biblical and traditional situations are used to describe injustice. The harrow, a farming tool, but also the verb for plunder, is used instead of pit tools. The ghoulish descriptions of the coal owners are exceptional, and perhaps derive from the auto-erotic Methodist hymns about Christ's blood. Hatred of the owners usually found expression in more openly vindictive images.

In contrast to the artificial language and metre of 'The Pitman's Complaint', revenge had a vigorous spontaneity. The most militant language came in the isolated letters and proclamations made by miners attacking hated individuals or symbols of power. A viewer for the Cowpen Colliery received the following letter in April 1831 after a group of miners broke into his house; they ate and drank, but did no damage to the furniture and occupants.

> I was at yor hoose last neet, and myed mysel very comfortable. Ye hey nee family, and yor just won man on the colliery, I see ye hev a greet lot of rooms, and big cellars, and pleny wine and beer in them, which I got ma share on. Noo I naw some at wor colliery that has three or fower lads and lasses, and they live in won room not half as gude as yor cellar. I don't pretend to naw very much, but I naw there shudnt be that much difference. The only place we can gan to o the week ends is the yel hoose and hev a pint. I dinna pretend to be a profit, but I naw this, and lots o ma marrows na's te, that wer not tret as we owt to be, and a great filosopher says, to get noledge is to naw wer ignerent. But weve just begun to find that oot, and ye maisters and owners may luk oot, for yor not gan to get se much o yor awn way, wer gan to hev some o wors now. I divent tell ye ma nyem, but I was one o yor unwelcome visitors last neet.[9]

Although union leaders sought to minimize these incidents, they were effective in frightening those who might oppose the men. The letter was a sign of the individual miner's growing sense of personal and class rights; the task of the union was to channel this confidence into productive ends.

Unoon leaders heartily approved attacks on blacklegs. It was essential to teach each miner the importance of communal action; social ostracism and physical violence were used against those who could not be convinced by reasoning. 'The First Drest Man of Seghill, or the Pitman's Reward for Betraying his Brethren' appeared in March of 1831, after the decision to strike had been taken, but before the bond fell due and the men were out. It is a single-minded attack on a blackleg, showing the confidence and active pursuit of justice absent from 'The Pitman's Complaint'. The author used the flexible Irish Come-all-ye form, with a rollicking metre, but his serious message is never lost:

> Come, all ye Miners, far and near,
>   And let us united, o,
> In bonds of love and unity,
>   And stand out for our right, o.
> Like Israel, these many years,
>   In bondage we have been, o.
> And if we do not still stand out
>   Our truth will not be seen, o.
>   With my fal, la, la etc.
>   . . . .
> Man a weak frail being is,
>   And easy to deceive;
> And by a man call'd black J. R.
>   Was made for to believe —
> It was on March the nineteenth day,
>   Eighteen hundred and thirty one,
> A man from Earsdon Colliery
>   His brethren did abscond.
>
> And to the Seghill binding he
>   Did come with all his might
> For to deceive his brethren dear,
>   He thought he was but right.
> But when he came to Seghill town
>   The men were standing off;
> He thought that he would then be bound,
>   And he would make a scoff.

As other men were standing off,
    He would not do the same;
That idle work would never do,
    He'd rather bear the shame.
Black J. R. made him believe
    That he was in no danger,
And to the office he might go,
    Because he was a stranger.

      . . . . . .

And at the hour of two o'clock,
    As I was sitting cobbling,
A rout there came unto our house,
    I heard the women gabbling.
Away I went with all my speed,
    As hard as I could hie,
To see if I could catch the hares —
    It was my will to try.

But there were some upon the chace
    Long ere I got there:
With running I lost my breath,
    And I could run ne mair.
But I will tell his travels here,
    As he went from the binding;
They stript him there of part of his clothes,
    And left his skin refining.

Black J. R. was all the blame,
    He lost all but his lining:
But when he came to Hallowell
    His skin so bright was shining.
They left him nothing on to hide
    That good old man the priest,
But there they put him on his hat,
    He was so finely drest.

They set him off from there with speed,
    To an ale-house by the way,
And there the Earsdon men did sit,
    A-drinking on that day.

> But of their minds I cannot tell
>> When they did see him coming.
> The priest he had within his hat
> And he was hard a running.
>
>   . . . . . .
>
> And so remember, you that come,
>> Unto Seghill to bind
> You may think upon the man
> That we have treat so kind.[10]

The song is part of the comic broadside tradition discussed in Chapter 1. The stereotypic beginning and conclusion, the mentioning of an exact date, time and place, and the mocking refrain all place the song in the miners' traditional pit culture. The approach to the subject is also traditional, and in many ways similar to 'Jone o' Grinfilt, Jr.' in the bitingly comic treatment of a serious situation. The blackleg is 'forgiven' for his frailty, but is still punished for betraying his brethren. The central figure is 'black J. R.' who misuses his power in luring the Earsdon collier to Seghill, and so is most deservedly chased to an ale-house where all the Earsdon men see him covered only with his hat (the sexual reference to "priest" may also carry connotations of anti-Irish feelings).

One of the characteristics that distinguishes this song from its predecessors, and from the hymn-based 'Pitman's Complaint', is the individual narrator who participates in the action he is describing. Traditional folk songs were usually about individual lovers, desperadoes or heroes, but the writers were anonymous. Many folklorists have argued that the songs were written communally. Industrial songs, on the other hand, were usually signed by the author, and were generally about and by particular individuals within a given community. The emphasis was upon shared, communal values. Union propaganda, by and large, was not anonymous after 1831 since it was important to identify a writer as a union member to give his song credibility among his fellow unionists; the writer was often a well-known individual, and his subject matter was about and for working people in praise of solidarity.[11] 'The First Drest Man', with its first-person narrator and anonymous author, is a transitional work, pointing the way to the more individualized pit songs of the later nineteenth century.

The disorganized coal owners within two months capitulated to the United Association's demands. In August 1831 a huge celebration was held on Bolden Fell, on the border between Northumberland and Durham. The occasion was similar to the traditional miners' Whitsunday revels and a foretaste of the annual miners' gala of the present. Men from different collieries carried banners, bands played and songs were composed for the occasion. The day was used to demonstrate publicly the miners' strength and unity; every effort was made to impress outsiders with the reasonableness and good behaviour of the men. Unlike the secular Irish metre used for the anti-blackleg 'First Drest Man', on this public occasion, hymn tunes were sung, showing the religious base of the union's precepts.

'The Pitman's Union' expresses the miners' attitude of well-earned peace and prosperity:

> Now let the colliers' hearts be glad
>   While plenty round them shines,
> And blest contentment flows along
>   The banks of Wear and Tyne.
> Brave Hepburn and our delegates,
>   Like rays of virtue shine,
> Their fame shall long be echoed round
>   The banks of Wear and Tyne.
> On Bolden Fell our flags shall wave,
>   Like victory's wreaths entwine,
> But peace shall be the motto still,
>   With lads of Wear and Tyne.
> We envy not the rich and great,
>   Whose dazzling greatness shine;
> While we the hardy sons of toil,
>   Can labour in the mine.
> Our happy wives and children now,
>   All former cares resign,
> And sing with joyful mirth and glee,
>   The lads of Wear and Tyne.
> May he, who rides upon the storm,
>   Protect with care divine,
> From all the dangers that surround
>   The lads of Wear and Tyne.
> Here's health unto the King,
>   Likewise the Queen sublime,
> Who gave the pitmen their applause,
>   That dwell on Wear and Tyne.

> Now to conclude and make an end,
> May luck around them twine;
> O, bless the happy collier lads,
> On both the Wear and Tyne.

Chorus

> Still round our banners we will stand,
> In love and truth combine,
> And children yet unborn shall sing,
> The lads of Wear and Tyne.[12]

This song is typical of the miners' commemorative songs; it is factual, with few metaphors or poetic devices, and has a flat, unvaried rhythm. The alternating use of iambic tetrameter and trimeter quatrains is a survival of a popular eighteenth-century hymn structure, often employed by Cowper in his poems about the poor. The language is rooted in the more formal religious traditions of the past, rather than the new economic and political traditions forming around class consciousness and class warfare. 'The hardy sons of toil' praise a world where the traditional social order reigns and he 'who rules upon the storm/Will protect with care divine.' The union was not outwardly revolutionary, but emphasized loyalty to the crown, faith in God and love of family.

Success made the pitmen cocky, and in April 1832 they struck again, though their funds were depleted both from the previous strike and from sickness benefits. The main issue was recognition of the union. The owners declared they would bind no union men, and were united against the Association far more thoroughly than in the previous years. They had learned to combine against the men, and to stockpile coal before a threatened strike, so they could sell it at inflated prices, while purposely stalling the miners with unfavourable offers. Feelings ran high throughout the spring. The miners assaulted many blacklegs, and the owners evicted strikers from company housing. In June a magistrate was beaten to death by two miners; Joseph Skipsey's father was killed by a policeman during a disturbance. In spite of a policy of selective striking, enabling working miners to support their fellow strikers, the union could not stand up against the owners' combination.[13] The newly developed loyalties to fellow workers and the union were broken, and traditional loyalties toward one's superiors temporarily reasserted. The bitterness of failure led many to attack the union leaders instead of the overviewers. Hepburn was totally ostracized in the ensuing months, and finally forced to swear off organizing to get a job. In one of his last public speeches, however, he spoke confidently of a brighter future:

> If we have not been successful, at least we, as a body of miners, have been able to bring our grievances before the public; and the time will come when the golden chain which binds the tyrants together, will be snapped, when men will be properly organized, when coal owners will only be like ordinary men, and will have to sigh for the days gone by. It only needs time to bring this about.[14]

II
The Miners' Association 1842–4: Testing the Bonds of Union

The crushing defeat of 1832 temporarily destroyed all efforts to form a miners' union in the North-east, but by the late 1830s several followers of Hepburn were forming friendly societies. Their efforts were hampered because owners and overviewers blacklisted former union men. An early song to 'The Miners' Philanthropic Society' vowed 'Never let it be said that we are afraid to join the union', a sentiment to provide badly needed encouragement. Conditions deteriorated rapidly in the period from 1837 to 1842, however, and soon many risked joining again. By late 1842 individual mining unions throughout Great Britain and Ireland were strong enough to amalgamate, and the first national miners' union was formed. It was led in the North-east by Martin Jude, a pitman turned publican. Among the leaders were men who had been blacklegs in 1832. The Miners' Association was remarkable for its size (estimated to be 60,000 at its height) and varied methods of promoting the miners' cause.[15] Parliamentary pressure, legal defense and paid organizers were all used extensively. The union, nevertheless, paid a price for its size and strength; its goals were confined to those all members could accept, regardless of their religious and political beliefs.[16] Despite the Chartist background of many of the leaders, they carefully avoided radical politics as detrimental to harmony (this did not prevent the press and the owners from accusing union members of being dupes of the Chartists). Only after the strike did the Association openly support the Chartist Land Scheme and the Chartist-led plan to create a National Association of United Trades.

The propaganda distributed by the Miners Association both before and during the four-month long 1844 strike was far more varied and sophisticated than that of 1831 and 1832. The comic Bob Cranky had become 'Peter Fearless' who cogently argued the union's goals. Two regular papers, the monthly *Miners' Magazine* and the fortnightly *Miner's Advocate*, kept members abreast of legal battles, union income and membership, the intricacies of safety and ventilation, and all union meetings. Popular songs were reprinted and with altered lines about the union, such as 'The Bonnie Pit Lads', in which the 'lovely maid' asks 'Pray do you belong to the brave Union' before she will consent to marry her wooer (see Appendix). Songs from earlier strikes were updated and countless new ones were issued as broadsides. Replies to the owners and their minions were printed, in addition to pamphlets and verses aimed at the general public. The recurring problem of reluctant printers was solved by employing a Newcastle printer full time. Both sides took each other's propaganda seriously, challenging and answering by every means.

The presses had barely begun running when events brought about a crisis. In 1843 wages had fallen 15 per cent. Early in 1844 the union leaders presented an alternative bond, embodying many of their demands, and in particular a guaranteed wage of 3s. a day for hewers. Coal owners had long been outraged by the miners' continued policy of labour restriction, dating from the 1820s. In a glutted labour market and with the falling price of coal, they refused to answer the union. At the March national delegate conference the North-east received support to strike, and 33,000 men and boys went out when the bond fell due in April. Within a month all funds were gone, and theowners began publishing a weekly report of union defections and newly arrived workers. Despite ruthless evictions and minimal supplies, the men struggled on for nineteen weeks. In 'a trial between the long purses of the owners and the hungry guts of the pitmen', the union suffered almost total loss.[17] Although the Association survived another three years, by 1845 it was an ineffectual shadow in the North-east.

The union's rapid growth during 1843–44 and its extended strike placed unusual demands upon the leaders. Education for union solidarity and understanding had to be effective and fast. It was estimated that three-quarters of the National Association's membership could not read; by necessity songs were a vital form of propaganda.[18] Union propaganda among members focused on developing self-confidence, retaining loyalty under stress, and teaching the terms of the bond and general political economy. Two main psychological approaches were used: first, self-respect and self-improvement were emphasized, and second, hatred of the coal owners and of blacklegs was intensified to strengthen union loyalty.

A major problem the union leadership faced was rebuilding the miners' self-confidence. The repeated admonitions to break the shackles of slavery were not simply rhetorical; through the strengthening of group loyalty would come strength and self-respect. An intensive campaign was launched in 1842–3 to make real the motto 'Union is strength/Knowledge is power'. *If* the 'Sons of Toil' were true to their own interests, and felt confidence in each other and in themselves, 'no earthly power [could] prevent them from raising themselves to that position in society, to which by their industry and usefulness they so justly deserve to be risen.'[19] During the strike the union confidently published 'A Dialogue Between Three Coal Viewers After Being in Search of Men', in which one of the viewers comments, 'they have long been called ignorant, but they are quite the contrary: they can lay their case so plain before the public as to make a very weighty impression.' It was this image that the union particularly wanted to propagate.

One of the ways in which the Association developed the miners' self-confidence was teaching them about the details of their annual bond. For years the men had blindly signed on without attempting to read the minute regulations; viewers had often taken advantage of them by adding penalties and fines each year. The union's bond, which the owners refused to look at, was circulated widely and its conditions explained. Poems were written outlining a just relationship between masters and men. If many of the union songs of the past appeared to have little to do with coal mining, these new works found no detail of underground life too trivial to be forced into metre and rhyme. Some poems read like a rhymed version of the proposed bond:

> Neither laid out nor set-out shall stand in our bill,
> For both round and small in the tub we shall fill;
> Eight hours and no longer we'll stop in the mine;
> Then we will come to bank without fear of a fine.[20]

This matter-of-fact information helped men to memorize the various issues in the union's struggle. No one now was to be victimized through ignorance.

Stronger emotions, however, were needed to pull the men together. Hatred of blacklegs and false friends became an important element in the survival of the union. A great many songs and poems were written against blacklegs. A few were in the formal language of political verse, but most continued the tradition of 'The First Drest Man of Seghill'. In the tightly-knit pit communities every man's position in regard to the union was known; every stranger was recognized instantly. Songs attacked specific individuals for violating the miners' code or for outright hypocrisy. After a broadside circulated attacking a person, he either left the village or joined the union; the only other alternative was ostracism for him and his family that might last for years. William Hornsby's 'New Song' describes the enemies in Shotton Moor:

> At Shotton Moor we have some tools, for men it is not fit to call
>   them,
> They think that every one is fools, but mark and see what will befall
>   them;
> There's some of them been much esteem'd, both far and near their
>   name is sounded;
> But little have they thought or dream'd how their character now is
>   wounded.
>
> There's one perhaps you know him well, a preacher was perhaps
>   you'wd heard him,
> For gain his principle did sell, for it the Lord will acre reward him;
> He has not kept the law so good, which we as well as him shall go
>   by,
> Do to thy neighbour as thou would, that thou would wish him to be
>   done by.
>
>   . . . . . .
>
> Then W   G   a Cockfield man, he is a base and treacherous
>   villain,
> To hurt us he'll do all he can, but to do us good he's never willing;
> A dirty useless tool is he always trying to deceive ye,
> He should be drowned in the sea, he is not fit to live believe me.
>
> Then W   T   next in the clan, for favour he'll do ought
>   that's dirty
> To undermine his fellow-man, but men like these can never hurt
>   you;
> False to his neighbour he has been, now mark and see what will
>   come on it;
> He'll rob his master 'twill be seen, give him the chance depend upon
>   it.[21]

The real bitterness of Hornsby's song is embodied in the word 'tools' — the union's struggle centred on the demand to be treated like men and not like tools. The indictment of W   T   cuts two ways: untrustworthy men might appear powerful, but their falseness against the coal owners makes them ultimately powerless as informers.

In order to reinforce the men's self-respect, hatred of the tyrant owners was encouraged. Just as with blackleg poetry, sometimes this hatred was expressed in formal language, appealing to God's justice. But a more common method was humour; by deflating the power of the owners it was easier to manage. One song between an old woman returned from Hell and a coal owner, warns that all the poor are being thrown out of Hell to make room for 'the rich wicked race', with the coal owners 'next in command'. Comic prose dialogues served a useful educational purpose. The two parts could be taken by different union members at a meeting or in a pub, and the entire argument could be dramatized, exploiting its comedy, while instructing those who could not read. Satiric portraits of local dignitaries, pompous ministers or grasping overviewers were very popular. William Johnson, a versatile writer and organizer from Framwellgate Moor, wrote a number of dialogues about 'Peter Fearless' and 'Harry Heartless', using the Bob Cranky image of the pitman for political ends. All of his dialogues show the advantages of sticking with the union, for 'The Maistors are stiff, aye as stiff as a prop,/But props sometimes crack, when the stone starts to drop.'

Religious parodies were also common. A parody for the non-reader insured easier memorizing than a dialogue and permitted greater humour and irony for the reader/listener, who would recognize the discrepancy between the original and the parody. Early in the 1844 strike the following 'Miners' Catechism' appeared. It is well worth quoting in its entirety as an example of the Association's sophisticated and effective propaganda:

1 Ques. What is your name?
Ans. PETER POVERTY.
2 Q. Who gave you that name?
A. My godfathers and godmothers in my baptism, wherein I was made a member of the Black Coal Pit, a child of Slavery, and an inheritor of the sunless mine.
3 Q. What did your godfathers and godmothers then for you?
A. They did promise and vow three things in my name. First, that I should renounce all opposition to my master's will. Secondly, That I

should believe that every Word and Action of the Viewers was said and done for my benefit. Thirdly, That I should obey them in every thing, work for their benefit alone, and live inpoverty and want all the days of my life.

4 Q. Dost thou not think that thou art bound to believe and to do as they have promised for thee?

A. Yes, verily, and by God's help so I will not. And I am very thankful that such a spirit of resistance is within me, for I see plainly that they would bind me to slavery to my life's end.

5 Q. Rehearse the articles of thy belief.

A. I believe that my master, who is a Coal Owner, sinks his capital in a coal pit in expectation of making a princely fortune in a short time, and that his Viewers are hard task-masters, and that it is them who make such hard laws as these: Thou shalt not send any foul coal, splint, or stone to bank among the good coals, or if thou dost thou shalt pay threepence a quart for it; and if thou sends a tub to bank not containing the quantity specified in the bond, thou shalt not have any pay for the same. I believe that the Overman is a tool in the hands of the Viewers, and that he will do anything the Viewers want him, such as not measuring the rank of the Putters, cheating the men out of their yard-work, and enforcing the fines contained in the bond.

6 Q. What dost thou chiefly learn in the articles of thy belief?

A. First, I learn to believe that the Coal Owner wants his work done as cheap as possible. Secondly, That the Viewer gets as much money as possible from the workmen so that he may accumulate as large a fortune as possible. Thirdly, That the Overman will do anything the Owner or Viewer tells him to do.

7. Q. You said that your godfathers and godmothers did promise for you, that you should keep your master's commandments, tell me how many there be.

A. Ten.

8 Q. Which be they?

A. The same that the Master spake on the day that he read the bond, saying, I am thy Master who hath bound thee to the Coal Pits, and for twelve months thou shalt remain in bondage to me.

I. Thou shalt have no other Master but me.

II. Thou shalt work for no other Master, neither shalt thou give thy services to any otherman, for I thy Master am a jealous man, and I will visit thee with heavy fines and punishments if thou break any of my commandments.

III. Thou shalt say no manner of evil of me, but shalt say I am a good master although I act as a tyrant towards thee; for I will not hold thee guiltless if thou say any manner of evil of my name.

IV. Remember thou work six days in the week, and bevery thankful that I allow thee the seventh day to recruit thy exhausted strength, for I, thy Master, want as much work out of thee as possible, and if it suits me to give thee only two, three, or more days in the week, be very thankful that I give thee any work at all, for I only look at my interest, not thine.

V. Honour me thy Master, honour my Viewers, my Overman, and my Agents, so that thy days may be long in my service.

VI. Thou shalt work thyself to death and commit self-murder.

VII. Thou shalt exhaust thyself with work to hinder thee from committing adultery.

VIII. Thou shalt not steal anything from thy Master altho' I give thee no money for working for me.

IX. Thou shalt not bear witness against me or any of my agents for any misdemeanor we may commit.

X. Thou shalt not covet thy Master's house, thou shalt not covet thy Master's wife, nor his servants, nor his lands, nor his carriage, nor his horses nor any thing that is his.

9 Q. What dost thou chiefly learn from these commandments?

A. I learn two things, my duty towards my master, and my duty towards myself.

10. Q. What is thy duty towards thy master?

A. My duty towards my master is to work honestly for him and not to waste his substance, while I remain his servant.

11 Q. What is thy duty towards thyself?

A. My duty towards myself is to work a fair day's work for a fair day's wage, and to hinder my master from being a tyrant overme.

Catechist. My good man you know your duty well; continue to pursue the path of duty, look well to your own interest and to that of your masters, and you will do well; train up your children to hate tyranny, love freedom, justice, and truth; and may the God of Heaven and Earth bless you to your life's end.

A PRAYER

Unto thy care and protection O most unmerciful Master, I commit myself this day. Preserve me from all fines, cheatery, deductions, either by weight or measure, or from any thing contrary to the justice of my labour; by thy *graceless assistance* enable me to receive my pay without any subtraction, division, or reduction from its true and rightful amount; and so conduct my *interest*, that neither sloth, idleness, drunkeness, nor the *ill-will-ness* of Overman or Viewer may occasion the neglect of it, that I may be dutiful and obedient to all Viewers, Owners, Masters, or Tyrants; that I may love them with that due submission and affection to which their dissimulation and tyranny so justly entitle them. Preserve me from all misfortunes and accidents. Leave me not to the wolfish and devouring fiends of despotism and *crush-down-ism*; but so guide me by common sense, that I may live without any fear of them now, or dread of them hereafter. Bless all those who are linked in the bonds of *Union*. Bless all those who *have*, or may relieve our necessities, and all associations of good feeling and humanity. Purge all collieries from the pestilential fever of proud, arbitrary, and domineering oppression. By thy condescension permit me to receive the full fruit of my labour this day, and defend me from all dark-dealing treachery in the night, so that I may be enabled to procure substantial food for myself and family, thro' the merits of my own diligence, industry, and perseverance. Amen.[22]

Too often in the nineteenth century both the church and the chapel exhorted the working man to remember his duties and his failures to perform them, rather than the rights and the injustices wrought against him by those in power and authority. Week after week during the strike various ministers issued broadsides and tracts telling the pitmen that their strike was a sin.[23] The miners replied with a catechism that speaks of duties and rights; in the proper performance of his day's labour, the worker would receive 'the full fruit'.

Union solidarity was as important as attacking the miners' enemies. The Association encouraged relationships among different branches and individual members. The most valuable 'organ of communication and defence' was the *Miners' Advocate* (see Plate 6). Edited in Newcastle by a Scots carpet weaver, William Daniells, it sold for 1 1/2d., as an unstamped paper, issued fortnightly from 2 December 1843 until 27 July 1844. Prosecuted for infringement of the stamp laws, Daniells then published it monthly until April 1846, when he was forced to flee to the Isle of Man and publish from there. The *Advocate* reported local union lectures, ran a series of articles on pit ventilation and safety devices, and featured biographies of self-made men. It included trials and the cross-examination by the Association's lawyer, W. P. Roberts, and thereby provided valuable information for miners confused about the legalities of court action. It also listed all donors to the strike fund. As the official voice of the Association the *Advocate* was more cautious in explaining policies than the broadsides and pamphlets quoted above.

From its inception the paper encouraged miners to participate in it by writing the editor about their grievances, sending poems and articles and aiding sales. The response was vigorous, if mixed. At one point Daniells woefully admitted, 'Our poetical friends must have patience, we are in possession of a great number of poetical epistles, many of which we fear, it will be impossible to prune into shape so as to appear in the *Advocate*.'[24] Most of the literary pieces are stilted and formal, lacking in the vehemence or humour of broadside verse.

The *Advocate* was the union's foremost educational tool; its strength lay in its vigorous and clear defence of the miners' rights. The editor and contributors built upon the traditional pit culture of tales, fables, folk heroes and biblical allusions to explain the union's position. The *Advocate* was read aloud and discussed in pubs, so each important point was carefully described in terms the miners would understand and enjoy. For example, in one editorial the necessity of working with the coal owners was explained using a well-known fable:

> The moral and physical consequences of a contentious warfare between capital and labour does appear to us to be fully illustrated by the fable of two noble animals combating or fighting for a piece of prey, and while the combat is going on, another animal of diminutive size and strength came and carried off the prize; while neither of the two, such was their state of exhaustion, could prevent him.[25]

The real enemy was the general public who wanted cheap coal, although it invested neither labour nor capital to procure it. The use of the fable here highlights its importance in working-class political writing. Fables were succinct and embodied an effective lesson based upon folk customs. Moreover, they carried connotations of a traditional and more justly governed society.

W. P. Roberts, 'the Pitman's Attorney General', also edited a journal for communication and information. In October 1843 he began the *Miners' Magazine*, to diffuse 'that knowledge amongst the Miners that they so much need, and [secure] to them a greater degree of power.' Like Daniells, he encouraged the miners to write about themselves and their mining experiences. Soon after the strike began he announced a

contest for the best song about the strike, to the tune 'Brave Old Oak'.
The prize was two guineas:

> The present time is idle and hungry and therefore well suited, in the
> opinion of those who understand these things; to the growth of
> poetical fancy. Now we want a good Song for the Pitmen — suitable
> to existing circumstances — and we want the Song to be written *by* a
> Pitman, or his wife, or daughter, or son.[26]

The winning entry and second prize were finally published in March
1845. The editor was lavish in his praise of the winning entries,
predicting a long career for both: ' "I dreamt that I dwelt in marble
halls" though good enough for people who go to concerts and theatres
and such like trash is altogether decidedly inferior to that which we
have just given.'[27] Whatever the editor might have thought, both
contributions were decidedly inferior to the strike broadsides, and
never left the pages of the magazine. (The snobbish puritanism of the
editor is an interesting side-note. Another means of building union
solidarity was to scoff at what was either too expensive or a waste of
hard-earned money.)

Roberts was immensely popular among the miners; broadsides
appeared throughout the North singing his praise. They paid him the
supreme compliment of reviving an 1831 song originally in praise of
Hepburn, and substituting his name. The coal owners, on the other
hand, hated him as a symbol of all the union stood for. Much of their
propaganda, distributed for free among the miners, attacked Roberts
and his assistant, William Beesley, as outside agitators who had duped
the men into leaving work. In addition to their tracts openly stating
their position against the union, on occasion they published broadsides
purporting to be by disillusioned miners. In August 1844 a broadside
entitled 'New Song' circulated widely in County Durham. In crude
dialect a 'miner' bitterly attacked Roberts and Beasley, 'May R   s,
B   y gan to h   l,/The unyen to the de'il', and requested a
friend to 'cut me throte' if he should think of joining the union again.
The true source of the work was William Armstrong, Jr, the overviewer
for Wingate Grange Colliery, against whom Roberts had defended the
pitmen in their refusal to descend into the pit by means of a frayed
wire rope. Armstrong wrote the printer a note accompanying a copy of
the poem: 'If I ever hear one word of my incognito being broken *not
one penny piece* will I pay you for the lot.'[28] The printer added the
promise 'My oath of secrecy shall not be broken', and filed the note

with his personal papers. The crudity of the coal owners' and overviewers' propaganda shows their attitude toward their workers. They had never found it necessary in the past to recognize the union and were indignant at the strength of the Association.

To counter this propaganda the union disseminated information and literature among both working men and the general public. Their outward-looking writing emphasized class solidarity and the courage of the miner. Part III is a discussion of this literature and its impact upon the miners, other workers and the public.

III
Reaching a Wider Public

The propaganda written to reach other workers was usually a straightforward explanation of wages, working conditions and the need to stand by one another. Pamphlets and broadsides were distributed regularly among strike breakers who had come North under the promise of good wages. Few, however, were sufficiently convinced to join the strike; hunger was the masters' most successful weapon in setting working men against each other. In August 1844 the Association sent twelve delegates to London to raise money and to publicize the strike; they placed great hopes on help from the better paid and more educated Londoners. The delegates visited a large number of Chartist and working men's associations, and were enthusiastically met, but they received little financial aid. Their failure was a blow to the morale of the rank and file and probably hastened the end of the strike.

Before leaving London the delegates published a tract calling for class unity. In language reminiscent of a religious meeting, they warned;

> And why have the sons of labour not come more nobly forward, to support their own cause? See you not that the Miners' cause is your cause? If they are crushed, you must follow, and that soon. Awake from your slumbers, rise and look to your own interests, ere it be too late. Capital is rampant, and unless it is met in a spirit of determination by the sons of toil united, it will assuredly sink lower every class of labour's sons.[29]

The cadenced questions, the war metaphors and the imperative tense all speak of a prophetic urgency felt even in the midst of defeat. The miners spoke with firm confidence about their struggles to a sympathetic audience: the language of religious battle had become thelanguage of class war. Whenever union writers dealt with their most serious issues they returned to religious language and imagery. The moral fervor of earlier times had been transformed under stress; class solidarity and God's justice were combined.

The Miners' Association put most of its effort into convincing a larger public — middle-class sympathizers as well as working people — of the justice of their cause. Writers emphasized the dangers underground and the constant presence of death — awe-inspiring facts everyone could feel. The Association held frequent public meetings in which thepitmen themselves described their working conditions, sang songs and gave readings. An early historian described one public meeting in Newcastle as 'a meeting which did great good by removing a vast amount of prejudice from the minds of the inhabitants concerning the miners, and convinced many of the justness of their cause.'[30] Such meetings were popular with the colliers who met persons outside the pit community and gained confidence in presenting their issues publicly.

The Association was fortunate in receiving support from many non-mining writers, including the well-known 'Bard of the Tyne and Minstrel of the Wear', Joseph Philip Robson (1808–70).[31] One of his most successful poems was 'The Miner's Doom', which was printed as a broadside with the comment 'Written expressly for "The Miners' Advocate" and recited by Mr Jos. Fawcett, a practical miner, at a concert held in the Lecture Room, Nelson Street, Newcastle-upon-Tyne, on Thursday, August 13, 1844, for the benefit of the unemployed miners of Northumberland and Durham.' In a suitably elevated style, the poem describes the fate of theminers in a pit explosion:

The choke-damp angel slaughters all — he spares no living soul.
He smites them with a sulphureous brand — he blackens them like
   coal.
The young — the hopeful, happy young fall with the old and gray.
And, oh, great God! a dreadful doom, thus buried to decay
Beneath the green and flowery soil whereon their friends remain,
Disfigured, and perchance, alive, their cries unheard and vain.
Oh, desolation! thou art now a tyrant on thy thone,
Thou smilest with sardonic lip to hear the shriek and groan!
To see each mangled, writhing corse, to raining eyes displayed,
For hopeless widows now lament, and orphans wail dismayed.[32]

It ends with the moral:

> Aye! this is he that masters grind and level with the dust,
> The slave that barters life to gain the pittance of a crust.
> Go read yon pillared calendar, the record that will tell
> How many victims of the mine in yonder churchyard dwell.

Whenever the miners and their sympathizers, such as Robson, returned to a religious framework for their poetry, they used a heightened and impersonal language, treating the miner and his situation as symbolic of what all men faced. The effect was to depersonalize the miner's situation, while generalizing it. Similarities between the miners and others were thereby emphasized. By reminding the public of death, the miner appealed to sentiments that were readily transferred to his earthly cause. While all pit accidents could not be eliminated, greater consideration could be given to the men who willingly risked their lives underground.

The pitmen wrote many imitations of 'The Miner's Doom', describing an anonymous miner who sacrifices his life to hew coal for the uncaring public and tyrannous masters. These elegies were often written to raise funds for the families of men killed in pit disasters. The formal language and high seriousness of the genre were not derived from literary sources, but from the traditional Irish Come-all-ye. The long lines of fourteen syllables and the rhyme scheme of AABB (broken into two lines each in 'The First Drest Miner of Seghill') were felt throughout the century to have sufficient dignity to be the most suitable form for pit elegies. Joseph Skipsey wrote in this form after the Hartley calamity of 1862, when 204 men and boys were killed. In 1882 Tommy Armstrong found the form suitable for his 'The Trimdon Grange Explosion', when seventy-four were killed. In time pit disaster songs came to be written about specific events and emphasized particular persons and the causes of the disaster, rather than portraying a generalized picture of A Miner. While retaining the lament style and easy recitative form, the later disaster poems were much closer to reportage than Robson's artificial and symbolic description. For example, two lines of Armstrong's 'Trimdon Grange' run 'Let's think of Mrs. Burnett, once had sons, but now has none – /By the Trimdon Grange explosion, Joseph, George and James are gone.'[33] In strike songs attacking blacklegs or coal owners the pitmen had developed an idiomatic, direct and explicit style; pit disaster songs, on the other hand, for a long time retained a static, fatalistic tone. It was easy for

the miners to see what they could do about blacklegs, and their songs
were dramatic examples of revenge. Pit disasters were more difficult to
control, even with proper safety methods, and so were described with
stoicism and muted anger.

The miner's doom became a reality soon after the failure of the
strike. In September 1844 the Haswell Colliery explosion killed 95
persons. The tragedy served to strengthen temporarily the miners'
loyalty to the Association, since Roberts demanded and obtained a
special government investigation. It revealed a serious neglect of safety
precautions, but no action was taken against the owner or the manager.
The miners reacted with fury at this continued carelessness, but their
anger had no outlet except an enfeebled union and poetry.[34] Generally
the memorial verses written were similar to Robson's piece — an entire
community stricken by death found consolation in the portrayal of
unidentified but typical sorrowing families. One of the most popular
recitation pieces of the time was 'The Pit Boy', by G. P. Codden:

> The sun is sinking fast, mother,
>   Behind yon blue hills,
> The signal bell has ceased, mother,
>   The breeze of evening chills:
> They call me to the pit, mother,
>   The nightly toil to share:
> One kiss before we part, mother,
>   For danger lingers there.
>
> My father's voice I hear, mother,
>   As o'er his grave I tread,
> He bade me cherish thee, mother,
>   And share with thee, my bread;
> And when I see thee smile, mother,
>   My labour light shall be;
> And should his fate be mine, mother,
>   Then heaven may comfort thee.
>
> Nay, dry thy tearful eye, mother
>   I must not see thee weep;
> The Angels from on high, mother,
>   O'er me their watch will keep.

> Then, oh! farewell awhile, mother,
>   My fervent prayer shall be,
> Amidst those dangers dire, mother,
>   That heaven may comfort thee.[35]

The poem was widely reprinted in mining districts. The first two verses were published in the *Miners' Advocate* soon after the explosion. The version quoted here was published as a broadside, with the author's name included for the first time, for a lecture on mining, 'in Aid of a Fund for the Relief of the Surviving Sufferers by the Explosion which occurred at Warren Vale Colliery [near Barnsley], on the morning of December 20th, 1851'.

Such poetry as this fulfilled a need shared by the miners, members of the Ten Hours Movement and other similar groups protesting against dangerous working conditions. The importance of 'The Pit Boy' was not its factual accuracy, so vital in the strike poems, but its emotional accuracy. The devoted pit boy sustained a positive self-image, confirming an inner ideal held by many union men seeking a better life for themselves and their children. Moreover, it gave outsiders a favourable impression of miners and their plight.

From a modern perspective, however, poetry such as 'The Pit Boy' functioned to defuse frustrations. It portrayed suffering and death in a distant and formal manner that relieved the reader of any responsibility. The metre and tone of such poems were often at odds with the overt intention: while calling attention to an evil in need of change, the poems actually create an atmosphere of static, unchanging conditions. The reader could enjoy his sensitive response without feeling any need to intervene. This do-nothing sentimentality was particularly popular among many middle-class readers. In working-class readers it operated to reassure and to remind them of eternal verities, without focusing on the origins of the evil described. Since all agency is avoided, all action is irrelevant.

'The Pit Boy' contrasts sharply with Joseph Skipsey's poem, written after the age of entry of boys into the mines had been raised to thirteen. In his poem the young boy is eager to go to work, while his parents are unhappy about a dangerous necessity. The reader is expected to understand and sympathize with theparent's point of view. In Codden's poem the sympathy is more explicit. The boy is resigned to performing his duty and pleased with his reward, his mother's love. Death isfar away for Skipsey's boy, though not for his parents, while Codden's boy expects to die soon. Skipsey creates a sense of danger and death in the midst of youth and vigour which makes a more powerful impression upon an outsider than the more direct fatalism of Codden's poem. Both, however, play upon the expectations of a general readership by emphasizing family love and faith, combined with the most praised trait of the pitmen, their courage in facing danger.

An interesting contrast to 'Mother Wept' and 'The Pit Boy' is a poem collected by J. R. Leifchild, and published in his popular survey of mining life, *Our Coal and Our Coal-pits: The People in them and the Scenes around them* (1853). Leifchild was the sub-commissioner appointed to examine the pits and pit villages of Northumberland and Durham for the 1842 Parliamentary Report on children's employment. His report was considered by many to be the most thorough, as he alone learned the pitmen's dialect and went underground to speak with them.[36] Leifchild was deeply sympathetic to the pitmen's grievances, but he remained adamantly anti-union. His descriptions of pit life seem to be very accurate, yet the songs he claims to have heard pit boys singing appear to be counterfeit. Folklorists agree that miners did not sing while at work; their labour is too difficult and the air too foul.[37] Yet Leifchild records that his songs came from hewers and others while at work. Moreover, his songs touch all the points he wished to emphasize in his official report. He gives, for example, 'The Trapper's Petition':

> Father! must I go down with you
>   Into that dark and dismal hole,
> And leave the sky ever so blue
>   Buried amidst the blackest coal?
>
> Father! I want to go to play.
>   I've had no play since Monday last.
> O! let me have one hour to-day,
>   And then I'll work and do a vast!
>
>   . . . . . .
>
> They never let me come and sail,
>   My little ship upon the pool,
> Or read that pretty little tale
>   My mother got me from the school.

> But if I must go down beneath,
>   Don't let the putters beat me sore;
> I tremble so, it stops my breath
>   To hear them coming to the door.
>
> . . . . . .
>
> Well, father! if I must go down,
>   Just hold me tight upon your knee;
> But get me work in yon big town,
>   And let me life and daylight see![38]

This is the middle-class sentiment of an outsider. Unlike the previous two poems, this trapper boy regrets leaving his childhood and shows little courage. He asks his father to find him a position away from the pit village — an improbable request, considering how tightly knit mining communities were. The poem sounds like a versification of the 1842 report; its purpose seems to be to encourage the passage of more stringent child labour laws. It appears likely that Leifchild made up all or most of the songs appearing in *Our Coal and Our Coal-pits*. He was considered one of the most reliable and informed reporters about coal mining for the middle class, and yet he felt it necessary to write fake songs to gain sympathy for his major points. Although the union agreed with Leifchild about the need to limit child labour, their perspective was considerably different. A major goal of union literature was educating middle-class sympathizers about the true nature of mining life; the misunderstandings perpetrated by Leifchild were typical of what the union fought.

The next generation of miners reacted fiercely against unnecessary danger in the pits; 'rampant Capital' would not long be left unchallenged. The foundations laid by the 1831 and 1844 strikes proved to be strong enough to build yet another union. The works discussed in this chapter reflect a narrow but potent and persistent use of literature. Class pride, self-respect, a love of union leaders and a belief in improvement mark the writings of union members. Under straitened circumstances pitmen wrote with a sincerity few professional writers could hope to convey. The most suspicious characteristic of Leifchild's poem is the plea to leave the coal field; no miner's poem either beforeor after the 1844 strike ever suggested a better life could be found elsewhere. Such an option was open to some, but the proud miners had coal dust in their blood. Trade-union literature throughout the century celebrates this solidarity.

Notes

1. Dante G. Rossetti, 29 October 1878, as quoted in Joseph Skipsey, *Songs and Lyrics*, coll. and rev. (London: Walter Scott, 1892). 'Mother Wept' was originally published in *A Book of Miscellaneous Lyrics* (Bedlington: George Richardson, 1878).

2. 'The Effects of Literature on the Moral Character', *Miners' Advocate*, 6 April 1844.

3. Literature, of course, had long been used by the Religious Tract Society as a means of inculcating very different values. Hannah More in response to those who believed that reading matter among the labouring poor was bound to be inflammmatory, insisted that a ballad broadside had prevented a riot among miners near Bath. See R. K. Webb, *The British Working Class Reader, 1790–1848* (London: Allen and Unwin, 1955), p.25.

4. Thomas Wilson, in a preface written in 1843 to his collected poems, *The Pitman's Pay and other Poems* (London: George Routledge and Sons, 1872), p.vii, describes the following as common practice in the eighteenth century: 'Whenever they considered themselves aggrieved, they "struck"; or, in the language of that day, a "steek" took place. These "steeks" generally originated on the Wear; and, by the way of enforcing their demands, the malcontents immediately "laid in" all the pits in the district. The mode of proceeding in such cases was this: – The men with whom the strike commenced, visited all the neighbouring collieries; and on their arrival at each pit, they hung on a corf [basket], filled with stones, at the same time hanging on the clog. The weight of the corf moved the gin; and as the former descended, the latter gained velocity, until the clog, flying out in the air, knocked away the supports of the gin, and laid it on its side, thus rendering it totally unfit for use, and thereby putting a stop to all work for some time to come. This was the mode then generally resorted to, for compelling redress of grievances -- practice that would not be even thought of in the present day'. While Wilson is correct in saying that the practice 'would not be even thought of in the present day', the local papers in 1831, 1832, and 1844 were filled with court cases about miners arrested for beating blacklegs, attempting to destroy pit property, etc. After 1844 such instances became less common.

5. E. J. Hobsbawm, 'Methodism and the Threat of Revolution in Britain', *Labouring Men: Studies in the History of Labour* (London: Weidenfeld and Nicholson, 1964), p.26.

6. For information about the early miners' unions, see Richard Fynes, *The Miners of Northumberland and Durham* (Sunderland: Thomas Summerbell, 1923 [1873]); E. Welbourne, *The Miners' Unions of Northumberland and Durham* (Cambridge: University Press, 1923); and Sidney Webb, *The History of the Durham Miners (1662–1921)* (London: The Fabian Society, 1921).

7. Colliers of the United Association of Durham and Northumberland,

A Voice from the Coal Mines, or a plain statement of the various grievances of the pitmen of the Tyne and Wear, addressed to the coal owners, their head agents and a sympathizing public (South Shields: J. Clarke, 1825), n.p. See also the replies, *Brief Observations in Reply to 'A Voice from the Coal Mines'* (1825) and *A Defence of 'A Voice from the Coal Mines'* (1825). See also *A Candid Appeal to the Coal Owners and Viewers of Collieries on the Tyne and Wear* (Newcastle: John Marshall, 1826).

8. 'The Pitman's Complaint' (Newcastle: W. Fordyce, printed for the author, n.d.), Bell Collection, University of Newcastle Library. In Bell's handwriting the date 'May 13th 1831' has been added.

9. Quoted by Fynes, p.21.

10. (Newcastle: J. Marshall, n.d.). Bell Collection, University of Newcastle Library. Dated 'March 31st, 1831', with the note '10 quires, Crown 3 on a sheet' in the printer's handwriting.

11. A. L. Lloyd, *Folk Song in England* (London: Lawrence and Wishart, 1967), pp.340–2.

12. (Gateshead: Stephenson, n.d.). Newcastle Central Reference Library. Dated 'July 1831' in Bell's handwriting.

13. Matthias Dunn, author of *An Historical, Geological and Descriptive View of the Coal Trade of the North of England* (Newcastle, 1844), kept a diary while manager of the Hetton Colliery. He comments as follows about the end of the 1832 strike (unpub. diary, Newcastle Central Reference Library):

    'Sept. 1: Fresh alarm of cholera at Hetton which threatens to thin our ranks of strangers again. Ten in a dozen of the Union men have come in during the week but at a general meeting today upon Bolden fell it is determined to stand firm, and 1/-p. £ making 7 to be levied upon the workers.

    'Sept. 20: Having got no encouragement from Mr. Mowbray or the Committee [of coal owners] they this day surrendered at discretion and allowed us to pick out as many and whom we pleased binding them under the declaration contained in the Bond against becoming members of any society acting against the free exercise of their working powers, etc. Notwithstanding great feeling prevails for some Union of their own – which will I believe be carried on in spite of fate – '

    Also, see Fynes, pp.26–36 and Welbourne, pp.33–44 and Webb, pp.28–39.

14. Fynes, p.36.

15. For a full discussion of the economic and political policies of the Association, see Raymond Challinor and Brian Ripley, *The Miners' Association: A Trade Union in the Age of the Chartists* (London: Lawrence and Wishart, 1968); and A. J. Taylor, 'The Miners' Association of Great Britain and Ireland, 1842–48: A Study in the Problem of Integration', *Economica*, n.s. XXII (1955), pp.45–60. See also Fynes, Welbourne and Webb.

16. In a letter to the editor of the *Miners' Advocate*, 3 December 1843, 'AMO' described the situation as follows: ' . . . never until now

have they [the miners] had an object placed before them, on which men of all religious and political opinions could so universally unite. The object to which I allude is the uniting together all the miners of Great Britain in one common body, for the godlike purpose of improving their social and moral condition through the medium of a society, to protect their labour against the inroads of capital.'

17. This comment is commonly attributed to W. P. Roberts, the miners' lawyer, but it was actually said by a Wingate collier. For a correction, see 'The Colliers' Strike', *Northern Star*, 18 May 1844.

18. The estimate of three-quarters illiterate was given by the *Manchester Guardian* in its report of the Manchester National Delegate meeting of the Association. The *Guardian* article is reprinted in full in the *Miners' Advocate*, 17 January 1844. Some of the difficulties faced by the union in educating its members can be seen from the following excerpt from 'Instructions to Lecturers, by order of the conference held at Burslem, Staffs., on July 15th and four following days'. (*The Miners' Advocate*, 27 July 1844). A lecturer [an organizer] is instructed 'to improve his mind and those he is placed among, to remove prejudice, intolerance, and all paltry feelings which tend to retard the progress of the Association, in order that we may be enabled to give a proper direction to our industry and Association . . . you are recommended to direct the whole of your energies, physical and mental, to the promulgation of the principles of the Association, not to interfere in political or religious controversy in the advocacy of those principles, nor to engage in the forwarding or getting up of any law suits, but your sole object to be to show miners that before they can engage successfully in the task of bettering their condition they must engage in a body, anxious to discover the true and useful for the common advantage of all, to show them the advantage of just practice and consistent principles, until this be done and acted upon the reign of tyranny and suffering must continue. Then by all legal means endeavour to properly throw open their minds in pursuit of knowledge, as it is that alone which will enable us properly to remove the causes which at present impede our progress, and to the discovery of themeans best calculated at once to remove such impediments, and to advance us in the cause which it is our interest to pursue, at the same time learning to know that the interest of each is the interest of all, as that which is ruinous to some is injurious to all . . . '

R. K. Webb, in *The British Working Class Reader*, p.22, estimates the literacy in northern colliery districts to be well over fifty per cent. Lawrence Stone points to the particularly high level of literacy in Northumberland, Cumberland and Westmoreland in 1840 (81 per cent) in his article 'Literacy and Education in England, 1640–1900', *Past and Present*, 42 (1969), pp.122–3. He does imply that the demand for child labour in the coal-mining areas may affect literacy rates among miners. Michael Sanderson shows the literacy rate of Lancashire miners in the 1830s to be 13.94 per cent in 'Literacy and Social Mobility in the Industrial Revolution in England', *Past and Present*, 56 (1972), p.90. Whatever the correct figures, miners were notorious for their general lack of formal schooling. It is safest to say that reading was probably a difficult chore for three-quarters of the miners.

19. *Miners' Advocate*, 2 December 1843.
20. James Purdy of Winlaton, 'The Miner's Right' (n.p., n.d.), 'Pitmen's Strike, 1844', unpub. scrapbook, Wigan Central Library.
21. William Hornsby, 'A New Song' (n.p., n.d.), 'Pitmen's Strike, 1844'. Wigan Central Library.
22. 'The Miners' Catechism' (n.p., n.d.), 'Coal Trade: Pitmen's Strike, 1844'. unpub. scrapbook, Newcastle Central Reference Library.
23. See John Burden, late incumbent of Castle Eden, 'To the Pitmen of the Wingate Grange and Castle Eden Collieries', 1 May 1844 and 26 June 1844 (n.p., 1844); John Besley, *Sermon on the Respective Duties of Master and Servant* (Long Benton: n.p., 9 June 1844); and the broadside 'May A Christian Join the Union?' (n.p., 18 May 1844), all in 'Coal Trade: Pitmen's Strike, 1844'. Newcastle Central Reference Library.
24. *Miners' Advocate*, 20 April 1844.
25. op. cit., 2 December 1843.
26. *Miners' Magazine*, May 1844, p.47.
27. op. cit., March, 1845, pp.56–60.
28. Emphasis in the original. I am indebted to Robert Wood, of West Hartlepool, for permission to examine the printer John Procter's personal papers, which include the original copy of the 'New Song'.
       The *Durham Chronicle* parodied Roberts' contest, offering two guineas to anyone who could write a song showing the truth about the union, to the tune 'Brave Old Oak'. First prize went to 'Tommy Wiseacre' for his 'Farewell to the Union and the Men at Heed on't'. (*Durham Chronicle*, 26 July 1844). One verse runs,

> Also, O Lord! give men to see
> That strikes and kick-ups winna dee;
> But best when men an maisters gree
>   Upon each place,
> To bargain for his sell, be free,
>   Each knows his case.

> So farewell Union, and farewell Roberts
> And farewell Beesley and all sic lobarts.

Tommy, of course, is a figment of the editor's imagination.
29. *An Address to the Public by the Delegates from the Coal Miners of Northumberland and Durham, now in London* (London: R. Thompson, n.d. [1844]) p.11.
30. Fynes, p.71. Some measure of the distance between the miners and

their 'betters' can be judged from 'The Mayor and the Miners' in the *Tyne Mercury* (13 July 1844): 'On Saturday afternoon between two and three o'clock, Sir John Fife rode into the midst of a great crowd of pitmen, who were bowling on the town-moor, Newcastle. He was immediately surrounded, and most attentively listened to for some time. He told the men that he was anxious they should know that bowling on paths and roads was against the law, and could not be suffered. His worship mentioned some fatal injuries that had occurred from this practice to parties not engaged in the game, nor even present as spectators, but passing on roads. The mayor then pointed out to them the superiority of the game of cricket, and offered to assist the pitmen in obtaining ground and implements for the game, if they would establish cricket clubs. They did not seem to relish the change from their old and favourite game; but asked if they might be permitted to play on the moor, if they confined themselves within the circles of the race-course. The mayor asked if they would pledge themselves, in that case, not to cross the ditches. To this they assented by a unanimous shout, and the mayor accepted the condition; afterwards saying, that he would not proceed further against those men to whom summonses had been issued. They then gave three hearty cheers and separated.'

31. Robson was a plane-maker turned schoolteacher. To supplement his meagre earnings he wrote a great many songs for the music hall and in the '50s and '60s contributed a regular dialect column in the *North of England Advertiser* as 'The Retiort Keelmin'.

32. Broadside, 'Pitmen's Strike, 1844'. Wigan Central Library. All of Robson's poems for the Miners' Association were reprinted in one of his volumes of verse, *The Monomaniac and Minor Poems* (Newcastle: Robert Ward, 1848).

33. A. L. Lloyd, *Come All Ye Bold Miners: Ballads and Songs of the Coalfields* (London: Lawrence and Wishart, 1952), pp.70–1. *Tommy Armstrong Sings*, intro. by Tom Gilfellon (Newcastle: Frank Graham, 1971), pp.9–10. See also chap. 5.

34. The *Miners' Advocate* editorialized on the event in nearly every issue after the explosion. The *Northern Star* (19 October 1844) ironically commented, 'We must no longer call the premature death of ninety-five working men *"accidentally"* hurried from existence into eternity, a MURDER. No. It was purely *"accident"* notwithstanding the *"insufficient dams"*, the *"absence of wastemen"*, or the insufficient pillars to support the superincumbent weight of the roof. O, it was all "ACCIDENT", quite an "ACCIDENT": and the jury of viewers, clod poles, understrappers, overlookers, and the whole tribe of Coal King dependents, have declared, ON THEIR OATHS, that proper verdict was *"accidental death"*: and not only so, but at the instance of Mr. CORONER, they further declared, that *"no blame was attachable to any person."* '

35. Broadside Collection, Barnsley Public Library. The poem is based upon an earlier poem by the ex-miner Thomas Wilson (1773–1858). See Chapter 5 for a discussion of Wilson's dialect poetry.

36. *Commission for Inquirying into the Employment and Conditions of Children in Mines and Manufacture* (1842), XVI, pp.513–16.
37. See in particular George Korson, the leading folklorist on American coal mining, *Coal Dust on the Fiddle: Songs and Stories of the Bituminous Industry* (Hatboro, Pa.: Folklore Associates, 1965 [1943]), p.119.
38. 'A Traveller Underground', *Our Coal and Our Coal-pits: The People in them and the Scenes around them*, 2nd ed. (London: Longman, Brown, Green and Longmans, 1856), pp.155–6.

CHAPTER 3 Chartist Poetry and Fiction: The Development of a Class-Based Literature

> Poetry is impassioned truth; and why should we not utter it in the shape that touches our condition most closely — the political?
>
> Ebenezer Elliott

The Chartist movement occupies as significant a place in working-class literature as it does in the history of working people. In literature as in politics, it represented the most imposing attempt by working people to take control of their lives. The Chartists wanted to transform England into a representative democracy where the working-class voice would be heard. Their famous six points were aimed at making it possible for all Britons to participate in the political process. Only then would working people obtain universal suffrage, social justice, a taxation system that did not tax the poor to maintain the rich, and — most important — their dignity. The Chartist promise was so total that for a time it absorbed all other working-class activity; political, trade union, and cultural. From Brighton to Aberdeen, working men and women met weekly to seek the salvation of their class through their Chartist Association; Chartism became a way of life, a rich and varied experience that had a profound impact on its participants. Literature was a valued part of this way of life, and the foremost Chartist writers sought to create a class-based literature, written by and for the people. Their efforts influenced not only working men aspiring to become writers, but also the popular press and such middle-class writers as Charles Kingsley, Thomas Hughes and Dante Rossetti. Out of the political turmoil of Chartism came a new respect for people's literature.

Each wave of Chartist activity created particular demands, and produced distinct types of literature.[1] Over the years came an outpouring of speeches, essays, prison letters, dialogues, short stories, novels, songs, lyrical poems, epics, and later in the century, auto-biographies. This variety grew out of many long-developing political and social movements. The language of class had developed in political struggles over the years 1790–1830, and with it a sharp and effective journalism.[2] The language of protest had developed from folk and religious sources, and found its literary outlet in broadsides. These two traditions joined in the propaganda of trade unionists and such groups as the Ten Hours Movement and the Anti-Poor Law agitation. Chartism alone attempted the development of a class literature, expressive of personal aspiration. Protest, politics and individual hope all came together.

Throughout the decade of 1838–48 the bulk of Chartist literature was exhortative and inspirational; it is similar to the works described in Chapter 2 and will therefore not be discussed here (see the Appendix for a sample of these songs and poems). The concerns of this chapter are with those writers who had read deeply in the radical literary tradition of England and the Continent and wished to express through their own writings the 'impassioned truth' of Chartist politics. At the same time they hoped to fulfill the aesthetic precepts they had learned from the mainstream of English literature. They were deeply concerned with the relationship between politics and art – whether literature should describe conditions in need of change, or the future brother- hood of man, resulting from changed conditions; whether it should give readers a soothing escape from this life or a foretaste of a better life. Their goal was a new, class-based literature.

Chartist poets articulated the ideals of the movement. According to the times they urged political change or educational improvement. In their poetry they taught men about a just and moral world, while emphasizing the heinousness of existing conditions. When radical change seemed remote, however, writers stressed self-education as a means of ameliorating conditions for the entire working class. Intel- lectual autobiographies describing the growth of the poet's mind and his coming to terms with himself and society became common by the end of the Chartist period. But the political inheritance was never forgotten, and gave their poetry a wider social context and under- standing. These poets will be discussed in part I.

The years 1848–53 were the richest period of working-class creativity until the dialect writers rose to prominence in the 1860s. Throughout England working men published each other's writing, started journals and took steps to strengthen class-oriented literature. The most important development of this period was the rise of fiction as a significant working-class artistic medium. The poets who composed serious verse had reached only a few of the best-educated Chartists; popular fiction, on the other hand, was more widely read by workers. The conclusion drawn by those interested in revitalizing political activity was to combine the idealism of poetry with the attractive plotting and characterization of fiction. The common man was made a hero, and his adventures were drawn from Chartist political and social events. Such fiction proved to be rare throughout the nineteenth century, and was not successfully attempted again until the very end of

the century. Part II will discuss the strengths and weaknesses of this
fiction of class struggle.

I
The Poetry of Impassioned Truth

The central task of Chartist poets, in contrast to Chartist propagandists
and song writers, was to create a new poetic tradition which embodied
their political ideals. The essentially private act of creative writing
found its rationale in serving the political needs of the people. Indeed,
the poet was most himself when he contributed to society poems that
would educate, move and enlighten. As early as 1840 the editor of the
Chartist Circular introduced a series entitled 'The Politics of Poets' with
the proclamation 'Poets and their Poetry have, and will continue to
exert an extensive influence on the destinies of Mankind.'[3] In
working-class circles that pursued most ardently the goals of self- and
class-improvement, poets were the acknowledged legislators of
morality. It was the duty of every true Chartist writer to contribute to
the great task of changing individuals, so they would change society.
   These ideas had their roots in the previous generation of Romantic
poets. Chartist writers eagerly imitated their subject matter and poetic
style. Under the influence of Wordsworth and Keats, Nature was an
unadulterated good, 'a poetry that never dies'; in turn the finest poem
was like a work of Nature. The political poetry of Byron and Shelley,
however, was most popular. Byron's fluid and colloquial style proved
an excellent model for writing conversational verse; the mocking prose
and verse dialogues between starving workers and the wealthy owners
owe much to him. The exposure of hypocrisy and folly, a central theme
in Byron, was transmuted by Chartists into descriptions of avarice and
misused power. Byron's melodramatic verse and misunderstood heroes
were less successfully imitated, often becoming bombastic posturing.
Shelley's idealism and faith in human potential were fundamental
tenets among all Chartists. He had been able to imbue such familiar,
and well defined, abstractions as Liberty and Freedom with a mythic
importance beyond specific battles for a free press or universal suffrage.
But in the hands of less skilful writers the descriptions of such ideals
too often became diffuse, static and even incomprehensible. Effective
verse is not necessarily made up of references to the soul, Bright
Liberty, tyrannous foes and hopeful tomorrows.
   The single most important predecessor of Chartist poets was

Ebenezer Elliott, the Corn-Law Rhymer (1781–1849), who paved the way for other 'poets of poverty'.[4] Elliott had been able to establish a very successful iron foundry in Sheffield and to retire to the country with £3,000, but throughout his life he wrote powerful indictments of the rich and their pernicious taxes on corn and other necessities. His descriptions and denunciations of poverty were popular among all classes, and so encouraged otherworking men to write about subjects closer to their personal experience than Nature. Moreover, Elliott always emphasized the concrete consequences of a particular evil, and not its place on a moral scale. The high price of corn meant forced emigration, overwork and child mortality, and not simply the transgressions of a callous government, as sometimes described by better-off Romantic poets. The virtues of concreteness, however, were offset by the accompanying emotional bombast. Elliott's fervid language and urgent appeals to God were appealing to those making their first attempts at verse. If reading Shelley encouraged personification and capitalizations, Elliott encouraged ranting and exclamation points

Elliott, in spite of his denunciation of Chartism after 1839, was admired as a living example of someone who wrote effective political poetry and who had portrayed sympathetically the sufferings of working people. Chartist poets were constantly reminded of their obligation to portray their own class in a favourable light, since many contemporary poets spoke of the 'unruly mob', or described the poor as naïve fools. It was the duty of every working-class writer, as one critic in the *Northern Star* explained, 'never to miss an opportunity of doing honour to the nobility of [his] order.'[5] Ernest Jones took this advice one step further, arguing, 'It is necessary that democratic poets should, in their pages, *elevate* and not endanger the dignity of the democratic character.'[6] The weight of this obligation may explain the general lack of humour among the most ardent poets. They, like Elliott, refused to condone society's more foolish moments, which for them were immoral, unjust or hypocritical. Writing after the death of Chartism, but exemplifying many of its attitudes, Gerald Massey judged Thomas Hood 'with the lofty conclusion, 'Lifeis too real, too earnest, too solemn a thing, to be spent in producing or reading such light literature . . . . Earnestness is at the root of greatness and heroism.'[7] Only an earnest literature could educate and inspire.

Chartist poets were given the responsibility of fitting a new subject — working-class ideals — into the traditional forms of English poetry. Unlike the writers discussed in Chapters 1 and 2, and Chartist song writers, they were forging a new *written* working-class literature.

As pioneers in creating a literature worthy of their people, they embraced the most respected styles of the time. They rarely used song metres or catchy rhymes; the sonnet, the epic and other complicated forms were preferred as more aesthetically important. Cooper wrote his epic, *The Purgatory of Suicides*, in the very difficult Spenserian stanza; it is a *tour de force* that earned him respect among the middle class and admiration among its few working-class readers. It is an extreme example of the problems all Chartist poets faced: how to write appealing and ennobling poetry that was intelligible to the working class. Some, like Cooper, settled for impressing their 'betters'. Most, however, addressed their verse to those educational Chartists anxious to master the riches of English literature. Despite their passionate political message, the difficulty of reading their poetry limited the audience of all Chartist poets. The division between oral and written literature –– songs and poetry – was only partially bridged by writers and readers.

I have concentrated in this section on the four best-known writers: W. J. Linton, Ernest Jones, Gerald Massey and Thomas Cooper. Their poetry and writing mirror many of the strengths and difficulties of pioneering a written working-class literature. They were the most skilful in adapting a variety of poetic forms to their political subject matter; their imagery, metre and language could be effective and sophisticated. The four had very different political beliefs and wrote very different poetry, but for a time each was looked upon as an important poetic voice within the Chartist movement. Linton belonged to the radical tradition of the 1820s and early '30s, in which both the middle class and the working-class could co-exist; his political enemies were the aristocracy, the church and privilege. After he was disillusioned with Chartism, he became a republican and was active in supporting Mazzini.[8] Gerald Massey's politics were a diffuse form of revolutionary sentiment, unenlightened by any ideological comprehension. After his initial fervour died, he no longer wrote political poetry. Cooper's life was a series of conversions; although he briefly converted to Chartism and was an ardent leader, he was fundamentally most concerned with his own intellectual needs. Throughout his life he was an active proponent of self-help. Jones alone remained ideologically committed to Chartism. He was the only one of the four who was not self-educated, and he tried the hardest to write verse that was accessible to working-class readers. He used familiar metres, such as the ballad and rhymed couplets, and avoided recondite allusions and a literary tone.

The commitment to writing ennobling poetry went hand in hand

with an earnest desire to master the literary and political antecedents of
Chartism. The London engraver W. J. Linton (1812–97) (Plate 7)
wrote poetry for many years, first under his own name and then as
'Spartacus', which embodied his rather dated political beliefs and his
wide reading in French and English. He published a weekly journal, *The
National* (1839), in order to 'supply the working classes with political
and other information not open to them with their limited means for
purchase and time for study.'[9] He spent long hours copying out
sections of Godwin's *Political Justice*, translating Condorcet, Voltaire
and Robespierre, and preparing engravings for the cover. His series,
'Hymns to the Unenfranchised' are sophisticated and clear, albeit
poetically stiff, descriptions of the oppression of the poor. The tenth
hymn, showing the influence of Shelley and Elliott, is a good example
of the strengths and weaknesses of early Chartist poetry:

>Truth is no more the anarch Custom's prey;
>>Man, the poor serf, by kings and priests long hounded
>Into the den of Woe, now turns at bay:
>>The trampler is unhorsed, the hunter wounded.

>We sought for peace – ye gave us toil and war;
>>We begg'd for quiet bread – and stones were given: –*
>Tyrants and priests! we will be scourged no more:
>>The chains of loyalty and faith are riven.

>What bargain have your boasted victories bought?
>>Church-rates and gyves, corn-laws and desolation:
>Tyrants and priests! *we* need not *your* support; –
>>The Nation will work out its own salvation.

>We claim Man's equal rights; we will no ruin
>>Even unto the robbers: – Love, Truth-gender'd,
>Dwelleth with Justice: we to all men doing
>>That we require shall unto us be render'd.[10]

The form of this poem is far more complex than those works
intended primarily for singing (though obviously not all songs have easy
words – witness 'The Internationale'). The sharply broken lines, alternating masculine and feminine rhymes and intricate sentence structure

* Taxing us to build new churches in a time of famine [Linton's footnote].

force the reader to go slowly, savouring each phrase and considering its implications. Linton presents a vision of a better world that can be wrested from the existing unjust world through the concerted action of all truth-loving men. The static reified world of 'The Pit Boy' or 'The Miner's Doom' is the reverse of the world described here by Linton; social inequality and injustice are the result of human actions, and can be changed by human actions. The literary expression of man's ability to transform existing conditions and build a new society was Chartism's contribution to working-class literature.

Ernest Jones (1819–68) (Plate 8) was particularly successful in embodying Chartist ideals and actions in his poetry. A barrister from an aristocratic family, Jones had already published poetry before joining the Chartist movement.[11] Although not of working-class background, he belongs in this discussion because of his importance as Chartism's finest poet and novelist; his influence among working men who wrote both within and without the movement was great. Jones did not enter the Chartist movement until the spring of 1846; Chartist poets at this stage wrote about not only 'Tyrants and priests', but also about the future brotherhood of man. Their readers understood their own oppression, and wanted descriptions of the new world that political change would bring. Jones was a strong advocate of O'Connor's Land Plan as a means of establishing a just social order. All of his verse supporting the Plan urged a united assault on current conditions, and the rapid establishment of the new society. A popular recitation piece among Chartists was 'The Factory Town', describing the hideousness of factory life and the joys of rural life under the Plan.

> Fear ye not your masters' power;
>   Men are strong when men unite;
> Fear ye not one stormy hour:
>   *Banded millions need not fight.*
>
> Then, how many a happy village
>   Shall be smiling o'er the plain,
> Amid the corn-field's pleasant tillage,
>   And the orchard's rich domain!
>
> While, the rotting roof and rafter,
>   Drops the factory, stone by stone,
> Echoing loud with childhood's laughter,
>   Where it rung with manhood's groan![12]

The Ten Hours Movement had published many doleful verses describing the factory system, but their poets had never been able to give much life or energy to their static portraits of suffering. Jones, on the other hand, explained what individual workers could do to bring about change and to make possible theparadise of rural resettlement.

Jones was highly aware of the importance of intangible feelings and emotions in galvanizing the oppressed. Descriptions of injustice and oppression could anger workers, but appeals to their idealism could focus that anger and channel it toward political action. He believed working men wanted social change both to right their own injustices and to establish a world in which all people could flourish. Early in 1848, before the Continental revolutions, he published 'The Funeral of the Year and Its Epitaph', a long description of corruption, suffering and death. The poem ends, however, on an optimistic note, with a consideration of the battles undertaken for freedom and justice. European working men who have fought these battles have learned to act as brothers, and have therefore moved closer toward realizing their goals:

> Pause, reader! pause; *that* side the shadow lies,
> But turn on *this* as well thine equal eyes.
> This year has stirred the nations far and wide,
> And woke in slavery's heart a manly pride;
> Hark to the clank of chains, as yet untorn,
> But not as erst in tame supineness worn.
> As break the rivers at the thaw-winds' call
> The icy bondage of their wintry thrall,
> And dash their waves in volumes vast along,
> Sounding through many lands the self-same song —
> So one great pulse in nations' hearts has wrought.
> Beating harmonious to the self-same thought.
> Old rivals now no longer look askance,
> But England holds the olive branch to France.
> The Teuton walks the Rhine's contested strand,
> Nor fears the Lurlei's swan-eclipsing hand;
> The Celt and Saxon meet no more as foes
> But twine the hardy shamrock round the rose;
> And bigotry, oppression's bitterest rod,
> Sinks fast before the ennobling thought of God.

'All men *are* brethren!' how the watchwords run!
And now men *act* as such, then freedom's won.

Old year! old year! sleep peaceful in thy grave.
Thou camest to teach, to punish, and to save.[13]

Although Jones has not described the conflict between '*that* side' and '*this*', he has explained metaphorically the psychological changes occurring among the seekers of freedom; the images drawn from nature make their victory seem inevitable. By pointing to the idealism among working people of many nationalities, he justifies the Chartist cause and its struggle for a more complete victory. The poem presupposes fundamental social change, and denies the legitimacy of the existing social and political order. The rendering of justice, emphasized by Linton, is no longer sufficient, and the old social order is to be swept away.

The theme of class conflict was carried on in the later years of Chartism by Gerald Massey (1828–1907) (Plate 9). Massey's life is a remarkable example of politics and poetry yielding worldly success. The son of a canal boatman, his childhood was spent in unrelieved poverty, first as a silk factory operative and straw plaiter, and then as an errand boy in London. In 1849 he edited and wrote almost singlehandedly the Uxbridge *Spirit of Freedom*. His journalistic experience gave him valuable contacts, and he was soon publishing his verse in Chartist journals. In 1851 he published his first volume of verse, *Voices of Freedom and Lyrics of Love*, later issued as *Poems and Ballads* (1854). The middle-class literati saw the craggy well-built Massey as a prototype success story, made a bit more delicious by his righteous indignation at the sufferings of the less fortunate. Favourable reviews soon led Massey out of radical circles and into a career as a lecturer, specializing in mesmerism and phrenology.[14]

During his political phase Massey was unabashedly among the reddest of the red. He was strongly influenced by Julian Harney, who introduced him to the revolutionary movements of the Continent. He was even more enthusiastic than Jones about the brotherhood of man and the inevitable triumph of liberal democracies throughout Europe. In his political verse he emphasized ideals such as freedom and justice that would arouse men to political action. As the possibility of revolution faded, his poetry became more fervently optimistic:

> Fling out the red Banner! in mountain and valley
>> Let Earth feel the tread of the free once again;
> Now soldiers of Freedom, for love of God! rally,
>> Old earth yearns to know that her children are men.
> We are nerv'd by a million wrongs, burning, and bleeding;
>> Bold thoughts leap to birth, — but the bold deeds must come.
> And whenever Humanity's yearning and pleading,
>> One battle for liberty, strike we heart-home!
>
> Fling out the red Banner! its fiery front under
>> Come gather ye, gather ye, champions of Right!
> And roll round the world with the voice of God's thunder
>> The wrongs we've to reckon — oppressors to smite!
> They deem that we strike no more, like the old Hero-band,
>> Martyrdom's own, battle-hearted and brave,
> Blood of Christ! Brothers mine, it were sweet but to see ye stand,
>
> . . . . . .
>
> Fling out the red Banner! the patriots perish.
>> But where their bones whiten, the seed striketh root;
> Their heart's-life ran red, the great harvest to cherish,
>> Then gather ye, reapers, and garner the fruit.
> Victory! victory! Tyrants are quaking!
>> The Titan of Toil from the bloody thrall starts;
> The slaves are awaking — the dawnlight is breaking —
>> The footfall of Freedom, beats quick at our hearts![15]

'Our Symbol', or as it was called in later editions, 'The Song of the Red Republican', is far more inflated than anything Linton or Jones wrote. 'Millions of wrongs', but no one is specifically mentioned; the images of battle do not lead anywhere, except perhaps to a quickening of the reader's spirit. Yet the emotional impact is dissipated by the extravagant language. Moreover, the class struggle is reduced to 'soldiers of Freedom' and 'champions of Right', rather than specific, recognizable persons who have suffered injustice. Harney pointedly criticized Massey's political poems for 'a painful striving for effect by means of big words and monstrous fantasies', and for mentioning God more than a hundred times in an eighty-page volume.[16]

'The Song of the Red Republican' illustrates one of the main difficulties in writing political poetry: writers did not visualize clearly their message and its recipients. 'The footfall of Freedom' beating at

the heart gives no clear image of power or change, but instead a peculiar
sense of emptiness, as if Massey were not quite sure whom he was
addressing, or if anyone were listening anymore. This confusion was
accentuated by an unclear notion of the appropriate subject matter and
style at a time when Chartism was dying. At one point Massey had
declared, 'There is more poetry to be *lived* than to be written! There is
no poetry like that of a noble life, wrought out amidst suffering and
martyrdom.'[17] Yet Massey did not choose to write about noble
suffering or 'the byways and nooks of the world.' Instead his political
verse was either an idealistic exhortation such as 'Red Republican', or a
description of the world after 'glory' had been achieved. Unable to
dramatize the quiet lives he praised, Massey attempted to dramatize
artificially his political ideals, making heavy use of the command form,
personification and exclamation points.

Exhortatory literature loses its force very quickly; the harder Massey
and others tried to be passionate and powerful, the duller they became.
Ernest Jones had long warned novice authors, 'when the truths of a
principle are once established in the minds of millions, unless a *new*
argument is advanced against them, we cannot burthen our readers with
the repetition of an oft told tale.'[18] 'Something more' was needed. The
answer was poetry as a good in and of itself, offering delights that could
not be found elsewhere. The style and framework of political verse
were often kept, but the intentions had shifted. Harney, in recommending Tennyson, caught much of the new Chartist priority for
literature: 'His poetry is a very world of wondrous beauty – purifying
and ennobling beauty; and working men should be made acquainted
with it that they may get beauty into their souls, and thence into their
daily lives.'[19] To 'get beauty' would sustain a man through dark
political times.

Here again Massey reflected the mood of the time. In 'The Chivalry
of Labour Exhorted to the Worship of Beauty', he urged his readers to
look beyond themselves to Nature:

Come out of the den of darkness and the city's toil of sin,
Put on your radiant Manhood, and the Angel's blessing win!
Where wealthier sunlight comes from Heaven, like welcome-smiles
    of God,
And Earth's blind yearnings leap to life in flowers, from out the sod:
Come worship Beauty in the forest-temple, dim and hush,
Where stands Magnificence dreaming! and God burneth in the bush:
Or where the old hills worship with their silence for a psalm,

Or ocean's weary heart doth keep the sabbath of its calm
Come let us worship Beauty with the knightly faith of old.
O Chivalry of Labour toiling for the Age of Gold!

Come let us worship Beauty: she hath subtle power to start
Heroic work and deed out-flashing from the humblest heart:
Great feelings will gush unawares, and freshly as the first
Rich Rainbow that up startled Heaven in tearful splendour burst.
O blessed are her lineaments, and wondrous are her ways
To repicture God's worn likeness in the suffering human face!
Our bliss shall richly overbrim like sunset in the west,
And we shall dream immortal dreams and banquet with the Blest.
Then let us worship Beauty with the knightly faith of old.
O Chialry of Labour toiling for the Age of Gold![20]

The substance of this poem is little more than a series of images based
on that familiar Victorian cliché, man is closer to God in nature than in
the city. The final couplet of each stanza, however, shows the grafting
of Carlyle's work ethic on the Chartist idea of class pride. The poem
readjusts politics to serve literature, instead of vice versa.

The shift away from a political poetry describing fundamental
grievances and their redress was reflected in Massey's self-image. At first
he appears to have hoped to revive the people through his violent
language and fiery manner. He dedicated his 1851 volume to a fellow
Chartist, William Cooper (no relation to Thomas), with a long
introductory letter explaining why he had written such verse as 'The
Song of the Red Republican', 'The Men of Forty-Eight', and 'The Red
Banner':

> I shall be accused of sowing class-hatred, and yet, my friend, I do
> not seek to fling fire-brands among the combustibles of society. I
> yearn to raise my brethren into loveable beings, and when I smite
> their hearts, I would rather they should gush with the healing waters
> of love than the fearful fires of hatred: but looking on the wrongs
> which are daily done in the land, will sometimes make the blood
> rush to the heart, and crimson to the brow. Who can see the masses
> ruthlessly robbed of all the fruits of their industry, of all the sweet
> pleasures of life, and of that nobleness which should crown human
> nature as with a crown of glory, and not strive to arouse them to a
> sense of their degradation, and urge them to end the bitter bondage
> and the murderous martyrdom of Toil! Not he who feels concen-
> trated and crushing upon himself the slavery of millions.[21]

In this passage we are back to the language of 1839 and the physical-force rhetoric of necessary violence in the name of essential change – and yet conditions had changed, making such a call an impossible hope for a handful, in comparison to the thousands of a previous decade.

Massey, like his predecessors, argued that his purpose in writing poetry was to instruct men in how they could love and understand one another better. But, given the 'murderous martyrdom of Toil', he is forced to write inflammatory verse, urging toilers to rise up against their oppressors. His readers, however, did not join him singing 'Fling out the red Banner!' and Massey himself changed. In the preface to the third edition of 1854, the dedication to William Cooper was dropped and Massey's poetic purpose shifted to a form of amelioration in line with such poems as 'The Chivalry of Labour Exhorted to the Worship of Beauty'. He now calls his political poetry 'memorials of my past', kept as 'some worn out garment because he had passed through the furnace in it.' Through a long quotation by 'the rebel', Massey places himself at one remove from an altered version of the above quotation:

'It is not', says he, 'that I seek to sow dissension between classes and class, or fling firebrands among the combustibles of society; for when I smite the hearts of my fellows, I would rather they should gush with the healing waters of love, than with the fearful fires of hatred. I yearn to raise them into loveable beings. I would kindle in the hearts of the masses a sense of the beauty and grandeur of the universe, call forth the lineaments of Divinity in their poor wan faces, give them glimpses of the grace and glory of Love and the marvellous significance of Life,and elevate the standard of Humanity for all. But strange wrongs are daily done in the land, bitter feelings are felt, and wild words will be spoken. It is not for myself that I have uncurtained some scenes of my life to the public gaze, but as an illustration of the lives of others, who suffer and toil on, "die, and make no sign;" and because one's own personal experience is of more value than that of others taken upon hearsay.'[22]

The function of poetry, as well as Massey's self-image, has changed radically here. It is not a call to action, but a means to elevate and ennoble the masses. 'Nature', 'Divinity', 'Love' and 'Humanity' have replaced 'slavery', 'human nature', 'degradation' and 'nobleness'. The working-class is no longer denied justice by a corrupt system, but is in need of personal enlightenment and improvement. By reading the elevating poetry of a fellow worker, each would feel an answering chord of nobility in his heart, and become sufficiently strengthened to see 'beauty and grandeur' in spite of his poverty. In turn, the poet would educate middle-class readers about the ways and thoughts of the mute workers who 'suffer and toil on'. Massey now sees the working-class poet as a pacifier of his class – the poor must be taught not to speak 'wild words' or have 'bitter feelings', but to know 'the standard of Humanity for all', regardless of class divisions. The radical demand for more education and opportunity has become a conservative force, reinforcing existing values rather than those of a developing class.

One of the major difficulties faced by political poets was to combine literary enthusiasm and political beliefs in a manner attractive to their less educated peers. At every stage of the movement leaders encouraged self-education, particularly through literature. As one Barnsley Chartist explained in his introductory remarks to an evening school club rules, 'An extensive Literary Education, may be classified amongst the highest of all earthly enjoyments; not only, in its beneficial effects on the Individual who possesses it, but, in its application conducive to the welfare of society at large.'[23] The political justification for reading and writing poetry was its power as spiritual leavening among the mass of people. In a review of a volume of poetry edited by members of the National Chartist Association, the *English Chartist Circular* said, 'We rejoice . . . because we regard "Singing for the Million" as something to glory in – something towards the great work of regenerating the now mentally debased – to cheer the physically oppressed, – and to stimulate men to noble deeds for Truth and Freedom's sake.'[24] Educational Chartists were convinced that nothing would be more effective in strengthening working-class unity over time than a thoroughly moral education. Literature, which could be made readily available to all, provided the foundation.

The first stage in the literary education of working men was resurrecting their own heritage. Linton's *The National* was only one of many journals that published excerpts from politically sympathetic artists. The Glasgow *Chartist Circular* (1839–41) ran a series called 'The Politics of Poetry', including the major contemporary poets, Scots poets from all periods and minor poets with working-class backgrounds. At the conclusion of an essay on Wordsworth and Elliott, the editor, William Thomson, declared, 'Let the people bathe deep in the light of the accumulated genius of many ages, and armed at all points "with heaven-born knowledge" – let them enter boldly on the conflict between light and darkness, and tyrants alone have cause to fear the issue of the contest.'[25] He advocated Chartist schools (with a recommended one teacher for every 150 pupils) because he hated the literature he had been forced to read as a child. In thenew schools honest Burns and not the toadying Allan Ramsey would be taught. Throughout Julian Harney's editorship of the *Northern Star* (1845–50, 1852) long excerpts of radical English poetry were published; Milton, Thomson, Shelley and Byron were his favourites. In 1846 he published a series on American democrats and agrarianists, devoting much space to his friend and Chartist sympathizer, John Greenleaf Whittier. He encouraged readers to send in their own works, asking particularly for poems to commemorate the Hungarian and Italian patriots who had fled their native lands.

Educational Chartists also looked to the most famous writers of the day to provide a literature suitable for uplifting the working class. Ernest Jones rhetorically asked, 'Can Tennyson do no more than troll a courtly lay?' The 'cheap and nasty' products of serialized fiction, street broadsides and the music hall did not have sufficient literary merit, and for many Chartists they seemed to be specifically designed to drug the political consciousness of the reader.[26] The middle-class novels of industrialism, such as Mrs Trollope's *Michael Armstrong* (1839–40) and Mrs Gaskell's *Mary Barton* (1848), with their anti-union and anti-Chartist positions, were scarcely likely to win many readers among militant working men. Jones warned contemporary authors — the natural artistic leaders of society — of their duty to be relevant, 'We say to the great minds of the day, come among the people, write for the people, and your fame will live for ever. The people's instinct will give life to your philosophy, and the genius of the favoured few will hand down peace and plenty, knowledge andpower, as an heirloom to posterity.'[27] Literature honestly written about the working class would bring both the writer and his audience — from all classes — a better understanding of society.

Chartist educators put most of their energy into teaching fellow workers how to write a literature worthy of their class. As Thomas Cooper explained in a letter addressed 'To the Young Men of the Working Classes', it was,

> a matter of the highest necessity, that you all join hands and head to create a literature of your own. Your own prose, your own poetry ... would put you all more fully in possession of each other's thoughts and thus give you a higher respect for each other, and a

clearer perception of what you can do when united.[28]

He went on to give practical advice on how to write poetry, suggesting that young men should read widely to form their own poetic taste, and to remember to 'use plain words', and avoid 'inflation of expression – over-swelling words – sound without sense – and exaggerated sentimentalism.'[29] It was advice Massey – and Cooper himself – would have done well to accept. The pedagogical as well as moral benefits of writing poetry were emphasized by John Burland, a Chartist teacher from Barnsley. He found each part of poetry – the metrics, metaphors, word selection and logical construction – conducive to learning, and stated triumphantly, 'the person who assiduously endeavours to become a good poet, cannot do otherwise than become an elegant and accomplished scholar.'[30] The mastery of the forms of poetry encouraged both 'intellectual and moral progress' which in turn made men worthy of suffrage.

The best-known conjunction of literary education and Chartist principles was Thomas Cooper's Shakespearean Chartist Association, which flourished in Leicester in 1841 and 1842. Under Cooper's leadership classes were formed with such names as 'Major Cartwright Class', 'John Milton Class' and 'George Washington Class'.[31] He combined the teaching of poetry and politics by encouraging men to write political hymns and poems, which were published as a small six-penny volume (see Appendix). Events chastened many Leicester Chartists, and by the end of the 1840s the poets had turned from passionate hymns to poems of self-development. William Jones in the introduction to his dream vision *The Spirit; or A Dream in the Woodlands* (1849) explained his change,

... the earlier shapings of his subject were somewhat imbued with vindictiveness, couched in terms construable into personality; but sober reflection taught him to regard the enunciation of such feelings as calculated only to do mischief – whether resorted to by rich or poor. Besides, it is his firm conviction that social wrong, and the morally degrading causes which have pressed so long and so heavily upon working-men, especially in manufacturing districts, can only have permanent removal in proportion to the growth of te masses in Knowledge, Temperance and Self-Respect. If the subsequent thoughts, finding expression in rhyme, have a tendency to hasten such happy result, the end of their publication will be answered, and the writer have reason to rejoice that he embraced the opportunity to spread the principles of Progression and Peace amongst his fellow men.[32]

The working class is itself now blamed for the social wrongspressing down upon it — a conclusion very close to Gerald Massey's, and a long way from Chartist ideas about social oppression.

'Thoughts finding expression inrhyme' is a good description of Chartist poetry after 1848; Thomas Cooper (1805–92) (Plate 10), however, tried to combine his learning, personal beliefs and political hopes in his poetry. As a youth he had devoted himself to mastering six languages, science, mathematics and a variety of other disciplines, almost without companionship or encouragement. For several years he ran a large school in Lincolnshire, but his learning offended the more narrow-minded parents. In time he took up journalism and later lecturing, the two careers he was to pursue for the rest of his life. At the age of fifty he reconverted — on the platform — to Christianity, and devoted the remainder of his long life to the Baptist ministry. For a brief period he led a large Chartist association in Leicester, providing not only classes, but also a coffee-house, newspapers and general guidance. Convicted in 1843 of sedition, he was imprisoned for two years. During this time he wrote *The Purgatory of Suicides*, an epic in Spenserian rhyme, describing all manner of classical, medieval and modern suicides. A monument to Cooper's learning, it is virtually unreadable. The political content is murky because of the long digressions and descriptions, but several Romans speak in favour of Chartist principles, and in one of the more dramatic sections, Judas, of all people, heaps invective upon Castlereagh.

While Cooper was in gaol he received an anonymous offer of tuition at Cambridge, with the stipulation that he forego politics. He turned down the offer,but his epic was living proof that he was as learned as any poet with a Cambridge degree. A mixture of pride, self-seeking and abnegation characterized many of Cooper's litery efforts. In his introduction to Book II he compares himself, with some modesty, to the greatest of previous poets:

> Lyre of my fatherland! anew, to wake
> thy solemn shell, I come, — with trembling hand, —
> Feeling my rudeness doth harsh discord make
> With strings great minstrels all divinely spanned.
> How shall a thrall essay to join your band, —

Ye freeborn spirits whose bold music fired
My freeborn sires to draw the glittering brand
For home and England, – or, in arms attired,
To awe their lion kings who to sole power aspired?

How shall a thrall, from humble labour sprung,
Successful, strike the lyre in scornful age,
When full-voiced bards have each neglected sung,
And loftiest rhyme is deemed a worthless page
By crowds that bow in Mammon-vassalage?
Gray Prudence saith the world will disregard
My harping rude, – or term it sacrilege
That captive leveller hath rashly dared
To touch the sacred function of the tuneful bard.

. . . . . .

Poet of Paradise, – whose glory illumed
My path of youthful penury, till grew
The desert to a garden, and Life bloomed
With hope and joy, 'midst suffering, – honour due
I cannot render thee; but reverence true
This heart shall give thee, till it reach the verge
Where human splendours lose their lustrous hue;
And, when, in death, mortal joys all merge –
Thy grand and gorgeous music, Milton, be my dirge! – [33]

Cooper aimed to create a working man's epic, but he was unable to carry his idea one step further, and argue for a new literary aesthetic. Although he takes pride in his background of 'humble labour', he was determined to write an epic worthy of past giants, and not of interest to the 'crowds that bow in Mammon-vassalage.' In later editions this line was toned down to 'And Taste doth browse on bestial pasturage', but the connotations of an unenlightened, materialistic general public remain. For all of his Chartist commitment, Cooper saw himself as an intellectual leader, apart from the masses.

In his autobiography (1872) Cooper explained at length his difficulties in finding a publisher, for the benefit of other poor men seeking to publish their poems. Despite his inordinate pride, he was indebted to the kindness of many influential men; Disraeli, Harrison Ainsworth, John Forster and Douglas Jerrold all read the manuscript and offered advice, often accompanied by letters of recommendation to prominent publishers. Within three months of his release from prison Cooper found a sympathetic radical publisher; the epic went through three editions between 1845 and 1853, and was reviewed quite widely.[34] As Douglas Jerrold explained, a Chartist poet had a better chance of being listened to than a conservative, 'inasmuch as there is to be expected from him newer developments than can be hoped for from one of an expiring creed.'[35] A more difficult issue, discussed at greater length in the next two chapters, was whether middle-class reviewers took the work seriously, or patronized it as an interesting example of working-class talent.

In spite of many stirring passages, the political intention of *The Purgatory of Suicides* was obscured by the deliberately self-advertising display of information. Reviewers of every persuasion criticized the work for what Jerrold called 'its perpetual display of learning and allusions to subjects that can only be familiar to persons more than commonly well read, and not to the class with which the author so specifically delights to connect himself.' Cooper was trapped by his painfully acquired learning and his middle-class aesthetics. In the 1877 edition of Cooper's collected poetry he apologized for the political passages in *The Purgatory of Suicides*, and like Massey, defended his fight 'for Human Freedom', which his 'Mind-history' records. He claimed his most lasting personal gain from writing the epic was as an outlet against bitterness in times of personal depression. He had to be content with distant admiration from both the middle-class and the working class.

It was often a hard and lonely battle for such autodidacts as Cooper, who spent many hours of their youth reading into the night, breaking away from the lure of politics and comradeship to return to yet another book, mathematics problem or half-completed poem. Although their efforts might be praised by sympathetic men such as Jerrold, too often they found no place in the swirling events surrounding the Chartist movement, and were sent back into their isolated world of books after a brief foray into leadership. It was only in a later generation that such men could find a role for themselves within the complexities of working-class society — and even then, as Chapter 5 documents, they found many limitations, and changed their own high ideals about literature and art to suit their audience and its politics.

II
Chartist Fiction

Just as the better-educated Chartist had a taste for the dignities and forms of traditional poetry, so had he a distaste for the conservative social message of popular fiction. In 1841 William Thomson made a characteristic attack upon the publishers of serial fiction for encouraging a love of aristocratic romance among the poor. Whenever a hero appeared in humble life he was invariably found to be a long-lost son of an aristocrat whose innate nobility shone through in spite of his poor associates. Thomson called for 'a Radical Literary Reform', in which 'The virtues of the masses should be sought out and extolled; the iniquities of the *titled* honestly exposed and condemned. Every man should be praised or blamed as he merits, and false glory extinguished. All men are equal, distinction is artificial, and the vile press has spread the iniquity.'[36] His suggested solution proved too simple: 'the intelligent people' were to cease reading such works that 'wickedly trample on their rights, and unjustly elevate their oppressors.' But Chartist writers were not slow to recognize the need for their own literature to counteract the demeaning portrayal of working people and the adulation of the aristocracy. In addition to their poetry column, Chartist newspapers and periodicals ran sketches that 'sought out and extolled' the virtues of the working class. Particularly in the late 'forties fiction became more important for Chartists, and a number of writers tried their hand at sketches and novels.

Chartists used two basic forms of fiction: the moral fable and the popular novel. The fable appealed primarily to educational Chartists who sought a literature reflecting their best hopes and aspirations while condemning the social conditions that perpetrated so much suffering and lack of opportunity. Thomas Cooper is the best known exponent of this type of fiction, although many others wrote fables, including W. J. Linton and Ernest Jones. The more innovative form was the popular novel, particularly as written by G. W. M. Reynolds, a Chartist sympathizer and pioneer in combining romance and politics.[37] Writers placed in a class context such traditional ingredients as unrequited love, a hero of superior character and heart-stirring adventures. The latter came largely from the Chartist movement itself. Wheeler's *Sunshine and Shadow* (1849–50), published in the *Northern Star*, is the most narrowly political. Thomas Frost, who had written for Salisbury Square publishers, had several commissions from political magazines. Ernest Jones was probably the most outstanding writer in this group; his education and wealthy background enabled him to write about every level of society. *De Brassier: A Democratic Romance* (1851–2) and *Women's Wrongs* (1852) were his most widely admired political novels.

Chartists began writing novels based on popular fiction when the movement began to falter politically. They needed an alternative form of fiction to encourage potential members and to sustain the faithful. Their material was drawn from earlier Chartist agitation to remind readers of their rich political heritage, and to show the link between it and the less promising present. Readers could see the mistakes and strengths of the past and plan for more effective political work. Thomas Martin Wheeler in his introduction to *Sunshine and Shadow* pointed out the need to attract young people:

> ... the opponents of our principles have been allowed to wield the power of imagination over the youth of our party, without any effort on our part to occupy this wide and fruitful plain. Would that some of the many talented minds acknowledging our tenets, would achieve that supremacy in the novel which Thomas Cooper has done in the epic.[38]

Wheeler, like Cooper, wanted a fiction that working men would recognize as an intellectual achievement by one of their own class. Ernest Jones settled more openly for an entertaining plot, declaring, 'I do not see why Truth should always be dressed in stern and repulsive garb. The more attractive you make her, the more easily she will progress.'[39]

All Chartist fiction was built upon stereotyped characterization and plotting. Authors consciously broke away from the character development and unified action found in the bourgeois novel in order to emphasize the political implications of a situation. Readers were expected to identify with the hero only as a typical honest-hearted working man who embodied their best characteristics. A great many events befall the hero in order to document as fully as possible the oppression of the working class. Characters frequently die not simply as a convenient way to end a story, but also to bring home the inevitable conclusion of oppression left unchanged. The courage of the hero combined with his many misfortunes focuses the anger of the reader against those in power. It is a literature designed to increase social tension rather than to provide an explanation for injustice. Because both the characters and the events are familiar to the reader, he is not waylaid by a consideration of motivations and alternatives. Psychological analysis gives way to a political analysis of why good people are trodden down by circumstances. This fiction first quickens the reader's existing anger, and then channels it toward a political outlet.

Both the moral fables and the popular fiction shared a vision of society as corrupt and in need of change; they are part of what William Empson has called 'the realistic pastoral', in which the focus upon human waste and social injustice yields in the reader a fuller conception of the possibilities of life.[40] While writing in a realistic mode, all Chartist novelists expressed a hope for a better future which is close to a pastoral world where conflicts can be reconciled and the simple, natural human sentiments can reign unchallenged. In judging the contrast between what is — human waste — with what should and could be — human fulfilment — an author will soften at least some elements of class conflict in order to present the means of changing the old into the new. If he does not do so, the difficulties of affecting change seem insurmountable, and the reader will not believe in the promise of fulfilment. Moreover, if the potential conflict appears too destructive, the reader may consider the price of change,even when it brings improvement for himself, to be too high. Sympathizers from all classes are needed to bring about a people's revolution. At the same time the hope of a new society involves a simplification of the complex — a process which concentrates and makes more forceful the wrongs suffered by the people, and thereby heightens the sense of class conflict. These two contradictory tendencies are reconciled in the hero. Whether passive (as in the moral fable) or active (as in the popular novel), he embodies certain ideals which placed him at odds with the existing society, and closer to the envisioned new society. He is linked to the people through his common shared humanity, but separate from them through his superior political idealism.

The hero, as the mouthpiece of the author, often carried a very heavy share of the moral burden. Authors started with their political ideas and then tried to build characters and actions around them; the results were necessarily mixed. At its worst, a piece became wooden propaganda, but the best narratives combined emotionally-charged action with effective analysis. Jones, in *De Brassier*, describes the motivations and satisfactions of a mob plundering a banker's home; at the same time he analyzes the moral dilemma faced by the hero in this situation. If he defends the banker he will lose all credibility with the men, but if he permits them to continue he knows the general public will turn against the cause of democracy. Jones does not evade the implications of political activity and does not flinch from portraying

characteristics he sees as weaknesses of the people. The hero could also
be a means of demonstrating the relationship between personal
oppression and political change. Bitter poverty teaches Arthur, of
Sunshine and Shadow, the necessity of working for the realization of
concrete changes within his own lifetime. Unlike Chartist poetry, which
often simply asserted a position, in fiction writers could portray
characters and situations that brought to life complex political
problems.

The moral fable was adapted from religious and folk traditions.
During the early years of Chartism it was primarily a simple means of
explaining everyday injustices suffered by working people. Traditional
religious connotations gave the fable greater emotional and symbolic
weight than its simple form might indicate. Since fables and illustrative
anecdotes were frequently used in Chartist speeches, readers found an
immediate relation between their reading and what they had heard at a
political rally. Moreover, fables were built upon oral traditions; they
clarified and focused knowledge that had been shared among working
people in Chartist discussions and meetings. With this background the
connection between the disasters sketched in a tale and political action
was easily made. By sharpening the consciousness of oppression, fables
encouraged greater political commitment.

W. J. Linton published a characteristic series called 'Reords of the
World's Justice', told by a 'Hardwareman', in *The National* (1839).
Each sketch revolves around a particular case of the rich and powerful
destroying the poor and honest. Realistic descriptions of working
conditions and poverty are combined with allegorical characters and
plots. The characters act out their parts (Honest Age, Corrupt Parson,
Faithful Child, etc.) to formula, leading to a Chartist moral. The series
served as a model for other writers, and was reprinted in the *English
Chartist Circular* (1841–3) along with Linton's 'Hymns to the
Unenfranchised'.

In 'The Pauper' Ashton, representing Honest Age, is unable to pay
his church-rate of three shillings, and so the Law drives him from his
home. He had been a day labourer of 'irreproachable' character, whose
'little store' of savings had been exhausted by illness and hard times. He
lost two sons through impressment during the Napoleonic Wars; one
daughter had been seduced by Mr Euston and had died on the streets.
His remaining daughter is unable to earn enough by her needle to keep
them in food and pay the church-rate. His house is seized to pay the
rate and,

The Honourable Mr. Euston is now a Viscount with a pension of £5,000 a year, his wife having been, with his consent, one of the king's mistresses.He has never done a real day's work in his life. His hardest work has been legislating – I mean picking the pockets of industrious folk and endeavouring to demoralize the people: the last I am sure is easy to him. Now I don't like to differ from the world, but this is what I call a pauper: I may be wrong, for they say a pauper is one who lives on *charity*, and the *noble* Viscount lives by robbery. I am a rough plain man – some say I am as stiff and hard-hearted as one of my own steel pokers – yet I do wish for a somewhat better distribution of property (to be made in a spirit of good-will, on the live-and-let-live system,) so as to prevent all kinds of pauperism, which must be very unpleasant (to say the least of it) even to a Viscount.[41]

While the reader might identify with Ashton, he is not expected to agree with his Job-like patience; rather, the hardwareman's ironic rhetoric implies the necessity of political action.

Later authors of this form added more direct conversations and action, but the basic formula remained unaltered. For example, Jones's 'The London Door-Step' (1848)[42] describes the death of an honourable woman picked up for vagrancy when she rested momentarily on the door step of a mansion in Grosvenor Square, where the man within earns £15,000, has two country homes and a government position. Her husband had left Leicester some weeks previous in search of work. Attempting to stop a policeman from beating a woman after the famous Kennington Common meeting, he was struck with a truncheon and died. His wife, unable to find him, sinks onto the door step under the burden of hunger, fear and exhaustion. The 'proud aristocrat' within sends his 'powdered lackey' to expel 'that drunken woman'. Jones anathamatizes him as 'A SOCIAL MURDERER' for his unwillingness to share 'a trifle with that wretched victim'. The language is more lurid than Linton's, but the convention of piling indignities upon the poor victim, and the political moral are unchanged.

With the decline of Chartism the political message of fables changed. Educational Chartists were probably influenced by the rise of the new purified press of the late 'forties and early 'fifties. Fiction, previously refused by the uplifting educational journals, became their mainstay, albeit greatly chastened. *Eliza Cook's Journal* (1849–54), *The Family Economist* (1848–60), *The Family Friend* (1849–1921) and other journals sponsored by religious groups all contained stories and novels

that an ex-Chartist could use as a model for his own writings, rather
than the more inflammatory works of Linton or Jones. These journals
appealed to the better-educated working families who saw their
interests as divergent from the poorer members of the working class.
Their political fiction, therefore, conveyed a very different message –
one of self-help, improvement and ameliorating conditions within
society. Specific problems were to be solved by applying specific
solutions, and the general ills of capitalism were ignored.

Thomas Cooper's *Wise Saws and Modern Instances* (1845) is an
example of this kind of fiction. In his preface he defined the purpose of
art quite modestly, declaring, 'Higher merit than naturalness, combined
with truth is not claimed for any of the stories: they are, simply, such
as any man may write who has the least power of pourtraying [sic] the
images which human life, in some of its humblest, least disguised forms,
has impressed upon his memory . . .'[43] 'Naturalness' meant an accurate
portrayal of many plain folk, often going back to his early days in
Gainsborough, but 'truth' demanded a morally uplifting conclusion to
each sketch, and frequently disguised persons provided unexpected aid
in times of distress. Cooper clearly intended his stories to be read by
working people; many of them were published in the more respectable
political monthlies of the late Chartist period. But he also, as with *The
Purgatory of Suicides*, had his eye on sympathetic members of the
middle class. While critical of conditions that had led to extreme
poverty, his solution was largely dependent upon outside help from the
financially secure.

The difficulties of combining realism and instruction can be seen in
Seth Thompson, the Stockinger, written while Cooper was in jail.
After years of semi-starvation in the slums of Leicester, Seth and his
family are saved by the opportune arrival of a long-lost uncle:

> Seth blushed, as he took his dish of potatoes, and offered the
> stranger his fragment of a seat. And the stranger blushed, too, but
> refused the seatwith a look of so much benevolence that Seth's heart
> glowed to behold it; and his wife set down her porringer, and hushed
> the children that the stranger might deliver his errand with the
> greater ease . . .
>
> 'Are working people in Leicestershire usually so uncomfortably
> situated as you appear to be?' asked the stranger in a tone of deep
> commiseration which he appeared to be unable to control.
>
> Seth Thompson and his wife looked uneasily at each other, and
> then fixed their gaze on the floor.

'Why, sir,' replied Seth, blushing more deeply than before, 'we married very betime, and our family, you see, has grown very fast; we hope things will mend a little with us when some o' the children are old enough to earn a little. We've only been badly off as yet, but you'd find a many not much better off, sir, I assure you, in Hinckley and elsewhere.'

The stranger paused again, and the working of his features manifested strong inward feeling.

'I see nothing but potatoes,' he resumed; 'I hope your meal is unusually poor to-day, and that you and your family generally have a little meat at dinner.'

'Meat, sir!' exclaimed Seth; 'we have not known what it is to set a bit of meat before our children more than three times since the first was born; we usually had a little for our Sunday dinner when we were first married, but we can't afford it now!'

'Great God!' cried the stranger, with a look that demonstrated his agony of grief and indignation, 'is this England, – the happy England, that I have heard the blacks in the West Indies talk of as a Paradise?'[44]

Seth is given £50 and a half-yearly remittance, with which he sets up a shop, employing stockingers at a fair rate. He regularly lends money to theman from whom he rents the stocking frames, until a business reversal sends him into bankruptcy, leaving Seth with the bills. Disillusioned with England, Seth and his family decide to join his uncle in the West Indies.

This story compares poorly with a similar incident described in Cooper's autobiography (1872). As a newly-arrived journalist he had attended a Chartist meeting in Leicester, and on the way home around eleven o'clock, he overheard the sound of stockingers at work:

'Do your stocking weavers often work so late as this?' I asked of some of the men who were leaving the meeting.

'No, not often: work's over scarce for that', they answered; 'but we're glad to work at any hour, when we can get work to do.'

'Then your hosiery trade is not good in Leicester?' I observed.

'Good! It's been good for nought thismany a year,' said one of the men: 'We've a bit of a spurt now and then. But we soon go back again to starvation!'

'And what may be the average earnings of a stocking weaver?' I asked, – 'I mean when a man is fully employed.'

'About four and sixpence,' was the reply.

That was the exact answer; but I had no right conception of its meaning. I remembered that my own earnings as a handicraft had been low, because I was not allowed to work for the best shops. And I knew that working men in full employ, in the towns of Lincolnshire, were understood to be paid tolerably well. I had never, till now, had any experience of the condition of a great part of the manufacturing population of England, and so my rejoiner was natural. The reply it evoked was the first utterance that revealed to me the real state of suffering in which thousands in England were living.

'Four and sixpence,' I said; 'well, six fours are twenty-four, and six sixpences are three shillings: that's seven-and-twenty shillings a week. The wages are not so bad when you are in work.'

'What are you talking about?' said they. 'You mean four and sixpence a day; but we mean four and sixpence a week.'

'Four and sixpence a week!' I exclaimed. 'You don't mean that men haveto work in those stocking frames that I hear going now, a whole week for four and sixpence. How can they maintain their wives and children?'

'Ay, you may well ask that,' said one of them, sadly.[4][5]

Cooper has vividly recreated his personal shock, leaving the reader to draw his own conclusions. Unfortunately he was never able to dramatize the difficulties of working-class life as well as this in his fiction. Seth Thompson seems more remote than the anonymous stockingers of Cooper's autobiography. The ignorant reader is able to identify and learn with Cooper, but in *Seth Thompson* the feelings of the stockinger and his uncle remain artificial and stereotyped. Both utter the clichés of the time – the stranger echoes Oastler's attack on 'white slavery' in northern factories, and Seth accepts contemporary Malthusian arguments against premature marriage. The uncle asks all the questions in order to do something for his relative; Seth does not save himself, in direct contradiction to the basic tenets of Chartist education.

In 'The Autobiography of Timothy Twinckle', written for the *Northern Tribune* (1854–5), Cooper carried the doctrine of self-help within a just capitalist society one step further. In so doing he joined the many working men who had turned to trade unions, co-operative organizations and the Liberal Party following the decline of the Chartist movement. Young Timothy, after being wrongfully accused of theft by his master, is sent to 'a good plain school' by 'the son of my mother's old master, Squire Heartwell'. In due course he is apprenticed, applies himself 'assiduously' and becomes a 'freeman'. He saves money, is made manager of a business, and eventually becomes the owner. In old age he reflects,

> All I need say is — there is money to be made in old England without going to the gold-diggings. Economy — strict economy, in the outset — Industry and Perseverance — these are qualities which can scarcely fail to lead to Independence. Let the reader cultivate them, keeping his conscience clean of wrongdoing and oppressing his follows, and he may reach the vale of life with the sun shining clearly and lightly overhead — not withstanding that when he first set out to climb that hill the storm threatened to overwhelm him.[46]

Within a decade Cooper changed from seeing poverty as inevitable and emigration a solution to a full acceptance of self-help combined with help from above. However, he did not consider how one could accumulate capital from the labour of others without 'wronging and oppressing' them. The labour theory of value has been rejected for individual self-improvement. Moreover, Cooper assumes harmonious relationships between the classes. Without obligation the son of the squire helped the son of a former servant; the boy proves himself worthy of trust when he comes to treat his own workers justly. The tone of self-congratulation, so evident in the story, was frequently part of a respectable working man's writing at this time.

Cooper's short stories about working-class conditions emphasized the underlying similarity of all men, rich or poor, a position emphasized by Dickens and many lesser novelists of the mid-century. In 1851–2 he wrote a Chartist novel, which he implied in his autobiography was much better than Charles Kingsley's *Alton Locke*. The manuscript has not survived; there is no way of knowing whether the political perspective was different from his short stories. The refusal in later years to write a specifically political novel, despite the urgings of his friends, may have been because of his distaste for reluctant publishers, but it is undoubtedly symptomatic of his shift from political activity to educational work.

Others, more committed to the Chartist movement than Cooper, were not willing to concede a unity of interests, but they were forced to justify their cause in a way that had not been necessary earlier. Since they did not write for money or fame, they were not constrained by market conditions, but they could not veer too far from the familiar, lest they repel the average novel reader. Moreover, they wished to teach their readers about the strengths and weaknesses of the past, and to encourage the faltering to continue their political activities. They had to create attractive stories that could carry their political message realistically and forcefully.

Chartist novelists readily borrowed the conventions of popular fiction: the heroine was a passive victim; the villain was brought to justice by fortuitous events; the hero was manly, idealistic and honest; the aristocracy was selfish and cruel, but had its heartaches. Vague democratic principles rather than particular Chartist demands made up most speeches and actions. Emotionally charged situations carried the political burden; class conflict was justified through the villainy perpetrated by a careless and selfish member of the ruling class. Seduction of an innocent servant girl, the dismissal of a faithful retainer, or a more personal cruelty all pinpointed his perfidy, which was then declared to be typical of his class. A tortuous plot frequently led up to a confrontation between the hero and the villain; a fair damsel was the reward. Often enough the villain won her, but the forces of democracy, it was implied, would eventually triumph, and so the brave hero continued his political work despite a heavy heart.

Unable to control much of their situation, working people found emotional satisfaction in these conventions. They could identify more readily with a hero or heroine who was largely a victim of circumstances; such a character showed how misfortune was not a reflection of one's own personal worth. At the same time, melodrama often showed the joys of goodness rewarded through a *deus ex machina*. The appearance of Seth's rich uncle is emotionally, if not rationally, satisfying. And yet, Chartist novelists wrote out of a belief in the possibility of change. As Jones insisted,

> It is folly to say 'we can't help it,' 'we are the creatures of circumstances' — 'we are what society makes us.' We *can* help it — we can *create circumstances* — we can make *society* — or whence the efforts to redress and reform — moral, social, political, religious?[47]

The problem was how to graft a sense of political instrumentality upon a melodramatic plot. The less skilful sacrificed their political message to the exigencies of romance. The machinations of the upper-class villain gave opportunity to pillory those in power, but the emotional interest centres on the young lovers. The overall impression is of thwarted love, with political principles often reduced to a hatred of the upper-classes. The more sophisticated writers altered conventions in order to show men working together, creating circumstances. A disaster, such as the burning down of a factory, was used to show men organizing for a better tomorrow. The superior knowledge and good character of the hero occasionally enabled him to influence the course of events. The constraints of the plot, however, were most frequently broken by an authorial interruption calling for united political action on the part of the readers.

Thomas Frost's *The Secret* is an example of an adventure story that provided readers vicarious revenge against the ruling class. Frost (1820–89?), a Croydon printer turned journalist, had been active in the Chartist movement while earning his living writing serial novels, political essays and miscellaneous pieces. In 1850 he was hired by the *National Instructor* (1850) to write a tale that would appeal to its Chartist readers.[48] 'The secret' revolves around an incident that occurred twenty years before the novel opens. An embittered Vincent had exchanged his granddaughter for that of the aristocrat who had seduced his sister. Over the years he chuckles at the results. His 'granddaughter' Lizzie is seduced by her employer's son, and has an illegitimate child. In the meantime his true granddaughter has grown up with an unusually firm and charitable character, and happily marries a wealthy earl of like mind. All is then revealed to the Duke. He attempts to 'save' Lizzie by placing her with a family in the country to learn proper manners and speech. But she has fallen in love with Ernest Rodwell, an upright Chartist compositor, and in the face of the Duke's wrath, marries him. Her happiness thereby foils the artful Vincent and solves all for the Duke, who has found nurture stronger than nature. The only variation from the standard plot is Lizzie's marriage; a few seduced, but modest, women might find happiness with an understanding Chartist.

In a similarly melodramatic series, *Women's Wrongs*, Ernest Jones describes the plight of a poor working man's wife, a young milliner, a tradesman's daughter and a lady of title. He insisted he was painting 'life *as it is* – no poet's fancy, no romancer's dream . . . the romance of fiction cannot equal the romance of truth.'[49] 'The romance of truth' actually betrays a remarkable number of characteristics drawn from the popular novel – lovers are totally unable to reveal their affection and endure tortured lives; aristocratic society is decadent and depraved, but its finest heroes and heroines survive virtually untouched; innocent and faithful love is invariably distorted by society, and the penalty falls most cruelly upon women, etc. For all of the variety of classes represented, Jones does not describe women from the same class as the majority of the readers of *Notes to the People*. The question of how politically aware men treat their women is not posed. The reader can look upon the mistreatment of women in other classes with disgust, but can avoid considering too closely his own possible failings.

What strikes the reader most about both these works is the emphasis upon the violent and vengeful. In the first sketch of *Women's Wrongs* the labourer murders his former employer, and his wife is hanged for concealing him. The gory details, including burying the mutilated body, are spun out through several episodes. Social criticism remains oblique; the husband is fired because he is drunk and inefficient, and not for political reasons. The story points to how society's injustices warp men. Melodrama reaches the depths of bathos in 'The Young Milliner' episode. The medical student has deserted the pregnant milliner, and she dies in a charity hospital. Her body is then used during a medical lecture; the story ends as the student faints in moral anguish. Like Jones, Frost insures that all the enemies of the workers are portrayed at their most venal and gullible. Vincent leers and snickers over the fate of Lizzie and the torments of the Duke. Like the woman in 'A London Door-Step', Lizzie is mistaken for a drunken prostitute and spends a hideously degrading night in jail. The ambitious sister of Lizzie's seducer marries a forger masquerading as an exiled French marquis; she ends her days the mistress of a local merchant.

Such stories as *Women's Wrongs* and *The Secret*, like so many popular novels, permit the reader to have his cake and eat it. The corruptness of the aristocracy is denounced at the same time long passages are devoted to dramatizing the delights of wealth. In *The Secret* much of Vincent's pleasure comes from seeing his grandchild ensconced amidst all the luxuries of the day. Jones describes with relish how Lady Honora's 'better impulses' are 'polluted' by her environment. She is depraved by attending balls that appear extraordinarily attractive:

It was at that hour of the evening, in which the imagination, heated by a thousand voluptuous images, conjured up by the ball, loses itself in wild and ardent vision — before fatigue tames down its warmer impulses. There seemed something dreamily intoxicating in the air — the mingled atmosphere of scents and flowers, throbbing with the rapid pulse of music. A burning dew glistened on the purest, fairest brow — and while the gay brilliancy of the hot saloon stimulated and excited, the quiet, warm gloom of the half-seen country wooed to voluptuous and mysterious retirement.[50]

Her poor, spurned lover stands by, commenting bitterly about the 'band of moral assassins' at the ball. The reader is encouraged to enjoy the immoral scene while condemning it — and confirming his prejudices.

Women's Wrongs and *The Secret* share many characteristics with moral fables. In order to portray clear examples of good and evil both types mixed sordid details, the victimization of the innocent and the timely juxtaposition of characters. The irrational accusation of dishonesty against Timothy Twinckle is less obviously dramatic than the contemptuous treatment of Lizzie by her seducer, but the emotional intent is the same. Both the fable and popular fiction point to the unjust attitudes and behaviour of the powerful against the powerless. The melodrama and moralizing in all of these stories was designed to encourage anger and resistance in the reader. Cooper channels these feelings toward Timothy's wordly success as an adult; Frost toward Lizzie's eventual happiness with Ernest. Frost affirms the superiority of an upright mechanic in comparison with the Duke's hypocritical world, and thereby affirms the values of his own readers, and not that of the middle class or the aristocracy. Neither Jones nor Linton provide any solutions outside a continued political commitment. However, in their works the need for change is overwhelmingly clear.It only remains for the reader to take up the issues they have clarified in their fiction.

Two Chartist novels, both the work of leaders, are important because they sought to make Chartists aware of the complexity of radical political action. Ernest Jones, in *De Brassier: A Democratic Romance*, and Thomas Martin Wheeler, in *Sunshine and Shadow*, each wrote about the Chartist movement in fictional form while it was still alive. Wheeler (1811–62) had been a baker, gardener and school teacher, but from 1840 until the mid-'fifties he held a variety of posts in the Chartist Association. He served as secretary of the Chartist Land Company, and was a successful participant in the settlement at O'Connorsville. He had written verse in praise of the experiment, but had done no other writing before beginning his novel.[51] Ernest Jones had considerable experience in Chartist writing and speech making, in addition to the creative writing he had done from childhood. Both men were convinced that the events in which they themselves had participated would interest readers if described in the guise of fiction. Whatever disadvantages there might be in choosing such familiar and recent events were offset by the advantages of placing politics at the heart of their plots.

The Secret and *Women's Wrongs* encouragd class conflict through hatred of the ruling class. *De Brassier* and *Sunshine and Shadow* have their full share of selfish and oppressive aristocrats, but the focus is upon the people's own movement. Jones and Wheeler concentrate on examining the basis of a class-divided society, even to the detriment of the forward movement of the plot. This places the behaviour of individuals in a political and social context; hatred of the ruling class arises out of a class analysis. For example, both writers include scenes of crime. They do not excuse the criminals, but argue that great poverty and great wealth cannot exist together in a healthy state. Hatred and crime are the inevitable result of England's unhealthy condition. Until a just society exists, class solidarity is the workers' only protection against the economic, social and political power of the wealthy. This perspective differs sharply from the middle-class protest novels of the 1840s. Mrs Gaskell, Disraeli and Dickens all sought a solution to social problems through better understanding between the classes. In their works conflict is reduced to a failure of communication or to the weaknesses of individuals within each class. Unions, Chartism and any other form of organized class solidarity are treated with fear and distortion; indeed, these middle-class writers were unable to believe that the working class was capable of organizing itself for social betterment. Christian fellow feeling and gradual amelioration are their solutions to social problems. Jones and Wheeler, as champions of class conflict, followed a new course in their presentation of the social system from the perspective of the politically aware working man.

The purpose of *De Brassier* was to examine 'why democracy has so often been foiled', or as Jones explained more explicitly in Part II, 'The object of "De Brassier" is to show the People how they have but too often been deceived and betrayed by their own presumed friends. Deceived and betrayed, not by an individual selling them to the government, but by the individual *selling them to himself*.'[52] Although he insisted that the novel contained no portrayals of Chartists, many of the characters and episodes appear to be modelled after well-known persons, and the opinions expressed by the two heroes, Edward and Latimer, are clearly those espoused by Jones. Readers may have mistaken the demagogic, self-seeking De Brassier for Feargus O'Connor. But rather than reading the novel as a *roman à clef*, it is more interesting as a tale of 'the dangers from within' the democratic movement. Jones shows every known weakness of the movement and gives every possible strength to the government and the forces of oppression. He saw the novel as a warning to his readers not to repeat either the errors of the past or the worst evils described in the novel.

The plot of *De Brassier* is exceptionally complicated, with many sub-plots designed to drive home particular political points. The action centres on the well-known aristocrat, Simon De Brassier, who tempestuously leads the people forward in massive marches, appeals to parliament and other activities similar to the Chartist movement of 1838–9. De Brassier successfully blackens the reputations of upright and committed leaders, such as Latimer, a middle-class sympathizer, and Edward, a mechanic. As social tensions come to a head, De Brassier temporizes, and the democratic cause loses the initiative; the government easily defeats a divided and dispirited people. The oppressive treatment of tenants and farm workers by De Brassier's older brother forms an important sub-plot. In this case, revenge is enacted by an embittered woman who has plotted against her seducer, De Brassier's brother, for over a decade. In another sub-plot Jones attacks the banking and factory interests, while adding a romantic touch. Latimer's beloved is the daughter of a selfish and avaricious self-made banker, Henry Dorville. Edward, in the meantime, pines after a woman who loves Simon De Brassier. Jones did not finish the novel; it ends with the successful destruction of the people's movement by the government, and the sentencing of every leader except De Brassier, who escapes into parliament, where he mismanages government funds with impunity.

The novel contrasts the lack of foresight of the people with the well-developed sense of cause and effect of the rich. Repeatedly the people are moved to act without considering the long-range implications of their actions, while the rich always look ahead. De Brassier invests in stock when the market falls as a result of his agitation; he sells at a great profit when his failures in leadership steady the market. Henry Dorville insures his factory for twice its value, hoping his workmen will burn it down and save him the cost of buying new equipment and making necessary repairs. He then retires to a safe seaside resort. Only avarice brings him back; it leads ultimately to his death, but Dorville's weakness is that of a self-made man. The aristocracy may fear the people on occasion, but it always has plenty of toadies and spies who keep it informed of the divisions and weaknesses within their movement. At one point the Cabinet meets to discuss quelling the people, after a luxurious dinner at Lord Weathercock's mansion. Sir Gaffer Grim speaks of 'anarchy and infidelity', and Weathercock mocks him for wearing a mask amongst the Cabinet members — 'Call all things by their right names here — truth and enlightenment.' Jones gives the rich no honest motivations, but always credits them with hypocrisy, greed and a love of power. Moreover, they always know how to control those without power. Weathercock had formerly led a popular movement, and accurately assesses how to defeat the democrats:

> Believe me, my dear Grim, — temporise — procrastinate. Popular enthusiasm is at its height now. It never lasts long. Give them no pretext for an immediate outbreak — don't interfere with them — let them commit outrages, they have not done so yet — they will be sure to do so when non-interference and the presumption of self reliance intoxicate them a little more. There are still many of them whom the first act of violence will estrange — it will cause bickerings among themselves, personal antagonisms will ensue — some will be for standing still, merely because others are for going on, and *vice versa*; then the masses will be disgusted at their own leaders — numbers will go home; and then, at last, the time will have arrived to strike a blow. Then, and not till then, the leaders must be seized — and a blow struck, the blood of which shall not be wiped from the memory of the people for a hundred years.[53]

His advice, of course, yields complete success. Although Jones repeatedly speaks of the working class uniting to gain power, his presentation of the united upper classes appears overwhelming. Indeed, at times the only logical action seems to be the long maturing revenge against a single person such as Vincent and the seduced Maline commit. Jones gave the upper classes so much power in order to warn working people against underestimating their enemies. In the past fiery Chartist speech makers had told their followers that firmness of purpose and moral superiority would bring down the government. These simplicities angered Jones, who hoped through his novel to encourage a more analytic and considered political position among his readers.

While the rich appear totally selfish and their spies totally powerful, the workers compound their own powerlessness through a love of drama, style and blood. Jones, like Thomson a decade earlier, chastises the poor for their fascination with the aristocracy. Much of De Brassier's initial appeal comes from his dashing aristocratic manner and well-known connections. Latimer loses favour when he sacrifices the advantages of birth to the people's cause. The most common political mistake is following false leadership while denying the true. 'The fitful, selfish, and uncertain guidance of De Brassier' enchants them. Even when his thundering rhetoric on behalf of arrested men yields more severe sentences, the prisoners are proud of his speech and their own self-importance; they give no thought of the years away from home, but yield to the drama of the moment. Repeatedly the people see De Brassier's manner and not his message; in spite of patent lies and prevarications, as long as he appears noble, they forget the past and obey his rulings. Latimer and Edward, in contrast, must suffer mockery, accusations of spying, poverty and general disrepute for their efforts to aid the people. Speaking out of personal experience, Jones describes the reluctance of the people to support their own leaders, particularly when their advice is unpopular; the ordinary organizer or editor was expected to live by his wits while the people fought for a fair day's wage. Finally, Jones was particularly scathing about the petty divisions within the movement. Time and again in *De Brassier* divisions from within prevent the defeat of the oppressors.

In spite of all these weaknesses, Jones remains resolutely loyal to the people. They are deluded and misguided, but never depraved or dishonest. In the fury of just revenge they hold back from harming a woman, 'in angry generosity – one of these chivalric touches, nature's true romance, in which the sons of toil outvie the famed knighthood of the proudest aristocracy'. All possible sneers and attacks on the working class and its movement are examined and analysed without attempting to explain them away. In contrast to the middle-class novelists of the time, Jones never presented the working-class as children in need of instruction; whatever their faults, from ignorance or delusion, they were adults who must learn from their mistakes.

Thomas Martin Wheeler's *Sunshine and Shadow*, published in thirty-seven parts in the *Northern Star* (1849–50), is more narrowly concerned with the career of a single working man than *De Brassier*. Wheeler wrote his novel because 'Our novelists – even the most liberal – are unable to draw a democrat save in war-paint.' *Sunshine and Shadow* would

> 'prove that Chartism is not allied with base and vicious feelings, but that it is the offspring of high and generous inspirations – that it looks not to self but to mankind: that whilst working for the Present, it holds the future in its grasp, that it is founded upon justice and true to nature, and, therefore, must ultimately prevail.'[54]

Throughout the novel Wheeler emphasizes the high idealism that impels men to join the Chartist cause; the truly degraded are the unprincipled, who are guided solely by selfish desires.

The novel goes from the beginnings of Chartism until 1850. The difficulties of dealing with a subject all his readers knew are overcome by avoiding most of the major controversies and by leaving the hero's actual political activities vague. The plot revolves around Arthur Morton, a typical idealistic working man, who is drawn into the Chartist movement at an early age. He is first forced to flee England in 1839; in a storm he saves the sister of his boyhood friend, Walter North. A pure and holy love grows between him and Julia, married to the dastardly Sir Jasper, governor of a West Indies island. Soon after Julia's premature death, Arthur returns to England and once again throws himself into Chartism. He happily marries a young woman who ardently follows Chartist principles, but misfortune dogs him. After months of unemployment, Arthur succumbs to temptation, and robs a drunken merchant – his former school friend. 'His pure feelings of morality' have been 'broken and disturbed', but he is able to pay his bills and find work. Arthur bitterly returns once again to politics, determined to remove the evils besetting his ownclass 'with the iron weapons of reality' and 'the demonstrative power of practical experiment.' He becomes leader in the Land Plan, but once again government repression drives him into exile. The novel ends with his wife and daughter faithfully waiting his return, hopeful of the future.

The novel falls into two parts: in the first Arthur undergoes a series of romantic adventures in the manner of G. W. M. Reynolds, but in the second part his career becomes a paradigm of the idealistic working man beaten down by economic circumstances. Unlike Jones, Wheeler did not have any close knowledge of the upper classes, and he is at his weakest when attempting to dramatize their lives. Julia's forced marriage to Sir Jasper is the result of an unbelievable deception practiced by Sir Jasper and her brother. Walter dismisses all his servants one night, fills Sir Jasper with drink, and pushes him into Julia's bedroom. Once raped, she agrees that her only alternative is to marry the man. Wheeler appears to have contrived this brotherly sadism not so much out of hatred for the merchant class, as from his effort to keep Julia perfect. If she is beautiful and intelligent, she will not agree to marry Sir Jasper, so she must be tricked by an ambitious brother. Wheeler further titillates his audience with an extended discussion of the moral implications of Julia's love for Arthur.

Let not the censorious or the prudish blame my heroine. Love in her
was no crime, albeit she was the bride of another, – it was the result
of feelings as pure as nature ever implanted in human breast; the
treachery of her relatives, and the baseness of Sir Jasper, were the
circumstances which caused it to verge upon crime – or rather,
should we say, retributive justice. Let the saint and the hypocrite rail
on – we write not for their perusal, we heed not their censure, we
picture human nature as it is – veritable flesh and blood – glowing
with warm and ardent feelings – feelings which are apt to overpower
the judgment; but far better is it so than for us to fall into the Dead
Sea waters of apathy, or wallow in the mire of cold and frigid
selfishness.[55]

Several panting scenes later 'the pure and youthful pair' must part. This
leads Wheeler into a long digression on society's cruelty to true lovers,
hinting at the possibilities of love conquering all. But Julia chooses
'wealth and respect, but a blighted heart and an early grave', and 'the
world's wisdom hallows her choice.' Perhaps, sighs Wheeler, her
example may help to reform the world and change those customs which
hallow a perverted marriage. As a final gesture toward his reader's
vicarious sexual satisfaction, Julia is placed in quarters resembling a
harem, where she pines away in spite of numerous black slaves catering
to her every whim.

Fortunately Arthur is made of sterner stuff, and the novel returns to
its political objectives. Jones's work is most interesting when he is
dealing with the dilemmas of leadership; Wheeler is most interesting
when he explores the problem of poverty and the respectable worker.
Month after month of unemployment drives Arthur to the edge of
insanity:

Had he been alone in the world he could have battled with poverty,
or if the struggle became too painful he could easily have withdrawn
from the conflict, but his wife and children now bound him to life,
he had their lives and welfare to protect, with the maddening
knowledge that he was unable to perform it, – that he was a drag
upon his wife's energies, a recipient of the infinitessimal sum that is
doled out to the poor sempstress, and to reflect upon it was to
endanger the sanity of his intellect. Misery had set her mark upon
him – the terrible struggles of his mind were visible in his
features, – his former acquaintance would not have recognized him,
in the emaciated and haggard-eyed shadow that might occasionally

be seen wandering through the streets of the metropolis, seeking
bread but finding none; exploring, with ardent gaze, the very
pavement of the streets in the vain hope of finding something . . . [56]

Wheeler is too honest to pretend that love strengthened under
adversity. While Arthur and Mary do not cease to love each other, they
no longer see the other as perfection embodied, nor do they find the
same perfect congeniality in each other's company. Arthur torments
himself watching Mary eke out a living he feels to be his duty to earn,
and Mary must suffer from his moody bitterness. Absolute poverty
reduces Arthur to 'apathetic dullness', dividing him from the rest of
humanity, whose relative success only deepens the shadow of his own
misery. Unlike the hand-loom weavers and stockingers of the North,
Arthur is cut off from all companionship during his period of
unemployment. Only after he is again at work does he have the energy
to look about him and rejoin the Chartist movement. Wheeler's
language is plain and harsh when he describes Arthur's descent into
'outcast humanity', with none of the falsely heightened tone he felt
necessary for important occasions. It is a stark and moving account of a
life many readers must have recognized.

After Arthur robs his old school friend, and feels he has desecrated
the memory of Julia, Wheeler muses upon the effects of conscience on
those 'driven by stern necessity' to thievery. While Arthur may suffer
inwardly, he is not so overcome with remorse as to throw himself into
the arms of bourgeois justice. The overwhelming guilt that seems to grip
most Victorian heroes or heroines when they have transgressed society's
laws, no matter what the circumstances, is seen as artificial and wrong
by Wheeler. He does not excuse Arthur, but points to 'the laws of
nature', which led him to take the only recourse open for survival.
Attacking conventional morality, Wheeler explains,

[B]ut better far to our ideas of religion and morality is the victim to
one great and solitary crime, than the man of the world, -- the
respectable villain, whose whole life is a series of meanness and
hypocrisy, unrelieved by magnanimity of any description, -- true, he
evades the law and the law's justice, but he is none the less a
villain, -- the gold that he accumulates may be encrusted with the
gore of his starving victims, -- the respectability of which he boasts
may be based on the ruin and prostitution of hundreds, -- the
blighted hearts he has trampled upon may be thickly strewn about
his path, -- but he recks it not, the world smiles on him, he has no

remnant of natural religion in his soul, and he knows no remorse;
with demure and sanctified countenance he worships in the temple
of his God, and boasts, with the Pharisee of old, 'that he is not a
sinner like othe;men' . . . [5][7]

Throughout the novel Arthur consistently acts out of idealistic
principles, whereas Walter North is utterly self-seeking. Arthur's wasted
talents, idealism and leadership are but a single example of the price
working people pay for society's injustices. The triumph of the
democratic movement will bring a return to a natural state where man's
natural impulses for goodness and happiness will flourish. Until then
Arthur's life will be only a 'shadow' with a gleam of 'sunshine' in the
distant future.

Sunshine and Shadow and *De Brassier* differ from the other stories
discussed in this chapter in several ways. In these two novels Wheeler
and Jones have kept political issues in the fore, and have not given easy
solutions to the problems raised. Emigration, Heaven or an inheritance
never occur; love is difficult and lovers do not live happily ever after.
These authors attempted to recast the conservative plotting and
characterization of the popular novel in order to create a new radical
novel. Wheeler and Jones believed in the eventual triumph of
revolutionary forces, but since change had not yet come and did not
appear imminent, they left their novels open-ended. The only possible
ending is revolution. Arthur's 'fate is still enveloped in darkness, what
the mighty womb of time may bring forth we know not.' Edward and
Latimer languish in jail. Unlike *The Secret* or Cooper's fables, there is
no personal solution for these three heroes because their lives are
entwined with the fate of Chartism.

Sunshine and Shadow and *De Brassier* raise the question of whether
it is possible to write revolutionary fiction using a traditional form. The
English bourgeois novel has been about a hero (or heroine) who tries
and fails to surpass an objectively limited destiny; he becomes
chastened and usually adjusts to his fate within a faulty society. In
these two works the heroes attempt to change society rather than
themselves. They are held back by conditions which the authors
consider temporary – the ignorance and selfishness of men, or the
power of their oppressors. Once these conditions change, society must
necessarily change. But oppression and ignorance are so powerful in the
novels that the reader is uncertain about the possibility of revolution.
When the processes of change are shown, such as rioting and burning,
they are fearsome and destructive of the people's cause. Melodramatic

interventions, beyond the control of the heroes, only reinforce the hegemony of the ruling class. In both novels the possibility of a more perfect future is ever-present, but the process of class struggle takes its toll on the heroes. Since they must be left still believing in the cause, and unadjusted to a faulty society, the novels must be left unfinished. Had Chartism continued to develop culturally, it might have developed new fictional forms descriptive of working-class political life and future.

The thread of working-class fiction *by* working men remained slight throughout the century in England; sketches and poetry abound, but full length novels were more difficult and were susceptible to the latest fads. Wheeler and Jones were not able to free themselves entirely from the romantic clichés of the time, but they did establish a new standard of realism based not on the presuppositions of Mrs Gaskell, Disraeli or Dickens, but upon the realism of felt experience. Poverty and its numbing effects were often more powerfully described by Dickens, but Dickens did not give up his fairy-godfathers and happy endings, nor did he see the working man, united with men of his own class, as a source of social improvement. Jones dared to imagine the possibility of working men seizing power by insurrection, a position few other English writers took by 1850. His extremism was never imitated by contemporary working-class writers, with the possible exception of Gerald Massey, but he can be considered kin to William Morris and other late nineteenth-century socialists. Wheeler had more limited literary goals; he recognized the intrinsic interest of his own life and that of his fellow workers, and insisted that such a subject would interest his own class. In this, along with other Chartist poets and novelists, he looked forward to the dialect writers of the North, who flourished in the second half of the century.

Wheeler and Jones established the right of future working men to write a fiction of class solidarity. The importance of *struggle* as a part of literature was often forgotten by working-class writers, anxious to write about the idyllic moments of home life or to escape into poetic realms. The loss of struggle and conflict in their work was linked to the fate of the Chartist movement: co-operation among working men and the middle-class became the necessity of the 'fifties. The single-minded emphasis upon class struggle combined with the stereotypes of the popular novel had not been a wholly successful artistic venture. The safest course appeared to be that of the apolitical praisers of Nature, home and country. And so, with few exceptions, the working-class political novel ceased to be written orpublished.[58] The political use of literature continued along the lines outlined in Chapter 2, while the course of self-development can be traced in the poets described in Chapter 4. 'The Reform of Literature' demanded by Thomson involved more than a boycott, a few new novels, a discussion of needs – it demanded talent, time and political understanding. These qualities were seldom found together in the nineteenth-century working-class artist.

Notes

1. The fullest discussion of Chartist literature to date is Y. V. Kovalev's introduction to his *An Anthology of Chartist Literature* (Moscow: Foreign Languages Publishing House, 1956). It has been translated twice: 'The Literature of Chartism', trans. J. C. Dombreck and Michael Beresford, *Victorian Studies*, II (1958), pp.117–138; and 'Chartist Literature', *Our History*, 17 (Spring, 1960). John Miller discusses a few Chartist songs in 'Songs of the Labour Movement', *Our History*, 30 (Summer, 1963) and 'Songs of the British Radical and Labour Movement', *Marxism Today*, VII (1963), pp.180–6. Kovalev's collection, in spite of a number of errors, is an important source of material which has unfortunately never been followed up by scholars. He has, however, emphasized the physical force and revolutionary elements of Chartism disproportionately.
2. See Asa Briggs, 'The Language of "Class" in Early Nineteenth-Century England', *Essays in Labour History*, eds. Asa Briggs and John Saville (London: Macmillan, 1960), pp.43–73; and Patricia Hollis, *The Pauper Press: A Study of Working Class Radicalism in the 1830s* (London: Oxford University Press, 1970). See also E. P. Thompson, *The Making of the English Working Class* (New York: Vintage, 1963), pp.709–46. For a discussion of the efforts of the middle class to educate their 'inferiors' in a very different set of beliefs, see R. K. Webb, *The British Working Class Reader, 1790–1848* (London: Allen and Unwin, 1955), pp.103–57.
3. [William Thomson], 'The Politics of Poets', *The Chartist Circular*, 42 (11 July 1840), p.170.
4. Ebenezer Elliott was the most famous 'poet of the people' in the 1830s; there was extensive commentary on him and his poetry at the time in all the journals. See Simon Brown, *Ebenezer Elliott: The Corn Law Rhymer, A Bibliography and List of Letters* (Leicester: Victorian Studies Centre, 1971) for a complete listing of sources. See in particular Thomas Carlyle's review of his works in the *Edinburgh Review*, LX (1832), pp.338–61; W. J. Fox's review in the *London Review*, I (1835), pp.187–201; and Louis Etienne, 'Les poètes des pauvres en Angleterre; III Ebenezer Elliott', *Revue des deux mondes*, XXIII (1856), pp.387–400. The standard biography is John Watkins, *Life, Poetry, and Letters of Ebenezer Elliott, the Corn-law Rhymer; with an abstract of his politics* (London: John Mortimer, 1850).
5. 'William Thom, the Poet of Inverury', *Northern Star*, 14 September 1844.
6. Ernest Jones, 'Literary Review: Ebenezer Jones', *The Labourer*, II (1847), p.237. Italics in the original.
7. 'Thomas Hood, Poet and Punster', *Hogg's Instructor*, n.s. IV (1855), p.323. Quoted in Donald J. Gray, 'The Uses of Victorian Laughter', *Victorian Studies*, X (1966), p.158.
8. For a discussion of Linton's career, see F. B. Smith, *Radical*

Artisan: *William James Linton 1812–97* (Manchester: University Press, 1973).

9. W. J. Linton, *Memories* (London: Lawrence and Bullen, 1895), p.75.
10. *The National: A Library for the People*, I (1839), p.289.
11. Jones's life and political career are discussed in John Saville, *Ernest Jones: Chartist: Selections from the Writings and Speeches of Ernest Jones* (London: Lawrence and Wishart, 1952).
12. *The Labourer*, I (1847), pp.47–52. Italics in the original.
13. *The Labourer*, III (1848), pp.1–8. Italics in the original.
14. The third edition of *Poems and Ballads* (New York: J. C. Derby [based on the 3rd London ed.], 1854) contains a biographical sketch by Samuel Smiles, reprinted from *Eliza Cook's Journal*. See also Buckner Trawick, 'The Works of Gerald Massey', unpub. diss. (Harvard University, 1942). For Massey's later career, see Trawick and also B. O. Flower, *Gerald Massey: Poet, Prophet and Mystic* (New York: Alliance Publishing Company, 1895). In the period of Victorian self-confidence of the 1860s, George Eliot could model her hero in *Felix Holt* (1866) after Massey, whereas the novelists of the 1840s saw Chartism as a threat to traditional values. The educational Chartists' plea for personal dignity was received sympathetically by Mrs Gaskell, Dickens, Disraeli and others, but the cry for freedom and power struck fear in their hearts (See part II, below).
15. 'Our Symbol', *Voices of Freedom and Lyrics of Love* (London: J. Watson, 1851), pp.9–10. *Poems and Ballads*, pp.181–2.
16. 'Poetry for the People', *The Friend of the People*, II (3 May 1851), p.196.
17. 'Bandiera' [Gerald Massey], 'Poetry to be Lived', *The Red Republican*, I (6 July 1850), p.19. Italics in the original.
18. 'Literary Review', *The Labourer*, II (1847), p.94. Italics in the original.
19. 'Critic and Poet', 'Our May Garland', *Northern Star*, 8 May 1852. In the dialogue the poet is Gerald Massey; most of the arguments are excerpted from 'Poetry to be Lived'. Harney plays the role of the practical critic.
20. *Poems and Ballads*, pp.77–80.
21. *Voices of Freedom and Lyrics of Love*, p.i. Also quoted in Harney's review, 'Poetry for the People', *The Friend of the People*, II (26 April 1851), p.177.
22. *Poems and Ballads*, pp.x–xi.
23. *Rules of the Barnsley Franklin Club* (Barnsley: J. Elliott, 1845), n.p.
24. *English Chartist Circular*, II (1842), p.156.
25. *The Chartist Circular*, 43 (18 July 1840), p.182.
26. For a discussion of popular fiction and its political and social implications, see Margaret Dalziel, *Popular Fiction 100 Years Ago* (London: Cohen and West, 1957); and Louis James, *Fiction for the Working Man, 1830–50* (London: Oxford University Press, 1963).

See also Richard D. Altick, *The English Common Reader 1800–1900* (Chicago: University Press, 1957).

27. 'Literary Review', *The Labourer*, I (1847), p.96.

28. *Cooper's Journal*, I (1850), p.129.

29. op. cit., pp.129–32, 209–13.

30. *Poems on Various Subjects* (Barnsley: J. Elliott, 1865), preface.

31. Thomas Cooper, *Life* (London: Hodder and Stoughton, 1872), pp.164–76. See also 'Poets of the People, III: Thomas Cooper', *Howitt's Journal*, III (1848), pp.226, 242–7.

32. *The Spirit; or a Dream in the Woodlands* (Leicester: Joseph Ayer, 1849), preface. See also the review of *The Spirit* in *The Leicestershire Movement: Voices from the Frame and the Factory, the Field and the Rail, etc.*, I (1850), pp.78–9.

33. *The Purgatory of Suicides, A Prison-Rhyme* (London: Jeremiah How, 1845), pp.51, 56.

34. Cooper, of course, thought he did not receive enough attention. But see Philarete Chasles, 'De la poesie chartiste en angleterre', *Revue des deux mondes*, XII (1845), pp.326–339; [Charles Kingsley], 'Burns and His School', *North British Review*, XVI (1851–52), pp.149–83 [authorship per Wellesley Index]; Douglas Jerrold, 'New Books', *Douglas Jerrold's Shilling Magazine*, III (1846), pp.95–6.

35. Douglas Jerrold, p.95.

36. 'Literary Reform', *The Chartist Circular*, 71 (30 January 1841), p.299. Italics in the original.

37. Very little work has been done on G. W. M. Reynolds. See 'Mischievous Literature', *The Bookseller* (July, 1868), pp.445–9; J. V. Hunter, 'Reynolds: Sensational Novelist and Agitator,' *Book Handbook*, IV (1947), pp.225–36; Dalziel, pp.35–45; and James, passim.

38. *Northern Star*, 31 March 1849.

39. Preface, 'The History of the Democratic Movement, Compiled from the Journal of a Demagogue, the Confessions of a Democrat, and the Minutes of a Spy', *Notes to the People*, I (1851–52), p.20.

40. William Empson, *Some Versions of the Pastoral* (New York: New Directions, 1960), pp.17–20.

41. 'A Hardwareman', 'Records of the World's Justice: A Pauper', *The National*, I (1839), p.26. Italics in the original.

42. First published in *The Labourer*, III (1848), pp.228–32. Reprinted in *Notes to the People*, I (1851–52), pp.207–9.

43. *Wise Saws and Modern Instances* (London: Jeremiah How, 1845), I, p.vii.

44. *Wise Saws*, I, pp.222–3.

45. *Life*, pp.138–9.

46. *The Northern Tribune: A Periodical for the People*, I (1854), p.199. Reprinted in *Old Fashioned Stories* (London: Hodder and Stoughton, 1874), pp.354–65.

47. Introduction to *Women's Wrongs*, Bk. IV, *Notes to the People*, II (1851–2), pp.913–14. Italics in the original.

48. Thomas Frost wrote two incomplete autobiographies, *Forty Years' Recollections, Literary and Political* (London: Sampson, Low, 1880), and *Reminiscences of a Country Journalist* (London: Ward and Downer, 1886). For a discussion of Frost's involvement with Salisbury Street fiction, see *Forty Years'*, pp.77—95, and *Reminiscences*, pp.65—84. In later life Frost was the editor of a series of small weekly and daily newspapers. *The Secret* appears during the weeks of 25 May 1850 through 19 October 1850 in the *National Instructor*. As soon as it was finished he started another apolitical serial, which was never finished. He also published several sketches and short stories in the *National Instructor*.

49. *Notes to the People*, II (1851—2), p.515. Italics in the original. *Women's Wrongs* appeared regularly throughout vol. II; the fourth episode ('The Lady of Title') was not finished when the periodical died. The novel was later published separately as *Women's Wrongs: A Series of Tales* (London, 1855).

50. op. cit., p.939.

51. A complete account of Wheeler's life is given by William Stevens, *A Memoir of Thomas Martin Wheeler* (London: John Bedford Leno, 1862). Wheeler's enthusiastic support of the Land Plan earned him a number of enemies within the Chartist movement. Wheeler ended his days as an insurance salesman, a job, according to Frost, that many political organizers took as a means of meeting working people and of avoiding reprisals from factory owners.

52. *Notes to the People*, II (1851—2), p.833. Italics in the original. *De Brassier* appeared regularly throughout vol. I, and was started again midway through vol. II. It wasunfinished when the periodical died, and Jones appears never to have finished it. In the introduction to part II Jones disclaims representing 'particular individuals under the various characters he introduces in the work', and warns in characteristically florid style, that his readers must learn from the novel 'PREVENTION IS BETTER THAN CURE'.

53. *De Brassier*, Ch. 18, *Notes to the People*, I (1851—2), p.284.

54. Ch. 37, *The Northern Star*, 5 January 1850.

55. Ch. 12, op. cit., 23 June 1849.

56. Ch. 30, op. cit., 27 October 1849.

57. Ch. 33, op. cit., 1 December 1849.

58. Nineteenth-century novels about class conflict from a working-class perspective are so few that a nearly complete list can be given here: W. E. Tirebuck, *Miss Grace of All Souls* (1895); H. J. Bramsbury, 'A Working Class Tragedy', published in *Justice* in 1889; John Law [Margaret Harkness], *A City Girl* (1887), *Out of Work* (1888) and *In Darkest London* (1890); and Robert Tressell [Robert Noonan], *Ragged Trousered Philanthropists* (completed 1911). See P. J. Keating, *The Working Classes in Victorian Fiction* (London: Routledge and Kegan Paul, 1971).

CHAPTER 4   Literature as a Vocation: The Self-Educated Poets

> He . . . must carry about with him the pain of knowing that all he
> did could only be judged after allowance made . . .
>
> Edward Burne-Jones on Joseph Skipsey

For the working classes literature had two main uses which often seemed contradictory. The previous two chapters have shown it was a vital part of trade union and political movements. The readers and writers of such poems, dialogues and novels wanted them to reflect their lives in language, attitudes and subject matter. In contrast, those who were primarily interested in elevating their class by education preferred writings imitative of the masters of English literature. They saw literature as an apolitical, personal outlet. They rarely attempted anything besides verse. Poetry was considered the highest form of creativity, and seemed the ideal medium for personal thought. Its demands were not great in terms of plotting, characterization and form, and it could be written between periods of work at the loom or workbench. Working men who wrote poetry for intellectual and spiritual fulfilment became known in their communities as 'the weaver poet', or 'the bard of Craven', or simply as unusual men who spent their leisure time writing. Most were content with this limited sphere, but a few cherished the belief that writing was their God-given vocation. Rarely able to become full-time writers, they still hoped for recognition as true poets.

Literally thousands of working men wrote poetry. Virtually every newspaper in the country ran a poetry column; editors were inundated with verse from individuals of every class. Unlike trade union or dialect literature, the poetry discussed in this chapter can be found throughout England. Every Chartist who wrote poetry at one time or another tried his hand at verse imitative of his favourite writer, and dialect writers reserved their most serious topics for standard English. The desire to participate in English literary culture was almost universal among self-educated working-class writers. The best approach to the enormous quantity of material is through a few representative poets who achieved more than passing fame. Although those who never published outside their local paper did not have the same expectations as these men, they shared aesthetic values, writing styles and many of the same problems. I shall first discuss the self-image and subject matter of working-class poets; the attitudes revealed are key to an understanding of their relationships with their peers. Writers formed literary circles to teach and encourage each other. The support of friends would often lead a poet to publish a volume of verse. This brought about the problems of sales, reviews and a further divorce from one's class. Because the upper classes largely controlled the publishing houses and literary journals, writers trimmed their verse to suit them. In the final section I discuss the difficulties of patronage and the distortion of the poet's verse and life.

I
The Writer and His Muse

Two main groups of poets were struck by the Muse. By far the largest group were those operatives, mechanics, weavers and clerks who turned to poetry for personal enjoyment, and never considered themselves anything more than poetasters. Generally the stronger the local literary tradition, the better the poetry and the larger the number of working men interested in writing. Some of the largest groups were in Manchester, Bradford, Barnsley, Nottingham and Blackburn. The better known part-time poets that I will discuss were William Heaton (1801–71) from Halifax, Stephen Fawcett (1805–76) from Bradford, Elijah Ridings (1802–72) from Manchester and William Billington (1827–84) from Blackburn. The second group were far and away more talented than the pleasing versifiers around them. Under more auspicious circumstances they might have become men of some literary stature. The four major figures in the North were Robert Story (1795–1860) from Northumberland, later of Gargrave, in the West Riding, John Nicholson (1790–1843) from Bradford, John Critchley Prince (1808–66) from the Manchester area, and Joseph Skipsey (1832–1903), a Northumberland miner. These 'major' writers were all capable of interesting minor lyrics, and attempted such ambitious works as epics, verse tragedies, Pindaric odes and the like. All working-class poets of this period shared the same definition of poetry, its powers and the role of the poet in society; they differed only in talent, expectations and opportunities.

One can speak of a 'Burns syndrome' among the most serious writers; many had careers similar to his on a smaller scale. They went to work at an early age, gained an education with great difficulty, wrote verse for friends in pubs for a number of years, and then published a serious work with the help of a patron. This led to lionization by the local society, including mill owners and the squirearchy, easy access to drink, a breakdown of steady working habits, a subsequent lowering of poetic effort and death in poverty. Having made great sacrifices to further their education and to write poetry, they eagerly accepted any attention they received as justly deserved. Poetry was, in their eyes, an honourable means of improving their economic and social situation, whereas their work was often valued only as a curiosity. Too many believed the flattery they heard, only to be disappointed when it was withdrawn. In contrast, Burns was able to recognize the true nature of his lionization, and, in part, use it to his advantage.

The difficulties of self-education cannot be underestimated. Obtaining copies of the English literary masters remained a persistent problem, aggravated by a lack of leisure time. Reading material *per se* was not particularly difficult to come by; the development of cheap paper, faster printing methods and an enlarged reading public had all led to an immensely increased production of broadsides, religious tracts, cheap periodicals, novels, advertising and the like. But cheap editions of the great poets were not widely available until the 1830s, and even then contemporary poets were often unobtainable. Working-class autobiographies speak of foregoing meals and walking dozens of miles to buy a book, or surreptitiously reading at a bookstall. Young readers also frequently met family and peer opposition. John Nicholson, a journeyman wool-sorter, found his candles were hidden because he stayed up late reading and was perpetually late to work.[1] The father of John Critchley Prince beat him for reading because books were dangerous and unnecessary for a working man. He was forced to apprentice as a reed-maker to his father; the trade was dying as rapidly as hand-loom weaving, so the family worked excessively long hours for less and less money. Time and money were not available for luxuries such as books, paper and pens.[2] Yet, Prince could speak of his youthful escape into literature as his happiest childhood memory. In a series about poets for a working men's journal, he reminisced,

> From the first dawn of poetic taste in our minds, the amount of pure enjoyment and elevating instruction we have received from these 'the living of the earth' makes us grateful to that power which inspired them, and sent them into the world as the prophets and purifiers of their race. . . . How often in our thoughtful boyhood have we stolen away from too early and too painful toil; from the miseries and privations of our paternal dwelling, to snatch a brief mental feast from the pages of a Pope, a Prior, a Gay, and more

especially a Goldsmith![3]

Such enthusiasm — and exaggerated language — characterized many working men who found their only escape from the constrictions of 'too early and too painful toil' in reading, and perhaps in writing poetry.

Prince's list of favourite poets is revealing. Since the more famous Romantic poets were unavailable until the 1830s, or to be read only in snippets in magazines, the majority of working men were introduced to poetry through the works of Milton, Shakespeare and the many minor eighteenth-century versifiers. Robert Story speaks of picking up a copy of Watts's *Divine Songs for Children* as a shepherd boy, and memorizing every hymn in his eagerness to enter its poetic world. He spent many years imitating Mrs. Barbauld, Hervey and Watts before turning to Burns as his model.[4] Nicholson's verse usually sounds like a debased version of Thomson's descriptions of the sublime and the beautiful. He attempted to give his verse the patina of a classical education through references to Greek and Roman myths; the main characters in his narrative 'The Poachers' (1824) have Latin names, although the poem is set in contemporary Yorkshire. As late as the 1840s and '50s Joseph Skipsey found his greatest inspiration in Milton and Shakespeare; he memorized long sections of their works, and could discuss them as learnedly as any of his patrons.[5] Yet, by then, he and his associates were imbibing great draughts of the Romantics, taking from them that which most closely resembled their predecessors — their emphasis upon Nature.

Despite this grounding in Renaissance and eighteenth-century poetry, all these writers were at home in the nineteenth-century tradition of moral verse which elevated writers and readers from the common significance of common things. In his introduction to a cheap edition of the popular and influential Felicia Hemans (1793–1835), William Rossetti described her as 'a leader in that very modern phalanx of poets who persistently co-ordinate the impulse of sentiment with the guiding power of morals and religion.'[6] Self-educated working-class poets belonged to that phalanx. The more controversial beliefs of Milton, for example, never touched them; instead, they saw poetry as perennially soothing and uplifting. Unpleasant or divisive issues were by definition unpoetic. Aside from a few Church of England poems written by Story and Nicholson as Tory propaganda, these writers never took a sectarian position on religion. The morally safe was morally correct. They eagerly wrote about the platitudes of the day as superior virtues to be embraced by all.

The combination of pre-industrial poetry and contemporary moral sentiments resulted in a poetry little attuned to working-class life. These poets did not offer insight into their urban and industrial communities, but gave instead idealizations of Nature, Poesy and Love.[7] Nor did they look to their own experiences to describe fear, frustration or anger; rather, they wrote about emotions they had learned in books. The moral clichés that dot their works were embraced along with everything else that seemed to be a part of the richer cultural world they longed to enter, for they were certain its values were the highest. Their self-education had taught them to doubt their own judgments, but not to question the accepted literary masters, much less the accepted moral values. Working-class poets who wanted an entrée into literary circles imitated what they were certain was approved. Yet no matter how hard they tried, these writers were always out of touch with current literary trends and powerful social centres. They could never feel fully confident that their imitations of long-dead writers were acceptable to the working class or to those they most admired.

As a partial solution to this conflict, working-class poets endorsed the Romantic conception of the poet. Alienated from every class, they promoted their own special poetic sensibility. As recipients of higher moral tones they were lifted beyond the class barriers of society to a more perfect communion with the Muse. The metaphors describing this highly personal escape usually involved a movement upwards and outwards from the city, to a pastoral world of Nature, innocence and childhood; and upwards by means of poetic inspiration. The portrait of John Nicholson (Plate 12) portrays this escapism perfectly. The Byronic flowing tie, eyes heavenward, and the bit of sublime nature in the background all speak of a man belonging to a class apart from ordinary mortals. The contrast is obvious with Blind Willie (Plate 3) or Joe Wilson (Plate 29), traditional working-class song writers. Both men are shown surrounded by everyday objects, familiar to working people, whereas Nicholson is shown surrounded by 'poetic' scenery, demanding an imaginative response. Unfortunately the reality for Nicholson was a series of short-lived jobs, repeated requests for money from sympathizers, and finally escape through alcoholism.

Escape on the wings of Poesy compensated Nicholson for his lack of recognition:

She leaves all earthly grandeur and o'er the hills she soars —
What cares he then for slander when every star adores:
Here, singing strains unborrowed, the poet's verse can claim
A wreath that's everlasting, of never-dying fame.

In his own path of glory he sweetly chants along,
And every son of genius can comprehend his song;
Beyond the reach of slander he sings in loftier strains,
His verse has greater grandeur as higher heights he gains:

Till lost in the creation — surrounded by its gems —
He sees the heaven of heavens bedeck'd with diadems;
And though sometimes in sorrow despised and turned to shame,
He wins his wreath of glory, composed of endless fame.[8]

The poem is a compendium of Romantic clichés on the role of the poet: he is misunderstood by ordinary mortals, but is loved by men of genius; his special power is angel-like, and in the end he gains immortality. But the form of the poem is seriously at odds with the content. The use of irregular hexameters with a uniform caesura, marked by internal rhyme or a syntactical pause, makes the lines drag, whereas they should move quickly to accentuate the idea of the poet mounting on the wings of inspiration. The rhymed couplets make the long lines end with a jerk, instead of the supposed smooth movement of the 'numbers'. The images are insufficiently visualized or are plainly incongruous. Precisely what is 'the heaven of heavens'? If it is Heaven, is the poet knocking at the gate to join theangels, or is he merely soaring around among the stars? Nicholson's poem does not bear up under close scrutiny, but reveals how far apart theory and practice were.

Working-class poets also subscribed to the Romantic belief in a spontaneous, uncontrollable poetic inspiration as the sign of a true poet. Despite their difficulties in combining metre, rhyme, sense and naturalness, poets felt they had not been struck by the Muse unless their poetry appeared unpremeditated. Elijah Ridings said in his defence of 'The Poet's Dream' (1858):

I could not suppress or resist the temptation to write something, I knew not what, without predetermined rule, or laboured commonplace. The result is the following simple poem, almost unstudied, and certainly not bearing the richness of an exuberant or overflowing fancy, nor the poverty of a studied and *mediocre* accuracy. Whether the production will be considered the offspring of a legitimate visitation of the Muse, the most liberal scholar will be the best judge . . . .

Perhaps I have not always succeeded in the true poetic diction; although I perceive, myself, an occasional freedom of syntactical arrangement, I hope that all will not be found a kind of rhymed prose, nor a specimen of the spasmodic school, nor an overflowing cup of sugared words, to pall upon the taste, and satiate before it gratifies or satisfies. A happy negligence is to be preferred to a fastidious care, for the Muses brook no chains but those of their ownselection or adoption . . . ?

Unfortunately the virtually unreadable poem shows more spasms than inspiration. Ridings' enthusiasm for 'a happy negligence' arose in part from his own writing style, but in large measure it was due to his imitation of accepted poetic standards. A 'visitation of the Muse' was expected of true poets, and so he felt it necessary to justify himself in such terms. Ridings was betrayed by his poetic models; lacking a training in the fundamentals of prosody and composition, spontaneity should have been eschewed.

Not all working-class writers were as disengenuously confident of their ability as Ridings or Nicholson. Their extreme seriousness is offset by others who looked upon poetry as a pleasant pastime. Ben Hardacre (*c*. 1820–80), a factory operative from Bradford, wrote a humorous account of waiting for a visitation from the Muse. Sitting at his desk, pipe in hand, instead of falling into a trance, he is interrupted by tom cats fighting for the local 'goddess':

> [I] craved that the Muse would come and inspire
> With sweetly attuned and classical lyre . . .
> She came, but instead of the poet's ideal,
> A heavenly Muse, she was earthly and real:
> No airy-light being for Bard to adore,
> But a hairy young jade whose mews were a bore.
> She had in her train, in lieu of the lyre,
> A lewd, lurking lot, a squalling queer quire;
> Nor harp, nor sweet lute, nor lyre did they use,
> But vocal responses they made to her mews.[10]

The punning, the galloping rhythm and the repitition of words usually associated with the sacred Muse beautifully undercut Hardacre's pretensions and those of his peers. He was quite aware of the absurdity of an induced spontaneity or of high claims about a special vocation, and so set his poem against the realities of a working-class neighbourhood.

A dose of Hardacre's debunking was needed by many self-educated writers who were disappointed with their poetic reception. Nevertheless, their high seriousness was invaluable for extending the range of working-class literature. They imitated the literary establishment in order to overcome the restrictions of comic verse, bawdy songs and propaganda which their own culture offered as literary models. At a time when popular fiction and even literary critics denied the working man higher moral sensibilities,[11] these writers stood firm for the finest values they knew and expressed them consistently in their works. The ideal they presented of the poet and his lofty position in society may have been untenable in a modern industrial setting, but it was a valuable reaction against 'the general devotion to Mammon seeking', as Story defined the spirit of the age.

II
The Role of Nature

Escape through poetic inspiration was important for working-class poets because it affirmed the existence of a richer, more rewarding world. This other, better life was most easily found in Nature, so poem after poem was written about 'that great teacher'. Pre-industrial rural bliss was a recurrent topic, but equally important was a nature available for all their readers – the occasional country walk, parks, country customs and even gardening were popular subjects. This simple descriptive verse was a fulfilment of Julian Harney's exhortation to working men 'to get Beauty' in their souls. But many writers felt an obligation not only to portray the beautiful, but also to show a world where beauty was the norm, and man could follow nature's laws. Just as the Chartists had described the life they hoped to bring about through political change, these writers created idyllic worlds within the imaginative grasp of every reader. They were an alternative, if only poetic, refuge from the cares of daily life. In this section I shall examine the major themes of both types of nature poetry as important reflections of the cultural and moral attitudes of a large portion of working class.

In the earlier part of the century many poets grew up in touch with a traditional rural society. Robert Story, from a Northumberland peasant family, belonged to the still-living tradition of border minstrelsy. When nine years old he spent a month as a fiddler's callant, or assistant. It was then customary along the Scottish border during seed-time to dance and sing at the end of a day's planting; music was supplied by an itinerant fiddler. He and his callant were paid in lodgings and a bag of seed.[12] Story's best lyrics hark back to the border songs he had learned as a child. Many of them describe a countryside loved by first generation city dwellers. As he wrote in 1826 soon after leaving Northumberland:

> Through the vales where my fate bids me wander,
>   The streams may flow on wi' mair pride,
> But nae charm will they hae, when I ponder,
>   The charms o' my ain Beaumont-Side,
> When wave their green woods in the dews o' the morning,
>   I'll think o' the lang broom that yellows yon glen;
> When they talk o' their high hills and brag o' them scorning,
>   I'll think o' the Cheviots, and scorn them again.
>
> Farewell to thee, land o' my childhood!
>   When far frae thy beauties I dee,
> My last wish, dear land o' my childhood,
>   Shall rise for a blessing on thee —
> 'Healthy,' I'll cry, 'gush thy streams frae their fountains,
>   Birds in thy broomy glens sing the lang day,
> Lambs bleat alang the green sides o' they mountains,
>   And lasses bleach claes by ilk bonnie burn-brae!'[13]

The images lack freshness and the sentence structure is too complicated, but the energy of a traditional ballad is behind 'I Gang frae Thee'. The beauty of Beaumont-Side is well expressed, particularly in 'I'll think o' the lang broom that yellows yon glen', where "yellow" as a verb evokes an image of the glen covered with yellow broom. Unfortunately Story is unable to sustain this kind of simple description. His self-conscious blessing concludes the poem on an artificial note; even the image of the girls laying clothes out to dry seems contrived because of the excessive alliteration of 'ilk bonnie burn-brae'. However, the poem's vigorous provincial patriotism and strong sense of place make a pleasant contrast to the heavy moralizing on a generalized scene found in much working-class poetry.

Story's nature was not possible for weavers and operatives further south born at the same time or a little later. Village weaving customs of the 1790s, described by Samuel Bamford in *Passages in the Life of a Radical* (1844), lived on only as memories among nostalgic factory workers of the nineteenth century. William Heaton of Halifax spoke longingly of the time when he worked at home, with a view of the village cemetery from his window. He felt its proximity gave him a ready source of poetic subject matter. Pent up in a factory, listening to the ceaseless clatter of machinery, he found it difficult to think about poetry at all.[14] The nature Heaton remembered was not the primitive agricultural community of Story's childhood, but a countryside already integrated into a mercantile system. His memories were of a less disciplined time when he could combine hand-loom weaving with gardening and poetry. However, his desire for appropriately 'poetic' subject matter, such as Death, placed him with his Victorian contemporaries, rather than in the tradition of folk songs. His learning did not enable him to go beyond applying ready-made poetic interpretations to what he saw.

'I love to walk in the twilight grey' expresses Heaton's nostalgia, evoked by a self-conscious response to romantic scenery:

> I love to walk when the twilight grey
> Hath tinged the scene in the month of May;
> When the sun hath sunk in the western sky,
> And streaked the clouds with a crimson dye;
> When the lasses play on the village green,
> When the hearts of all are blithe and gay,
> I love to walk in the twilight grey.
>
> . . . . . .
>
> I then can think of departed years,
> Of childhood's hopes and bygone fears,
> Of friends that moulder with the dead,
> Of joys and sorrows gone and fled,
> Of youthful sports and pretty flowers,
> And parents loved in childhood's hours,
> Who now are laid in the silent clay
> While here I roam in the twilight grey.[15]

The seasonal changes of nature remind the poet of time destroying everything, whereas in 'I Gang frae Thee' the beauty of Beaumont-Side seems permanent, despite the poet's absence. A sense of impending disappointment characterizes all of Heaton's verse, as if he were oppressed by time and change, even before entering the factory.

The small garden, the cemetery and his family working together, described by Heaton, belong to the brief golden age of handloom weaving. For a man who began life as a factory operative at ten or twelve, nature was either a rare stroll in the country on a Sunday or it was a newly-created public park. Although the first Public Park Act was enacted in 1847, town councillors were reluctant to open costly parks, which might give opportunities for immoral behaviour. Parks which were locked at night and well policed during the day, however, gradually became an accepted part of industrial cities. They proved to be very popular with many workers who urged others:

> Then come ye toiling thousands forth,
>   Your daily labour done;
> And view these beauties of the earth,
>   These glories of the sun.
>
> You here in sinous paths may thread
>   Green lands and shady bowers.
> Inhaling healthful odours, spread
>   From trees and fragrant flowers.
>
> And oh! ye heedless ones, come forth,
>   False pleasure's cup dash down;
> Your powers of eternal worth,
>   Why madly seek to drown.
>
> Come here, and quaff pure pleasure's cup,
>   Nor fear a base alloy;
> Imbibe, 'twill bear your spirits up,
>   Drink deep of nature's joy.
>
> . . . . . .
>
> Yet he who views this grassy lawn,
>   Or marks each flowery sod,
> Must feel his spirit upward drawn,
>   From these, to Nature's God.[16]

So wrote one poet praising Bradford's new Peel Park, in 1861. The nature described stands apart from the sinful city, beckoning men to a purer life; escape has become limited, but more readily available to all. Both Story and Heaton wrote nostalgically about a past they remembered and could never regain, but by the 1860s working men more commonly wrote about a defined and easily comprehensible portion of Nature, making the best of what was available to them. A quick foray into the park after work was considered sufficient to reinvigorate working men.

The emphasis upon appropriate poetic themes in working-class verse resulted in a relative lack of interest in human relationships. Men and women were placed in a setting where they learned from Nature, or the poet addressed his readers directly, exhorting them to follow a particular moral lesson. Human emotions were kept at a distance by means of generalities. Although much verse was intensely personal, the poet was most concerned with his own soul, and showed little awareness of his relationships with others. Narratives about people were similar to moral fables, treating characters and emotions as stereotypes. Only occasionally in nostalgic poems about the past do individuals come to life. Personal isolation and a distaste for their peers only increased the bookish quality of these poets' work.

Nature as the basis for an idyllic world, where beauty was the norm and man could follow nature's laws, can be seen in three important poets – Nicholson, Prince and Skipsey. In 'Airedale in Ancient Times' (1824), Nicholson speaks of the Aire valley as a man familiar with the countryside from daily walks. Prince wanders through an unspecified rural setting in 'The Poet's Sabbath' (1841), seeking refuge from the city where he spends his other six days. For Skipsey nature became a vehicle for describing human emotions. In his 'Psychic Poems' (1886) flowers and insects speak, suffer and rejoice. But for each writer nature was the chief source of spiritual regeneration and morality.

'Airedale in Ancient Times' is a long narrative predominantly in rhymed couplets (in one section the bard sings a ballad) describing the fourteenth-century raids by Scottish chieftains into the Craven valley, and the successful repelling of them by Yorkshiremen under the leadership of the local squirearchy. Sections are also given to musings on the valley during pre-Christian times, the general beauty of nature and the poet's role in society. Nicholson exhibits a becoming tolerance of dead religions and hatred for the living alternatives to the Church of England. He described fourteenth-century rural Yorkshire with loving care:

Though history has shaded o'er with crimes
The long past period of the feudal times,
Here foreign luxuries were yet unknown,
And all they wished was in the valley grown, —
Their wholesome food was butter, cheese, and milk,
And Airedale's ladies never shone in silk;
The line* they grew their own soft hands prepared
The wool unheeded to the poor was spared; —
But few the poor, unless by age oppressed,
At little rent some acres each possessed.
When from the fields the golden sheaves were led,
The lovely fair could glean their winter's bread;
The husbandman could to his cottage bear
The withered boughs, his frugal hearth to cheer,
Or oft at eve his willow basket, stored
With wholesome viands from his lib'ral lord;
Or did he want for Lent a proper dish,
Aire's silv'ry streams produced unnumbered fish;
Their fruitful boughs the mellow apples bore,
And plum-trees bended with the sable store; —
The ills which crowded population brings,
Had never broke, sweet rural bliss, thy wings!
Then on the green the nymphs and swains would dance,
Or, in a circle, tell some old romance . . .[17]

This section is a pleasant evocation of an idealized past; the moral
implications are clear, but not oppressive. Nicholson was familiar with
rural customs (he insisted he could never write poetry unless he
rambled along the Aire first), and could discuss them in some detail.
While 'nymphs and swains' undoubtedly danced on the village
green — they were still doing so in Heaton's poem — 'sweet rural bliss'
existed only in the minds of men oppressed by 'The ills which crowded
population brings'. The self-sufficient rural community Nicholson
describes was infinitely preferable to the worst slums of Bradford where
he ended his days. It is stable under the rule of the Church and the lord
in his manor; Yorkshiremen fight only in self-defence, and until such
outsiders as 'Commerce' and foreign luxury' corrupt them, all is well in
the valley.

The golden past Prince describes in 'The Poet's Sabbath' is quite

*line: linen

different from Nicholson's. The poem tells how Prince spent his
Sunday, rising early, walking into the country, attending a church
service (where he mildly wonders how sincere the worshippers are),
wandering about dreaming of the past, and then returning home to his
happy hearth for an evening with his family and friends. The moral and
aesthetic glories of nature are all contrasted with the evils of the city:

> Sabbath! thou art the Ararat of my life,
> Smiling above the deluge of my cares, –
> My only refuge from the storms of strife,
> When constant Hope her noblest aspect wears –
> When my torn mind its broken strength repairs,
> And volant Fancy breathes a sweeter strain.
> Calm season! when my thirsting spirit shares
> A draught of joy unmixed with aught of pain,
> Spending the quiet hours 'mid Nature's green domain.
>
> Once more the ponderous engines are at rest,
> Where Manufacture's mighty structures rise;
> Once more the babe is pillowed at the breast,
> Watch'd by a weary mother's yearning eyes:
> Once more to purer air the artist flies,
> Loosed from a weekly prison's stern control,
> Perchance to look abroad on fields and skies,
> Nursing the germs of freedom in his soul, –
> Happy if he escape the thraldom of the bowl.
>
> . . . . . .
>
> Now Fancy wafts me to that golden age,
> When blessed our fathers in the days of yore;
> Whose semblance lingers on the poet's page,
> And in the prophet's visionary lore:
> Perchance some future age may yet restore
> The lost reality, more pure and bright,
> When man shall walk with Nature, to adore
> The God of love, of loveliness, and light,
> And truth shall teach his heart to worship Him aright.

With thee the earth was ever rich and fair;
No Summer scorched, no Winter chilled her breast;
Nor storm, nor dearth, nor pestilence, were there,
To break the holy quiet of her rest;
Eternal Spring, with constant beauty dressed,
Walked in a paradise of buds and flowers;
Eternal Autumn, with abundance blest,
Smiled on the fields, and blushed upon the bowers,
Fed by a genial sun and fertilizing showers.

The world was one Arcadian realm, and rife
With graceful shape, soft tint, and pleasing sound;
Unwet by sorrow's tears, unstained by strife,
An Eden bloomed on every spot of ground:
Mankind, a mighty brotherhood, were bound
By the strong ties of Charity and Truth:
With equal hand spontaneous Plenty crowned
The universal feast; no care, no ruth
Furrowed the brow of Age, nor dimmed the eye of Youth.

. . . . . .

As yet gigantic Commerce had not built
Cities, and towers, and palaces of pride —
Those vast abodes of wretchedness and guilt,
Where Wealth and Indigence stand side by side;
Man had not ventured o'er the waters wide,
To deal in human thraldom, nor unrolled
His hostile banner to the breeze, nor dyed
His selfish hands in kindred blood, nor sold
The joys of Earth, and Heaven, for thrice-accursed gold![18]

The slow, stately Spenserian stanza suits Prince's attempt to describe an ordered world where every man has his place and is linked with other men by all the virtues. The harmony so absent from the city can only be recaptured through an imagined Eden, springing out of Prince's country ramble. 'The Poet's Sabbath' has a powerful cumulative effect, though at times the reader feels bludgeoned by personifications and sublime adjectives qualifying every noun. Mills become 'Manufacture's mighty structures', slavery 'Human thraldom,' and Eden is blest by 'Eternal Spring,' 'Eternal Autumn,' 'a genial sun', and 'Fertilizing showers', etc. The strength of 'Airedale in Ancient Times' over 'The

Poet's Sabbath' is its accurate eighteenth-century descriptions of real
places; Nicholson was equally guilty of straining for a moral effect, but
his rhymed couplets were less pompous.

Prince clearly expects his readers to learn from his journey through
the country and into his imagined utopia. As he concludes his section
on 'that golden age',

> Transcendent Fiction! though we cannot find
> That aught so beautiful hath ever been;
> Though thou art but a vision of the mind,
> Fancied but felt not, – sought for but unseen;
> Yet hope is with us, – let us strive to wean,
> Our hearts from selfish influences, and go
> Together in the fields of truth, and glean
> All it behoves the hungry soul to know,
> Creating for ourselves a Paradise below.

Upon returning home Prince rejoices in his family and exclaims '[I]
wish that human life were one long Sabbath day', with a permanent
escape from the city and 'the thraldom of the bowl.' His paradise is an
escape into an unspecified Nature where perfection already exists. In
Nicholson's medieval idyll the good is made easy and natural, but it has
not yet been achieved. He describes a historical past, grounded in the
idealized customs of a particular time and place; in contrast, Prince's
utopia is a timeless product of his imagination. Although Prince has
obviously drawn many characteristics from traditional rural life, the
poem remains a compendium of all he personally considers to be
spiritual and physical perfection. In both poems nature and society
contain order and hierarchy, leading to contentment and goodness. For
Nicholson, however, each man works and earns his place in society,
gaining the respect of those above and below him. In Prince's world
self-help and work are both rejected for a Sunday excursion, where
unselfishness and beauty are found. His escapism – while meant to lead
the reader into a higher poetic and spiritual life – becomes a means of
avoiding spiritual decisions. He has romanticized moral improvement,
making it seem simple and easy, or, in his descriptions of a past Eden,
so perfect as to be unobtainable.

Nicholson and Prince believed that the social order should reflect a
higher God-given order, bodied forth in Nature; their longing for utopia
grew out of the disordered worlds of industrializing Bradford and
Manchester. Thirty years later for Skipsey nature reflects society as it

is. The reader learns from the follies, rather than the perfection, of human nature as acted out by flowers and insects. Glimmerings of a transcendent world which reaffirm the existence of a better life can only be seen by those who know this nature. The incipient allegory in 'The Poet's Sabbath' became the dominant mode for Skipsey, in spite of Dante Rossetti's advice that he continue his 'real-life pieces', such as 'Mother Wept' (see page 60).[19] Skipsey was unwilling to limit himself to poems describing working-class life, and insisted upon taking his own path. Isolated from his fellow miners, and without even the companionship of a literary club, he turned to writing poems about various abstractions — the soul's immortality, Spiritualism, Destiny and similar phenomena. Such poems as 'The Mystic Lyre', 'The Inner Conflict' and 'Omega' were never popular with his readers, but he persisted, convinced that he had found a means of expressing his innermost thoughts without betraying the inadequacies of his education or gaining the label 'pit-poet'.

In 1878 Skipsey wrote that a poet's consciousness of his art enabled him to spend his life 'in obscurity, poverty, or subject to the calumny & obliquy of a world who is ever ready to bow the knee to the idols of Fashion while [his] by-many-degrees inferiors in poetics and artisitc worth are riding the gilded car of wealth and notoriety.'[20] So he confidently asserted the superiority of his allegories, in which he could show the moral potential of the idealist. In one of his favourite 'Psychic Poems', Skipsey described the beneficent effects of his guardian angel:

> I'm the spirit of Emmalina, thy guardian angel, and
> Drawn hither by a subtle law but few can understand —
> Thy golden cord of sympathy, I leave the summer-land,
>   Thy aching brows with lilies to entwine.
>
> I've watched thee late and early, I've watched thee on the morn;
> And when the sun has left the sky, and Luna like a lorn
> Dejected maid has brought the hour most prized by hearts, grief-torn,
>   I thy aching brows with lilies have entwined.[21]

Prince and Nicholson were able to create a 'summer-land' on earth, but Skipsey finds only the 'cord of sympathy' linking him with Heaven. Nature cannot be an all-encompassing escape, but instead, through various manifestations offers both a description of mankind's unhappy life (the moon), and a symbolic promise of life after death (the lilies). While the earlier poets seem to be parading their personal and poetic problems before the reader, Skipsey's allegories keep the reader at an emotional distance. Romantic self-revelation has given way to a universal spiritualism; nature is a treasure house of symbols for the human psychic state.

In the more direct allegory of 'The Brooklet' Skipsey describes the distrust and dislike of poetry he found among so many of his peers:

> A little brooklet trilled a song
> As merry as the day was long,
> At which a music-hater stung
> To frenzy said: 'I'll bind thy tongue.
> And quell they merriment:' That night,
> A dam check'd babbler's song and flight;
> But blind are ever hate and spite!
> And so it fell, the brook did swell —
> Ah, truth to say, ere dawn of day,
> Had grown a sea, unquelled would be,
> And soon with ruin, down the dell,
> Dashed with a fierce triumphant yell;
> And cried, 'Ha, ha! ho, ho! oh, la!
> Where now thy skill, my voice to still? —
> Ah, dost thou find that he who'd bind
> The tongue e'en of a rillet, may
> Be doomed to hear instead, one day,
> What shall with terror seize, control,
> And wring with agony his soul? —
> In very deed then, reck the rede!'
> Thus yell'd the flood and onward swept;
> And music-hater heard and wept:
> And so weep all who'd try, or long,
> To render dumb the child of song.[22]

'The Brooklet' is a most unusual work, despite its many technical faults. The imagination brought to bear on the subject is far more original than anything seen previously in this chapter. Rather than the usual personification of human virtues against a backdrop of Nature, the poet as a brook is central. Moreover, poetic power is *natural*; when blocked it becomes a disruptive power that cannot be halted, just as a brook cannot be checked. Nicholson and Prince had presented Nature as a redemptive force. Skipsey, in contrast, pictures his creative energies in terms of Nature's destructive force. Beneath the unskilful surface of the poem lies his intense personal frustration; his creativity must burst forth, destroying the unnatural boundaries of society, despite 'music-haters' or his own technical limitations.

Skipsey has taken a common theme of countless working-class poets – the supremacy of the poet in the face of society's indifference or hatred – and has used familiar images drawn from nature, but he has gone beyond these clichés to a new poetic sensibility. In all the poets discussed previously poetry was seen primarily as soothing and elevating; Skipsey alone mentions the possibility of fear and strength. His anguished obscurity and loneliness find their justification not only in a greater sensitivity, but also in greater power. He believed that a just recognition of his powers could come only if he had faith in himself. Other writers told their readers poetry could be a force for change; Skipsey shows it. Yet one senses with Skipsey more than any other poet a straining to overcome his limitations. As Burne-Jones had said, he knew he could be judged only after due allowance was made for his lack of formal education. Skipsey was reaching beyond society's definition of him as a pit-poet, attempting to fashion his own self-definition. This course of lonely self-development was not pursued by others; indeed, had Skipsey had as many companions as Nicholson or Prince he might well have chosen the course of simple imitation that they took. No other working-class writer throughout the century wrote as he did. In isolation, Skipsey remains a poignant example of the inadequacies of a literary self-education in a culture demanding political and organizational genius, but making little room for experimentation in literary expression.

III
The Writer and His Public

When Skipsey described himself and his writing, he portrayed an almost isolated struggle against countless adversities. His psychologically bleak picture, however, can be placed in a wider social context. Informal clubs, sympathetic publishers, well-to-do patrons and like-minded friends played a large role in the development of a poet. The majority began composing verse as part of a course in self-education. As soon as they had a reputation as versifiers, they were asked to write for various organizations and ceremonies. The more ambitious also published poems in local newspapers and magazines. Their poems were then frequently collected for a volume of verse. Publication brought the complications of patronage, a subscription list, reviews, sales and local fame. Whatever his talents, a self-educated writer was dependent for success upon his friends and sponsors rather than upon the favour of the general public, and therein lies the central problem of the writer and a satisfactory literary life.

Having tasted intellectual riches, working-class poets longed to join the cultural circles where such matter was daily fare. Few were as successful as Thomas Cooper. It took little experience to discover that the real cultural life of one's city was class based, and part of a social world a working man could never enter. The humiliations of an inadequate education were reinforced by social denial at every turn. The newspapers and book shops were filled with descriptions of literary dinners, social gatherings, famous visitors, and other events well out of the social and financial range of any worker. Charles Swain, a lithographer known as 'Manchester's Tennyson' was honoured to sit on the platform with other dignitaries when Charles Dickens spoke at the Athenaeum Club, but he was not asked to join the guests at dinner. Although it might be possible to meet the cultural and social leaders of one's town on special occasions, working men did not have access to the circles that made discussion, writing and publication easy and natural.

Despite these disadvantages, literary enthusiasts started many small discussion groups that encouraged and publicized the interests of the most educated members of the working class. In the smaller towns these groups became the focus for local literary and historical interests, and participation from all classes was welcomed. Occasionally literature made a common ground for friendships across class lines. A few groups, particularly after the 1860s, survived several years, but most were short lived, and left their members struggling once again to reconstruct their intellectual and social life. These groups were important because they fostered not only self-education, but also self-expression through oratory, essay writing and verse. Every member was expected to performregularly, no matter how self-conscious he might feel about his dialect, appearance or voice. The experience gained in reading and writing for a sympathetic audience gave many young men the confidence to go on to better jobs, to write poetry and to court a woman they admired.

One of the most interesting of these literary circles met at the Sun Inn, Long Millgate, in Manchester, off and on through the 1830s and '40s. This group was the forerunner of the still existing Manchester Literary Club. The leading figure was John Critchley Prince, who lived

across the street for several years. Included in the group were Samuel
Bamford (1788–1872), the well-known Radical weaver, John Bolton
Rogerson (1809–59), a local editor of short-lived magazines, George
Falkner, editor of *Bradshaw's Journal* (1841–3) and later a publisher,
Charles Swain (1803–74), the lithographer, R. P. Procter (1816–81), a
barber, spare-time antiquarian and poet, and Elijah Ridings (1802–72),
an ex-silk hand-loom weaver, turned jack-of-all-trades.[23] This
remarkably close-knit group flourished during years of severe crisis in
Lancashire. Economic and political differences little affected it,
although many suffered from prolonged unemployment. Years later
Prince wrote a friend,

> Yet thou wilt not forget the pleasant hours
> Which we in social intercourse have spent,
> When Poesy has strewn her magic Flowers,
> And calm Philosophy has wisdom lent . . . [24]

Many poets, like Prince, had received their first encouragement at the
Sun Inn. Poesy, Philosophy and beer were a heady combination.

In July, 1841, the informal Sun Inn group took on the title
'Lancashire Literary Association', and elected officers. Invitations were
sent out proposing an organization for 'the protection and encouragement of British authors' and 'the meeting of men of congenial ideas and
sentiments.'[25] Plans were made to hold regular soirées, and to found a
magazine to aid Lancashire writers. Unfortunately funds were not
available for a periodical, but quarterly meetings were held for about
eighteen months, with usually more than forty attending. On one
occasion Isabella Varley (later the author of the popular *The
Manchester Man*) hid behind curtains to hear her poem read to the
company. For the 24 March 1842 soirée poems were especially
composed. Alexander Wilson, of 'Johnny Green' fame, sang a humorous
song about those present; Prince read a 'Poet's Welcome', and toasts
were made to one and all. George Falkner was particularly praised
because he edited *Bradshaw's Journal*, the only local magazine catering
to their poetic interests. The event was described in detail in the local
newspapers, and later the poems were published in *The Festive
Wreath*.[26] The favourable publicity helped to promote the sale of
poetry in Manchester and to dispel the notion that the city had no
native literary culture beyond its dialect writers.

Members of literary circles encouraged each other to publish in
newspapers and local periodicals. Although they had a smaller

readership, magazines carried greater prestige and often paid contributors a small sum. Many journals, similar to *Howitt's Journal*
(1847—8) and *Eliza Cook's Journal* (1849—54), encouraged amateurs
to submit their work. Their influence was disproportionate to their
circulation or longevity because they popularized the Romantic poets,
and Romantic ideals, such as the poet as a moral guide. All were
marked by the same high seriousness as the poetry they published. The
sober format of *Bradshaw's Journal* (Plate 14) is characteristic. Fiction
was admissable, but pictures were printed only for educational reasons.
While the content generally emphasized working-class interests, the
manner of presentation was close to the expensive middle-class
quarterlies. By and large their ideas and cultural values were an
imitation of the leading journals of the day.

Bradshaw's Journal (1841—3) and *The Bradfordian* (1860—2) are
two examples of local literary journals that made a conscientious effort
to publish the writings of working men. In addition to poetry they
carried articles on recent inventions, biographies, local history and
fiction. The fiction comprised either moral tales along the lines of
Harriet Martineau and Maria Edgeworth, or accounts of industrial life.
John Bolton Rogerson combined fiction and the familiar essay in his
series 'Walks in the Streets', written for *Bradshaw's Journal*. He
described the people he met on city streets, and speculated about their
possible life histories; people familiar to his readers are given a
mysterious or adventurous life. Out of kindness to Prince, *Bradshaw's*
offered to pay him for a series of letters describing a trip to London. He
walked much of the way, writing about the countryside he passed
through. Prince's prose was as artificially mellifluous as his poetry, and
he could not resist the opportunity to play a Wordsworthian role, but the
letters may have encouraged readers to explore the country south of
Manchester.

Abraham Holroyd's *The Bradfordian* was started to give local writers
an opportunity to publish more easily. Holroyd's stationery shop
attracted all the leading intellectuals of the 1850s and 1860s in
Bradford. They included Stephen Fawcett (1805—76), the Ten Hours
Movement poet, James Waddington (1829—61), a power-loom weaver,
Ben Preston (1819—79), a dialect writer, George Ackroyd, a banker,
John James FSA, a local historian and biographer, and William
Scruton, another antiquarian. Holroyd was an enthusiastic local
historian; he wrote a number of books and assisted with Rev. Baring-
Gould's research on Yorkshire customs. His efforts to promote local
literature through his magazine, publications and meetings were vital to

the development of the culture of Bradford, which at the time had no
public museum or free library and no antiquarian, philosophical or
historical societies.[27]

After publication in *The Bradfordian*, or a similar journal the next
step was a volume of verse. Bringing out a book was facilitated by
patrons devoted to local culture and by the steadily falling cost of
printing and paper. With the backing of a patron and a good subscriber's
list, a poet was virtually assured of meeting his expenses. The profit on
an edition of 350–500 is difficult to calculate. William Heaton insisted
that he made no profit, but Nicholson is said to have earned and spent
vast sums during his prime. An indication of the costs of printing a
book of verse can be gleaned from the record of George and Alexander
Falkner's publication of George Richardson's *Patriotism and other
Poems* (1844). The original account books shows the following
expenses for the volume of 152 pages:

			£	s.	d.
undated,	1843	400 copies of prospectus of *Patriotism*		15	6
April 29,	1844	500 copies of *Patriotism*, 10 sheet post work, with considerable manuscript alterations and additions.	35	0	0
May 8,	1844	300 title pages as prospectus for *Patriotism*		11	6
May 18,	1844	500 cases (hard covers)	11	8	0
		conveyance from London		3	6
May ?,	1844	240 bindings		4	10
		Folding and gathering of 500 copies of 10 folio sheets		8	4
Oct. ?,	1844	2 bottles of whisky for Richardson		7	0
undated,	1844	cost of posting books to subscribers		15	4

The total cost, excluding the whisky, for 500 copies, was £49 7s.0d.,
which Richardson did not finish paying until 1846.[28] The maximum he
could have cleared is £35 to £50, if every book sold at 3s.6d. or 4s. per
copy, and if he had no additional expenses for advertising and the like.
This would be a sizable sum for a man accustomed to earning about a
pound a week, but was scarcely enough to encourage further
publication as a sole source of income.

The costs of book publication were generally high enough to cut a
poet off from his working-class audience. Nicholson's *Airedale in*

Ancient Times (1824) was approximately the same size as *Patriotism*, and sold for 6s. per copy, including two steel engravings. In 1851 a subsidized edition of Prince's *Hours with the Muses* was sold for 2s.6d. While the cost had been cut, poetry inthe 1840s was still priced beyond the means of many working men. Poetry could not be both profitable and accessible for working-class readers without patronage or a return to broadside selling.

Once a book had been published, review copies were sent to the major local newspapers and periodicals, and sometimes to London and Edinburgh. The inclusion of a short biography helped to gain the attention of the critics, who could then praise the verse in the light of the poet's circumstances. The most common critical response to working-class poetry was that it was remarkable as verse written by a self-educated man, but was not particularly remarkable as verse. A number of reviewers optimistically predicted an enriching of English literature through 'new blood from the working classes', as William Howitt declared, but the majority praised what they could. Prince's *Hours with the Muses* (1841) was reviewed favourably by such well-known papers as *Tait's Magazine, Chambers' Edinburgh Journal, The Spectator, Westminster Review*, and the *New York Tribune*. The reviewers all concentrated on Prince's unhappy life, and commented on how little bitterness he expressed, and how untouched by poverty his poetry was. Some considered this a virtue, but others pointed to his 'dread that plainness and poverty are inconsistent with poesy.'[29] The *Westminster Review*, however, sounded the warning against Prince and all self-educated poets who expected national fame and fortune for their literary efforts:

> Had such a volume of poetry as the one before us been produced twenty years ago by a poor cotton weaver, its author would have been accounted a prodigy. As it is, he must be content to take his stand amongst the numerous *Dii minores* who overflow the realms of print: to him, poetry must be its 'own exceeding great reward;' and but little of that fame his heart pants so fiercely after can be expected to sweeten his lot; but, if sympathy and unfeigned admiration can supply its place, he may reckon upon receiving it from the small circle of his readers, among whom we classify ourselves.[30]

Indeed, twenty years before Nicholson had been greeted as a prodigy, and had received an impressive amount of money from patrons, particularly after good reviews pushed *Airedale in Ancient Times and other poems* into three editions within eighteen months. However, even he was treated as a curiosity by the London literary establishment, and everywhere told to remain at his work as a journeyman woolsorter.

Working-class poets did receive almost entirely laudatory reviews from local papers, who were proud of their self-educated men, and saw them as permanent residents on Parnassus. They were often effusive in their praise and promise of future success. The *Midland Counties' Herald* ended its review of *Hours with the Muses* with the comment, 'We hesitate not to predicate that the name of J. C. Prince can never die'.[31] Robert Story was so lavish in distributing free copies of his *Poetical Works* (1857) that he was left with scarcely any profit, but he had the consolation of uniformly good reviews, and letters from such distinguished men as Carlyle, Macaulay and Aytoun.[32] In no case did favourable reviews lead to concrete assistance in the form of a job; at most they improved sales and created an atmosphere in local areas that encouraged publication by other working men. This fostering of the arts was a valuable service in industrial towns, but most working men had higher hopes for their own future.

Good reviews attracted attention to a poet's work, but distribution beyond the immediate city of publication was difficult. Subscribers often refused to buy a book once it was published. It was essential to canvass widely to sell as many copies as possible. Nicholson went from inn to inn throughout the West Riding selling his books for drink and money. He would first show his talent for impromptu versifying to convince his audience that he was a genuine poet, and then would proceed to persuade his listeners to buy his book or at least give him a drink. Nicholson's methods of selling link him with the town eccentrics such as Blind Willie, yet he took himself more seriously than they, and never permitted the publication of his pub verse. His hawking was brought to an abrupt conclusion by the bankruptcy of his publisher; the stock was auctioned off at a greatly reduced price, glutting the market with his books.[33]

Selling broadsides on street corners or in public houses was never favoured; writers preferred to use contacts in other towns or to sell from door to door. Elijah Ridings, in addition to his outdoor bookstall, tried selling among the Manchester merchants. The results were mixed, if the following is any indication:

Sir, – what would you do if every third or fourth week of your existence you were waited upon by a bard, and asked to pay 7s. 6d.

for his fomentations, I mean effusions? There stands the man before you; his fomentations, I mean effusions, in his hand, an intellectual hunger in his face, and a smell of 'sperrit' gradually stealing dishonestly over the counter house. Bard has been sent to you by an intimate friend, who, fomented himself, desires that the divine essence may also air your system. Bard tells you that Mr. Plank, of the Internecine Railway Company, has bought a copy of the 'Emulsion,' and given your name as the possible purchaser. With a sickly smile, as of one round whom a hexametric cobra is about to coil, you disclaim all sympathy with anything in the shape of Olympian oppodeldoc [sic] ; you say very distinctly, 'Bard, this is nothing in my way – it is a thickish volume for the money – but really I am not a buyer.' . . . He presumes upon your veneration for his craft to protect himself; but his own respect for his craft does not withhold him from attacking you . . . [34]

'Cranberry' goes on in this vein of heavy irony for several more paragraphs; despite his condescension, he admits to having friends from his own class who write poetry, and he shows some knowledge of poetical terminology. His attack on 'Bard' evoked replies from 'Fairplay', 'Gooseberry' and 'Unpensioned', all defending the sale of books among merchants during working hours. As 'Fairplay' said, ' . . . have they not a right to travel with their books, the productions of their own minds, as much as Mr "Cranberry" and his friends, if so employed, have to travel with their calicoes?' They may have had as much a right, but the informal sale of books from pub to pub or shop to shop fell increasingly into disfavour, and after 1860 most writers left their wares to be sold by a stationer.

Income and fame also came from poetry readings and lectures. However, more than enough amateurs were willing to read for prestige alone, and later the dialect writers cornered the penny-reading market. Lecturing on a small scale was undertaken by many serious working-class writers when the Mechanics' Institutes and other organizations hired speakers regularly. In later years these lectures often brought unexpected praise; a number of working men in the latter half of the century recalled how meeting a genuine local poet had kindled their interest in verse writing. Prince was invited once to lecture at the Sheffield Mechanics' Institute by an acquaintance; the event was a great success – he met Ebenezer Elliott and sold many copies of *Hours with the Muses.* He then proceeded to bombard his friend with flattering letters about the 'intelligent and sympathetic Sheffield people', asking

if he could lecture again, and about the possibility of a job or of editing
a volume similar to *The Festive Wreath*.[35]

Prince was never asked back to Sheffield because few Institute
members really cared about him or his poetry. Not only was the price
of books too high for most workers, they preferred to read popular
fiction or educational material. Reactions among self-educated poets to
their failure to gain a working-class audience varied. They always
pointed to those few they had inspired. Rare speaking engagements and
requests for occasional verse sustained many after their initial fame had
died. Some poets were convinced that with more education their peers
would recognize the beauties of poetry. Others sought comfort in
friends and drink, or in their special sensibility. A few denied their
roots and tried to gain acceptance by the middle class.

At the beginning of his career Prince was convinced of the potential
refinement of his fellow workers. It appeared to be only a matter of
time before the innate poetic taste of the people would flower:

> It is true that the greater portion of the people, the poor and
> uneducated, can neither understand nor appreciate the higher
> principles of Poetry; but, while they can be cheered by a simple air,
> and melted by a pathetic ballad; while they have joys and griefs,
> hopes and fears, feelings and affections in common with all
> mankind, they cannot be said to be entirely unmoved by its
> influence. The spirit of poetry is within them, and only requires the
> quickening breath of moral and mental culture to give it a more
> permanent and elevated character. I think that a day will come, and
> I look forward to it with the cheerfulness of constant hope, when
> the sayings and sentiments, beauties and truths, of the master-minds
> of every age and clime, shall become 'familiar as household
> words.'[36]

Like the early apologists for the miners' trade union, Prince bases his
argument on the existence of inalienable feelings and passions within all
men. Although he disliked much of what he found among his peers,
including their ballads and broadsides, he believed in their moral and
mental development. He did not, however, consider the rapidly
developing cheap press and its power first to follow and then to lead
the semi-literate. The commercial possibilities of popular fiction and
verse were just being realized when poets such as Prince were vowing
their faith in the intellectual potential of their class. Their plea for

adequate education was not answered early enough, nor creatively, and an interest in 'the higher principles of Poetry' remained the enthusiasm of a minority.

Prince became embittered in time, and waxed maudlin about his lack of recognition, terrible living quarters and noisy neighbours. Joseph Skipsey had fewer illusions about his fellow miners, and made little effort to share his poetry with them. He was in his forties before he met in Thomas Dixon another working man with whom he could share his secret hopes and intellectual ambitions. Dixon, the Sunderland corkcutter to whom Ruskin had written the letters published as *Time and Tide* (1867), sent copies of Skipsey's works to Ruskin, Rossetti, and several other Pre-Raphaelites. But Skipsey could only view his life sombrely, 'There is not a bit of doubt that I feel that want of harmony with my surroundings to my mental requirements and the lack of general appreciation most keenly but I know this will not last long, only it may be till this body is laid in its grave and perhaps not that. – '[37]

Ignored by most of their peers, self-educated poets depended emotionally and intellectually on a few friends, those 'best and most refined minds' who read poetry and understood its inspiration. When they met together, poets consoled themselves with the belief that they had some influence on society even when unrecognized. Story claimed, 'amid the general devotion to Mammon, there are still found some worshippers of the purer divinity – minds whose influence necessarily and incessantly mingles with and exalts the worldly spirit of the time.'[38] Alternatively, they argued that they wrote because they had to, and poetry was its own satisfaction. 'The true Poet is never duly appraised or understood by his neighbours or his contemporaries', wrote a power-loom weaver in 1883, 'The Bard is Nature's priest and needs must preach, and peal her glorious gospel in the world's dull ear. It may be deaf, but he must not be dumb . . .'[39] But as Skipsey knew all too well, it was difficult to sustain this optimism without friends. When poetic inspiration failed, self-educated writers put great strain on those who had originally encouraged them. Younger poets were shamelessly exploited for a drink or a handout. Edwin Waugh spoke with embarrassment of 'that old sponger' Elijah Ridings, and tried to avoid him. Miserable at their own failures, writers were not always able or willing to support each other during hard times.

William Billington was correct in saying that poets were 'never duly appraised or understood', but he blamed the materialistic spirit of the age. These poets were ignored by their peers, however, because they attempted to give an alien and irrelevant culture to their working-class audience. They did not take the best qualities of working-class life and make them attractive and desirable to their readers, as did dialect writers, but rather, they wished to uplift their readers into a different culture. They denied much of what their peers appreciated as literature, and offered instead a borrowed culture that aped the morals and sentiments of those holding social and political power. They saw and accepted a class-based society; the very metaphors they used to describe their fellow workers reinforced the superiority of the culture 'above' them. For example, William Heaton speaks of himself as well paid 'if these my humble endeavours should gratify my friends and tend to raise the class to which I belong.'[40] The upper classes controlled all access to publication – patronage, publishing houses, publicity and reviews – forcing these poets, consciously or unconsciously, to write what they knew would be acceptable. They could expect virtually no audience among their own class outside a few fellow poetasters, and so vied for attention from sympathetic patrons and middle-class readers.

IV
The Writer and His Patron

The English literary establishment had long patronized 'the uneducated poets', as they were usually known before the 1830s. John Taylor (1580–1653), the 'Water-poet', Stephen Duck (1705–56), a thresher, and Anne Yearsley or 'Lactilla' (1756–1806), a dairymaid, among many others had been taken up by various literati and taught proper manners and versification, only to be later dropped. Experience had shown, as the *Edinburgh Review* said, that such persons become 'literary mendicants', totally dependent upon their sponsors.[41] But in the nineteenth century working-class poets found greater encouragement as it became socially necessary to foster working men who accepted middle-class superiority. Everyone admired a helping hand extended to those who helped themselves, and bookish poets rarely bit back.

Distant sympathy rather than distinct encouragement, nevertheless, marked most writers' responses to working-class poets. Although Robert Southey helped Henry Kirke White, the son of a Nottingham butcher, and John Jones, a Yorkshire butler, he positively discouraged others who wrote to him. He corresponded for years with Ebenezer Elliott, warned him against premature publication and suggested a long apprenticeship of publishing in local papers where criticism would not damage his reputation. He did not suggest bringing Elliott into his own circle, and was not particularly pleased when success came to the iron-master.[42]

A typical example of prestige without concrete help is William Wordsworth's formal thanks to William Heaton for dedicating a poem to him. Heaton, in turn, received both permission to publish the letter and payment for one copy of *The Flowers of Calderdale.*

Rigdal [sic] Mount, Ambleside
New Year's Day, 1844

I cannot suffer this day to pass without thanking you, my worthy Friend, for the good wishes you have expressed for me in your Verses of the 23rd of last month. Pray accept mine in return. May it long be permitted you in your humble station, to enjoy opportunities for cultivating that acquaintance with literature, of which the effects are shown, greatly to your credit in the lines you have addressed to me.

I remain, with much respect,
Sincerely your's, [sic]
Wm. Wordsworth.[43]

For all his interest in the common people, Wordsworth responded withpolite gratitude and good wishes; the example of his friend Southey was sufficient to warn him from promising assistance that might lead to future disappointment on both sides. A letter from England's poet laureate must have been immensely satisfying to a man who had modeled his most solemn works after Wordsworth's descriptive lyrics. Even though the letter makes no comment about Heaton's verse, it acts as a kind of imprimatur at the front of *The Flowers of Calderdale,* calling attention to the respectability and ability of thepoet. Perhaps it also helped sales.

Joseph Skipsey was one of the few working men taken up by a literary circle. Unlike the writers in Manchester, Bradford and other northern towns, Skipsey wrote in almost complete isolation, except for his friend Robert Spence Watson, a manufacturer and one-time president of Armstrong College. From 1859 Watson attempted to find more congenial employment for him than mining, but each job was short-lived. In 1886 Edward Burne-Jones had obtained £50 for him from the Royal Bounty, and an annuity of £10, later raised to £25.[44]

Finally, in 1888 with the assistance of Rossetti and other Pre-Raphaelites, Skipsey, at fifty-five, was appointed custodian of Shakespeare's home. But Skipsey missed Northumberland, and hated to guide unbelieving American tourists; he soon returned home. Although well treated whenever he visited London, Skipsey was never invited to settle there, or to attempt full-time writing. Rossetti and others recognized that he could never become a journalist, and would never earn anything from his verse. Without the training to become a secretary or librarian, the only alternative was a respectable unskilled job. But his repeated failure to settle into various positions discouraged further aid. In 1878 Skipsey dolefully predicted, 'I am sometimes afraid that I shall die as I have lived, a coalminer.'[45] This was indeed his fate.

With the doors of established authors closed, a writer was forced to make his own way. For Ebenezer Elliott, the political importance of his corn-law rhymes combined with excellent reviews made possible national fame – but he wisely remained in Sheffield. Others followed the example of Nicholson, who in 1827, flushed with the success of his two volumes of verse, walked to London. Yorkshire friends introduced him to a number of working-class sympathizers, including Dr. Birkbeck, but he was not invited to participate in the literary world of the capital. He fell in with a group of Yorkshire roustabouts and had a brush with the law for disorderly conduct; he managed to escape with a reprimand and unfavourable reports in the northern newspapers. The trip was turned to some profit, however, when Nicholson wrote the pamphlet 'The Yorkshire Poet's Journey to London', in which he compares the natural beauties of Airedale with the ugliness of the great metropolis. The next year he tried to crash the London literary world, and again met with failure, though friends solicited £10 for him from the Literary Fund Society, and he had a few verses published in the Morning Advertiser.[46] Robert Story lived for twenty years in London working as a clerk at Somerset House, but he did not attempt to join a literary group. Whenever he went North he visited his literary friends, content to remain important among minor poetasters, rather than be humiliated by the mighty in London. A similar fate was met by other northern working men when they went to London; a few Cockney poets might be supported by the mighty, but outsiders were not welcome.[47]

A more promising course was to seek patronage among those gentry anxious to encourage local culture. Some local politicians and clergymen were sympathetic and their names show up repeatedly. Elijah Ridings dedicated The Village Festival and other Poems (1848) to Lord Ellesmere, the Conservative M.P. for South Lancashire who had helped Robert Story to a sinecure at Somerset House. Nineteen years previously Ridings had led the Miles Platting radicals on the day they marched to Peterloo, but now he was grateful for any assistance he could get in publishing his verse. Thomas Lister of Barnsley was well known as an ornithologist and poet when Lord Morpeth 'in the true spirit ofhis illustrious ancestors . . . stretched forth his fostering arms to shelter modest merit.'[48] He offered Lister the position of postmaster of Barnsley in 1832, but Lister was a Quaker and could not take the required oath of office. Impressed with his modesty, the post was again offered by Morpeth when the oath was no longer mandatory, and Lister filled it from 1839 to 1870. Sir Titus Salt was particularly generous in aiding Bradford's factory operatives; he assisted Nicholson, his wife, Holroyd, Story and Waddington. Other patrons were less well known, but equally anxious to encourage the talents of bookish working men. Against the flood of verse, the *Edinburgh Review* took a minority position in arguing 'of all the things in the world which are not immoral, one of the least deserving of encouragement was indifferent poetry.'[49]

Unable or unwilling to become journalists and reluctant to return to physically exhausting work, writers turned gratefully to their patrons for assistance. In the early stages of his career the sponsor found a publisher, corrected his grammar and helped get up a subscription list. Later he was often called upon to find the poet another job, to assist his family and to keep him out of the public house. At its best the relationship was marked by a friendship on both sides reminiscent of the pre-industrial master-man relationship so many poets mourned. Elevated by a wealthy sponsor, the poet usually felt he had to represent himself and his beliefs in the best possible light both to those above and below him. For a time his self-esteem sustained him, even when his poetry continued to receive limited recognition.

Prince's first patron was J. P. Westhead, M.P. for York, whom he addressed with gratitude in a long autobiographical poem:

> Before I lay my lowly harp aside —
> My constant hope, my solace, and my pride,
>   Through all the changes of my grief or glee —
> Before its powers grow weaker and depart,
> I weave the inmost feelings of my heart
>   In one true song of thankfulness to thee.

> Daily I laboured for uncertain food;
> But yet my dearest hopes were not subdued
>   By stern Misfortune's unrelenting frown;
> A bright but distant future cheered my way, —
> Oh! how I yearned to breathe a living lay,
>   And win the glory of a Bard's renown!
>
>   . . . . . .
>
> A kind advisor thou hast been to me,
> Leaving me still in thought and action free;
>   Oh! let me thank thee for such just regard!
> For I believe that thy superior aim
> Is but to raise to comfort and to fame
>   A long-distressed, but now aspiring Bard.[50]

The humble aspirations expressed here tell exactly Prince's expectations: fame, financial security and the opportunity to develop further his poetic powers.

It was, of course, essential to avoid the imputation of being a social climber, even if this were the intention. Prince emphasizes that his only hope is to be a player of 'the lowly harp', encouraged by Westhead's sympathy. Working-class poets nearly always apologized in their prefaces for possible errors of prosody or grammar, and insisted their writing had not been done during working hours. The justification of intellectual pleasure and moral solace runs through all of their appeals to the middle class. As Stephen Fawcett explained:

> The following work has been composed in the evenings, after the author's toil at the plough and flail. In it the fatigues and vicissitudes of poverty were forgotten. The muse often caused drooping misfortune to smile; never failed to put to flight those taloned harpy-sorrows with which thought worn human nature is too often infested. May she soothingly shed her Aonian balmy dews upon the heart of the reader, and teach him or her, humanity, charity and loyalty.[51]

Fawcett wrote in a style that was hardly intelligible to the average reader, but his message of 'humanity, charity and loyalty' was appealing to those looking for humility and respectability among the poor.

Gratitude for attention and favours — or the expectation of

favours — led working-class poets to write about controversial subjects in a manner they thought would please their mentors. Sincerity and genuine feeling were lost under a layer of heavy moralizing. This was nowhere clearer than in poems about two vital working-class issues: the New Poor Law of 1834 and drink. A fear of the workhouse hung over men who preferred writing verse to working steadily, and intemperance was almost an occupational hazard. Yet they had difficulty in coming to terms with their own personal feelings and the known expectations of their readers.

The workhouse was a central symbol for the working class of their alienation and hatred of industrial conditions. Broadside writers wrote popular attacks on the 'Bastilles', but these poets equivocated. They had hated the workhouse, yet they could not advocate protesting against it lest they lose their wealthy readers. The poetic solution was to distance the moral dilemma emotionally, and make the grim image of the workhouse an admonishment to work hard and support one's family. All sense of agency is lost in their poems. The workhouse is regarded as a symbol of personal failure, and the individuals and institutions responsible are never blamed, or even mentioned. Dependent on middle-class patronage working men themselves advance the argument that working men are to blame for the evils of the workhouse.

Robert Story, a staunch Conservative, wrote about how his family would feel being forced into the Bastille. The language and tone are fervent and colourful, but the style betrays an aesthetic, educated distance from the situation:

> A House they've built on yonder slope
>   Huge, grim, and prison-like, dull!
> With grated walls that shut out Hope,
>   And cells of wretched paupers full.
> And they, if we for help should call,
>   Will thither take and lodge us thus,
> But ELLEN, no! Their prison wall,
>   I swear it, was not built for US!
>
>   . . . . . .
>
> They shall not go — to pine apart,
>   Forgetting kindredship and home;
> To lose each impulse of the heart
>   That binds us wheresoe'er we roam!

And we, whom GOD and LOVE made one,
　　Whom MAN and LAW would disunite,
We will not, Famine's death to shun,
　　Sleep there, or wake, a single night!

Still is their act — in something — *mild*:
　　Though *I* no more must share your rest,
They would *permit* your *infant child*
　　To — *tug* at an *exhausted breast*!
And Jack would cease, poor boy! to scream,
　　Awed by some keeper's rod and threat;
While, sunk in cribs, the rest would dream
　　Of days — too well remembered yet!

Away! on ENGLAND'S soil we stand;
　　Our means have, erst, supplied the poor
We *have* claims on our father-land: —
　　No, no — that right is ours no more!
But we will die a Beggar's death,
　　Rather than pass their hated wall!
On some free hill breathe out our breath —
　　Our nameless grave receiving all![52]

He does not attempt to analyse the economic and social causes of the abomination, but only loudly declaims that his family will starve together on a 'free hill' before they will cross its threshold. He briefly mentions having paid taxes, which give his family 'claims on our father-land' (and separates them from the 'wretched paupers'), but he does not explain why this 'right is ours no more'. The concluding lines seem hollow rather than courageous because so little time is spent on *why* society has denied the rights of taxpayers, and is no longer obligated to them in hard times. Like Jone o' Grinfilt, Story assumes certain God-given rights, but he does not provide any frame of reference for these rights by which to condemn either society or individual men for creating the Bastilles.

　　Nicholson writes of the workhouse from the point of view of an outsider; yet he nearly ended there himself, and only the kindness of his patron kept his family out after his death. He wrote 'On Visiting a Workhouse':

Allowed to walk into the sad retreat
Where tott'ring age and foolish fair ones meet,
I heard deep sighs from those bent down with years,
Whose cheeks were deeply furrowed o'er with cares.
To see their locks by ruthless Time turned grey,
Melted my heart, and took my pride away:
For who was seated in the corner chair,
But one who in my youth I held most dear . . .

I spoke, but John my words could scarcely hear;
At length he cried, in exclamation strong,
'Ay! is that thee?' for still he knew my tongue.
His age-dimmed eyes then brightened with a ray,
Which like a wasted taper died away.
Dotage had seized upon his feeble brain,
As he revolved to infancy again.
A while he spoke of heav'n and things divine,
Then laughed — and stopped a moment to repine;
Wished for the grave — next talked of things to come,
Then wept — and thought of his once happy home,
But his poor heart was most of all subdued
With daughters' pride and sons' ingratitude.
'Alas!' said he, 'that those who owe me all,
'Should know me thus, and yet refuse to call
'To spend one hour, to mitigate my grief,
'To bring one cordial, or afford relief.
'Though they neglect a father, old and poor,
'Yet oh, avert it, Heav'n! Blessed may they live;
'Oh teach an injured father to forgive!'
Touched with the scene, I turned aside to weep,
And like a child he camly fell asleep! [53]

Nicholson has shifted the problem away from the obligations of society
and the government (i.e. the inadequacies of the law), to the injustices
of ungrateful children. Nothing really needs to be changed after reading
this poem except human nature, and nobody — it is confidently
implied — can change that. The law itself is unfortunate, but if children
will not care for their parents, then such 'wasted tapers' must be put
somewhere. The old man's sorrow is softened by his senility, so that
Nicholson and his readers are further excused from taking any action
against his pitiful condition. Like trips to the madhouse in previous

centuries, a visit to the workhouse has an excellent chastening effect on
Nicholson. The moral is not 'Look at this and strive to change it', as in
propaganda verse, but 'Look at this and consider your sins.'

Story and Nicholson have taken an all-important subject for working
men, and have evaded examining it. Instead, they concentrate on their
own states of mind: Nicholson on his sympathy for an old friend and
Story on his virtuous fear of seeing his family divided. They direct
attention away from the workhouse as a living symbol of degradation
and toward themselves. Story and Nicholson cannot admit to feeling as
other working men lest they lose their hard-won artistic sensibility. This
sensibility went hand in hand with middle-class attitudes toward the
workhouse and other working-class abominations. The price of their
struggle for self-expression was isolation from their emotional roots and
emasculation of their poetry. Although these poems concentrate on the
state of each writer, their cumulative effect is of reified human
emotions bearing little relation to the reality described. The avoidance
of moral confrontation and the accompanying loss of emotional
understanding was a very high, yet inevitable, price to pay for
middle-class acceptance.

Working-class poets were more successful in describing the horrors of
drink, and its root causes. Their literary lives were led in pubs, and they
had witnessed scenes of destruction and degradation that shamed them,
and quickened the urgency with which they advocated temperance.
Elijah Ridings wrote a poem about a friend who had died from delirium
tremens, imploring in a note, 'I beseech the attention of the reader to
this effort against vice in its primary source, the very fountainhead of
crime and immortality [sic].'[54] Unlike temperance propaganda,[55] these
poems were intended for working-class readers, but the more educated
and self-conscious poets were also able to illustrate the roots of
intemperance, and to suggest solutions that would appeal to a
middle-class readership. Since drunkenness was a social evil agreed upon
by members of all classes, they were able to describe it without
compromising themselves to their patrons.

As one would expect from men who placed such importance on
writing as a morally regenerative force, education was regarded as the
principal means for combating the influence of alcohol. While not
accepting the entire social milieu of the teetotal associations, poets such
as Ridings and Prince did see the necessity for viable alternatives to the
public house. As Prince pointed out in his 'An Appeal on Behalf of the
Uneducated', few alternatives to drunken brawling existed for the
ignorant:

> Seek ye the drunkard at his sober toil,
> Tending the loom, or sweating o'er the soil –
> An unenlightened slave your glance shall greet,
> Scarce wiser than the clod beneath your feet . . . .
> They cannot feel the pure delight that springs
> From constant converse with all nobler things;
> Bound to a beaten track, they cannot know
> How many flowers along its margin grow;
> They reap no joy from wit or wisdom's lore,
> But toil, eat, drink, and sleep – and nothing more.[56]

The solution suggested is to send teachers to the poor, 'Go to the sons of Labour, and inspire/Their sluggish souls with intellectual fire.' Although less attractive than the temperance propaganda verse, the contribution of such works as Prince's 'Appeal' should not be underestimated. He presents the working man in a sordid slum, with no other recreation but drinking to give him respite from long hours of work. By showing the causes of drunkenness he validates his criticism of both the drunken labourer and of those who fail to provide education. Prince's work was effective for educating not only the working class, but also his sympathetic middle-class readers. Published in 1841, years before such popular novels of social protest as *Mary Barton* and *Sybil*, the poem offers an explanation of social ills in a language and tone palatable to the middle class. In well-defined topics like the endorsement of temperance, poets such as Prince fulfilled their desire to elevate morally their own class and to educate their 'betters'.

The intellectual juggling act of elevating working-class readers and appealing to middle-class patrons could not always be sustained. Trouble came between a writer and his patron after the passing of a brief moment of fame and the dropping off of sales. A lucky few obtained appropriate sinecures. William Heaton was well enough known as a poet of nature to be made the caretaker of Halifax's first public park.[57] But more commonly a poet was dropped when he showed signs of independence or of overstepping his station in life. When Lactilla enquired about Hannah More's investment of her profits, she was quickly dropped and 'the wild vigour of her rustic muse' denied.[58] Westhead and his friends found Prince a job as postman in South-hampton for 15s. per week. Prince, however, thought he deserved better, and sardonically remarked that at the very least the job would make him 'truly *a man of letters*'. Upon further investigation he turned down the position, and thereby lost favour irretrievably with his most valuable sponsors. A second attempt was made to assist him in 1856 by the Manchester 'Prince Testimonial Committee'. They paid off his numerous debts and subsidized another edition of *Hours with the Muses*, but they were unable to find him 'permanent healthy employment with moderate remuneration,' which had been their original goal.[59] Prince does not seem to have had the necessary combination of honesty and humility that Thomas Lister impressed upon Lord Morpeth to gain his position.[60] He managed to alienate all who helped him, in spite of his many flattering poems.

It was humiliating to Prince and other poets to be 'literary mendicants'. In order to bear their social degradation and intellectual isolation they turned to drink. But they also drank to socialize with other writers and to sell their books; they frequently spoke to each other about adopting more temperate behaviour. Elijah Ridings wrote to Prince that he was giving up the company of poets for a while in order to 'abstain for a short time from those positions which Comus gave his crew of satyrs, because I feel myself at times so much inclined to make a satyr of myself.'[61] Nicholson wrote in defence of poets who drank,

> The public answer, they should not drink; but the very persons who are advising them, the next sentence is — come take a single glass with me, a single glass cannot hurt you. The poet refuses — again is pressed. He knows it hurts him, but is afraid to disoblige his friend — he is a subscriber; — points out the beauties, the defects, &c., of the work. The next gentleman he meets does the same: perhaps another enters — another glass is the consequence: the poet's heart warms — forgets his constitution — Till in a few years, like lime with water, he falls away and drops into the earth.[62]

Nicholson and Ridings treated their weakness for drink as predetermined by their vocation. They had no other explanation of why drink had become important to them, and why so many of their friends ended life as dipsomaniacs. But from a modern perspective their ideals and realities conflicted at every turn, and their only harmony was achieved through the temporary escape on the wings of poesy or the camaraderie of drink — and neither could drown out their failure to achieve the promise of their youth.

If the verse of nineteenth-century self-educated poets seldom rose above the most conventional clichés, it expressed a hope of stability and moral improvement through literature that was a more personal alternative to politics, religion, temperance and other more familiar working-class institutions. These poets extended the scope of working-class literature and gained recognition for self-educated writers among a wide range of men. Moreover, poetry was an ever-present personal consolation. Against all difficulties, Story could still say at the end of his life:

> My Muse . . . taught me to embody my feelings in verse, the very act of which is an exquisite pleasure. It directed my boyish eye to the beautiful in nature — a never-failing spring of enjoyment. It diffused a purity through my youthful amours. It shed a charm round my domestic hearth. It poured a light over many a scene, the dearer for being distant. It threw a rainbow on the gloom of political strife. It made me hundreds of friends, whose friendship has been repeatedly proved by the most trying of all tests. It introduced me to circles, from which my birth and breeding would — but for it — have excluded me.[63]

Notes

1. W. G. Hird, 'The Life of John Nicholson', *The Poetical Works of John Nicholson*, ed. W. G. Hird (London: Simpkin and Marshall; Bradford: Thomas Brear, 1876), p. xxx. Hereafter cited as *Works*, ed. Hird; and John James, 'Life of John Nicholson', *The Poetical Works of John Nicholson*, ed. W. Dearden, 4th ed. (London: W. H. Young, Bingley: J. Harrison, 1859), p. xii.
2. R. A. D. Lithgow, *The Life of John Critchley Prince* (Manchester: Abel Heywood, 1880), pp.7–10. Hereafter cited as Lithgow, *Life*.
3. 'Random Readings from Poets of the Nineteenth Century', *Bradshaw's Journal*, III (1842), p.233.
4. John James, 'Sketch of his Life and Writings', *The Lyrical and other Minor Poems of Robert Story* (London: Longman, Green, Longman and Roberts, 1861), pp.xxiii–xxiv. Hereafter cited as *Minor Poems*; and *The Poetical Works of Robert Story* (London: Longman, Green, Longman and Roberts, 1857), p.vi. Hereafter cited as *Poetical Works* (1857).
5. Robert Spence Watson, *Joseph Skipsey: His Life and Work* (London: T. Fisher Unwin, 1909), pp.20–2.
6. *The Poetical Works of Mrs. Felicia Hemans* (London: Ward, Lock, n.d. [1879], 'Moxon's Popular Poets series'), p.xxvii. There are ninety-five entries for Felicia Hemans' works in the British Museum catalogue; throughout the century she remained a perennial favourite for family anthologies.
7. For an analysis of how poets avoided the city in their poetry, see Martha Vicinus, 'The Literary Voices of an Industrial Town: Manchester, 1810–1870', *The Victorian City*, eds. H. J. Dyos and Michael Wolff (London: Routledge and Kegan Paul, 1973), II, pp.739–61.
8. *Works*, ed. Hird, pp.280–1.
9. *The Poet's Dream* (Manchester: J. J. Sale, 1856), preface.
10. *Miscellanies in Prose and Verse* (London: Simpkin, Marshall; Bradford: T. Brear and W. Morgan, 1874), pp.107–9.
11. See Margaret Dalziel, *Popular Fiction 100 Years Ago* (London: Cohen and West, 1957), pp.137ff.
12. John James, 'Sketch', *Minor Poems*, pp.xi–xv.
13. *Minor Poems*, pp.43–4.
14. 'Sketch', *The Old Soldier, etc.*, p.xiii.
15. *The Flowers of Calderdale; Poems*, p.10–11.
16. George Davidson, 'Thoughts on Peel Park', *The Bradfordian* I (October, 1861), p.198.
17. *Works*,ed. Hird, pp.19–20.
18. *The Poetical Works of John Critchley Prince*, ed. R. A. D. Lithgow (Manchester: Abel Heywood, 1880), I, pp.1–17. Originally published in *Hours with the Muses* (1841).
19. Watson, *Joseph Skipsey*, p.53–4.
20. Unpub. letter, Joseph Skipsey to Thomas Dixon, 10 December 1878. I wish to thank Ronald Marshall, the Stone Gallery,

Newcastle-upon-Tyne, for permission to quote from the collection of Skipsey letters in his possession.

21. *Carols from the Coal-Fields and other Songs and Ballads* (London: Walter Scott, 1886), p.254.
22. *Carols*, p.145.
23. For details of the Sun Inn poetry group, see R. P. Procter, *Memorials of Bygone Manchester* (Manchester: Palmer and Howe, 1880), pp.145–250; and Lithgow, *Life*, pp.124–36.
24. Prince, II, p.295. Originally published in *Miscellaneous Poems*, (1861), a collection of verse dating back over twenty years, published solely to raise money.
25. Lithgow, *Life*, p.129–30.
26. See Procter, *Bygone Manchester*, p.124ff.; Lithgow, *Life*, pp.129–30; and J. B. Rogerson, ed., *The Festive Wreath* (Manchester: Bradshaw and Blacklock, 1843); and 'Poetic Festival', *Manchester Guardian*, 30 March 1842.
27. 'To Our Readers', *The Bradfordian*, I (November, 1860), p.30.
28. All information comes from George and Alexander Falkner's 'Private Journal and Weekly Balance Sheet, 1843–7'. In 1843 George Falkner gave up editing *Bradshaw's Journal*, and with funds from his father, began a printing house with his brother, specializing in handbills, invitations, calling cards, etc. They also published the poetry of a few friends. Richardson still owed them £7 14s.4d. in 1846, which may have discouraged them from helping other poets. I wish to thank W. B. Blackburn for permission to examine this journal, the only remaining document from the firm's early days. George Falkner and Sons, Ltd suffered almost total loss of their premises, plant and records by enemy action in 1941. The original account book survives because it was kept in the company safe. At the present time the firm prints cheques for banks and private companies.
29. *The Spectator* XIV (1841), pp. 570–1.
30. XXXVI (1841), pp. 264–6.
31. Newspaper cutting, 'The Olio', Prince's commonplace book, Manchester Central Reference Library.
32. John James, 'Sketch', *Minor Poems*, pp.lxix–lxx.
33. John James, 'Life', *Poems*, ed. W. Dearden, pp.xxiv-xxvi, xxxiii.
34. *Manchester Examiner and Times*, 16 August 1858–21 August 1858. The entire correspondence is in Elijah Ridings' commonplace book in the Manchester Central Reference Library, with the marginal remark, 'Elijah Ridings told me that that letter was written about him, but that he had not drunk any intoxicating drink for some time previously. J. P.' Samuel Bamford had just retired from Somerset House in the spring of 1858, and had returned to Manchester where he hoped to earn enough to keep himself and his wife (he received no pension) by selling his works and giving readings. He indignantly wrote the editor of the *Examiner and Times* disclaiming any part in the letters. The newspaper assuaged his ruffled pride by publishing his letter with

the comment 'We insert with pleasure Mr. Bamford's disclaimer, though we were not aware that he was suspected of having a hand in the "bardic" controversy'. A copy of this correspondence can be found in Samuel Bamford's unpublished diary, 28 February 1858–26 December 1861, Manchester Central Reference Library.

35. Unpub. letters to John Fowler, dated 1 November 1841 through 23 August 1842, Manchester Central Reference Library. The last letter in the collection was written during the Plug Plot Strikes. Prince commented, 'Things have been in so disturbed a state that writing or business has been out of the question. At present things wear a more tranquil aspect, and under the protection of the Police, the people are resuming their employment.'

36. 'Random Thoughts on Poetry', *Hours with the Muses* (Manchester: J. B. Rogerson, 1841), p.24.

37. Unpub. letter, Joseph Skipsey to Thomas Dixon, 10 December 1878.

38. *Love and Literature* (London: Longman, Brown, Green and Longmans, 1842), p.11.39.

39. William Billington, *Lancashire Songs with other Poems and Sketches* (Blackburn: J. G. & J. Toulmin, 1883), proem.

40. 'A Sketch of the Author's Life, *The Old Soldier; the Wandering Lover and other Poems* (London: Simpkin, Marshall; Halifax: T. & W. Birtwhistle, 1857), p.xxxiv.

41. T. H. Lister, 'Review of *Attempts at Verse, by John Jones, an old servant; with some Account of the Writer, written by himself; and an Introductory Essay on the Lives and Works of Uneducated Poets*, by Robert Southey', *Edinburgh Review*, 54 (1831), p.79. [Authorship per Wellesley Index]. Also see Rayner Unwin, *The Rural Muse: Studies in the Peasant Poetry of England* (London: George Allen and Unwin, 1954).

42. Their complete correspondence has been reprinted in E. R. Seary, 'Robert Southey and Ebenezer Elliott: Some New Southey Letters', *Review of English Studies*, XV (1939), pp.412–21.

43. *The Flowers of Calderdale; Poems* (London: Longman and Co.; Halifax: Layland & Son, 1847), p.vi.

44. Watson, *Joseph Skipsey* pp.71–76.

45. Unpub. letter, Joseph Skipsey to Thomas Dixon, 26 September 1878.

46. John James, 'Life', *Poems*, ed. W. Dearden, pp.xxii–xxxii.

47. Charles Dickens' well-known assistance of John Overs, a carpenter who wrote verse, follows the same pattern as that described above. See Edgar Johnson, *Charles Dickens: A Biography* (New York: Simon and Schuster, 1952), I, pp.309–10, 344, 346–8, 502, 536–7.

48. *The Rustic Wreath: Poems, Moral, Descriptive and Miscellaneous* (Leeds: Anthony Pickard, 1834), p.xi.

49. 54 (1831), p.81.

50. Prince, I, pp.147–52.

51. *Edwy and Elgiva and Other Poems* (Bradford: W. Byles, 1843),

preface.
52. 'The Union Workhouse' (1837), *Minor Poems*, pp.110–12. Italics in the original.
53. *Works*, ed. Hird, pp.192–3.
54. *The Village Muse*, 3rd ed. (Macclesfield: Thomas Stubbs, 1854), p.123.
55. The majority of temperance verse followed the format pioneered by teetotal reformers: vivid and horrendous descriptions of drunkards, dipsomaniacs and those possessed by delirium tremens, were combined with a heavy-handed moral about the destruction of the individual and of his family. Henry Anderton, a Preston founder of the temperance movement, wrote the following lines on 'A Peep into the Tap-Room and its Visitors':

> With long snarling face, and awful grimace,
>   *There* growls a political patriot;
> Yon brace with black eyes, and lips of such size
>   Are 'good uns' – at tapping the claret!
> Those scheming old rooks, in opposite nooks,
>   Fresh tricks with dice-box are playing;
> That wild-looking youth is 'spouting' forsooth,
>   And rivals the jackass in braying!

> . . . . . .

> 'Go home!' how absurd! to spend that sweet word
>   On four crumbling walls is a mockery!
> The 'bum' has been there and stripp'd them quite bare,
>   'My uncle' has taken the crockery!
> In closets below, on trusses of straw
>   Exposed to the wind and the weather
> Enclosed in old rugs, wife, children, and bugs,
>   Are lovingly huddled together!

The temperance movement used the forms of entertainment connected with the public house, such as the music-hall routine, light-hearted songs and comic acts, to combat its culture. Only by offering attractive recreation could the movement hope to appeal to large numbers of working men and women. As one of the earliest teetotal song writers and performers, Anderton was famous for his vulgar heartiness and breezy presentation of the cause. For an examination of the social and cultural life of temperance, see Brian Harrison, *Drink and the Victorians* (London: Faber and Faber, 1971). For Anderton's life, see *The Temperance and Other Poems with a sketch of his life*, ed. Edward Grubb (Preston: W. & J. Dobson, 1863). 'A Peep into the Tap-Room' appears on pp.1–3.
56. Prince, I, pp.102–8.
57. 'Halifax Poets', newspaper cutting from the *Halifax Courier*, 1913, compiled by W. H. Harwood, Halifax Public Library.

58. Unwin, *The Rural Muse*, pp.76–81.
59. Lithgow, *Life*, pp.151–7, 174–96.
60. John Burland commented on Lister's appointment in his 'Annals of Barnsley and Environs, 1744–1864': 'By sedulously courting the patronage of the great, he got an appointment more agreeable to his feelings' (I, p.324). Unpub. MS., Barnsley Public Library.
61. Unpub. letter, 6 September 1842, in 'The Olio'.
62. John James, 'Life', *Poems*, ed. W. Dearden, pp.xxix–xxx.
63. *Poetical Works* (1857), p.vii.

CHAPTER 5   An Appropriate Voice: Dialect Literature of the Industrial North

> ... if you'n gether reawnd, aw'll try my hond at a sung; It may
> shew a guidin' glimmer to some wond'rer astray, Or, haply, gi'
> some poor owd soul a lift on the way...
>
> Edwin Waugh

The modern poet Robin Skelton writes of 'begging from door to door the dialect', seeking out the idiosyncrasies of Lancashire speech with a tape recorder in order to preserve them forposterity. Conscious of how local culture is dying, he predicts that his sons will come to him when he is old, asking 'What/Do you call that? Call that?' Yet dialect was a major vehicle for literary self-expression among working-class writers inthe nineteenth century. Before the middle of the century, it was used almost exclusively for comic and satiric poems, with the exception of the followers of Burns, 'Jone o' Grinfilt, Jr.' and a few other works that rise above such a narrow classification. The literary poets discussed in Chapter 4 occasionally turned to dialect writing, but they always kept it distinct from their serious work. The outstanding period of dialect was 1860–85, a time of consolidation and rediscovery of working-class values and traditions by literary men. They took their subject matter from the half-submerged culture of industrial folk songs and learned poetic skills from writers of standard English. Their aim was to join old traditions with the new industrial and urban values. The result was a popular indigenous literature that spoke to and for the prosperous working class of the industrial North.

I
The Roots of Dialect

Dialect writers of the mid and late nineteenth century drew upon a mixed heritage of broadsides, antiquarianism, the cult of Robert Burns and their own spoken language. Before the late fifteenth century and the consolidation of standard English, literature flourished in a variety of dialects. But after this time, outside of Scotland, regional dialects were rarely used in literary works. Only in the orally transmitted ballads (many of which were published) did dialect continue. Printed broadsides often contained dialect words or turns of phrase, added consciously or unconsciously by a compositor. On the other hand,

many songs printed in standard English must have been bent quite
naturally to fit the singer's dialect, for pronunciation does not
invariably follow accepted norms. Throughout the sixteenth, seventeenth and eighteenth centuries the writing and printing of dialect songs
continued unabated in Northumbria, where the influence of Scotland's
separate vernacular tradition was strong.[1] But even in this region dialect
was rarely used for prose writing, nor was it commonly used by
educated writers; and the main growth in dialect songs occurred after
1750. The vernacular during these three centuries was the language of
rural folk; printed dialect was limited to songs, a few examples for the
upper classes and the ever-popular pithy aphorisms.

The rise of dialect for conscious literary purposes coincided with the
rise of antiquarianism. Henry Bourne's *Antiquities of the Common
People* (1725) was the first of many collections of folk speech, songs
and miscellanea. Gentlemen folklorists were soon assiduously tracking
down the words, songs and memories of their own servants, old
women and other rural folk. A love of 'popular antiquities', as folklore
was called in the eighteenth century, remained a minority enthusiasm
among the literati, but the popularity of Macpherson's Ossianic poems
(1760, '62, '63) and Percy's *Reliques of Ancient English Poetry* (1765)
speaks of an interest that was rapidly becoming respectable. The
followers of the cult of medievalism, enthusiasm and untutored genius
eagerly published minstrel pieces. Pseudo-dialect songs and epics
brought fleeting literary fame to more writers than the ill-fated
Chatterton. But despite this widespread interest in dialect combined
with traditional lore, few self-educated writers outside Scotland
attempted a career of providing 'reliques' for an eager London
audience. Rather, they followed the models of accepted poets, outlined
in the previous chapter, writing carefully constructed rhymed couplets
about familiar abstractions.

Nevertheless, the ground was laid for a future generation. Although
primarily interested in the heroic and tragic – love and battle were the
most acceptable topics for the untamed muse – the antiquarians of the
eighteenth century encouraged the collection and dissemination of
literature written and sung in a local dialect. Their approval meant easy
publication and respectability, two assets to an ambitious writer. On
the other hand, as collectors they could encourage but not direct the
development of local literature. Without widespread popular interest
dialect could never have grown in the eighteenth century. Working
people in both the cities and country were eager to buy broadsides and
chapbooks written in their spoken language. The new songs of the

eighteenth century, unlike traditional ballads, usually dealt with the work and leisure time of the people. By the nineteenth century dialect literature cannot be considered folk culture, but is the conscious product of literate individuals who wrote for their own class with encourage- ment from a wider audience. These writers, moreover, had first learned to read and write in standard English, and then returned to their native tongue and relearned its cadences, vocabulary and thought structure.

In the late eighteenth and early nineteenth centuries entertainment in Northumbria centred on the writing and singing of songs in pubs, clubs and at home. Individuals from every walk of life dashed off songs. Local antiquarians, such as John Bell (1783–1864) were intimately acquainted with every aspect of daily life on the Tyneside; in contrast to the majority of wealthy collectors, Bell and others were constantly reprinting songs they found.[2] Well-to-do dabblers in song writing enjoyed an exaggerated reputation for their mock heroic verse in dialect. John Selkirk's 'Bob Cranky' (pp. 34-6) teeters between realism and parody, half-admiring and half-amused with the activities of pitmen. This widespread interest in local songs and lore encouraged working men to write and perform in the pubs of Newcastle and the surrounding area. They were particularly successful at adapting older traditions; regional customs lived on far longer than in other parts of the country.

Dialect writing was not revived south of the Trent until well into the nineteenth century, and then only under the influence of northerners.[3] The resurgence of dialect in Lancashire and Yorkshire was slower than in Northumbria, but in the end proved to be more varied. Far more prose was written in these two counties than any other area. Under the influence of antiquarians, many authors supplied a glossary, an explanatory introduction and other scholarly paraphernalia. Even so, dialect remained very much the voice of the working people. It came to be the literary language of the well-established factory workers who sought a reflection of their ideals and customs.

Broadsides in Yorkshire and Lancashire dialect appeared with increasing frequency after the late seventeenth century. A York printer, Stephen Bulkely, published the poem 'A Yorkshire Dialogue in Yorkshire Dialect; between an Awd Wife, a Lass and a Butcher' in 1673. The poem describes in realistic detail the misadventure of an ox on the way to the slaughter-house – a subject lacking any heroic possibilities, but defining dialect's greatest strength, a resilient, realistic comedy that did not bow to snobbish literary or social assumptions.[4] In 1746 the most famous eighteenth-century dialect work appeared under the title *A View of the Lancashire Dialect; by way of Dialogue between Tummus o' William's o' Margit o' Roalphs and Meary o' Dick's o' Tummy o' Peggy's*, by 'Tim Bobbin' (John Collier, 1706–86). The sone of a poor curate, Collier lived most of his life in the village of Milnrow, serving as the schoolmaster. He supplemented his earnings by painting grotesque comic signs for local public houses, giving flute lessons and composing satiric songs. 'Tummus and Meary', as it became known among its readers, was an instant hit, although later dialect writers criticized Collier's crude realism and distasteful characterization. Collier was one of the first writers to write a sustained prose piece in flexible and vivid dialect; his main intention, however, was not literary but philological and antiquarian.[5] Devoted to Lancashire, from an early age he noted down every odd expression or word he heard. The country bumpkin, Tummus, undergoes varied misadventures so Collier can use as many of his collected expressions as possible. The result is a humorous and easy way to learn the Lancashire dialect. 'Tummus and Meary' remained popular among working people for its comic and vivid action; the success of the work, moreover, encouraged others to try their hands at similar dialogues. By 1800 in Yorkshire and Lancashire dialect dialogues and songs were firmly established as the principal genres for comedy and realistic descriptions.

The comic, even brutal, style of eighteenth-century dialect was carried over into the nineteenth century by political satirists as propaganda for the new trade unions and political organizations. John Doherty, an organizer of the cotton spinners in the 1820s and '30s affected a thick accent when writing and speaking about the self-made masters who tyrannized the spinners. Irish accents, often borrowed from the theatre, were a continuous source of amusement. The Tory press never tired of mocking Feargus O'Connor, while the Chartist press frequently attacked Daniel O'Connell by means of heavy-handed dialect conversations. The educational possibilities of dialect were not ignored — comedy coated the pill of political economy in much political propaganda. 'Sally Bobbinwinder' wrote in 1838 *A Conversation between Peter Pickenpeg, Jack Shuttle, and Harry Emptybobbin*, about the labour theory of value. Intellectual Harry has the final speech, attacking the government's system of taxation and war policies, in standard English. The comedy comes from Harry's long-winded explanations in standard English, Peter's self-education and Jack's shrewd native understanding. Indeed, at one point, the author emphasizes the discrepancy in speech and manner — and unity of interests — among the three by rebuking Harry with the comment 'Hey,

Harry, an Oi wist Oi cut interrupt thee e' t'same way – If Oi wor as good a scollar az thee Oi'd let sumbady naw.'[6]

Bawdy realism was generally less popular in the nineteenth century than previously. Romanticism in its various forms demanded an aura of the moral, or at least of the exceptional found in the commonplace. Dialect might have remained limited to the comic dialogue and popular song in England, but for Robert Burns (1759–96). Combining realism and romanticism, he became the single most important influence on nineteenth-century English dialect writers. In his public life and works he represented all a self-educated poet might become. The handsome ex-ploughboy's literary and social success was also handy evidence for the well-to-do that the talented poor would be recognized.[7] As the first poet many working men knew, he inspired the newly educated to speak in their own language about their own thoughts. The shoemaker to whom Thomas Cooper apprenticed introduced him to Burns, whose pathos 'took possession of my whole nature almost as completely as the fire and force of Byron.'[8] Edwin Waugh saw Burns as his literary mentor, repeatedly reading his moral verse for guidance and encouragement. To his inexpressible delight, on one occasion he discovered an unemployed mechanic who knew Burn's work thoroughly; they sat in a pub for hours exchanging favourite poems and anecdotes.[9] The pervasiveness of Burn's works, and his importance during crucial years of self-education and discovery insured a widespread acceptance and admiration for dialect.

After the death of Burns in 1796 until approximately 1850 literary dialect writing went into decline. During these years the self-educated writers described in Chapter 4 lacked sufficient confidence in themselves and their own culture to write seriously in dialect. Elijah Ridings' thick accent, for example, was mocked in his literary circle. Most written literature and songs in dialect appeared in such ephemeral forms as broadsides, and these writers wanted acceptance from the established literary order. But the next generation of writers embraced their own peculiarities of speech and behaviour, and trimmed their literary expectations.

Dialect flourished after 1850 in industrialized urban areas such as Newcastle, Manchester and Leeds. Large sections of the working class had achieved defined social roles by mid-century; a variety of working-class institutions were well established. While the old fears of unemployment and political instability persisted, relative prosperity had changed the focus of class interests. Entertainment came to hold a larger place in life. Reading material, lectures, plays and the music hall were all eagerly supported; dialect was particularly popular as family entertainment. The average reader might have had difficulty in deciphering the irregular spelling of dialect works, but he was attracted to a world close to his own in plot, conversation and character.

Although the use of dialect meant speaking to a limited audience, it had the advantage of building upon local feeling — *my* region and its culture against the rest of the country. Unlike Scots, the various English dialects differed very little from standard English in regard to vocabulary and sentence structure; only pronunciation and idioms marked them off. The most successful writing, however, was integral to a particular locality and could not be translated without a loss. Unfortunately, the extraordinary popularity of dialect until the end of the century led many weak versifiers to cloak their inadequacies in a kind of pidgin English that passed for dialect. When both the form and the content of a work became too general, dialect was as artificial as any other literary device. It was essential to retain the particularity of place and object to make dialect meaningful. Nevertheless, the stiff or exaggerated standard English used by many working-class writers is negative evidence that they found dialect their most natural and artistically effective language.

The most interesting characteristic of the new dialect was the mingling of the old and the new, the urban and the rural. Writers fashioned a language that grafted the new vocabulary of the city streets, factories and mines to the older rural vernacular. The large numbers of country people who came pouring into the industrial cities provided a link with the country, and in turn they found their old customs still living in the works of such writers as Waugh, Brierley and Hartley. Like Collier, Waugh collected rare sayings and words which he put in his works. His intention was to combine the best of the old traditional vernacular with the most amusing bits he actually overheard. Thomas Wilson hewed as closely as possible to spoken conversation in his rhymes, but he usually set them back to the time of his own childhood. He described the passing of old customs and adversities in a language combining the past and the present.

A rural setting was not always important in dialect tales, but often authors shifted a character from his hearthside or pub-corner to the moors or an ancestral village. The spoken dialect belonged to the past and to the country in the minds of many city dwellers who themselves spoke a dialect altered by contact with a wide variety of class, geographical and occupational accents. The richest source for a story often turned on a day trip to an old village, where the city dweller lapses into an old-fashioned dialect, conversing with the country folk about the changes they have seen and their memories of a harsher, but more satisfying life. He is pleased to find how little things have changed in spite of 'progress', and happily returns home. A variation on this theme was the story placed in an indefinite rural past. The traveller-persona was a necessary intermediary, taking urban readers back to an authentic dialect and a traditional way of life. For all the confidence and rapport felt by dialect writers with their readers, they were often happiest dealing only indirectly with contemporary conditions. They preferred to link descriptions of modern working-class life with a traditional rural life that still survived in the memories of the new migrants or of older relatives — and in the urban mythology of the mid-century.

Much dialect prose and verse was set in a pub or around the hearth. The factory or the mine was less important than leisure time, partially because working people did not relish the monotonous and regimented life of the factory or modern mine. A more important reason, however, was the increased acceptance of values and customs favoured by the middle class. Regularity of habits, close family ties and a romantic courtship leading to a happy marriage were all part of the better life espoused by advocates of self-help. The change in personal values was accompanied by a demand for reading matter that emphasized these priorities. This shift in setting and theme was not limited to dialect verse after 1850; domestic happiness or sorrow, chaste courtship and the general beauties of nature were all themes found in the minor writers of the Victorian age. Popular magazines of the day filled their pages with these sentimentalities by Eliza Cook, Felicia Hemans and a variety of long-winded novelists. Dialect writers, however, were saved from the worst excesses because regionalism gave point and purpose to their commonplaces.

Dialect writing was not always presenting idealized versions of life among the better-off workers. Some of the very best pieces come out of the political tradition of satire and comic irony, best exemplified by 'Jone o' Grinfilt, Jr.' Throughout the century working men wrote songs about their workplace, condemning the petty tyrannies of the boss, celebrating feats of strength or shrewdness, and praising all master-hewers, keelmen, weavers, etc. The tradition of satirizing the dominant values of the day was strong not only in trade union and political songs, but also in almost all literature about work. Tommy Armstrong's 'Row between the Cages', about a quarrel between a new patented lift and the old-style lift combines characteristics from the music hall and the traditional broadside, with an oblique comment on working conditions in the mines (see Appendix). Such works are far more lively than the rather stilted political pieces described in Chapter 2. However attractive they seem in comparison with the domestic dialect pieces, they remained occasional verse, best described as a link between traditional folksong and the music hall. Most dialect writing was apolitical, emphasizing the home life and local customs of northern workers and rural folk.

II
The Literary Life of Dialect Writers

Working-class dialect writers were unusually numerous and came from a wide variety of occupations. As with the poets discussed in Chapter 4, the majority wrote as an intellectual outlet and to supplement their income; only a few had successful full-time careers as writers and public readers. The most famous were Edwin Waugh (1817–90), from Rochdale and later Manchester, Ben Brierley (1825–96), from the Manchester area, and John Hartley (1839–1915), from Halifax and later Bradford. Waugh and Brierley exercised great influence over the course of working-class literature, assisting and inspiring many others to write in dialect, including Hartley. The two most successful Northumbrian dialects writers, Ned Corvan and Joe Wilson, had careers in the music hall and are discussed in the next chapter. A few fluent and confident individuals combined journalism with their dialect writing; James Burnley (1842–1919) wrote for the Leeds *Mercury*, Bradford *Observer* and several London newspapers. He also edited a number of localhumour magazines, including the dialect *Saunterer's Satchel*, and wrote a number of plays, popular entertainments and dialogues. The last years of his life were spent in London, where freelance journalism paid more consistently than in Yorkshire. The Newcastle schoolmaster J. B. Robson (1808–70) wrote poetry throughout his life, publishing many volumes of insipid verse; the last ten years he wrote a weekly local letter under the name 'th' Retiort Keelmin'. Among the best-known writers who combined work and writing were Thomas Wilson (1773–1853) of Gateshead, Tommy Armstrong (1848–1920) of Durham, J. T. Staton (1817–75), Samuel Laycock (1826–93), John Trafford Clegg (1857–95) and John T. Baron (1856–1922) From Lancashire, and Ben Preston (1819–89), Thomas Blackah (1825–95) and Joseph Eccles (1824–95) from the

West Riding.

Waugh, Brierley and Hartley (Plates 15, 16, 17) survived as full-time writers through sheer hard work. They wrote voluminously, frequently repeating the same plots, themes and characters. Each established certain characters and situations which identified his work; purchasers looked forward eagerly to the next instalment about 'Besom Ben', 'Ab-o'-th'-Yate' or 'Sammywell Grimes'. In addition to innumerable threepenny and sixpenny pamphlets, they all had regular outlets for their work in local newspapers, dialect magazines and almanacs. They also kept their names before the public by means of the expanding penny-readings circuit. Even so, life was never easy; all three men were dependent upon friends and donations during their last years.

Penny readings were one of the most successful forms of working-class entertainment in the nineteenth century. Culture of every sort was made available at a price and in a form that appealed to respectable families, courting couples and ambitious young men. With the theatre and music hall considered off-limits to the respectable, readings and soirées, as they were often called, became an increasingly popular substitute.[10] The educational demonstrations of phrenological skill or the elaborate dioramas of the Holy Land or dialect readings attracted audiences because of their colour, action and drama. Most evenings combined amateur performers drawn from a chapel, temperance group or co-operative society, and a professional reader or performer as the main attraction. Unlike lectures and events sponsored by the Mechanics' Institutes, penny readings did not have reserved seats or a separate section for 'the better class of people'. Although different prices were charged for seats, they were not based on class differences. A typical evening's programme is the Stackstead Co-operative Store's soirée (Plate 18). Waugh, at the height of his fame, wasparticularly appropriate because he had been associated with the Rochdale Co-operative and was sympathetic to the movement. He probably was paid between £1 and £2 for his evening's work — better than a skilled factory operative, but not munificent in comparison with music-hall artistes.

An organization such as the Stackstead Co-operative held a soirée for fund-raising purposes, which was also the culmination of a periodof practicing together in preparation for a special occasion or celebration. The evening was a ceremonial coming-out for the organization, declaring its place in thecommunity and reminding members of the communal pleasures to be found within. Thus the songs and recitations had to be a combination of outward-looking good will, community feeling and confidence. The usual entertainment included humorous verses mocking marital life or courting, a comic sketch in prose, a few poems to pull the heart strings (usually about children dying young), an occasional soliloquy from Shakespeare or another dramatist and selected songs rendered by the local choir. Audiences expected to feel comforting emotions, drawing the family, or lovers, closer together through the shared relaxations of humour and song in contrast to the pathos and fears melodrama could arouse and exorcise. Almost everywhere Waugh went he was expected to read his most famous works, either 'Come Whoam to thy Childer an' Me' or a 'Besom Ben' tale. His more sombre works, closer in tone and style to the starker industrial broadsides, rarelyappear on an evening's programme. Penny readings brought drama to the familiar, rather than the excitement of the novel or strange.

Every dialect reader had a public persona that he projected through his works and performances. The popularity of nicknames, such as 'the Lancashire Lad' or 'the Rachde Felly' made the identification of favourites easy on billboards and advertisements. Once on stage a reader usually appeared in his everyday dress, although late in the century, when the influence of the music hall was much stronger, a reader might appear in evening dress or comic garb fitting to his recitation. (Plate 16 is a caricature of Ben Brierley in his recitation dress.) Waugh was well-known for his homely style. He always wore thick tweeds and carried a heavy gnarled walking stick, evoking an image of the traditional countryman. He usually began by reminiscing about his childhood adventures in Rochdale and the surrounding moors. He recited in a great booming voice, sometimes thumping his stick at important turning points. Sam Fitton (1868–1923), an Oldham cartoonist, won many local competitions for dialect reciting, and was a favourite at readings. His style was more 'professional' than Waugh's, borrowing from music-hall techniques. When reciting his own pieces, particularly 'My Owd Case Clock', he ran the entire gamut of emotions, carrying his audience with him. The clock watches over the family through the years, giving Fitton ample room to draw out the pathos and humour of family life in industrial Oldham.

No performer could expect a regular schedule of recitals in conjunction with local organizations. It was also necessary to perform independently, renting a hall and paying for all the costs out of the gross profits. This could be very speculative since attendance was often dependent upon good publicity and the weather. A beautiful evening at a seaside resort could mean no one wanted to come indoors, but if it rained, no one ventured out of his lodgings.[11] With good luck, however, the profits could be greater than when participating in a sponsored programme. Samuel Bamford upon his retirement from Somerset House chose dialect readings as the only means of earning a living at his age. In 1859 he recorded in his diary 'Three readings at Oldham. Gross £16.18.2 Net £14.8.9.'[16] This magnificent sum, however, never appears again. Two years later he commented, 'Reading with Ben Brierley. Gross £1.0.2 Expended 12/- in costs.' In spite of Brierley's assistance, Bamford was a poor reader and attendance dropped as his reputation for dullness grew. Indeed, it appears that readings were never a reliable form of income. Without the large sales of their publications Waugh, Brierley and Hartley could not have survived. Bamford, fortunately, was given a regular subsistence income by friends in 1862.

Authors were almost totally dependent for publication upon mass circulation newspapers, journals and almanacs. Patronage came only after fame, and then usually in the form of short assignments to 'translate' excerpts into or out of dialect. Writers usually started by sending their pieces to the local newspaper; the more talented might be asked to contribute regularly. Almost every newspaper in the North had a weekly section devoted to local news, including jokes, commentary and anecdotes by 'Uncle Owdem [Oldham] ', or 'Jack o' Ann's', for Jack, son of Ann, a familiar mode of address in the Lancashire moor district. A regular paid column looked like security for a writer with an established reputation, but any newspaper editor wishing to cut costs could fill his dialect page with readers' contributions. Fortunately most readers preferred to read verses and stories by familiar favourites rather than the efforts of amateurs. Another source of income was the occasional assignment to write on current events in standard English, such as Edwin Waugh's series in the Lancashire factory operatives during the Cotton Famine, 1861–5. Popular tales and poems were reprinted by the newspapers as penny broadsides and threepenny pamphlets; the wide sales of these reprints spread the fame of both the author and the newspaper. If a piece were exceptionally popular a writer might venture the publication of a volume of poetry or stories.

The sale of these books, pamphlets and broadsides was carried on in the traditional manner of hawking from door to door or pub to pub, although increasingly the main shops and bookstores were outlets for reading matter. Obviously no reader went to a recitation without a handful of his best publications. Edwin Waugh's first publication was a series of essays on the Lancashire countryside, that he printed in penny numbers to pay off his debts; he appears to have sold the works to the very friends he owed money to, since he lacked the confidence of Elijah Ridings to go about hawking his wares to strangers. An established writer often found he had remarkably good sales among homesick Englishmen in the United States and the colonies; to improve sales both Brierley and Hartley toured the United States and wrote about their adventures. If a writer could guarantee a certain number of sales or good distribution he could count on extra income by including advertisements for local products, halls and other dialect publications.

In the West Riding dialect almanacs became the most common publication of a local writer, although it was necessary both to seek out local advertising and to sell a good many in order to realize a profit since their price remained 3d. to 6d. throughout the century. In 1877 the English Dialect Society found that out of forty-odd dialect almanacs all but four came from the West Riding; two came from Lancashire and two from Northumberland, the other strongholds for vernacular writing.[13] The two earliest almanacs were Abel Bywater's *The Shevvild Chap's Almanac* (1837—53) and *The Bairnsla Foaks' Annual*, edited by Charles Rogers under the name 'Tom Treddlehoyle' from 1838 to 1875, when it was taken over by Isaac Binns until 1883, with the additional title *an Pogmoor Olmenack*. Bywater wrote prolifically in dialect; most of his works were dialogues, best described as chastened versions of 'Tummus and Meary', but also including a good deal of Sheffield cutlery lore. In 1839 he published a collected edition of his works for 3s.6d., with a glossary and explanation of his use of dialect. Rogers, a paper-hanger by profession, was a high Tory who filled his annual with glowing accounts of the local squirearchy. Sally Bobbinwinder's political dialogue is in part an attack on the widely-sold *Annual* and its anti-worker propaganda. The two purest dialect almanacs were Rogers' *The Bairnsla Foaks' Annual* and Thomas Blackah's *The Nidderdill Olminac an' Ivvery Body's Kalindar*, later called *T'Nidderhill Comic Casket, Comic Annual and Almanac* (1864—80), edited under the pseudonym 'Nattie Nydds', after the river Nidd.[14] Blackah, a lead miner from the Yorkshire dales, supplemented his meagre earnings by setting up a shop in his front room, where he sold his own works and the woollen socks he had knitted.[15] These three, along with John Hartley's *Halifax Original Illustrated Clock Almanack* (1865—1956) became the best known almanacs among the Yorkshire working class.

All almanacs were basically variations on Cruikshank's *Comic Almanac*, but they can be divided into two general categories: the more factual, often with political or religious content, and the purely entertaining. The former were smaller, carried less advertising and almost no fiction or poetry. For their sale publishers relied either on party loyalty or on their value as sources of information. These almanacs were packed with statistics on annual temperatures, crop yields, phases of the moon, famous events, well-known people, holidays and local officials. The Miners' Association in 1843 and 1844 published almanacs with explanations of mining ventilation systems, first-aid underground and other helpful information for union members. The second group of almanacs, which includes all dialect almanacs, was filled with short, easily understood stories, local lore and advice; almost everything was humorous, including the calendar itself, with such spellings as 'Janewerry', 'Munecipal Matturs', and 'Fowert Sundah after Epifany'. When a formula of humour, homely advice and a calendar was found to sell, it was repeated everywhere. The biggest space filler was humorous sketches about the past year's major events, such as 'Mally Mufindorf's Letter tut Queen abaght t' yung Prince', in *The Bairnsla Foaks' Annual* after the birth of the Crown Prince. (The Queen is delighted to receive homely Yorkshire advice.) Proverbs and sayings ran along the lines of 'A chap 'at's niver had a struggle doesn't know his strength.' Almanacs contained an increasing amount of advertising as the century wore on, to the point where the calendar was a few thin pages scattered among full page drawings and the alluring promises of patent medicines, 'Vital' books ('Manhood! How lost! how regained!') and 'the latest Malthusian devices', in addition to the more familiar products, such as Cadbury's cocoa and Pears' soap.

The 'best seller' of almanacs was the *Original Illuminated Clock Almanack*, begun in 1865 by Thomas Wilson, a Bradford hatter whose place of business was under an illuminated clock. He soon found himself too busy to edit it, and two years later let his son-in-law John Hartley take over. Hartley added, and later took away, the name of his home town, Halifax, and used both Bradford and Halifax dialects. He was editor for nearly forty years except for two brief periods when he was in America. His first edition sold over 5,000 copies in less than a month; by 1887 circulation was up to 80,000.[16] The same red and yellow cover was used from 1868 until 1947 (see Plate 19); the only changes were the year and the story in the centre picture frame. The drawing is a conventional cartoon of the writer and his reader, a canny Yorkshire woman with the symbols of the West Riding's main industries at her feet. This gay cover contrasts sharply with the sober front page of *Bradshaw's Journal* (see Plate 14). The purpose of a

dialect almanac was, of course, entirely different from that of a serious
magazine, bent upon intellectual improvement. Yet often the same men
wrote for both types of publications; they sought self-improvement
through the more literary periodicals, and an income through popular
almanacs or journals.

John Hartley wrote prolifically about the virtues of Yorkshire. Most
of his stories were about Sammywell Grimes, who visits London,
America, Paris, Royalty and a variety of Yorkshire places and persons.
First appearing in the *Clock Almanack*, Sammywell was successfully
launched in a series of shilling books, furthering Hartley's fame. Unlike
Waugh or Brierley, Hartley rarely wrote in standard English; even his
descriptions and background information were in dialect. Moreover, he
was closer than they were to spoken conversation and everyday realism
in his subject matter and presentation. In *Seets i' Lundun* (1874)
Grimes visits Cremorne Gardens and describes the 'actresses' and other
women who are waiting for customers. The chapter ends with a long
scene between two quarrelling drunken women, and Grimes's
evaluation of their behaviour and what his wife would have thought of
it. Waugh and Brierley, in contrast, emphasize marital fidelity, courtesy,
if not total sobriety, and general good behaviour.

Hartley also played much more upon existing comic stereotypes in
his stories. The drunken Irishman, canny Scots, wise provincial-in-
London, cunning Cockney, etc. dot his pages. While the language of
Yorkshire is spoken, its proverbs, aphorisms and images have been
played down. The writing is flat and conventional – but easily
understood – in all of his works. As Grimes patriotically declares upon
arrival in London:

> A Yorksherman i' Lundun is considered by a gooid monny to be
> as mich aght o' place as a bull in a china shop (aw've often wondered
> whose bull that wor), but aw find th' fowk 'at hold that nooation
> know varry little abaat Yorkshermen or else varry little abaat
> Lundun, for ther's nooa place wheer it's easier to settle daan an' feel
> at hooam, an' aw'm sure a Yorksherman can mak' hissen at hooam
> onnywheer if onnybody can.[17]

This kind of local chauvinism was immensely popular. The humour
depended upon well-known clichés; familiarity with the subject matter
and characters enhanced the reader's amusement, rather than detracting
from it. Comedy in almost all dialect literature – and particularly in the
Sammywell Grimes stories – was based on a general acceptance of

1. An eighteenth-century broadside seller and chaunter from Yorkshire.

2. 'Watkinson's Thirteens'

W———'s THIRTEENS.
Indicted By Five PENKNIFE CUTLERS.

Orbe reformato, terras astrea revisit.
Redeunt Saturnia Regna, cum novo progenies cælo demittitur alto.

THAT monster oppression behold how he stalks
Keeps picking the bones of the poor as he walks
There's not a mechanic throughout this whole land,
But what more or less feels the weight of his hand
That offspring of tyranny, baseness and pride,
Our rights hath invaded and almost destroy'd,
May that man be banish'd who villainy screens,
Or sides with big W—— with his thirteens.
CHORUS.
And may the odd knife his great carcase dissect,
Lay open his vitals for men to inspect,
A heart full as black as the infernal gulph,
In that greedy blood-sucking bone scraping wolf.

This wicked dissenter expell'd his own church,
Is render'd the subject of public reproach,
Since reprobate marks in his forehead appear'd,

We all have concluded his conscience is sear'd,
See mammon his God, and oppression his aim.
Hark! how the streets ring with his infamous name,
The boys at the playhouse exhibit strange scenes,
Respecting big W——— with his thirteens.
And may &c.

Like Pharaoh for baseness that type of the d—l,
He wants to flog journeymen with rods of steel,
And certainly would, had he got Pharaoh's pow'r,
His heart is as hard and his temper as sour;
But justice repuls'd him and set us all free,
Like bond slaves of old, in the Year jubilee.
May those be transported or sent for marines,
That works for big W——— at his thirteens.
And may &c.

We claim as true Yorkshire-men leave to speak twice,
That no man should work for him at any price,
Since he has attempted our lives to enthral,
And mingle our liquor with wormwood and gall.
Come Beelzebub take him with his ill got pelf,
He's equally bad, if not worse than thyself:
So shall every Cutler that honestly means,
"Cry take away W——— with his thirteens."
And may &c.

But see foolish mortals! far worse than insane,
Three fourths are return'd into Egypt again,
Altho' Pharaoh's hands they had fairly escap'd,
Now they must submit for their bones tobe scrap'd.
Whilst they give themselves and their all for a prey,
Let us be unanimous and jointly say,
Success to our Sovereign who peaceably reigns,
But down with both W———'s twelves & thirteens.

And may the odd knife his great carcase dissect,
Lay open his vitals for men to inspect,
A heart full as black as the infernal gulph,
In that greedy blood sucking bone scraping wolf.

3. Blind Willie Purvis

FAIR PHŒBE,
AND HER
Dark-Eyed
SAILOR.

Printed, and Sold Wholesale and Retail, by G.
Jacques, Oldham Road Library, Manchester.

IT'S of a comely young lady fair
Was walking ut to take the air,
She met with a sailor upon her way,
So I paid attention to hear what they did say.

Said William, lady why, roam alone,
The night is coming, and the day near gone,
She said, while tears from her eyes did fall,
It's a dark-eyed sailor that's proving my downfall.

It's two long years since he left the land,
I took a gold ring from off my hand,
We broke the token—here's part with me
And the other rolling at the bottom of the sea.

Said William drive him from your min
Some other sailor as good you'll find,
Love turns aside, and soon cold does grow,
Like a winter's morning when lands are clothed
with snow.

These words did Phœbe's fond heart inflame,
She said on me you shall play no game,
She drew a dagger and then did cry,
For my dark-eyed sailor, a maid I'll live and die.

His coal-black eye, and his curly hair,
And pleasing tongue did my heart ensnare,
Gentel he was but no rake like you,
To advise a maiden to slight the jacket blue.

But still said Phœbe I'll ne'er disdain
A tarry sailor, but treat the same,
Drink his health—here's a piece of coin,
But my dark-eyed sailor still claims this heart
of mine.

Then half the ring did young William show,
She seemed distracted 'midst joy and woe,
Oh, welcome William, I've lands and gold,
For my dark-eyed sailor, so manly true & bold.

Now in a village down by the sea-side,
They're joined in wedlock, and well agree,
So maids be true when your ove's away,
For a cloudy morning oft brings a pleasant day.

Fortunate
FACTORY GIRL.

Printed, and Sold Wholesale and Retail, by G. Jac-
Oldham Road Library, Manchester.

THE sun had just risen one fine summer's morning,
When the birds from the bushes so sweetly did sing
When the lads and the lasses so merrily moving,
Unto those large buildings their labour begins:
I espied a fair damsel, far brighter than Venus,
Her cheeks red as roses none could her excel,
With a skin like a lily that grows in the garden,
Had this lovely young goddess, a factory girl.

I stepped up to her, this beautiful creature,
She cast upon me a proud look of disdain:
Stand back, sir, she cried, and do not insult me,
Though poor and in poverty, that is no sin,
I said, my sweet damsel, no harm is intended,
But grant me one favour, pray where do you dwell,
At home, sir, she answer'd, and wasgoing to leave me
I am only a hard working factory girl.

I stood all amazed, and at her I gazed,
Such modesty and prudence, I never did see,
You are my sweet charmer, my soul's great a rmer,
If you will consent, you a lady shall be,
But she said, sir, temptations are used in all stations
Go marry a lady and you will do well:
So let me alone, sir, the bell is a ringing,
I am only a hard working factory girl.

I stood in a flutter, knew not what was the matter
Little Cupid the whole of my heart it trepann'd,
My life I will waste in some foreign land,
Lovely girl replied, if you'll not be my bride,
For what pleasure's in treasure when love is a wanting,
Your beauty upon me it has cast a spell;
I'll marry you speedy, and make you a lady,
If you will become mine, dear factory girl

She gave her consent, when a license was purchased
The bells they did merrily echo and ring:
To church then they went, and as they retrn'd
They bride's man and maidens so sweetly did sing
Now this loving young couple live happy together,
She blesses the day that she met with her swain
So this factory girl she is made a great lady,
And married to a squire of honour and fame.

[No.61.]

4. 'Fair Phoebe, and her Dark-eyed Sailor' and 'Fortunate Factory Girl'

5. Street Melody: London, 1903.

THE MINERS' ADVOCATE

UNION IS STRENGTH — KNOWLEDGE IS POWER

LET US LIVE BY OUR LABOUR.

No. 1.   SATURDAY, DECEMBER 2, 1843.   PRICE 1½d

TO OUR READERS.

"We will a new order, we abjure oppression of every kind."

6. *The Miners' Advocate*

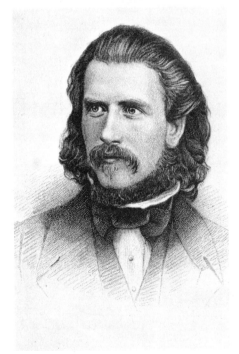

7. *(top far left)* W.J. Linton

8. *(top left)* Ernest Jones

9. *(far left)* Gerald Massey

10. *(left)* Thomas Cooper

11. *(above)* John Critchley Prince

12. *(top right)* John Nicholson

13. *(right)* Joseph Skipsey

14. *Bradshaw's Journal*

Vol. III. Number 2.]   SATURDAY, 14th MAY, 1842.   [Price 1½d.

RAMBLES OF A RHYMESTER;
OR, WANDERINGS THROUGH ENGLAND.
IN OCCASIONAL LETTERS TO THE EDITOR.
BY JOHN CRITCHLEY PRINCE.

LETTER FIRST.
Newcastle, Staffordshire, 20th April, 1842.

DEAR SIR,—On the 18th of this month I set out from Manchester partly on business, and partly for pleasure, to perform a pedestrian journey to the great Metropolis and back again. I had built up some wild but indistinct schemes of stepping out of the main track, so far as my limited means would permit, to look upon the beautiful and picturesque; to gaze upon all which, from its loveliness or its associations, might be deemed worthy of the notice of the poet or the painter. I thought of meditating amid the walls of time-shattered castles, and beneath the roof-trees of old baronial halls,—of reflecting and moralizing on the evils of populous cities—of scaling the summits of lonely mountains—loitering in cultivated vales —and threading the leafy labyrinths of dark majestic woods. I contemplated lingering in all kinds of imaginable places—of penetrating rocky and savage passes—of traversing wild and irreclaimable moors—of dreaming on the banks of song-celebrated streams—of resting during the night in snug wayside hostleries, and rising in the morning, with renewed mental and bodily vigour, to look for fresh charms, and undiscovered sources of pure intellectual pleasure.

How far my wishes may be realized, or my intentions carried out, is yet uncertain; but I will transmit to you, from time to time, the thoughts and feelings resulting from my peri-grinations, wherever circumstances, or the impulse of my own fancy, may lead me.

The weather on the morning on which I com-menced my rambles was exceedingly propitious, and up to the present time, not a cloud has arisen to darken the blue serenity of the skies. In the company of my wife and a much valued friend, I went by railway from Manchester to Stockport. From thence, leaving the smoke of that much suffering town behind us, we walked on to the clean and comparatively re-tired village of Cheadle, where, after half an hour's rest, I parted, not without a feeling of regret, with my beloved wife and my respected friend. Jogging on at a brisk pace, and hum-ming the fragment of an old song to drown my sense of loneliness, I passed through the village of Wilmslow, and got fairly into the country.

What relief it was to me, after vegetating for twelve months amid the gloom, the filth, the squalid poverty, and the dissipation of Manchester, to find myself surrounded by green fields, luxuriant hedgerows, and trees just opening to the breath of Spring! What quiet rapture to hear the lark carolling in a *pure* sky —to listen to the prattle of *pure* waters—to exchange the stench of manufactories and dirty alleys, for the delicious odour of dairies and the breath of uncontaminated flowers!—what natural joy to pass by the end of old elbow-

15. *(below left)* Edwin Waugh

16. *(below)* Ben Brierley

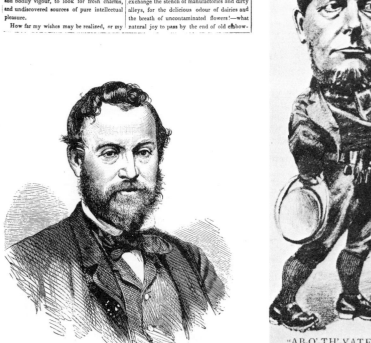

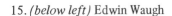

"AB-O'-TH'-YATE."

17. John Hartley

18. Stackstead Industrial Co-operative Store: Twenty-fifth annual festival

STACKSTEADS

INDUSTRIAL CO-OPERATIVE STORE

LIMITED.

THE TWENTY-FIFTH

ANNUAL FESTIVAL,

Saturday, November 20th, 1875.

THE CHAIR WILL BE TAKEN AT HALF-PAST SIX O'CLOCK BY

MR. S. TURNER,

PRESIDENT OF THE STORE.

PROGRAMME

GLEE	"Victoria"—*H. Smart*	
	CHAIRMAN'S ADDRESS.	
SONG	"Sing, Birdie, Sing"—*Gans*	MISS WRIGLEY.
SONG	"Shake of the Hand"—*Blockley*	MR. C. L. HOLDEN.
SONG	"I Don't Believe They Do"	MR. BOUVERIE.
	REPORT.	
SONG	"Doctor Quack"	MR. T. BUCKLEY.
READING	"Besom Ben"	MR. E. WAUGH.
GLEE	"Sisters of the Sea"—*Jackson*	
	ADDRESS BY MR. J. C. FARN.	
SONG	"The Batch of Receipts"	{ MR. BOUVERIE. MISS WRIGLEY.
DUET	"Syren and Friar"—*L. Emanuel*	{ MR. T. KERSHAW. MR. E. WAUGH
READING	"The Old Woman's Ring"	MR. E. WAUGH.
SONG	"Home Bound Sails"—*W. H. Cummings*	MR. T. KERSHAW.
	ADDRESS.	
SONG	"Robin's Return"—*T. Gabriel*	MISS WRIGLEY.
QUARTET	"The Letter"—*J. L. Hatton*	{ MESSRS. HOLDEN, BUCKLEY, HOWORTH, AND KERSHAW.
SONG	"Passing Events"	MR. BOUVERIE.
READING	"The Barrel Organ"	MR. E. WAUGH.
	ADDRESS.	
GLEE	"Come where the Cowslips"—*Buckley*	
READING	"A Striking Story"	MR. E. WAUGH.
SONG	"I want to go Home to Mamma"	MR. C. L. HOLDEN.
SONG	"The Twins"	MR. BOUVERIE.

FINALE - - - GOD SAVE THE QUEEN.

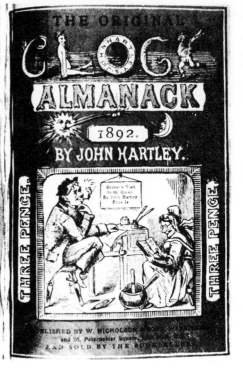

19. *(above) The Original Clock Almanack*

20. *(left)* J.T. Staton

21. *(top right)* Thomas Wilson

22. *(top far right)* Tommy Armstrong

23. *(bottom right)* The Oxford Music Hall, ca. 1860

24. *(above)* The gallery, London
    Music Hall, 1903

25. *(left)* Bessie Bellwood

COSTERMONGER
JOE.

I'm Costermonger Joe, and as my round I go.
  For many miles the girls will smile at Coster-
    monger Joe.
With mind devoid of care and spirits light as air,
  I whistle and sing and cabbages bring from
    Covent Garden, oh !
I started young in trade, and a nice connection
  made,
  Around the streets and terraces and squares,
And all I have to do, is to call a thing or two,
  While Ned, my little pony, draws my wares—
  While Ned, my little pony, draws my wares.

I'm Costermonger Joe, and as my rounds I go,
For many miles the girls will smile at Costermonger Joe.

I'm Costermonger Joe, and many people know.
  The lusty bawl and morning call of Coster-
    monger Joe,
For be it wet or dry, I never can forget,
  That many's the maid a waiting to trade,
    with Costermonger Joe.
For dinners must be had, be whether trade good
  or bad,
  And when it rains fresh customers I see.
For then without a doubt the ladies can't get out,
  So they make their little purchases of me.

I'm Costermonger Joe, no money do I owe,
  For not a crust is had on trust by Costermonger
    Joe;
But yet to barely live, why I must credit give,
  Or none would deal or grease the wheel with
    Costermonger Joe.
I'm Costermonger Joe, and tho' I'm rather slow,
  I find the fast don't longer last than Coster-
    monger Joe,
The steady going pace just suits the human race,
  It's better to stop than gallop and drop, says
    Costermonger Joe.

Your tradesmen in their shops, who live on
  mutton chops,
  Are often more unhappy I'll be bound,
Than I with bread and cheese, and a drive out
  at my ease,
  And the wholesale 20 shillings in the pound,
    in the pound, and the wholesale 20s. in
    the pound.
It's not the likes of me, that you in the paper
  see,
  Petitioning in the court for a divorce,
But those who can almost, College education
  boast,
  So morality with learning loses force.

I'm Costermonger Joe, and pleasantly I row
  This stream of life but wants a wife, does
    Costermonger Joe,
His humble lot to share, and be she dark or fair,
  She'll always be sure, of affection pure, from
    Costermonger Joe.
In summer after tea, how happy I should be,
  To drive my little Wifey round about
The green lanes in the cart, and with feelings
  proud at heart,
  That I could own what I was driving out

I'm Costermonger Joe, and now would have you
  know,
  All are not fools from ragged schools, says
    Costermonger Joe;
For that's where I began to learn that ev'ry
  man
  His mind must give to work, and live like
    Costermonger Joe.
I've told you all my mind, in hopes that I should
  find,
  Some folks to own the roughest may be true.
And that humble corduroy covers hearts that
  beat with joy.
  And respectfully I bid you now adieu.

26. 'Costermonger Joe'

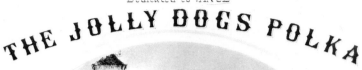

27. 'The Jolly Dogs Polka'

28. Marie Lloyd

29. Joe Wilson singing
'Geordy, Haud the Bairn'

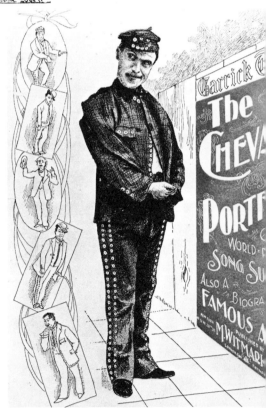

30. Albert Chevalier, 'the
Costermonger's Laureate'

31. 'If it wasn't for the 'Ouses in Between'

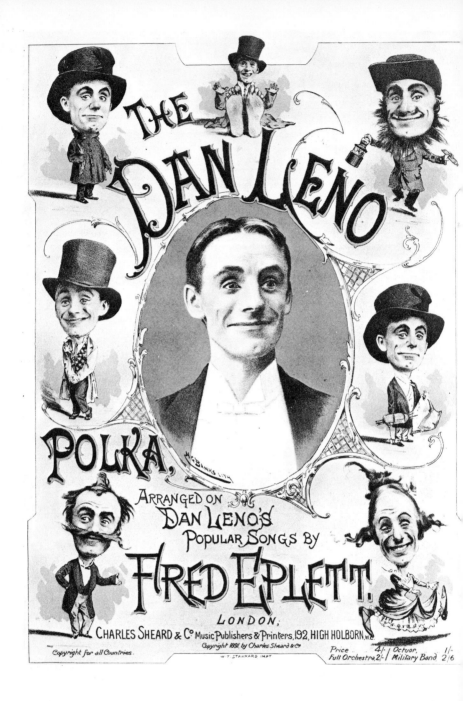

32. 'The Dan Leno Polka'

shared attitudes and values.

After undergoing the usual adventures in London, Grimes returns to Bradford fully expecting to be greeted with a brass band and crowd. Instead, he finds his neighbours scarcely aware of his absence, and his wife anxious to send him back to work. In a fit of pique, he withdraws £20 from his savings and leaves for America without telling his wife. He roams about working at odd jobs and writing letters periodically about how to avoid cadgers and crooks to his London friend, a middle-class gentleman formerly from Yorkshire. After a year or so, he returns gratefully to his family hearth. Hartley was caught between his desire to make Grimes typical of any Bradford worker, and yet freer and more comically articulate. Grimes's quarrel with Mally and his master, trivial in themselves, are alluded to frequently in the book. Hartley seems worried lest his readers condone such behaviour, yet it was a convenient device for freeing Grimes from his working life. The artistic dilemma is sharpened by Hartley's crude technique; most of his tales are a series of dialect letters about individual adventures or anecdotes through which Grimes must somehow be propelled while recording them.

The event which sets Grimes off to America reveals a curious attitude about work and 't' maister'.

... T' maister tell'd me t'other day 'at he thowt it 'ud seem me better to pay moor attention to my wark an' leeave letter writin' to mi' betters, sich as him, an' t'ovverleuker an' me couldn't hit it, an' when aw grum'led this mornin' becoss aw'd getten a rotten warp 'at noa chap livin' could ivver weyve, he tell'd me 'at if aw' didn't like it aw could lump it. Soa aw tell'd him to ax me aght, an' aw'd goa, an' nivver put mi nooas i't' shop agean. Soa he did, an' for t'first time i' mi life aw walk'd throo t'streets wi' mi hands i' mi pockets, aght o' wark.

Aw could ha getten ovver that, becoss tha knaws aw'wm nooan withaat a paand or two, but when aw gate hooam an tell'd awr Mally, expectin' 'at shoo'd clap me o' t' shoolder an' say 'Come thi ways! Tha did reight lad! We'll let 'em see tha'rt nooan to be put on,' shoo lewkt at me as faal as a mewl an' sed, 'It's just what aw expected, for ther's nivver been noa livin' wi' thi sin tha coom throo Lundun, an' my belief is, if tha had ony sense when tha went tha lost it afore tha coom back.'[18]

We are explicitly told that Sammywell had never been out of work before, so we know he is a reliable and steady worker. But the key

ambiguity rests in whether it is appropriate for a working man to
write – the master arrogantly tells him to 'leeave letter writin' to mi
betters, sich as him,' and his wife supports this view. Whatever secret
hopes any of his readers might have had are fostered through an
identification with Grimes against his society, as exemplified by his
wife, peers and master. It is unnatural for Grimes to be interested in
writing, and so it has upset his usual good sense (further evidence of
this was his comic expectations of a triumphal welcome home). Hartley
appears to imply that Grimes cannot be a typical working man, simply
because he writes, and enjoys doing so. 'Putting on airs' is inappropriate
for a working man, so he should not aspire to write or to be
independent, but should go to work daily. Hartley does not overturn
this ethic through satire, but by means of indirect irony and humour,
he both admits it is an important working-class belief and provides an
antidote against it. Going off to America must have been the dream of
many readers caught in a monotonous routine. *Grimes's Trip to
America* (1877) provided the necessary outlet without undercutting
existing mores. Literature by and for the working man, thus, acted to
limit his aspirations to what was appropriate and possible, while
providing a socially safe release to his feelings of constriction.

Ben Brierley wrote about his tours of America in 1880 and 1884,
but he more cautiously had Ab-o'-th'-Yate accompany him, rather than
be the main hero. Long sections of *Ab-o'-th'-Yate in Yankeeland* are
first-person narratives in standard English by Brierley. The dialect
sections, written as Ab's letters home to his wife, deal more strictly
with Lancashire interests or comic situations. For example, Ab visits
Lowell, Massachusetts, a mill town to rival any in Lancashire. He
declares roundly that he prefers 'Lanky lasses', and that the famous
factory girls should learn housewifery and not play pianos and write
novels. While echoing common opinion, Ab also is in agreement with
Mally Grimes about the appropriate behaviour of working-class
persons – creativity is not something in which they ordinarily should
indulge.

A trip away from home – impossible for an earlier generation – was
now a possibility for many working-class readers. Most almanacs and
periodicals carried at least one such story, usually about railway travel.
What characterized them all, however, was an acceptance of this
freedom to travel within carefully proscribed limits. Ab and Sammywell
saw the places they visited through 'Lanky' or 'Yorksher' eyes, and
returned unchanged to their cottages and families. Dialect travel
stories, whether to Blackpool or America, are holidays in which the

resilience and resistance of the hero are tested. He survives cadgers and sharpers because of his native shrewdness, but he also resists any change of familiar patterns of behaviour. This combination was humorous and self-protective. Everything observed is put into the context of life back home, reducing new experience to a selective rejection of the unknown and acceptance of the known. Readers could laugh at Sammywell or Ab and feel superior in their sophistication, while recognizing their own faux pas or fears when away from home.

In Lancashire the threepenny pamphlet and penny journals served in place of almanacs. The weekly journals shared many characteristics with the West Riding's almanacs. They depended heavily on advertising for profits, were written and edited almost entirely by one man, and most of the material was discouragingly repetitive. One of the earliest, and best, dialect journals was J. T. Staton's *The Bowton Loominary, Tumfowt Telegraph un Lankishire Lookin' Glass*, sold for one penny weekly, 1852–62.[19] Staton, trained as a skilled printer, had been an orphan scholar at Chetham's College, Manchester, and was better educated than most working men (see Plate 20). He always championed working-class causes, and made the *Loominary* more overtly educational than other dialect periodicals. While the poetry he published came from the well-known Lancashire poets of the time, Staton wrote all the prose sketches. Their titles are self-explanatory: 'Mary Mason, the Factory Lass, or Love un Drink', 'Knowledge un Wisdom', and best of all, 'Beware uv Wolves in Sheep's Clothin': Look to yoar Berryin' Clubs'. He was most concerned with Bolton ('Bowton') and its problems, and every issue had comments on current events there. One sketch, 'Bobby Shuttle's Visit to th' Mechanics' Institutshun Eggsibishun', included humorous incidents plus a detailed description of the educational purposes and membership qualifications of the Bolton Mechanics' Institute. Staton particularly pointed out that only one-fourth of is members were mechanics, and not a single one was a cotton spinner. Since he made no attempt to regularize his spelling or that of his contributors, who were required to write their letters-to-the-editor in dialect, reading the *Loominary* is sometimes difficult. It was probably most popular as a paper to be read aloud in Bolton's working-class pubs, where it reached the poorly educated who did not know all of their rights or oportunities.

Dialect journals could be quite successful, despite their limited potential readership. *Ben Brierley's Journal* ran for sixteen years (1869–85) as an 8- to 16- page penny weekly, with a maximum circulation of 13,000.[20] Before starting the *Journal* Brierley had assisted Charles Hardwick in editing *Country Words*, a weekly similar to *Bradshaw's Journal*. It died after only seventeen weeks, despite publishing some of the North's best-known writers. This failure convinced Brierley of the necessity of appealing to a more specific audience, yet offering less serious subject matter; the obvious answer was his forte, dialect. His *Journal* was rather like a Lancashire working man's *Punch*, composed of jokes, anecdotes, light reading matter, and a high percentage of local advertising. He also carried many items found in almanacs, such as a monthly calendar, household hints and factual information.

The success of the paper, however, was founded on the creation of his comic working man, 'Ab-o'-th'-Yate'. For years Brierley pretended that Ab was a different person from himself, enjoying the comparisons made between them. A typical tale is 'Ab-o'-th'-Yate Insures his Life, Communicated by an Eavesdropper'. At the suggestion of his canny wife, Ab goes to buy insurance. A friend warns him that he will have to fight with the doctor to prove he is in good health. Of course he does so, and provokes the dismay and anger of the doctor he knocks down. All is easily explained, and he leaves satisfied with his insurance. The potentialities of the situation are not explored – for example, the possibility that the insurance company might cheat Ab is never considered, though this was a problem for many working men confronted with the technicalities of buying insurance. Even the fight with the doctor is minimized for greater humour; the doctor could have thrown Ab out of the place or knocked him unconscious or 'unhealthy'. The story, like all five volumes of Ab-o'-th'-Yate's collected works, bears the signs of hasty work and half-realized ideas.

Brierley never mastered sophistications of plot and style; he depended heavily on conversations, with a little standard English holding the narrative together. The opening lines of 'Ab-o'-th'-Yate Insures his Life' illustrate Brierley's style:

'Ab,' said the 'better-three-quarters' of our friend the philosopher of Walmsley Fowt, as she sat looking at him in the dim light of a winter gloaming, 'theau'rt gettin' very meaudly abeaut th' toppin. Thy summertime's o'er, I think. It'll be Candlemas-day, if no' deep winter, wi' thee soon.'

Ab raised his head, which he appeared to have been roasting at the bars, whilst poring over, and committing to memory, a favourite song of Burns, and folding down a well-thumbed leaf of the book he was nursing, replied: —

'Theau'rt reet, owd crayther! Peggy Thuston wur sayin' nobbut
yesterday ut my yead wur gettin' very mich like a thurn-hedge ov a
frosty mornin'. I reckon th' sap winno' rise five-feet-six-an'-
three-quarters neaw; so wheere it conno' raich mun wither, as if I're
a tree i' th' cloof.'

'An' if theau withers deawn to thy toes, heaw then?' demanded
the wife, casting her eyes towards her husband's clogs, as if the
process of recidivation had already set in in that quarter.[21]

The humour and charm rest entirely in the dialect conversation, which
moves slowly and repetitiously over a simple point. The repetitiousness
aided slow readers, and it also reproduced more accurately everyday
conversation, which tends to move in and around a topic, with ample
asides. A fast-paced and witty dialogue might have been better
artistically, but it would not recreate so well the atmosphere of a
working-class home or the charm of a comic conversation. Brierley
seems more distinctly old-fashioned than Hartley with his talk
of 'Candlemas-day' and 'a tree i' th' cloof', but so too is the language
more vigorous and authentic. Brierley, by making Ab so distinctly
old-fashioned, gave his stories stronger roots in the traditional
vernacular of Lancashire; even though he might tell us less about
factory life in the 1870s, his works ring truer artistically than
Hartley's. Grimes is very much the comic Yorkshireman, living in his
own times, but he cannot therefore draw so naturally upon old customs
and sayings.

Penny readings, almanacs and journals were all written for a
working-class audience, and were priced and marketed accordingly.
However, the better dialect writers were also very successful in gaining
literary recognition and social acceptance from a wider public. In the
earlier part of the century, patrons and critics had generally
condescended to working men who wrote as curiosities worth
encouraging as long as they kept their place. With the rise of interest in
local history and customs, dialect writers were hailed as valuable
repositories of regional traditions. Even those with an upper-class
accent were anxious to claim their local culture; expensive northern
anthologies from the 1870s always included dialect works and some
commentary on provincial customs. Antiquarians now numbered in the
scores; all eagerly consulted working-class writers on the most authentic
vernacular words and expressions. Edwin Waugh was appointed to the
board of the English Dialect Society soon after its founding, an honour

he shared with such famous philologists as W.W. Skeat, Henry Sweet and
W. E. A. Axon. Prince Louis Bonaparte went through the northern
counties commissioning 'translations' of the 'Song of Songs' into all
varieties of dialect.[22]

Dialect writers were seen both as repositories of a dying rural
culture, and as representatives of the new working class. Public-spirited
businessmen turned to them for advice on the state of the factory
workers, or more commonly, for confirmation of the self-help ethic.
The recognition of dialect writers as artists in their own right also helped
to strengthen those literary ties first developed at the Sun Inn among
men of different classes. New clubs were formed in opposition to the
rigid and conservative 'Lit. and Phil.' societies. Often meeting in a local
pub, men from a variety of backgrounds came together informally to
discuss their own literature and the development of a local literary life.
Individual writers benefited personally from this interest through
contact with antiquarians, businessmen and professionals interested in
encouraging the arts. In the major cities no dialect writer needed to
complain of the lack of intellectual stimulus and encouragement.

Many of these loosely-knit groups became clubs with dues, regular
gatherings and annual publications. The hopes of the 1841—2
'Lancashire Literary Association' were realized in 1862 with the
founding of the Manchester Literary Club by Edwin Waugh, Ben
Brierley, R. R. Bealey, Charles Hardwick, Joseph Chatwood and John
Page. All six were professional writers themselves; the first four were
working men, the latter two, businessmen. Membership quickly
expanded to include such Sun Inn devotees as Charles Swain and
Samuel Bamford, in addition to a number of manufacturers, teachers
and journalists. At first the group met informally at the Clarence Hotel
for a convivial meeting, but from 1865 minutes were kept and
regulations governing fines, dues and attendance were made formal. In
1867 a magazine was started to publish the papers read and their
business proceedings.[23]

For the next thirty years membership varied between fifty and
seventy-five persons, with dues set at 10s. a year. The Club soon
included more businessmen interested in the arts than actual writers,
but it kept to its original purpose of assisting literary men. The
Club's objectives were reaffirmed in 1875:

1) To encourage the pursuit of Literature and Art; to promote
research in the several departments of intellectual work; to protect
the interests of the authors of Lancashire.

2) To publish from time to time works illustrating or elucidating the literature and history of the county.

3) To provide a place for meeting where persons interested in the furtherance of these objects can associate together.[24]

The Club was highly successful in all three ways. Talks were given on a wide range of subjects, including science, local history and contemporary writers; favourite events were the Christmas parties and conversazione, where women were permitted to attend. Several members were active in the English Dialect Society; through it they published a dictionary and a bibliography of Lancashire dialect. In 1876 after Waugh's health began to fail a committee was formed to hold his copyrights and guarantee him a monthly income. In 1886 Club members were successful in placing his name on the Civil List to receive a pension of £90 per year, enabling him to retire to a seaside spa.[25]

The Manchester Literary Club was sustained by close friendships among writers and businessmen; they frequently wrote teasing verses and sketches about one another. A favourite was Ben Brierley'spoem to Waugh, asking him how he had been of late:

> What ails thee, Ned? Thou'rt not as twur *
> Or else no' what I took thee for,
>   I' this quare pleck.†
> Hast' flown at Fame wi' such a ber, +
>   As t' break thy neck?
>
> Or arta droppin' fithers, eh?
> An' keepin' th' neest warm till some day,
> Toart○ April-tide, or sunny May,
>   When thou may'st spring,
> An' warble out a new-made lay,
>   On strengthened wing?
>
> For brids o' sung mun ha' ther mou't ,⊕
> As well as other brids I doubt:
> But though they peearch beneath a spout,
>   Or roost 'mong heather,
> They're saved fro' mony a shiverin' bout,
>   Bu hutchin' □ t'gether.

*twur: as you were   †pleck: place   +ber: force   ○ Toart: toward   ⊕mou't:
mouth, voice   □ hutchin': fidgeting

> Bring in thy train those brids o' note,
> Blithe 'Charlie,' * with his wattled throat,
> An' 'Dick,' †who never sang nor wrote
>   To hurt his fellow;
> With him, + who aye wi' 'seed-box' sote
>   To mak' brids mellow.[26]

And so on through the other literary members of the Club, ending with the moral 'Thus may we flutter through life's grove,/Nor crack't wi' glee, now steeped i' love'. All the 'brids' in Brierley's aviary have their places, but no soloists are permitted. While only a humorous rebuke, the poem points to some of the social forces holding back a working-class writer. Communal feeling and good will were hard-earned assets in nineteenth-century Manchester, and not to be lightly scorned, or escaped. Even when rivalry and dislike were strong, as in the case of Brierley and Waugh,[27] professional dialect readers projected an image of affability and friendship. Congeniality mattered more than originality.

Fellow poets and friends demanded loyalty and not too much ambition from each other, but in return they often gave financial and social assistance. In addition to the aid given Waugh, a fund was established for Brierley in 1885 at the end of his long writing career. The son of a hand-loom weaver, Brierley began life as a weaver and then a warehouseman, but from 1855 he had worked full time as a journalist. He served as a town councillor for a working-class ward in Manchester (1875–81), and was widely admired among all classes for his humour and good will. When he lost his savings in a bank failure a special testimonial fund brought in £650. At the dinner in his honour the following eulogy was read:

> ... Born in the midst of poverty, such as even the 'unemployed' nowadays cannot realise, with little or no incentive in the right direction, but with every temptation to become a vagabond, he steadily set his face to the improvement of himself and his class. ... Making the most of his exceptional abilities by steady application and sheer hard work he lifted himself into a position which honoured him and the class from which he sprung. ... The

*'Charlie': Charles Hardwick, author of *The History of Preston* (1857) and other local works. †'Dick': R.R. Bealey, author of *After Business Jottings* (1865) and other verse. +him: Joseph Chatwood, president of the Manchester Literary Club.

poor for whom he has written and striven have received from his life and his writings many a lesson of honesty and frugality and unaffected simplicity which only come with force from Mr. Brierley and such as he . . . [28]

This speech reflects commonly held attitudes about a working man who has risen: he is congratulated because he has educated himself and risen above his environment, which is described as providing 'every temptation'. Yet, it is this very heritage that was the source of Brierley's literary inspiration; without his early days spent as a silk hand-loom weaver he could never have written his many stories and poems of old village life and customs. 'Honesty and frugality and unaffected simplicity' make working-class dialect poets acceptable in the company of Manchester merchants. Nothing could less endanger the status quo. Brierley approved of this view of himself, and replied that he had indeed attempted to be a good member of society and not a bohemian. All present were perfectly united in their self-congratulation of those who had risen, as Brierley used to say, by first making their own ladders in order to climb.

Misunderstandings over the uses of dialect, nevertheless, abounded when patrons sought to give dialect writers advice. Friends seeking a civil pension for John Hartley had difficulty convincing London civil servants of his importance, so one wrote to Hartley:

I respectfully submit that you have made one great mistake as a litterateur: that your literary efforts have been solely confined to the writing of works in the Yorkshire dialect, or to be more accurate, in the West Riding's dialect . . . this fact limits your audience to not more than three million people at the very most who can understand today the West Riding's dialect and that is assuming even at the outset that they can read such dialect when it is written and printed. . . . Yes, you have shut out those who would otherwise have been only too glad to be your audience and therefore your financial supporters, if your literary efforts or the major part of them had been indited in pure English, I submit.[29]

The emphasis is on the widest possible circulation, yet ironically Hartley's dialect almanac sold 50,000 to 80,000 copies annually – far more than most works in standard English. Captain Haigh-Smith went on to recommend translating Hartley's best-known works into standard English to raise money through sales in London. Blind to the purposes of dialect, he calmly offered this condescending advice to a man who had spent nearly fifty years earning his living by writing. Hartley's imagination worked best within the West Riding dialect, so any 'translation' destroyed whatever was unique in his writings, and therefore worthy of a civil pension.

Hartley's difficulties were more common than Brierley's lionization. Their careers were almost identical, though Hartley probably reached a wider audience. But class boundaries were not ignored as easily as the successful might think. The self-congratulatory world of the Manchester Literary Club did not determine the course of dialect: working-class buyers did, and the subject matter they wanted and bought was what ultimately mattered. Part III is a discussion of the most popular themes, and their relation to the growing acceptance of the self-help ethic among workers.

III
The Subject Matter of Dialect Writing

Self-help is the best phrase to describe the vast majority of dialect works – self-help may have meant a strong sense of local class pride against 't'maisters', or family pride in hard times, or ambition that would lead a young man out of the slums. Whatever form this optimistic message took, the subject matter revolved around the daily life of working-class readers. The best dialect works offered a detailed examination of hard-won domestic serenity, love and confidence. The humorous and sardonic treatment of courting, marriage or working conditions remained popular. Writers chose their vernacular speech in order to recreate the world they knew best, avoiding some of the pitfalls of those who imitated Thomson or Wordsworth. Others found in dialect a refuge from the cares and problems of the present, escaping into a country idyll. And, of course, many wrote because dialect was popular and could be sold easily.

Edwin Waugh wrote in Lancashire dialect to restore the vitality of a rural past to an industrialized people. Until the age of forty Waugh had worked as a journeyman printer, secretary and salesman, primarily in industrial Manchester, which he hated. When he was at last freed to write full time he drew his inspiration almost entirely from his childhood experiences in Rochdale and from the many days he had spent roaming the moors, escaping the drudgery of his daily work. In the preface to his first published volume, *Lancashire Sketches* (1855), Waugh argued that the potentialities of dialect had only begun to be explored: ' ... all that has hitherto been done in this way is small in amount compared with that which is left undone. The past, and still more the disappearing present, of this important district teem with significant features, which, if caught up and truthfully represented, might, perhaps, be useful to the next generation.'[30]

The lessons Waugh taught,and the strengths and limitations of his dialect, can be seen in an example from *Lancashire Sketches*. Although describing recently taken rambles, he frequently set them back in time. A 'Ramble from Bury to Rochdale' is a first-person narrative in standard English. Waugh stops to eat at a quiet inn, where he records the following conversation about the Corn Laws between a carter and the couple who own the inn:

Jone. .... Iv they winnot gi' me my share for worchin' for, aw'll have it eawt o' some nook, – iv aw dunnot, damn Jone! (*striking the table heavily with his fist*). They'n never be clemmed* at our heawse, as aw ha' si 'n folk clemmed i' my time, – never whol† aw've a fist at th' end o' my arm! Neaw, what have aw towd yo!

Sam. Thea'rt reet, lad! Aw houd thi wit good, by th' mass!+ Whol they gi'n us some bit like ov a chance, we can do. At th' most o' times we'n to kill 'ursels (ourselves) to keep 'ursels, welly; but when it comes to scarce wark an' dear mheyt,○ th' upstroke's noan so fur off.

Mary. Ay, ay. If it're nobbut a body's sel', we could manage to pinch a bit, neaw an' then; becose one could rayson abeawt it some bit like. But it's th' childer, mon, – it's th' childer! Th' little things at look'n for it reggilar; an' wonder'n heaw it is when it doesn't come. Eh, dear o' me! To see poor folks bits o' childer yammerin'⊕ for a bite o' mheyt, – when there's noan for 'em, – an' lookin' up i' folk's faces, as mich as to say, 'Connot yo help me?' It's enough to may (make) onybody cry their shoon full! (p.114).

Waugh has successfully portrayed three rural characters considering a perennial fear: how to provide sufficient food for a growing family. Jone forcefully threatens to take his share for working, even if he must steal it, rather than let his family starve as he has seen others do; Sam

*clemmed: starved   †whol: while   +by th' mass: by the [Catholic] mass, a common medieval expletive   ○ mheyt: meat, food in general   ⊕ th' upstroke's noan so fur off: the end is not far off   □ yammerin': crying and complaining.

admits that in the best of times 'we'n to kill 'ursels to keep 'ursels', so that the high cost of food pushes one over the edge; and Mary sentimentally cries her shoes full of tears when she thinks of yammering children. The ease with which Waugh has delineated each character through his or her speech illustrates the resiliency and strength of dialect in the hands of a skilled writer. The inarticulate carter — normally unheard in the rush and bustle of city life — can speak strongly and emotionally in a language that would appear artificial and even demeaning in standard English.

Waugh's fame rested equally on his ability to portray the domestic life of his readers; indeed, his career as a full-time writer and speaker was launched with the publication of a home-piece, 'Come Whoam to thy Childer an' Me', in 1856. Within days 20,000 copies were sold as a penny broadside; it was widely reprinted on calendars, in church bulletins, temperance pamphlets, anthologies, and of course, in newspapers. Although read by many as a temperance poem, the emphasis is not on teetotal principles, but on the positive values of the home.

> Aw've just mended th' fire wi' a cob;*
> Owd Swaddle has brought thi new shoon;
> There's some nice bacon-collops o'th hob,
> An' a quart o' ale posset† i'th oon;+
> Aw've brought thi top-cwot, does to know,
> For th' rain's comin' deawn very dree○;
> An' th' har'stone's as white as new snow; —
> Come whoam to thi childer an' me.
>
> When aw put little Sally to bed,
> Hoo cried, 'cose her feyther weren't theer,
> So aw kissed th' little thing, an' aw said
> Thae'd bring her a ribbin fro' th' fair;
> An' aw gav her her doll, an some rags
> An' a nice little cotton-bo'⊕;
> An' aw kiss'd her again; but hoo said
> 'At hoo wanted to kiss *thee* an'o'.

*cob: lump of coal †ale posset: warm ale and milk +oon: oven ○dree: wearily continuously ⊕bo': bow

An' Dick, too, aw'd sich wark wi' him,
    Afore aw could get him up stairs;
Thae towd him thae'd bring him a drum,
    He said, when he're sayin' his prayers;
Then he looked i' my face, an' he said,
    'Has th' boggarts* taen houd o' my dad?'
An' he cried till his e'en were quite red; —
    He likes thee some weel, does yon lad!

At th' lung-length,† aw geet 'em laid still;
    An' aw hearken't folks' feet 'at went by;
So aw iron't o' my clooas reet well,
    An' aw hanged 'em o'th maiden+ to dry;

When aw'd mended thi stockin's an' shirts,
    Aw sit deawn to knit i' my cheerO,
An' aw rayley did feel rayther hurt, —
    Mon, aw'm *one-ly* when theaw artn't theer.

'Aw've a drum an' a trumpet for Dick;
    Aw've a yard o' blue ribbin for Sal;
Aw've a book full o' babs,⊕ an' a stick
    An' some 'bacco an' pipes for mysel';

Aw've brought thee some coffee an' tay, —
    Iv thae'll *feel* i' my pocket, thae'll *see*;
An' aw've bought tho a new cap to-day, --
    But aw al'ays bring summat for *thee*!

'God bless tho', my lass; aw'll go whoam,
    An aw'll kiss thee an' th' childer o' round;
Thae knows, that wherever aw roam,
    Aw'm fain to get back to th' owd ground;
Aw can do wi' a crack o'er a glass;
    Aw can do wi' a bit of a spree;
But aw've no gradely☐ comfort, my lass,
    Except wi' yon childer and thee.'³¹

---

*boggarts: hobgoblins †lung-length: a weaving term, the end of a piece of woven
material +maiden: clothes-horse O cheer: chair ⊕ babs: babies, pictures
☐ gradely: proper, right.

The poem's strength lies in the building of concrete details symbolic of the love felt by husband and wife for each other and their children. The ale-posset, bacon-collops and clean house all show the necessary care of a good wife, which is in turn reciprocated by the husband with his gifts for each member of the family. Yet, the poem teeters on the edge of sentimentality, and Waugh evades the question of why the husband has been gone so long if he prefers his own hearth; it would seem that he has been gone longer than 'a crack o'er a glass' would warrant, and has been gone for more than this one occasion.

The sentimentality of the poem was exploited by other writers, anxious to sell their work. Many went on to write even more mawkish poems on the virtues of the home; the taste for such verse was almost inexhaustible. Others, however, parodied Waugh's idealization of a woman's power over her husband and told the 'true' story — a shrewish woman and drunken husband fighting in a pub and on the streets. Brierley replied to Waugh with 'Go, Tak' thi Ragg'd Childer an' Flit', spoken by a sharp-tongued second wife complaining about her husband leaving her on the edge of starvation with his children. The unhappy situation is treated with high good humour, addressed to 'theaw great dhrunken slotch', who has no chance to defend himself from her verbal onslaught. Other parodies were 'Go Whoam an' Boyle thi' Yed', William Billington's 'A Tay an' Rum Ditty, illustratin' t'other side o' Waugh Celebrated Pictur', J. W. Mellor's two poems, 'Aw'll ne'er be Fuddled Agen', and 'Thae'rt Come Whoam Fuddled Agen', and Joseph Cronshaw's 'Aw'm Lonely, an' Weary, an' Sad'. The rollicking good humour of these poems link them with Anderton's temperance works; although the latter carried a different social message, both types of poet wished to provide working people with amusing entertainment.

Waugh's celebration of the family was echoed everywhere in dialect literature. Ab is blissfully contented with his wife and Sammywell Grimes certainly learns to appreciate his Mally. Many other stories deal with happy family outings on a warm Sunday, the hard-won contentment of the family hearth or the family as a refuge midst an industrial slum. The humorous relief found in some of the parodies of 'Come Whoam' were an antidote to so much praise, without attacking marriage as an institution. A typical satire on marriage was the popular recitation piece by John Eccles, 'Deein be Inches'. Eccles was frequently criticized by the Yorkshire Dialect Society and other purists for his use of non-dialect words, but his poems and almanac, called *T' Leeds Loiners' Comic Olemenac* (1873–82), sold well for many years.

A'm deein be inches tha knaws weel enuf,
    But nee e'en a fig duz ta care;
A'm a get aght road* sooin as I like –
    Ma cumpany I knaw tha can spare.
Goa fetch me that bottle ov fizzick daan stairs,
    An bring me that noggin ov gin;
I really feel ready ta faint inta t'earth –
    Tha knaws what a state I am in.

I cuddn't quite finish them two mutton chops,
    A'm az weak as wumman can be;
I hav all soarts ov pains flyin thro' ma boans,
    But then tha's noa pity for me.
A'l try an get t'doctor to giveme a chainge –
    Sich pain I noa longer can bide;
A mun hev sum owd port ta strenthen me up,
    An a drop ov gud brandy beside.

                . . . . . .

It's a queer piece ov bizziness (sed John tull hizsen;)
    It's cappin what wimmin can du;
Shoo's been cryin aght fer this last twenty years,
    An saying at shoo woddn't get through;
Yet shoo eats an shoo drinks all 'at cums e her waay,
    An lewks weel an strong az can be;
Wal hear 'Am hauf pined, 'an get nowt but crusts,
    It's noan here at's deein, it's ME!³²

This poem was particularly effective for recitation because of the range
of comic conversation. Although Eccles wrote a pidgin-English dialect,
he accurately captured the tone and style of a shrewish wife and a
submissive husband; the reader or reciter could always supply a more
authentic dialect through his own accent. The two characters are
sufficiently exaggerated to keep them at an emotional distance, but
sufficiently familiar to give them a satiric bite.

    Comedy remained one of dialect's strongest assets – particularly in
the portrayal of the self-confident, swaggering Lancashire lad or
Yorkshireman. One of Waugh's funnier stories is about a member of the

*get aght road: going out right

Lancashire Volunteers who makes friends with George III while he is
stationed in London. One day the King visits his home and notices,
'Jone, thou's a lot o' th' finest, fresh-colour't childer 'at ever clapt e'en
on'. His own children are 'o' as yollo' as marigowds', so Jone
recommends feeding them 'porritch'. 'Our Betty' then goes and teaches
'owd Charlotte' how to make it, and the story ends happily with the
comment, 'I believe thoose children o' th' king's han never looked
beheend 'em sin' they started o' aitin' porritch'.

Any small mishap made good material for a comic story. In
'Mrs. Shuttle Worsted', J. T. Staton recounts a story of Bobby Shuttle
walking down the street one day with his wife. Looking behind her she
stumbles over a jug of milk a little girl had put down on the pavement:

> As may be imagined, aw rush't at wonst to Sayroh's assistance, un
> help't hur to hur feet; un then, th' true state uv affairs beein' clear to
> hur moind, wot wi' th' ding-dong uv hur tung, th' skroikes* o'th'
> wench, un th' heawse lowfs† o'th' foak ut gether't reawnd, there
> wur a foine howrow i' Darrun for abeawt foive minnits. Aw'm soary
> to say that Sayroh's temper geet temporarily th' mestur on hur; for,
> poikin' up+ th' mug wi' booath honds, hoo dash't it wi' sitch a
> fullock○ ogen th' pavin' stones that it went aw to pieces; un then
> hoo threotn't to lug⊕ one hawve o'th' wench's stock o' yure□ eawt
> uv hur yed, for placin' hur mug in sitch a place, un vowed that if
> hoo'd ha bin lawm't☆ hoo'd had th' wench tried at the soizes■ on a
> charge little short o' monslowter.
>
> 'Yoa shouldn't blame th' wench, missis,' said a woman, wearin' a
> bedgeawn, un a cap very loike wot maytrons used to wear tharty
> yers back. 'If yoa'd not bin gawpin' un starin' abeawt yoa un
> wawkin' backurts yoa'd ne'er ha leet by th' misfortin'.'
>
> 'Wot hand oa t' do wi' it, Missis Meddlepup?' said Sayroh. 'Eh,
> wot han yoa t' do wi' it?'[33]

Sayroh proceeds to make a scene, calling for allies among the growing
number of bystanders. But she is not on her home ground of Bolton.
When the girl's mother arrives, 'as slender reawnd th' waist as a looad
barrel', demanding eightpence for the milk, she is vanquished. After
more loud complaining, she concedes and pays the eightpence. Her
husband and the reader, enjoy a good laugh at her indignities, and her

---

*skroikes: screeches †heawse lowfs: hoarse laughs +poikin' up: picking up
○ fullock: heavy throw ⊕ lug: tear □ yure: hair ☆ lawm't: lamed ■ soizes
assizes.

excessive pride over her 'good bombazeen dress'. Humorous scenes such
as these – spilt milk or well-made porridge – spoke to a reader's
personal pride and class consciousness.

In dialect literature the family was a strong bulwark against social
forces that were beyond individual control. Repeatedly working people
are portrayed as individuals motivated by simple desires, pleasures and
ambitions; their staunch morality saves them from the tawdry
temptations of the pub or music hall. Sammywell Grimes fled a London
hall after hearing George Leybourne sing 'What would your wife
think?' – His wife would think he should leave. The hero of Brierley's
Out of Work saves a young country girl from a life on the music-hall
stage in the nick of time. A belief in the family was shared by all classes
in the nineteenth century, but often for different reasons. The middle
class hoped that family men would be docile and respectable, and leave
politics to their betters. Working men, however, saw the family as a
refuge within which a man could lead his own life, regardless of
external pressures to conform and obey. Yet from a modern perspective
the end results appear to be the same: the family insured the status quo
by giving it moral legitimacy.

The same literature could appeal to both middle-class and working-
class audiences, who interpreted a message of family love and
self-improvement quite differently. A good example of this is Thomas
Wilson's *The Pitman's Pay* (1826 and 1830), written fully thirty years
before 'Come Whoam', and fifty years before 'Deein be Inches'. Coming
from Northumbria, Wilson felt no need to justify his subject matter,
but confidently begins:

> I sing not of warriors bold,
>   Of battles lost of victories won,
> Of cities sack'd or nations sold,
>   Or cruel deeds by tyrants done.
>
> I sing the pitman's plagues and cares,
>   Their labour hard and lowly lot,
> Their homely joys and humble fares,
>   Their pay-night o'er foaming pot.[34]

From this epic assertion Wilson goes on to present a full picture of the
domestic and working life of a miner. Using standard English for his
own narrative and dialect for the conversations and reminiscences, the
rich dialect and informative footnotes immediately attracted Northum-

brian readers. From its initial publication in an expensive magazine, it was quickly reprinted in a cheap edition for distribution among the pitmen.

The miners liked *The Pitman's Pay* because of its detailed and sympathetic descriptions of their own lives. Wilson (Plate 21) had come by his knowledge first hand. He entered the pit as a trapper boy at eight, but through hard work taught himself enough to become a school teacher at nineteen, when he left the pits forever. In 1799 he accepted a position in a counting house, and in 1807 he became a partner in the Gateshead manufacturing firm of Losh, Wilson and Bell. Prosperity marked the rest of his life, but he never forgot his early days and contributed generously to theeducational and library facilities of Gateshead.[35] He shows mining in the eighteenth century without any safety or technical equipment as brute, exhausting labour, paid for at great human cost. But throughout the poem he also comments upon the wonders that progress has brought. He portrays mining as a joint enterprise shared by the employers and the miners, bringing about continual progress and advancement. Wilson had a life-long hatred of unions, and for all his realism, he presented the horrors of mining as a thing of the past (in 1826 and 1830), with a rosy future for all. Despite these ambiguities, Wilson was frequently imitated by pit-poets; 'The Pit Boy' (pp. 84-5) is only one example. A tribute to him appears in *The Northern Tribune*, 'A Periodical for the People', alongside stories by Thomas Cooper and poems by W. J. Linton, both of whom believed many of the values Wilson encouraged in his poetry.

Nevertheless, elements in *The Pitman's Pay* reveal the distance Wilson had travelled since his days underground. His own successful rise in the social scale led him to accept completely the ethic of self-help.[36] He worked to make educational opportunities more widely available, and at the same time argued that those who did not take advantage of them were surely content in the place God had given them:

> 'For happiness is not confin'd
> 'Te folks in halls or cassels leevin';
> 'And if wor lives be good, ye'll mind
> 'There'll nyen ax how we gat te heeven.

> 'We labour hard te myek ends meet,
> 'Which baffles oft the gentry's schemin';
> 'And though wor sleep be short, it's sweet,
> 'Whilst they're on bums and bailies dreamin'.

'There is a charm aw cannot nyem,
'That's little knawn te quality:
'Ye'll find it in the happy hyem,
'Of honest-hearted poverty.

'Yor high-flown cheps oft fyel and brick,*
'But we hev a'ways yet been yable
'Te keep the wheelband i' the nick,†
'Though oft wi' but a barish tyeble.+

. . . .

'Aw dinnet mean te brag o' this –
'It's but the way we a' should treed;
'But where the greet se often miss,
'We may luick up when we succeed.

'For raither sic disgrace te share,
    'An' bring a stain upon wor freends,
'We'd work, on breed-an'-waiter fare,
    'Till blood drops frae wor finger ends.
                                            (pp.49–50).

The colliers here heartily endorse keeping in their place, and do not
envy the upper classes who 'run up debts they cannot pay'. This differs
significantly from early trade-union propaganda. Wilson argues from the
precept that happiness can be found everywhere, and defines the
greatest happiness as 'honest-hearted poverty'. Contemporary trade-
union writers would agree that happiness can be found among all
classes, but that it is destroyed in a society permitting honest labour to
fall below a living wage. Wilson's pitman paying his bills while living on
bread and water was an anathema to union leaders who believed such
sacrifices unnecessary in the face of the pit owners' wealth. *The
Pitman's Pay* is based on the continuation of the economic status quo,
with gradual social and physical amelioration through technical
improvements, education and savings banks. The miners' union stood
for economic control of one's livelihood, a view that threatened Wilson

*fyel and brick: fall and break   †Te keep the wheelband i' the nick:
a proverbial expression meaning steady and uninterrupted progress in life or work.
+barish tyeble: a bare table.

and his manufacturing associates. The conflict and resolution of these two views during the nineteenth century forms an important background to the songs and poetry written for political purposes, yet they were largely ignored by later dialect writers, seeking a modus vivendi within the existing system.

The next generation of dialect writers were less successful businessmen than Wilson, and were caught in conflicting attitudes about the social injustice they saw everywhere. On the one hand they were clearly being rewarded by the system – their own self-education and self-sacrifice had paid off and given them a means of earning extra money and local fame. Yet they recognized the limits of their progress, and that those without a gift for versifying could work day and night and never put any money by. Moreover, the vote was not uniformly available, and the legal system clearly discriminated in favour of those with property. The family might provide a retreat for some, but not all were happily married, and some could not afford to marry at all. Ben Preston's poignant 'Aw nivver can call hur maw wife', written in 1856, recounts the injustice of a society that leaves a weaver so poor he cannot follow the Christian precept to marry and and multiply. The weaver feels 'Like an ivy-stem trailin' i' t'mire . . . deein' for t'want of a stay' (see Appendix). The poem offers no solution; the weaver goes on to say 'that Chartist wor nowt bud a sloap/Ah wor fooild by his speeches an' rhymes', and he accepts as morally correct Malthusian arguments that he should not marry on an inadequate income. He is reduced to 'roarin' ' – a position many dialect writers took when they came to consider social injustice. Even so, many middle-class lovers of dialect appear to have found *any* social criticism questionable. One commentator in an expensive anthology apologized for 'Aw nivver', explaining, ' . . . in the poet, wrath is intensified a hundred fold, and too often becomes undiscriminating.'[37] Although 'roarin' ' was an improvement over the emasculated Poor Law verse of Story and Nicholson, upper-class patrons fifty years later were just as unsympathetic to a working-class perspective critical of the existing social system.

As another alternative to 'roarin' ' many dialect writers were active in politics and in their local trade union. One such was the early I. L. P. leader, Joseph Burgess (1853–1934), born in Failsworth, like Ridings and Brierley. Burgess began work at six, as a piecer, earning 1s.6d. for a sixty-hour week. He rose to become a widely respected journalist, editing several Lancashire newspapers. Much of his poetry attacked inadequate child labour laws and the excessively long working days of

the time. Chartists and trade unionists of an earlier generation had
established poetry as a viable political medium that could be read and
enjoyed by workers. Burgess wrote dialect verse as a natural part of his
intellectual and politicaldevelopment. In a poem written in 1874 he
treats shoddy — reworked wool — as a hateful object, swearing no child
of his will live to be a piecer. In his autobiography he explained,

'The poem which follows is a composite picture of my
experiences as a piecer at Robin Ogden's, Sett; Benson's,
Droylsden; and Boundary Mill, Mills Hill. The ill-usage described
was all experienced at Robin Ogden's, where I had an Irish
minder named Dillon. He was the only man who ever laid a finger
on me in the way of chastisement. I was then under ten years of
age. Later on it would have been dangerous for any man to
assault me.'

> Aw'm a shoddy piecer 'at's singin' yo' this sung,
> Bu' tho' aw'm one at present, aw durn't intend't be lung,
> For, ere aw'll stop at piecin', aw'll tell yo' gradely streight,
> Aw'll start o' sellin' idleback,* an' sheawtin' 'weight for weight.'†
> For what wi' speed an' o'ertime, an' what wi' dust an' dirt,
> Workin' bar'foot upo' th' flooar, i' yo'r breeches an' yo'r shirt,
> Fettlin'+ ev'ry blessed mealtoime four an' five days in a week,
> If yo' say'n that is no' slav'ry yo'n a toidy lot o' cheek.[38]

The speed of the lines captures the rhythm of a power-loom, and
accentuates the narrator's bitterness; he makes no pretence that the
work is honourable or satisfying. In the final verse the young boy
roundly declares:

> Why! A fact'ry's loike a prison, yo' con noather see nor yer,
> (When yo'n getten insoide it) owt 'at's passin' eawt o' th' dur,
> For they're filled wi' frosted windows,an' built insoide a yard,
> Wi' a wall yo' conno' get o'er, an' a dur 'at's allus barred.
> So' aw'm beawn to save mi oddie○ 'at when aw get upgroon,
> Aw con bid good-bye to shoddy an' to workin' beawt mi shoon,
> An' hopin' yo' as yer'n me'll think aw'm doin' reet,
> An' clap me leawd an' heartily, aw'll weesh yo' o' good-neet.
>   (pp.58–59)

*sellin' idleback: selling broken plaster for whitening hearths. †sheawtin'
'weight for weight': a poor peddlar who exchanges goods 'weight for weight,'
dealing mainly in old clothes and bones. +Fettlin': cleaning, fixing the looms,
○ oddie: odds and ends, trifles

The easy, almost conversational tone makes this a very effective argument for a richer life for both the speaker and the listener. The very best dialect spoke out of personal experience, vividly recreating local customs and beliefs. However, most writers preferred to present a satisfied, optimistic view of life, most suited for recreational reading and entertainment. The political potential of dialect was not explored as fully as might be expected in Lancashire and the West Riding, except by activists such as Burgess.

The spirit of protest lived on in the person of Tommy Armstrong, the Tanfield (County Durham) miner, who has the distinction of being the only person discussed who could fit in any of the other chapters. Many of his songs were written for political reasons, particularly in support of the growing Durham Miners' Association. He drew most of his tunes from the music hall, and was a well-known amateur comedian; he could have become a professional, but instead wrote for his fellow pitmen in a manner similar to the ballad writers described in Chapter 1. Armstrong loved drinking and singing with friends; he paid for his beer by selling his songs in the pubs he visited.[39] In times of crisis unknown miners still wrote for their union as in 1844, but increasingly semi-professional poets such as Amrstrong were expected to provide the necessary songs. On occasion a sympathetic music-hall entertainer might write songs for the unions. Joe Wilson, the Tyneside singer, wrote several pieces for the Nine Hours Movement. Interestingly enough they are all from the perspective of the wife who must struggle for food, clothes and rent during the strike. In one she loyally concludes 'Time'll bring yor nine oors yit . . . An' show te' men an' maistors byeth/The world'll haud the two'.

Armstrong was less forgiving than Joe Wilson, perhaps because he suffered through the strikes himself, watching his large family edge toward starvation. All of his pieces, mostly written in the 1880s and '90s, are closer in feeling to the protest songs of an earlier generation. One of his best-known songs was written as part of a song-writing contest in the Red Roe pub against a William McGuire. The audience chose the subject, a recent strike at Oakey's pit, and Tommy wrote the following lines, to the tune of 'Th' Pride of Petticoat Lane':

> It wis in November en aw nivor will forget
> Th' polises en th' candymen* it Oakey's hoose met;
> John, th' bellmin, he wis thare, squinten roond eboot;
> En he plaic'd three men it ivory hoose te torn th' pitmen oot.

*candymen: rag-and-bone merchants, rag-tag of the village, hired to help with evictions from company-owned housing during a strike.

Chorus

Oh wat wad aw dee if ad th' poower me sel,
Aw wid hang th' twenty candymen en Johny thit carry's th' bell.

Thare th' went freh hoose to hoose te put things on th' road,
But mind th' didn't hort thorsels we liften hevy loads;*
Sum wid carry th' poker oot, th' fendor, or th' rake,
If th' lifted two it once it wis a greet mistake.

Sume theese dandy-candy men wis drest up like e cloon;
Sum ad hats wivoot e flipe,†, en sum wivoot e croon;
Sum ad nee laps ipon thor cotes but thare wis one chep warse:
Ivory time he ad te stoop it was e laffible farse.

Thare wis one chep ad nee sleeves nor buttins ipon hees cote;
Enuthor ad e bairns hippin lapt+ eroond his throte.
One chep wore e pair e breekso thit belang tiv a boi,
One leg wis e sort iv e tweed, th' tuthor wis cordyroi.

Next thare cums th' maistor's, aw think thae shud think shem
Depriven wives en familys of a comfortable yem⊕.
But wen thae shift freh ware thae liv,□ aw hope thail gan te th' well.
Elang we☆ th' twenty candy men, en Johny thit carry's th' bell.[40]

The song is an attack on the scum of the village – the candymen who
benefit from the hard-working miners' fight against 'th' maistors'. But
the principal political message is in the last stanza, when the coal owners
and their tools are both wished in hell (published euphemistically as 'th'
well'). The major difference between this song and those written during
the 1844 strike is a sense of self-pride that the candymen cannot
destroy, in contrast to the earlier poems that concentrate on gaining
that self-pride. However, like the earlier strike literature, Armstrong's
songs always had carefully defined goals based on economic justice. His
denunciation of the greed and hypocrisy of the coal owners and their
tools is contained within a context of cultural values accepted, if not

---

*th' didn't hort thorsels we liften hevy loads: they didn't hurt themselves
with lifting heavy loads. †flipe: brim +e bairns hippin lapt: a child's
napkin tied, laid ○breeks: breeches ⊕yem: home □wen thae shift freh
ware thae liv: when they move from where they live ☆Elang we: Along with.

adhered to, by nearly every stratum of society: the right of every family to a 'comfortable yem' undisturbed by unjust evictions.

Pride and patience ran through the poetry and songs written during the Lancashire Cotton Famine, caused by the northern blockade of southern ports during the American Civil War. Unlike other periods of economic depression there were no political goals directly related to the Famine; working men had few outlets for their anger except speculators and cheap Indian cotton. As essential members of the country's economy they felt none of the hatred that had marked such times as the Plug Plot Strikes of 1842. Nor did they have political leaders who galvanized them to protest against the government's refusal to offer the county emergency assistance. Yet many families were reduced from incomes as high as three and four pounds a week to ten shillings. In Preston applications for poor relief rose from 4.6 per cent of the population in November 1861, to 47.5 per cent one year later. In 1862 of the 350,000 cotton operatives in Lancashire, only 40,000 were on full-time, 135,000 on short-time and 180,000 were totally unemployed.[41] When Edwin Waugh visited Preston he remarked in his notebook, 'I wonder why they tolerate these conditions so much more now than twenty years ago?'[42]

The four years of suffering brought forth many poems and songs, often written to earn a few extra pence by singing and selling on street corners. Shameful as many workers found this, it was better than begging. A few of these ballads became enormously popular, selling 30 and 40,000 copies as penny broadsides. Many of these amateur productions bear a strong resemblence to Waugh's popular works, or such traditional songs as 'Jone o' Grinfilt, Jr.', which continued to be sold. Most songs expressed solidarity with other unemployed men, emphasizing the need for cheerfulness and confidence that 'good toimes' would come again. Little was said about the war and its implications beyond such sentiments as 'iv yon Yankees could only just see/ . . . Aw think they'd soon settle their bother, an' strive/To send us some cotton to keep us alive' (see Appendix).

The answer to Waugh's query can perhaps be seen in James Bowker's 'Hard Toimes, orthe Weaver Speaks to his Wife'.

> Draw up thy cheer*, owd lass, we'n still a bit o' fire,
> An' I'm starv't to deoth wi' cummin' throo th' weet an' mire;
> He towd a lie o' thee an' me, as said as th' love o' th' poor

*cheer: chair

Flies out o' th' kitchen window, when clemmin' cums to th' door.
Aw'm not ruein' — as thae weel knows — as ever I wed thee,
But I've monny a quare thowt* as thae mon sometimes rue o' me.

I'm mad at them America foos, as never hes enuff
O' quarrelin' an' strugglin', and sich unnat'rel stuff,
An' its ter'ble hard, owd wife, to ceawer bi' th' chimley jam,†
An' think if they keep on feightin', as thee an' me mun clam+,
An' not aar faut,○ its like breykin' wer shins o'er th' neighbours' stoos,
An' it shows us for one woise mon, ther's welly twenty foes.

But better chaps nor me an' thee hes hed to live o' nowt,
An' we'n hed a tidy time on't afoor th' war brok' out;
An' if I'm gerrin'⊕ varra thin, it matters nowt o' me,
Th' hardest wark is sittin' here schaming for th' choilt an' thee.
Th'art gerrin' ter'ble pale too, but fowk wi' nowt to heyt
Con't luk as nice an' weel as them as plenty hes o' meyt□.

Ther's lots o' hooams areawnd us whear wot they waste i' th' day,
'Ud sarve for thee an' th' choilt an' me, an' some to give away;
An' as I passes by their dooars, I hears their music sweet,
An' I con't but think o' thee till th' teears dim mi seet;
For if I'd lots o' brass☆, thae shud be diff'rent, never fear,
For th'art nooan so feaw,■ yet, wench, if thae'd gradely clooas●
   to wear.

An' aar bonny little Annie, wi' her pratty een so breet,
Hoo shud sleep o' feathers, and uv angels dreom o neet;
I fancies I con see her monny a weary heawr i' th' day,
As I shud loike her to be sin, if luv mud heve its way;▲
And if what's i' this heart o' moine cud nobbut cum to pass,
Hoo shud bi' th' happiest woman, as hoo is th' bonniest lass.

---

*a quare thowt: a queer thought   †to ceawer bi' th' chimley jam: to cower
by the chimneyside +mun clem: must starve ○aar faut: our fault ⊕gerrin':
getting □meyt: meat, i.e., food ☆brass: money ■feaw: few, i.e., lowly
●gradely clooas: proper or decent clothes ▲if luv mud heve its way: if love
would have its way

I'm a foo wi' clammin' soa, or I shudn't toke like this,
It nobbut meks wer teeth watter to think o' sich like bliss;
An' th' winter cummin' on so fast, wi' th' dark, an' th' snow, an' th'
   cowd,
For I heeard th' robin sing to-day as I heeard him sing of owd,
When thee an' me wur younger, an' i' wur soft cooartin days,
An' I cum whistlin' thro' the fields to yoar owd woman's place.

Thea loved me then, an' as wimmen's soft enuff for owt,
I do believe thae loves me neaw, mooar nor ever I'd hae thowt,
An' tha' hes but one excuse, if I'm ragg'd, I'm fond o' thee,
An' times, though hard, I connot think'll change thee or me,
For if we're true an' reet, an' as honest as we're poor,
We's never hev no wos* chap nor poverty at th' dooar. ⁴³

Bowker has absorbed the values implicit in a cash-nexus relationship,
and sees emotional security in terms of money and the necessities and
luxuries it provides a family. As a man who derived his identity from
the sale of labour, the weaver needs reassurance that his family still
loves him when he cannot fulfil this role. In turn, he promises gifts in
the future as representative of his own love for them. However,
alongside the cataloguing of material goods are realistic descriptions of
'clemming' and poverty that place the desire for presents and good
times in a convincing context. The poem barely rises above the most
platitudinous thoughts, but it undoubtedly provided solace for
Lancashire families suffering from what seemed like an endless period
of unemployment.
    The poem makes an interesting contrast with earlier protest poetry,
and 'Jone o' Grinfilt, Jr.' in particular. 'Jone' seems more pessimistic
than 'Hard Toimes', which is more passive and accepting of the status
quo. Unlike Jone, Bowker's weaver does not think in terms of
economic stability or of deliverance from his plight by outsiders as a
right, but accepts his unemployment as a temporary aberration with no
solution. Despite his sense of injustice about the rich who waste food,
and of the need for a minimum standard of living, in the final stanza
Bowker reduces all suffering to an acceptance of poverty as a greater
good than prosperity because it is a source of greater family love. This
self-justification in facing inexplicable or unavoidable problems easily
yields to a justification of the status quo as not only necessary, but the
best of all possible situations. While Jone accepted social differences,
his sense of social justice could not be softened by any notion of family

*wos: worse

love; he and Margaret took each other for better or worse, and their sufferings could not be solved or assuaged by looking inward.

'Hard Toimes' did not have forty years of oral circulation to smooth out its awkward lines, flat clichés, and weak metaphors; the poem lacks precision in comparison with 'Jone o' Grinfilt, Jr.' Emotions are not integral to the poem itself, but are evoked in the reader by means of familiar phrases and words. The most serious affect of poetry such as 'Hard Toimes' is that it forms the vocabulary and ultimately the emotions of the reader. With no other words to describe personal emotions than those provided by Bowker and his like, readers grow to define and describe them in his terms, so that they force individual thoughts and feelings into a generalized picture taken from their reading. That which does not fit this format becomes unreal and unacceptable; any variation from the familiar is suspect. Individuals no longer trust their particular feelings, and their own words to describe them, but draw upon preconceived and predescribed sources. Bad poetry becomes not an explanation of emotions, but a substitution for them.

IV
The Limitations of Dialect

Dialect was a powerful voice when describing the joys and sorrows of industrial workers, but it never fulfilled its original potential. For all of its vitality and humour, one senses struggle and thwarted progress. The causes of this failure to develop were two-fold: writers themselves tended to accept the standards of the literary establishment and to judge their works by them. They saw themselves as minor figures in comparison with the giants of English literature, and assigned to themselves and dialect a limited social and artistic role. A second and more serious problem, with ramifications in other areas of working-class culture, was the widespread acceptance of dialect among all classes. Dialect never became a form of mass entertainment, controlled by the powerful and wealthy, as did the music hall, but it did have a mass readership. Writers wrote repetitiously and simplistically about themes that would offend no one, rather than about the unique characteristics of their own class.

Toward the end of the nineteenth century the defenders of dialect attacked the effects of compulsory education in standard English. In 1890 J. H. Wylie, an inspector of schools for the Rochdale district,

suggested that dialect literature might profitably be taught in school to
preserve its distinctive characteristics among the youth of Lancashire.
His idea met vigorous opposition from teachers who feared that
encouraging the local vernacular would make it even more difficult to
eradicate provincialisms and further handicap children seeking better
employment. The debate was ended by two long dialect letters in the
Rochdale Observer from John Trafford Clegg, 'Th' Owd Weighver', who
insisted 'There's nobbut a tuthri* owd folk at Mildhro, or Shore, or up
o' th' moor ends, 'at talk i' th' owd road;† most on us han getten a
mongrel sort o' talk, 'at's noather good Lanky nor gradely English, but
just nowt at o, like Ab-o'-Joe's whom-brewed when th' bottle brasted.'
Clegg believed that the authentic Lancashire dialect had disappeared in
the industrial cities, and he could see no reason to preserve a mélange of
words and phrases. Quite aside from content, modern dialect was too
impure to have any artistic validity as a written language. He not only
saw no point in teaching 'Lanky' in comparison with French or
German, or even Latin or Greek, but he also believed that Waugh and
Burns had been handicapped by writing in dialect:

> Aw like th' owd Lanky − ah! it's come like music into my ears time
> an' time again, makin me fair laugh an' cry wi thoughts o' past doins,
> an' to yer it in a strange place brings whom, an' love, an' tender
> feelins into th' mind − but iv yor beaun to trim it deawn to rules an'
> teigch it 'systematically' yo'll just get a tuthri rough-seaundin words
> an' sayins, an' yo'll find 'at o th' flavour an' beauty an' power's
> flown away.
>
> Dun yo think aw'm ratchin+ t' truth i' sayin that? Well, just jow○
> yo'r yeads once an' think abeaut it. There's very little written i' th'
> Lancashire dialect 'at couldn't be as weel or better done i' good
> English; but con yo tell me ov ony good English 'at yo could mend
> by turnin it into Lanky? Con yo deny 'at eaur dialect's come to be
> moore thought on nor it desarves just becose a tuthri folk (an yo con
> count 'em o' one hand) wi brains, an' wit, an' fancy, an' rare
> thoughts han happen't to use it; an' are yo beaun to tell me 'at
> everyone on 'em couldn't ha done as good wark i' th' Queen's
> English?[44]

As the language of common speech, dialect could not survive the
scrutiny of formal study, nor could it open literary or commercial

---

*tuthri: two or three   †th' owd road: the old way   +ratchin: pulling apart
○ jow: push, shake

worlds for those who had mastered it. Such criticisms from the most skilled practitioners spelled the end of dialect as a literary language for the working class.

Dialect writers by and large agreed with Clegg when they considered their own creative work. Ben Brierley, in a lecture on Lancashire dialect and its advantages, defined himself as a 'setter', who had the skill to weave a story from the phrases, anecdotes and incidents he overheard or observed: '... These sayings [in dialect] are not purely my own invention. They are "unconsidered trifles" that I have picked up in my journey through life. Gathered bits of humour arranged in a form of setting. I claim only to be the setter'.[45] This antiquarianism goes far to explain Brierley's fascination with thehand-loom weaving culture of his past, and his relative slighting of the power-loom operatives who read his stories. The artist-as-collector immediately places severe limitations upon individual creativity; the best writing becomes that which is closest to what has actually happened or been said. Subject matter and characterization are also limited to what will easily embody the various words, phrases or conversations the author wishes to include. The meandering, anecdotal nature of most dialect prose was partly a result of this desire to be as close to real events as possible, and partly a failure on the part of artists such as Brierley to use their material in a creative rather than simply imitative manner.

Both dialect writers and the poets described in the previous chapter believed they could influence society, but they had very different conceptions of the function of the writer. Nicholson, Prince and Billington, for example, regarded themselves as 'Nature's priests', with a special God-given mission to spiritualize society. They hoped to convert people to a new and better way of life. Dialect writers, on the other hand, primarily saw themselves providing humour and sentiment. As Waugh said, they could offer 'a guidin' glimmer to some wond'rer astray/Or haply gi'e some poor owd soul a lift on the way.' The principal obligations of authors were amusement and uplift. But like the writers in standard English, dialect writers sometimes felt unappreciated. They did not have recourse, however, to the consolations of an escape on the wings of poesy because they believed in the importance of reaching an audience. They defined their place in society quite narrowly, but hoped to gain greater popularity than their more earnest peers. In 'Only a Poet' (c. 1885) Samuel Laycock describes common attitudes toward poets and his own self-justification:

He'll offer to lead yo through nature's sweet beawers,
An' bid yo admire her grand fruitage an' fleawers.
Very grand an' poetical; nice food for kings,
Or bein's 'at flutter abeawt us wi' wings;
But one couldn't weel offer to clothe a bare back.
Or feed hungry bellies wi' stuff o' that mak'.
'Only a poet,' like Bloomfield or Burns,
'At may happen amuse yo an' vex yo i' turns;
Neaw charmin' his readers wi' th' thowts fro' his pen,
Thus winnin' their heartiest plaudits, an' then,
It may be th' next minute yo'r filled wi disgust
At some sarcastic hit, or some pointed home-thrust!

'*Only* a poet!' What moor do yo want?
Some narrow-souled parson to rave an' to rant
Abeawt th' heat an th' dimensions, an' th' people i' hell,
Till yo fancy 'at th' chap must ha' bin' theer hissel.
Yet there are foalk i' th' world 'at don't think it amiss
To pay hundreds for sich twaddle as this;
While others, entitled to love an' respect,
Are treated too often wi' scorn an' neglect!
'*Only a Poet*,' what moor do yo crave,
To sweeten life's journey fro' th' cradle to th' grave?
Which is th' likeliest − think yo − to help us along, −
An owd musty creed, or a hearty good song?[46]

'A hearty good song' replaced insight into the larger problems of life or an understanding of life beyond the immediate and familiar. The constrictions of an industrial, class-bound society were accepted as part of 'life's journey' by dialect writers and their readers.

Dialect writing did not develop or regress during the period 1850−1914, but it probably declined in terms of the sheer quantity of verse written after about 1885. The same themes were repeated over and over, following the paths laid out by Thomas Wilson, Waugh and Brierley. In many ways dialect writers became victims of the popularity they so desired. Money and respectability could be gained by writing a great deal about uncontroversial commonplaces; most writers found the temptations of a mass readership irresistible.

Respectability went hand in hand with acceptance by the middle class. Since dialect writers still judged themselves by the standards of the literary establishment, they were eager for acceptance. They also shared many of the same values as their middle-class admirers. But the embrace of the upper classes led to the misunderstandings expressed by Captain Haigh-Smith, and more seriously, to separation from the working class. Once a writer had accepted the dominant beliefs of the day, and had been rewarded by those holding literary and social power, he was in danger of cutting himself off from the sources of his inspiration. In this situation writers such as Edwin Waugh drew upon their childhood memories to create a series of rural idylls set in the past that did not disturb their mentors and pleased their working-class readers. Brierley and Thomas Wilson idealized the working conditions of the hand-loom or pit villages of the previous generation; their tales and poems about contemporary life had little to do with work. Repeatedly dialect writers versified general situations common to every class, such as domestic scenes or local lore.

The popularity of dialect might have produced a growing acceptance of working-class values in society at large. Political conditions had changed, however, from the days of the Chartist movement and its demands for an egalitarian, democratic society. Large portions of the working class accepted the self-help ethic, based on individual improvement and the continuation of property-based political, economic and legal systems. Equally, popular dialect reflected the cultural domination of those with political and economic power. Dialect had originally been written out of a strong sense of place and class, but a writer who attempted to appeal to a mass audience diluted whatever made his writing unacceptable to his potential audience. The tough anger of Burgess's little piecer or Armstrong's strikers might turn away part of that massive audience. Only by writing platitudes acceptable to everybody could such a problem be avoided. Mirroring the dominant social and economic standards of the day, popular versifiers accepted and propagated the pervasive world view that social injustice and personal discomfort were minor aberrations in comparison with the fundamental decency of all human beings and the proper running of the social order. The consciousness of the working class could only be circumscribed by such literature.

The debasement of dialect can be seen in such early works as Bowker's 'Hard Toimes' and Eccles' 'Deein be Inches', but both are redeemed by their use of natural imagery taken from the daily lives of workers. Whenever a poet of equivalent talent took on a more serious subject the limitations of dialect become obvious. To take one example, the popular anthology piece 'Johnny's Clogs' appeared in the *Blackburn Times* in 1886, just after the author's son had died. John T. Baron, an iron turner and fitter, wrote over 1,700 rhymes for his column 'Rhymes in Dialect' during the period 1886–1919, in addition to uncounted numbers in standard English. All are similar to 'Johnny's Clogs':

Howd on theer! Dunnot use 'em rough, but put 'em gently deawn;
They're nobbut hawf-worn clogs to yo, wi' tops o' musty breawn;
To me, they're sacred links 'at bind my thowts to one i' th' mowd;
Eawr Johnny wore those clogs afooar Deeath med him stiff an' cowd.

They're but a pair o' little clogs, wi' irons rusty red,
Yet thowts they wakken i' my heart, o ov a life-star 'at's fled.
For th' gloom o' grief seems darker neaw, an' Life's nowt near as
     sweet
As when he used to welcome me wi' hooam smiles every neet.

                    . . . .

Last neet, aw see a little star, 'at fairly pleased my eye,
It seemed o ov a flutter theer, heigh up i' th' dusky sky.
An' then a thowt flashed thro' my mind 'at med my eyeseet dim.
He wur my child! aw stood on th' earth, an' looked tort Heaven on
     him.

Con he be waitin' for me theer, hawf-way fro' th' gowden Throne?
Wur them his wings 'at fluttered breet heigh i' thoose realms unknown?
His bonny face seems allus near, an' th' love for him shall be
Held sacred i' this heart o' mine reight to Eternity.[47]

Little in this poem makes it native to Lancashire, except the word 'clogs' and the occasional changes in pronunciation and spelling. the emotions are described in terms of the most common Victorian symbolism of material possessions or natural objects replacing the loved one; it is a working-class version of Queen Victoria preserving Prince Albert's possessions for the rest of her life. Death, the central fact of the poem, is cheapened by the colloquial style and strained images. More seriously, feeling has been manipulated to appeal to the popular imagination, and in the process has been falsified. Addressed primarily to a working-class audience, 'Johnny's Clogs' reduces personal feeling to something totally explicable and even common. For readers seeking a greater understanding of Lancashire's working men, it only confirms the existing stereotype. Rather than bridging class differences, it satisfies each class by providing the expected.

A steady diet of the clichés and sentimentality exemplified by 'Johnny's Clogs', and 'Hard Toimes' can deprive the poorly educated individual of his own vocabulary and self-expression. It blunts his emotional perceptions and his confidence in his own emotional judgments. For persons little trained in conceptual thinking, literature of this sort encourages reducing everything to the familiar and known, opting out of any consideration of larger issues.[48] The most common events are thereby given a magnified importance, as if they were some great moral leap forward – Sayroh's 'worsting' educates her to control her temper and the reader to see this as a wonderful advance not only in her self-understanding, but his own also. For an important event, such as the death of Baron's son, no language is available to express grief but the worn clichés. Language is not a natural growth, but is shaped by real people using words they think convey profound, important, or at least sincere, meanings. Writing that starts with the idea of appealing to everyone, in a language everyone will assent to, cannot help but promote insincere and meaningless literature. As George Orwell has said in describing the debasement of the English language, a man may drink because he feels himself a failure, and then fail all the more completely because he drinks. Hollow and debased language encourages hollow and debased literature. The consciousness of readers will be affected in the same way.

A judgment of dialect literature, however, should also rest upon an evaluation of its most talented writers – Waugh, Brierley and Staton wrote some of the finest working-class literature of the century. In contrast to those writers moving wholeheartedly into the mainstream of English literature their primary influence was among their own class. It was no small achievement to have made literature an important part of working-class life throughout the North. These men and their followers presented a narrow but idealized vision of life that encouraged their readers in hard times and made them laugh in good times. Despite their obvious literary limitations, they strengthened the tradition of local and class pride among working people which still flourishes in northern England. Dialect literature can be seen as one answer to the *Northern Star's* exhortation to working men that they should read and study the works of their own class, and feel proud to be a member of it. The results may be quite unlike what Harney and other Chartist leaders would have liked, but the fundamental popularity of dialect literature remains.

Notes

1. I have used the word 'Northumbria' to mean the counties of Durham and Northumberland. Although rural folk traditions endured much longer in Cumberland and Westmorland, their dialect traditions were under the influence of Lancashire, Northumbria and Scotland.

2. For a recent discussion of John Bell and northern antiquarians, see David Harker, 'John Bell, The Great Collector', introduction to *Rhymes of Northern Bards*, ed. John Bell (Newcastle: Frank Graham, 1971 [1812]).

3. An exception, although not a working man, is William Barnes (1801–86), the Dorset antiquarian and philologist. An extraordinarily learned man, Barnes spent his entire life in the Vale of Blackmore, quietly turning out school books, grammars, dictionaries and poetry. He appears to have been totally unaffected by the poetic currents of his day, and had no contact with any of the industrial writers described in this chapter. He was, however, influential in the study of the rural dialects of southern England, a pursuit that remained more purely philological than in the North.

4. For a brief account of the history of Yorkshire dialect, see F. W. Moorman, *Yorkshire Dialect Poems (1673–1915)*, 2nd ed. (London: Yorkshire Dialect Society, 1917).

5. See Peter Haworth, 'A Lancashire Classic', *English Hymns and Ballads and Other Studies in Popular Literature* (Oxford: Basil Blackwood, 1927), pp.58–70; and Thomas Heywood, *On the South Lancashire Dialect with Biographical Notices of John Collier, the author of Tom Bobbin*, vol. 57 (Manchester: Chetham Society, 1861). In the nineteenth century Tim Bobbin's works were generally published with a translation. Both Elijah Ridings and Samuel Bamford earned money publishing translations; see Samuel Bamford, *The Dialect of South Lancashire, or Tim Bobbin's Tummus and Meary with his Rhymes, and an enlarged glossary of words and phrases, chiefly used by the rural population of the manufacturing districts of South Lancashire*, 2nd ed. (London: John Russel Smith, 1854); Elijah Ridings, *Tim Bobbin Tales; or Thomas and Mary. Rendered into Simple English by Elijah Ridings* (Manchester: James Ainsworth n.d. [1860?]).

6. Sally Bobbinwinder [Joseph Crabtree], *A Conversation between Peter Pickenpeg, Jack Shuttle, and Harry Emptybobbin* (Barnsley, n.p., 1838), pp.9–10.

7. In oral tradition Burns has lived on as a witty, ribald hero; a more decorous idol appears in the various collections of Burnsiana published throughout the nineteenth century. See [James Gibson], *The Bibliography of Robert Burns with Biographical and Bibliographical Notes, and Sketches of Burns Clubs, Monuments and Statues* (Kilmarnock: James M'Kie, 1881) for a listing of this material. The centenary of Burns's birth was celebrated with numerous poetry-writing contests. Gerald Massey came fourth

in the most prestigious contest, the Crystal Palace Company's
Centenary Celebration, with a first prize award of fifty guineas.
There are over seventy references to centenary publications in
Gibson.

8. *The Life of Thomas Cooper* (London: Hodder and Stoughton,
1872), p.42. Cooper also speaks glowingly of evenings spent with
Willie Thom (1789–1848), the Inverury weaver poet whose
Rhymes and Recollections of a hand loom weaver (Paisley, 1844)
created a sensation among the London literati. He was induced to
come to London for work, where he soon drank himself to death.
Cooper praised particularly his singing, adding, 'it required an
effort to free yourself from the conviction that you were
conversing with a thoroughly educated man when you talked with
Willie Thom' (p.313). Thom's verse is no better than many other
weaver poets, who lacked the magical origin of Scotland to attract
attention.

9. Edwin Waugh, 'Diary: 21 July 1847–10 February 1851', unpub.
MS., Manchester Central Reference Library.

10. The other popular form of respectable entertainment was music-
making — brass bands, choral groups and singing classes flourished
under the aegis of various institutions. See E. D. Mackerness, *A
Social History of English Music* (London: Routledge and Kegan
Paul, 1964), pp.127–234.

11. Ben Brierley describes the difficulties he and Waugh encountered
when trying to give readings in Blackpool in *Personal Recollections
of the Late Edwin Waugh* (Manchester: Abel Heywood, n.d.
[1890]). See also Ben Brierley, 'Goose Grove Penny Readings',
Ab-o'-th'-Yate Sketches and Other Short Stories, ed. James
Dronsfield, III, pp.135–48, about the disastrous turn penny
readings took when 'Rev. Stiltford Priggins' decided to make them
uplifting. Sim Schofield in *Short Stories about Failsworth Folk*
(Blackpool: Union Printers, 1905), p.49, recounts the following
anecdote about the perils of giving readings: 'I remember Brierley
once telling me a good story of how he and Waugh had been giving
readings before a scanty audience at Blackpool. They had scarcely
drawn sufficient to pay for the room. Returning to their lodgings
after the entertainment, in a downpour of rain, they met a dog
slouching along the street, the very picture of misery as it went
with its tail between its legs. "Does theaw see that dog?" Waugh
said to Brierley. "Aye, aw do," replied Ben. "Well, it strikes me",
Waugh continued, "that dog's bin givin' readin's." ' In one of
Waugh's untitled notebooks, Manchester Central Reference
Library, Waugh has listed all the cities where he gave readings in
1869: Glossop, Bury, Rochdale, Huddersfield, Oldham, Manchester, Bolton, Preston, Chorley, Bradford, Halifax, Liverpool,
Beverley, Kidderminster, Crick, Derby, Hull, Thornton, Hindley
and Todmorden. He does not record how often he spoke, but the
list at least indicates an improvement in fortune from the
Blackpool fiasco. It is interesting to note how frequently Waugh

left Lancashire, and how exclusively his engagements were in industrial centres.

12. Unpub. MS. 28 February 1858–26 December 1861, Manchester Central Reference Library, undated ref. August, 1859. The figures may have been inflated because at the time a fund-raising committee had been set up in Oldham to assist Bamford. Bamford, who despised Waugh and distrusted Brierley, was intensely critical of the committee for suggesting that Waugh share the podium with him to improve attendance. He went on to add in his diary, 'Even Brierley's attendance interfered with my plans, which ought not to have been disturbed at all, whilst his reading, the personal noveltyexcepted, lent not any additional attraction to the performance: He does not read well, and his pieces in the Lancashire Dialect would have been better done by myself. All however passed off very well, and at the conclusion Mr. Yates [chairman of the Oldham Committee] made a long and highly complimentary address in approval of my performance. I was really afraid Brierley would feel slighted . . . ' The reviews pasted in the diary are complimentary enough, but all comment on how few representatives of the working class were present.

13. F. W. Moorman, pp.xxx–xxxi.

14. This judgment was made by Moorman and Charles Federer in 'Bibliography of the Yorkshire Dialect Literatures', *Transactions of the Yorkshire Dialect Society*, I, 3 (1901), pp.86–114.

15. Harald John Lexow Bruff, 'A Short Biography of Thomas Blackah', *Dialect Poems and Prose by Thomas Blackah* (York: Waddingtons, n.d. [1937]), pp.12–13.

16. W. J. Halliday, 'John Hartley', *Transactions of the Yorkshire Dialect Society*, VI, 40 (1939), pp.27–34.

17. *Seets i' Lundun* (London: W. Nicholson, n.d. [1874]), p.8.

18. *Grimes's Trip to America* (Bradford: Watmoughs, n.d. [1877]), pp.7–8.

19. The titles of Staton's works fill three pages of Archibald Sparke's *Bolton Bibliography*, according to Halstead, p.267. The *Loominary* closed on 22 February 1862 because of the Cotton Famine, or as Staton explained, 'until th' gloom which at present o'ershadows th' manufacturin' districts has passed away, un gien place to breeter toimes.'

20. Brierley, *Home Memories*, pp.80ff.

21. *Lancashire Dialect Poems, Sketches and Stories* (Manchester: Abel Heywood, n.d. [1902]), p.75.

22. Their authenticity is questionable since he often had a single person make several translations; the project was never completed, so it is difficult to assess. At least it provided money for many authors.

23. John H. Swann, *Manchester Literary Club: Some Notes on its History, 1862–1908* (Manchester: Manchester City News, 1908). In 1909 Teddy Ashton, a local dialect writer, organized the Lancashire Author's Association specifically to aid local writers and to encourage Lancashire writing.

24. *Proceedings of the Manchester Literary Club 1873–74* (Manchester: A. Ireland, n.d. [1875]), p.xii.
25. George Milner, 'Introduction', *Lancashire Sketches*, vol.I of *Collected Works*, ed. George Milner, pp.xxxii–xxxiv. Milner's introduction contains a complete biography of Waugh and a general discussion of dialect. For Waugh's early struggles and his unhappy marriage, see his unpub. diary, Manchester Central Reference Library. See also the many reminiscences of Waugh; among the most reliable are: Brierley, *Personal Recollections*, James T. Foard, 'Edwin Waugh', *Manchester Quarterly*, 17 (1890), pp.197–204; Abraham Stansfield. 'Recollections of Edwin Waugh', *Manchester Quarterly*, 37 (1911), pp.434–46; and the *Manchester City News* obituary, 3 May 1890.
26. Untitled poem, 'Personal Recollections', pp.10–13.
27. Bamford, who enjoyed gossiping, commented about a conversation with his friend James Dronsfield, 'Talked about Waugh and his song "Com Whoam to thy Childre an' Me" whilst his wife and children were at the very time in the Marland Workhouse and he living with another woman in Strangeways: This is rank hypocrisy and astounding impudence. Dronsfield said if Ben Brierley put confidence in Waugh, he would betray him as soon as it suited his convenience to do so.' (19 September 1858). On another occasion he sent his wife to warn a landlady not to rent to Waugh because of his 'general habits of profligacy and faithlessness in his engagements.' (19 August 1861). Bamford is not a totally reliable informant, and unfortunately few other private opinions about the lives of these writers, or any other dialect writers of the time, are still extant.
28. *Manchester Guardian*, 26 March 1884. The best accounts of Brierley's early life are his two autobiographical sketches, 'Failsworth, My Native Village', *Ab-o'-th'-Yate Sketches and Other Short Stories*, ed. James Dronsfield, III, pp.253–94; and *Home Memories*. See also, James Dronsfield, 'Preface', *Ab-o'-th'-Yate, Sketches and Other Short Stories*, I, pp.v–xxv; and Sim Schofield, *Short Stories about Failsworth Folk*.
29. Unpub. letter addressed to John Hartley from Captain J. Haigh-Smith, 26 February 1914, Bradford Central Reference Library.
30. *Lancashire Sketches*, I (1892), p.xliv. All further citations to Waugh's writings are to the 1892 *Collected Works*.
31. *Poems and Songs*, VIII (1892), pp.3–6.
32. *North Country Poets*, ed. William Andrews (Manchester: Abel Heywood, 1888), I, pp.172–3.
33. *Lancashire Dialect Poems, Sketches and Stories*, p.46.
34. *The Pitman's Pay and Other Songs*, p.3.
35. For the life of Thomas Wilson see 'A Memoir of the Life of the Late Mr. Wilson of Gateshead Fell', *The Pitman's Pay and Other Songs*, pp.xv–xxiii; 'Thomas Wilson, Author of "Pitman's Pay" ', *The Northern Tribune*, II (1855), pp.52–4.
36. Wilson's attitude toward the pitmen and toward his middle-class

readers is best shown in his footnotes to *The Pitman's Pay*. For
example, part I ends with a married couple planning how 'to ettle'
[to deal out sparingly] their pay on market day:

'The anxiety of "honest poverty" to make all ends meet on such
occasions, and to avoid getting into debt, was highly praiseworthy
in many of those sons and daughters of toil. It was not uncommon
to see the man and wife on a pay-night apportioning the money
they had for purchasing the various articles which they wanted at
the market next day. The calculation was often very difficult, not
less so than, "placing the wark", particularly when the sum total
fell short of the different items wanted, as then a fresh arrangement
had to be made after striking out some of the articles which could
be best spared, and it was often no easy matter to decide so
perplexing a matter.

'Eatables were considered first, as being indispensable. The tea
and sugar, being deemed luxuries, took extra care in fixing the
quantities. For a small family two ounces of tea and a pound of soft
sugar were thought enough for a week, taking care always to have
the latter in quarter pounds in order to secure four *cants* of the
scale in weighing.

'As the good wife's wheel could not stand still, a pound of lint
or two must not be forgot, as she had got her last stock off the
night before. The food and raiment being thus disposed of, what
was left was apportioned for odds and ends. Jackey wanted a pair
of clogs, Bobby a hat, father a pair of old boot feet for the pit, and
mother her backey.

'It would sometimes happen that an "awd furren little fellow
sitting in the newk" would put in his claim for a History Beuk or
Bullant, if deddy had a penny to spare. Such are the important
discussions and intricate calculations that took place in many a
well-regulated pitman's cottage after the goodman has handed over
his fortnight's earnings to his better half.' *The Pitman's Pay and
Other Poems*, p.25.

37. J. E. Preston [no relation], 'Benjamin Preston', *North Country
    Poets*, I, p.178. Joseph Burgess, *A Potential Poet? His auto-
    biography and verse* (Ilford: Publications, n.d. [1927]), p.58.
39. See A. L. Lloyd, *Folk Song in England*, pp.376–84; and Tom
    Gilfellon's introduction to *Tommy Armstrong Sings* (Newcastle:
    Frank Graham, 1971) for biographical information.
40. *Tommy Armstrong Sings*, pp.40–1.
41. John Watts, *The Facts of the Cotton Famine* (Manchester:
    A. Ireland, 1886), pp.121ff. For working-class reactions to the
    Cotton Famine, see 'The Diary of John Ward of Clitheroe, Weaver,
    1860–64', ed. R. Sharpe France, *Transactions of the Historic
    Society of Lancashire and Cheshire*, 55 (1953), pp.137–85; Edwin
    Waugh, *Home Life of the Lancashire Factory Folk During the
    Cotton Famine* (Manchester: John Heywood, 1867); James
    Ramsbottom, *Phases of Distress: Lancashire Rhymes* (Manchester:
    John Heywood, 1864); and Samuel Laycock, 'Lancashire Lyrics',

Warblin's fro' an Owd Songster, pp.41–66.

42. Unpub. notebook, Manchester Central Reference Library.
43. Harland and Wilkinson, pp.512–14.
44. *Stories, Sketches and Rhymes, Chiefly in the Rochdale Dialect*, pp.xix–xxii.
45. 'The Lancashire Dialect', a speech given before the Manchester Literary Club, 19 November 1883, reprinted in the *Manchester Literary Club Papers*, 10 (1884), p.404.
46. *Warblin's fro' an Owd Songster*, pp.214–15.
47. *The Poets and Poetry of Blackburn (1793–1902)*, ed. George Hull (Blackburn: J. & G. Toulmin, 1902), pp.363–4. Baron was a prolific poet in both dialect and standard English from an early age. In 1877 he attracted the notice of Waugh, who spoke warmly of the poem 'Art and Song'. In 1879 he received first prize (an 11-volume set of Tennyson) at the Montague Street Congregational Chapel May Festival for his poem 'May Time'. For a long time he published poems in standard English under his own name or his initials, and all of his dialect writings under thypseudonym 'Jack o' Ann's'.
48. For a full discussion of these problems in the twentieth century, see Richard Hoggart, *The Uses of Literacy* (London: Chatto and Windus, 1957), pp.141ff.

CHAPTER 6 The Music Hall: From a Class to a Mass Entertainment

> . . . the working men of England at the present day are nothing more
> or less than, than — than working men!
>
> Dan Leno

The appeal of dialect readings remained necessarily limited not only by the provincial character of the material, but also by the narrow treatment of acceptable 'family' subjects. Working men and women who sought greater variety of entertainment went to the free-and-easy taverns and music halls. The 1843 Theatre Act made it illegal to perform plays and serve refreshments on the same premises, but public houses could still offer singers and acts that did not involve more than one person on stage at a time.[1] In the early free-and-easies the emphasis was upon drinking and eating; the entertainment was often whoever happened to be available, with the greater variety the better. The music halls, however, shifted the emphasis to the bill of entertainment, and established a formula of five-minute 'turns', cheap admissions and accessible drink that did not change through the First World War. The sheer quantity of published material on the music hall and the importance and length of its history make it impossible to survey the entire field.[2] The emphasis in this chapter will be on the working-class characteristics of the songs and the artistes, and how they altered as the halls shifted from a class to a mass form of recreation.

This chapter can be linked with Chapter 1 as part of a consideration of popular entertainment divorced from specific class interests. Both street literature and the music hall were rooted in the working class, but subject matter, authorship and performance were not limited to it. Working men who sought to improve themselves or their class wrote literature to re-enforce class values or to escape from them personally. In contrast, broadside and music hall songs were written almost entirely for entertainment, with little direct didactic purpose. Both were attacked as sources of immorality, an accusation both outlived. Broadsides flourished during a period of economic and industrial growth accompanied by the rise in urbanization and literacy; they died when other media were found more exciting, accurate or interesting. The music hall rose at a time of economic consolidation and growth in imperialism; it died under the impact of American ragtime, jazz and variety revue. It tried at first to absorb these influences, but the new rhythms of New Orleans jazz were more powerful and all-embracing than the Stephen Foster imitations of Leslie Stuart.

Throughout the nineteenth century written and performed literature were divided, with only dialect able to bridge the two. By and large serious literature was written, popular literature recited or sung. The music hall marks the emergence of another form of oral working-class culture. Like street literature, it depended upon performers to bring out its special characteristics; at the same time songs were printed so listeners could sing them and revive the memory of hearing them. Moreover, the music hall was an assertion of the validity of the shared artistic experience, as opposed to the more private world of poetry and fiction. The artiste performed in public, seeking the approval of his audience, just as had the broadside seller and trade-union singer. But unlike the earlier singers, the artiste was a professional, usually working under contract, and his audience had paid in advance to hear him.

Beginning as an entertainment by and for the working class, with a sprinkling of bohemians, by the end of the nineteenth century the music hall had a mass appeal, and was produced entirely by professionals who realized immense profits. The major shift was away from a form of entertainment that spoke directly to the working class out of a shared experience to one that was provided for 'the masses' by those familiar with their experience, but apart from it. From the beginning the halls had glorified mateyness, paying your own way and good times now -- all of which infuriated some elderly ex-Chartists who wished to imbue their fellow workers with a greater desire for self-improvement and aspiration. Some social criticism from a class perspective had been a part of the performances of the earlier halls, but it became muted with the development of the stereotyped comic working man. The broadest humour, the most obvious dupes and the most widely accepted social pleasures came to form much of the subject matter of an artiste seeking fame and popularity.

Despite these limitations, many artistes portrayed a wide range of affectionate and realistic working-class characters. The popular coster-mongers of the 1890s pandered to many of the characteristics described above, but at the same time they were an assertion of the importance and validity of the ordinary street vendor as a subject for inter-pretation. The best artistes came to express through their song and patter many of the emotions of their audience, providing a means of communication and interaction for thousands who listened to them. Moreover, with so much emphasis upon self-help in society at large, the music halls provided an antidote in praising man as he is and not as he should or could be. The music hall is crucial to the study of working-class literature as the summation of an oral and communal art expressive of class interests.

I
The Rise of the Music Hall

The music hall came from three main sources: the tavern free-and-easies, the travelling theatrical companies and the song-and-supper clubs centred in London. Before the opening of the halls proper, the song-and-supper clubs had been for men only. Working women, however, had long attended the tavern free-and-easies, greatly elevating the moral tone, if one middle-class informant is to be trusted.[3] These free-and-easies were the most direct and important ancestors of the halls. Pub owners encouraged local singers to perform upon a rude stage at one end of the house; songs about beer, conviviality and good fellowship led patrons to stay longer. Working-class couples throughout England crowded into taverns on Saturday nights to hear the latest singers; it was only a matter of time before an entrepreneur built a separate hall and offered nightly entertainment.

Many proprietors of free-and-easies discovered that theirpatrons drank less when entertainment was provided, although a full house could be anticipated. They began to charge threepence to be redeemed on liquor to offset possible losses; once a patron began to drink he rarely bought only threepence worth. Another method employed in the smaller taverns was to hire a 'butler' who passed around a 'big jug' from table to table. When the vocalist or fiddler or dancer took his or her break, a hat was passed around, paying for the jug and the entertainment.[4] Most of the performers in such taverns were similar to Blind Willie and other early semi-professional entertainers who sang because some physical disability prevented them from earning a regular living. In Lancashire one of the most popular turns was clog, or step, dancing — a form of tap dancing with wooden-soled shoes. Factory workers of both sexes knew many elaborate steps, and could be seen practising after work on street corners with friends. They followed clog dancers carefully and were very critical of poor performances. In all of these free-and-easies the audiences engaged in a great deal of hooting, joking, clapping and singing. They often knew the performers personally, and so eagerly gave their approval of an act. Or they might havecome to see one of the many touring Irish tenors who had found their singing and fiddling skills brought more money than unskilled labour. Obviously as the nightly donations grew, more ambitious and talented individuals were attracted to a possible full-time career.

In chapter 10 of *Sybil* (1845), Disraeli describes a popular singing room. Admittance to 'The Temple of the Muses' was threepence, paid upon entering the Cat and Fiddle public house, and climbing to the first floor. The long hall was richly decorated on the walls and ceiling, with panels portraying various literary and musical scenes. Red velvet and gold stucco were plentiful. About three or four hundred persons were crowded together, eating, drinking, smoking and talking at tables. Most of the entertainment was a rather hit-or-miss affair, depending on who was passing through town and which local amateurs wished to try out their latest act or song. A proper tone was maintained by the manager, who watched the behaviour of his patrons carefully, and encouraged elegant good manners. For Disraeli the attraction of the place was obvious: the Temple of the Muses was warmer and jollier – and more cultured – than most working-class homes.

Singing every night or so in a free-and-easy, amidst smoke, noise and drink was arduous training for any young person with romantic notions about the entertainment world. But it was child's play in comparison with the life of a travelling actor. Travelling theatre companies, from as few as three or four persons to as many as thirty, followed the various fairs, race-meetings and hoppings from the early spring till the late autumn. Most of them dispersed in the winter, leaving the actors to find work as best they could; some certainly became paid performers in the free-and-easies. A few companies found it profitable to keep together, renting a hall for several weeks in each of the smaller industrial centres (in the larger ones they risked competing unsuccessfully with established theatres). A company on tour would arrive a day or so before the fair began and set up its tent-theatre in the best possible location. No seats were provided, but prices were low: 6d. front and 3d. rear. The shows were specifically designed to appeal to rural and small-town working people out for a good time. They were normally only twenty minutes apiece, running continuously, so the hawker in front could always assure waiting onlookers that a show was just about to begin. One travelling showman from Leeds bragged that his company gave *Richard III* twenty times in seven hours.[5] It was excellent training for a music-hall career, since rapid character changes, immediate characterization of a part and instant audience rapport were all demanded.

Travelling showmen survived on their wit and clowning skill; they could gauge a crowd immediately and begin talking and guying individuals. Billy Purvis (1784–1853), the most famous travelling showman in the North, loved nothing more than standing on the platform in front of his tent, encouraging passers-by:

> Spying some old acquaintance in the crowd below, he would shout out, 'Assay*, Marget, are ye not cummin' up to see wor show; how away, lass, an' bring aw yer bonny bairns wi' ye if is oney† for awd acquaintance s'yek; de ye not mind the time when we were sweethearts tegither. Its a lang time since, an aw've forgeen Geordy for knockin me heels out; but aw's glad to see ye l'uckin' as bonny as ivver! Howaway lass!' Then turning round, he would address his hearers on the other side. 'Walk up, ladies and gentlemen, we are just about to commence,you will have no time to wait; walk up! walk up! Or there is a side door behind, where any lady or gentleman may enter, who does not choose to cross the public stage.' This was said in as good English as could be desired -- and few could do it better when it suited his purpose. Then again, turning about, he added in the broadest vernacular, 'We hae te tawk to thor ignorint stuck-up gonials⁺ se as they knaw what yen says, but te ye, lads an' lasses, whe knaw thor muther tongue se weel, aw hev oney to say, that ye that are ower shemf'yced to cum up the lether○, can get in bi the door in Billy's backside.'⁶

Once in the tent a customer would see a shortened version of a Shakespeare play or a domestic comedy or a melodrama. The main event was usually preceded by a brief series of acts – singing, juggling, or clowning. Pantomimes were a popular substitution for a regular play. The fluid plot, constant action and variety made them easy to perform and pleased an audience that demanded colourful and dramatic entertainment. If a member of the company could not perform, his place was easily taken in a pantomime, or it could be rewritten to fit the talents of the substitute.

Billy Purvis's most famous comic routine was 'stealing the bundle'. A countryman would come on stage and carefully leave his bundle outside the door of a public house. Billy would enter in his clown's costume, with a solemn air of moral superiority. Bumping into the bundle, he would go into a long soliloquy of self-justification. Just as he made off with it the countryman would appear. Billy then explains, 'Aw thowt it wor lost, aw wis just teykin care on't, aw lives roond here.' The bundle

---

*Assay: I say   †if is oney: if it's only   ⁺gonials: stupid fellows   ○ lether: ladder

is replaced and the man goes back inside. Billy now makes no further
pretences, but kicks the bundle around the corner, knocks on the door
and warns the man that his bundle has been stolen. He runs after the
thief in the wrong direction, and Billy triumphantly picks up the
bundle and walks off stage.[7] The act invariably brought the house
down — Purvis's acting was superb, and through careful timing, amusing
asides (which changed in every performance) and comic skill, the act
remained an ever-fresh character study. The comedy rested on Billy's
moral duplicity but it was also an indirect attack on the moral
pretentiousness of society. It shared many characteristics with the turns
of later music-hall comedians. In large part the pleasure an audience
derived from watching Billy steal the bundle was the familiarity of the
routine — friends had told them all about it, and sure enough it was as
wonderful as they had said. The act, however, differed from the later
music-hall turns because Billy did not treat the foolish countryman who
leaves his bundle outside as a comic butt; he is simply the device that
sets the scene for Billy. Moreover, contemporaries commented on how
each performance differed, as Billy responded to different audiences.
The music hall was far more mannered, and audiences expected their
heroes and heroines to repeat the same turn without variation night
after night.

One music-hall artiste who particularly benefited from working
under Billy Purvis was Newcastle's Ned Corvan (1830–65). Like Purvis,
who had been trained originally as a carpenter, Corvan had no theatrical
background, but began as an apprentice to a sailmaker. He was so
impressed with Billy's show that he soon left to join him as a singer and
bit-actor. In 1850 when offered the post of 'local singer' at a new
concert hall in Newcastle, Corvan left acting. His early training,
however, led him to emphasize the dramatic routine accompanying a
song more than the song itself; he also had a weak voice and incipient
tuberculosis (which cut short his career), making it essential to conserve
his strength. Audiences throughout the North loved his parodies of
local characters, including Purvis and other famous actors. Corvan also
liked to draw sketches of sacred events and political celebrities, while
solemnly singing and playing his violin.[8]

The finest quality about Corvan was his unfailing sympathy for
working men and the families of the poor. His father had died when he
was less than five, so he grew up in the streets of Newcastle, doing odd
jobs to help his mother make ends meet. One favourite song was 'The
Toon Improvement Bill, or Ne Pleyce noo te play' (see Appendix).
Urban 'improvement' then as now did not take into consideration the

needs of slum children when a profit could be made — in this case a
new railway station. Even in his straightforward characterizations of
town eccentrics, Corvan's wit and understanding about the difficulties
of life on the edge of poverty come through. In 'The Soop Kitchen' an
Irishman, a Scotsman and a Tynesider compare notes, in their
respective dialects, onthe quality of the soup in comparison with their
national delicacies of oatmeal and Irish stew. The pain and frustration
of needing charity received Corvan's delicate humour and respect.

Equally, he was able to treat comically the follies and ambitions of
his audience. He had himself run away to the theatre, and so could
delight in 'The Stage Struck Keelman'.

Aw's Jimmy Julius Hannibal Caesar,
A genius born for shootin'.
Aw can recite Hamlick, King Dick, the Warlock o' the Glen,
The Lonely Man o' the Tatie Garth, the King o' the Leers, Othello,
The Smashed bug; or the blood-stained bowlster, my neyme is Norval;
Noo, aw's the lad for spootin*.
Aw've studied Shakenspear, aw ken his points or rather,†
Although the folks that's here little knaws it aw's an awthur.

SPOKEN — Yis, aws' an awthur, aw've wrote a play entitled the
Flash o' Thunder; or, the Desolate Tree by the Roadside: an' the
Lonely Man o' theblasted Heath: an' the four eyed Murderer. It's in
fourteen acts an' a half. The music arranged by Frederick Jimmy
Appollo Lumphead for 9 Gugaws. — Aw'll recite a' dark passage oot
ont, as a specient+.

Scene 1st, a coalpit — blue mountains in the distance. — We'll say
the mountains is in America.

'Twas a dark, very dark neet, the sun peep'd oot before the skies,
the wind fell in fearful torrents, the clouds fell to the earth, and the
donkeys turned ther backs on the comin' storm, and with thor
melodious noise, gave a tarrefic he, he, ha, he, ha. 'Twas then a
perused my way by the blasted heath, meditating Codjitation and
Silly Quisin○, when something seized me, a cold sweat came o'er my
sleeved whiscoat. I fell doon insensible, an' when aw recovered, aw
observed the four-eyed murderer gazin' upon me, aw seized him an'
cast him forth into the boilin' cauld water: at that excitin' moment
aw flew towards the ruins of the old abbey. Hush! whast as that?

---

*spootin: spouting, declaiming   †aw ken his points or rather: I know his
points all right   +specient: specimen   ○ Silly Quisin: soliloquizing.

Hark, I see a voice! no, no! tis the wind whistlin' through the air! In this tent I'll pitch my field! O let me behold the green fields of Sandgate, the blue mountains of Geyteshead and Jarrow, the tripe market where youthful fancy guided maw three halfpence a week pocket brass. Extacy – a shower o' black puddins thickens my imagination. Light! light! Richard's himself again.[9]

The piling up of details, comic inversions of famous titles and the parodying of melodramatic conventions create a vivid picture of a stage-struck keelman. Played with grandiose gestures and exaggerated costuming, the act invariably brought the house down. Yet, despite his zany wildness, like the later genius of Dan Leno, Corvan always respected the dreams of grandeur and hopes for improvement among working men and women. The theatricality of the music hall gave an individual performer the scope to interpret working men such as the keelman in different ways, playing to different audiences. In other hands than Corvan's such acts could degenerate into a mockery of working men.

It is more difficult to evaluate the impact of the legitimate theatre on the music hall. The two stages shared many characteristics and throughout the century often competed for the same audience. Few plays, with the exception of dramatizations of novels by authors such as Brierley and Waugh, were actually written by working men. Those workers who became actors, such as Ned Corvan, were more likely to start in a travelling show or free-and-easy, and then go into the better paying halls. However, many early music-hall performers did gain their initial training as minor actors and singersfor theatre companies. Shakespeare and domestic melodrama, with the occasional topical play, were very popular in working-class neighbourhoods. Amateur theatricals were also common among younger people. As the music halls developed in the 'fifties and 'sixties, they offered entertainment to customers who were probably already regular theatre goers. They did not replace the popular theatre, but since they served drink, they were more risqué and exciting. The theatre served the need for an emotionally satisfying drama in its comedies and melodramas; the music hall served the need for conviviality and a shared entertainment.

Theatrical influences continued throughout the century because many minor actors switched backand forth between the legitimate stage and the halls. When engagements were scarce, actors with varying success attempted a few turns on the boards. Leading artistes were frequently invited to play important parts in Christmas pantomimes, though few were ever given serious roles. Many comedians and character actors in the halls considered their acting skill to be superior to that found on the legitimate stage because they had only five minutes to present their piece and win over an audience. Moreover, an actor's achievement was judged by the completeness of his identification with the character portrayed, whereas an artiste succeeded only through the projection of his own unique stage personality. His act depended upon a close rapport with his audience, who demanded a stylized performance that was instantly recognizable. Despite these differences, actors and artistes both played roles, rather than themselves. Corvan was not a stage-struck keelman, even if some members of his audience were. He remained first an actor with an act, setting him off from his audience in a way that was much less characteristic of the amateurs and semi-professionals who performed in the free-and-easies. These entertainers were themselves first – the Irish tenor was Irish, and his stage persona was simply a smoother, public projection of himself. Although the distinction is fine, generally a full-time music-hall artiste took on many different roles, within a narrow range, acting out a persona suitable to the song. He projected a public image that was a combination of an act – the stage-struck keelman, maudlin cockney or country innocent – and himself as a familiar stage personality.

In spite of the continual cross fertilization between the theatre and the music hall, the inheritance from the song-and-supper clubs may have been more important because it set the tone of the halls for so long. An atmosphere of relaxed, slightly risqué social behaviour marked the halls until the end, even when strongly mixed with a self-conscious respectability. No matter what entrepreneur might claim that his Palace offered family entertainment, Marie Lloyd was ready elsewhere to remind him and her audience that 'a little of what you fancy does you good.' The song-and-supper rooms and the pleasure gardens of the 1830s and '40s had been fashionable resorts for the demi-monde and the bohemian; they were for all who sought pleasure outside the narrow boundaries of Victorian respectability. The songs sung at such famous places as the Cyder Cellars, the Coal Hole or Evans's supper-rooms reflect this raffishness apart from any class distinctions. W. G. Ross's famous 'Ballad of Sam Hall', about a chimney sweep waiting to be hanged, excited listeners for its brutal and unrepentent violence, not because it was a commentary on the life of a 'sweep or because they might find any identification with his plight. The thrill of difference – not similarity – united the audience and the performer.

A feature of the song-and-supper clubs was the varied backgrounds of the performers as well as the audience. Ned Corvan's staunch working-class background was matched by Sam Collins (1826–65), an ex-chimney sweep who sang comic Irish numbers (The most famous, 'No Irish Need Apply', was said to be a comment on thehiring practices of the Great Exhibition's management). Sam Cowell (1822–66), the star at Evans's, came from a professional acting family. His father had beena popular actor in America, where Sam began his career; through his mother he was connected with the Siddons and Kemble families. He sang and acted many long-winded burlesques at Evans's, but his most famous song was 'The Ratcatcher's Daughter', a mock-pastoral known as 'the most tragic of his comic songs'. It is a story of the love between the daughter who sells sprats and the man who cried 'Lily-vite sand'.

> Now rich and poor, both far arid near
> In marriage, Sir, they sought her;
> But at friends & foes she cocked her nose
> Did this pretty little Ratcatcher's Daughter.
> For there was a man, cried 'Lily-vite Sand',
> In Cupid's net had caught her;
> And right over head and ears in love,
> Vent the pretty little Ratcatcher s Daughter.
>> Heu! tu diddle u!
>> Heu! tu tiddle u!

She has a premonition of death, and sure enough, the day before the wedding 'she tumbled into the vater', and went 'down to the bottom, all smothered in mud'. This unheroic and unbeautiful end leads the lover to suicide:

> Vhen Lily-vite Sand he heard the news
> His eyes ran down with water,
> Said he, 'in love I'll constant prove;
> And -- blow me if I'll live long arter!
> So he cut his throat with a pane of glass,
> And he stabbed his Jackass arter;
> So here is an end of Lily-vite Sand,
> Jackass and the Ratcatcher's Daughter!
>> Heu! tu diddle u
>> Heu! tu diddle u![11]

In an earlier age ballads had been about the aristocracy, but for the

248 The Industrial Muse

common people; pastorals had been about shepherds and shepherdesses, but for the aristocracy. An urban pastoral mocks these conventions. Street callers can never be romantic figures. The poor are scorned for having genteel emotions, which themselves are derided. The song, said to be written by a clergyman, is typical of and the most popular among many tavern songs of the mid-'fifties. An uneasy alliance of the traditional broadside ballad with the newer self-mockery of the city pubs, the song needs an audience of more than one class for all its implications to be enjoyed; its appeal may have been greatest among those who were moving from one class to another. Although the music halls were the primary working-class entertainment of the later nineteenth century, they always retained an element of this anti-working class bias, from the declassé world of the rogue and the bohemian.

By the middle of the century 'Temples of the Muses' throughout England were offering nightly entertainment in return for a threepenny or sixpenny 'refreshment ticket', redeemable for liquor. Although many preceded him, Charles Morton, manager of the Canterbury Arms tavern, Westminster Bridge, London, is credited as 'the father of the halls', with his opening of the Canterbury Hall in 1852. Several of the features of Evans's supper-rooms were carried over, including the boy choristers, excerpts from light operas, and at the cost of £80 per week, Sam Cowell.[12] Morton's success led to the widespread investment in separately built halls, apart from taverns, with continuous entertainment and a charge of admission that was not redeemable. Enormous costs could be met because enormous profits were assured. For a time the public's demand appeared insatiable. Whatever control working-class audiences exerted on the form and content of this entertainment was soon lost to the managers and their stars. While audiences could make or break a performer – or a hall – their power was limited to acceptance or rejection.

The first Canterbury Music Hall held 700 persons, but was enlarged to hold 1,500, the size of most music halls until such magnates as Edward Moss, Richard Thornton, Maurice de Frece and Oswald Stoll began building Empires, Hippodromes and Palaces throughout England in the mid-1880s. The large halls were expensive to run, so managers introduced the 'twice-nightly' programme, emptying and filling the hall twice in an evening; this further separated the show from the drink provided. The greater emphasis on the former encouraged a reputation for respectability. These changes were gradual and occurred only at the larger halls; the traditional halls continued to exist into the twentieth century (for a comparison of early and late halls, see Plates 23 and 24).

In 1892 a journalist, F. Anstey, distinguished four types of music halls: the aristocratic variety theatre of the West End, around Leicester Square; the smaller West End halls; the larger middle-class halls, found in less fashionable districts and in the suburbs; and the minor halls of the poor districts. The most distinguishing characteristic among audiences, aside from the formal attire at the West End halls, was the degree of concern for the entertainment. At the first two attention was intermittent and languid, at the third, everyone was 'perfectly ready to be pleased with dull songs, hoary jokes, stale sentiments and clap-trap patriotism.' At the poorest halls the audience was young and largely male, the odours thick and pervasive, but the noisy approval or disapproval almost constant. Anstey felt that the level of performance among artistes and song writers was low at every class of hall, commenting, 'It would be infinitely more difficult to fail than succeed in satisfying a music hall audience.'[13] But he took for granted the idleness of time spent at the halls, and the essential similarity of intentions amongst all levels of society, regardless of their attire or the price of their ticket.

The 1890s was the golden age of the music hall. All classes were attracted and a sufficient variety of halls existed to cater to all tastes. Money was freely spent, not only to obtain a star, but also for rich decorations, electrical lighting and complicated stage apparatus. Yet the halls declined rapidly early in the twentieth century with the arrival of revue, ragtime and films. Although many halls staggered on until the talkies came in the late 1920s, most of the larger halls had already been converted into cinemas or theatres for spectaculars. The fancy palaces had to be filled or torn down. Crucially, the music halls were not replaced with newer forms of working-class entertainment, but with mass entertainment, attempting to reach an ever-wider audience. They were a brief but important part of working-class culture in the later nineteenth century, in which the movement from the local and particular to the metropolitan and national can be traced.

Early music-hall audiences were usually young, 18–25, and either unmarried or newly married. At the halls they could relax and enjoy the company of their mates and of the opposite sex. The more daring factory women and servant girls would occasionally go as a group to a hall, each hoping to meet a favourite young man, or a new prospect. Men were always in the majority; they came to the halls because they might be lonely and away from home for the first time, or because they wanted to dress up and be swells, or because their friends

all went. Music halls in the suburbs had family entertainment, and those
in the West End, where evening dress was required, had many more
raffish men and women looking for thrills. The halls themselves were a
variety of sizes, and had seats at several prices; the cheapest could go as
low as a penny for the rear of the gallery. Quite early tables were
replaced by rows of seats with ledges for placing drinks and snacks.
Beer or porter were the most popular drinks, but here again an
impressive young swell never drank anything less than whisky. Glowing
stories were told of the marvellous lamb chops and baked potatoes or
sausage-and-mash to be had at the early Canterbury Hall. But as the
halls became more dignified food became a smaller item on the bill of
fare. It was customary to shout, talk, and throw things in some halls,
but decorum was increasingly enforced. The halls were always described
as hot, smoky and crowded. The gas lights, noise and the constant
movement of waiters all contributed to this impression. For many
young men, cooped up in an all-male office or warehouse all day the
close proximity of women, drink and smoke made a giddy and inviting
atmosphere that broke down their natural shyness and difficulty in
speaking to women of their own class. Critics particularly fulminated
against this element in the halls. But even the most negative
descriptions could not avoid making the halls sound like alluring centrés
of dissipation:

> The weak young man who asks the Great Jack Bang to have a drink
> (he sings the wonderful song 'I didn't tell the missis where I'd been'
> with much loudness of voice and variety of facial contortion, and by
> extra hurry and roar glosses over the fact that the lines do not scan
> and the air clashes with all ideas of harmony) has an idea that it will
> enhance his importance in the eyes of his fellows to be seen
> hob-nobbing with so big a personage. The Great Jack Bang, who is a
> man with a blotchy face and a red neck, and wears a billy-cock hat
> and a tweedy-grey ulster reaching to his feet, accepts him by saying,
> 'Thanks. A brandy-and-soda and a cigar.' The 'Thanks' is the only
> part addressed to the weak youth, the rest of it being said in a
> jocular way to the barmaid; and whilst the great man takes no
> further notice of his self-constituted entertainer than by just
> nodding to him when he commences to drink, the latter, who of
> course has been unable to do anything less than order two
> 'brandies-and-sodas' and two cigars, as it would ill-become him to
> drink threepenn'orth of whiskey whilst his guest was regaling himself
> so differently, finds himself called upon for two shillings, when his

highest flight of fancy, before embarking on the enterprise, had been
reached to sixpence each.[14]

However sleazy the author of *Tempted London* makes it sound, many
of his readers would like to have been the weak young man
    Many performers were like 'the Great Jack Bang' and mingled with
the nightly crowd at the side-bar after their turn, but most did so in
order to boost their fame and to help the management improve its
liquor sales. Life backstage was hectic and competitive. Everyone
shared the crowded dressing rooms, which were often made more
chaotic by the presence of saleswomen who had bribed the side-door
guard to let them in; they offered such timely necessities as extra pairs
of stockings, collar buttons, studs and make-up. Almost all artistes
dressed in costumes suited to their song; they usually changed some
part of the costume after each song, so many women kept a servant just
off-stage to help with the quick changes. Some stars, such as George
Leybourne, Maria Lloyd and Vesta Tilley gained fame for their
meticulous dressing on and off stage. Make-up was always worn. Some
of the minstrels wore black-cork not only to imitate the American
Negro, but also to differentiate themselves from the mass of sentimental singers. It was considered bad form to watch other artistes, so a
performer usually arrived just before the end of the turn previous to his
own. The chairman would introduce the artiste before he appeared,
putting an edge on the audience's anticipation. Then the band would
start up and the artiste rushed forward. The famous could expect to be
greeted with a round of applause; beginners were usually permitted two
or three verses before the catcalls might begin. The success of a song
rested on the catchiness of the tune, so a performer always had the
band play an extra chorus. The song itself was sung with gestures
befitting the words; these actions could be quite subtle, although the
larger halls encouraged a broad, breezy style that the most distant
customer could see. Almost all turns included some audience
participation – one song might have a chorus for all to join in, or it
might only be the nods, winks and gestures of the artiste that caught
the attention of the audience. Some artistes in their patter would
appeal to a particular section of the halls, some picked out a dashing
young man to flatter, others waved kisses to the gallery. Once off stage
the lucky artiste quickly changed and went on to his next engagement
in the hansom waiting outside. The rest joined Jack Bang.
    An essential feature of the early halls was the chairman or master of
ceremonies. Dressed in immaculate formal attire he called out the turns

and addressed the audience with admonitions to order drinks, to appreciate a forthcoming beginner, or to applaud our next old friend. He received tips from all the artistes who wished him to say a few extra words in their favour; at the same time the management expected him to cover for the non-appearance of a star by means of his own singing and patter, often in the face of disgruntled threats and missiles. The height of social aspiration for many a young man was to sit at the chairman's table and pay for his drinks under the eyes of the entire audience. The chairman lent tone and dignity to the proceedings, yet the unruly members of an audience subjected him, and the young swells sitting with him, to jokes and a wrath aimed at all who represented authority and order. A relationship of wit and repartee based upon respect, and some dislike, developed between the most skilful chairmen and their audiences. In the larger halls, however, he could not be heard, and was replaced with a billboard announcing each turn. This change was an important break between the audience and the performance. Shouting to the chairman, joining him in a chorus or cheering his jokes were all means whereby an audience participated in the making of an evening's programme. Without the chairman to give unity to the evening, each artiste worked in isolation, controlling the responses of an immense hall the best he could. While the audience could still give a performer 'the bird', they became more passive onlookers in the new Palaces and Empires of the early twentieth century.

The mocking of the chairman was little in comparison with the treatment meted out to a new entertainer, should he or she falter or displease the crowd. Early halls usually had a net over the orchestra pit to protect the innocent players from missiles thrown at an unpopular performer. A comedian was expected to have a quick wit that could answer any harassment. One night as Ned Corvan started his chalkboard sketch a voice called out, 'Myek us a cuddy [ass], Ned.' Corvan immediately replied, 'All reet, stand up.'[15] Bessie Bellwood (1857–96) (Plate 25), noted for her brash manner, frequently entered into slanging matches. Making her first appearance at the Bermondsey Star as a replacement for a local favourite, she was hissed as she came on stage. The chairman attempted to shame a coalheaver into silence by declaring him no gentleman if he would not let her perform. Such mild tactics were useless, so Bessie took him on. Speaking for five and three-quarter minutes (the length of a turn),

at the end, she gathered herself together for one supreme effort, and hurled at him an insult so bitter with scorn, so sharp with insight into his career and character, so heavy with prophetic curse, that strong men drew and held their breath, while it passed over them, and women hid their faces and shivered.

Then she folded her arms and stood silent, and the house, from floor to ceiling, rose and cheered her until there was no more breath left in its lungs.[16]

Even granting poetic license on the part of the author, Bessie was clearly no one to trifle with. Audiences loved her and an atmosphere that permitted such fighting matches and open jollity between the sexes. These occasions also had a mythic importance, recalling ancient fliting-matches and folk tales about the devil and those with too quick a tongue.

During the early years of the halls most performers wrote their own songs and patter, choosing familiar tunes for the music. Occasionally they would collaborate with a local song writer; Joseph Robson, the Newcastle schoolmaster, supplied songs for artistes, the Miners' Association and respectable society. Arthur Lloyd (1840–1904), one of the last of the lion comiques (a swell), wrote over 200 songs with such memorable words as the chorus, 'Not for Joe, Not for Joe, Not for Joseph, if he knows it!'[17] Before songs were copyrighted a performer was frequently credited with those he had made famous. 'The Great Vance' (Alfred Vance, 1840–89) was described as the author of his popular 'Costermonger Joe' (see Plate 26), but so were a W. Bain and an Ernee Clark.[18] In time most artistes found it easier to buy songs. Marie Lloyd was sent thousands by hopeful admirers; she would go over themall, selecting whatever struck her fancy. Yet many of her turns were flops. Despite the difficulties in obtaining just the right song, the performer remained in command. Few artistes gave exclusive rights to any one publisher, so they had to be lured. Publishers sent them expensive gifts and encouraged them to drop by their offices to hear a new song.[19] A vivid portrait of the singer, and not the writer, was always on the cover of the sheet music in order to attract buyers (see Plates 31 & 32). The price, usually 3s., was too high for those in the gallery, but sixpenny popular editions and penny broadsides of the words were easily available.

The life of a song writer for the halls is difficult to document since so few historians have cared to investigate his career in comparison with the many biographies of stars. The majority appear to have been born to the halls, or at least to the entertainment world. Fred Gilbert and Joseph Tabrar started as boy choristers at Evans's. George Ware began

as a singer and finished as an agent. During his long association with the
halls he wrote 'The Dark Girl Dressed inBlue', Leybourne's first hit, and
'The Boy that I love is up in the Galley', performed by Jenny Hill,
Nelly Power and Marie Lloyd. Royalties appear to have almost
invariably gone exclusively to the singer.G. D. Hunt with difficulty
persuaded 'The Great McDermott' (1845–1901) to buy 'We Don't
Want to Fight, but by Jingo, If We Do', for a guinea – and in the
process boosted McDermott's career and the Conservative Party to new
heights.[20] Gilbert received a guinea, the usual amount at the time, from
Charles Coborn for the singing rights to 'The Man Who Broke the Bank
at Monte Carlo'. Messrs. Francis, Day and Hunter, publishers, gave him
£10 for his share in the publication rights; they refused Coborn the £30
he demanded, and settled for £5 plus a royalty. Coborn eventually
received £600.[21]

Most tales about song writers tell of their close, often amusing
relationships with various singers. Many were hangers-on who through
bravado or free drinks would manage to sell a song. One method of
reaching performers was tipping the stage-door guard to get backstage.
Once there the writer joined others selling various goods – hosiery,
grease paint, photographs and the like – and attempted to catch the
eye, or ear, of a star. One informant in the 1890s explained how
important it was to dress well and appear wealthy. He dropped by
'Poverty Junction', the York tavern in Waterloo Road, daily to drink
with the 'pro.'s', often standing rounds. He made it a rule never to part
with a manuscript until he had been paid in full – rarely more than a
guinea, although the more famous might receive as much as two
pounds. Some received as little as five shillings. Melodies were easily
bought from other writers or composers, for a price that varied between
three pence and ten shillings. A lucky writer would sell a topical song to
a performer and then be paid five shillings or so every fortnight for
updated verses.[22] Although a few writers did well, it was a precarious
living, demanding not only an acute sense of the market, but also many
of the qualities that made a star – pertinacity, an ingratiating manner
and boundless confidence. It was not an occupation any working man
could enter easily; far moreworking-class men and women were
performers than were writers, composers or managers.

II
The Music-Hall Entertainer

Anonymous broadsides were reflections of the attitudes and emotions of the poor and of working people. Their authors did not separate themselves from their audience; like the trade unionists who wrote songs under the stress of a strike, much of their best work was the result of experiences shared with their readers. Dialect writers, while honoured by the upper classes for specific works, usually remained a part of their working-class readership, and reflected many of its values. Although both music-hall songs and dialect verse often dealt with similar topics, the music hall style and perspective were essentially different. No swells, saucy comediennes or coons strutted across the penny-reading stage. In contrast to other working-class literature, the music hall depended upon the star system. Men and women went to the halls to hear their favourites, who, more often than not, remembered poverty and labour but now earned astonishing sums. These artistes did not so much reflect working-class values as integrate them into particular sketches. Vignettes of a Cockney come into money, or on holiday or sitting by a cradle all embodied particular ideals recognized by a Cockney audience, but each was stamped by the performers personality. Audiences identified with a familiar stereotype, but recognized the separate genius of the interpreter. The music hall was a *made* communal art, and not a natural expression of class life. The self-conscious urban working class could not return to the folk culture of the past.

Whatever his routine, an artiste was always known for his personal style – even Dan Leno and Maria Lloyd worked within a few types which they varied with endless imagination throughout their careers. Unlike modern audiences, the music-hall devotees demanded the familiar; a performer could not introduce a radically different style lest he risk losing his career. G. H. Chirgwin (1855–1922), 'The One-Eyed Kaffir', so called for the white diamond shape over one eye amidst burnt-cork make-up, during his long career performed his one-string fiddle routine without variation. Those who found they could not break from a particular stereotype, such as Albert Chevalier, occasionally attempted new character sketches as part of a one-man show on the legitimate stage or while on tour in foreign countries.[23] One hit made the name of a performer, and the ascent was usually rapid, but the gruelling hours, drink and living style destroyed many before they had to face a slow fall from fame. The rise in salaries could be equally spectacular. George Leybourne (1840–84) started at 30s. a week at the Canterbury Music Hall, and was soon given a year's engagement at £25 per week. After the success of 'Champagne Charlie' his salary rose to £120 per week.[24] Immediately after the First World War Marie Lloyd earned as much as £600 for a week's engagement; her annual earnings during these years averaged £10,000.[25]

Such wages were not, of course, typical. In the 'sixties when Leybourne and Vance vied with each other for greater fame and money stars usually worked only one house at a standard weekly wage. They were given several turns at prime times (9.30–11.00 p.m.), and in between would join friends at the bar or promenade. However, artistes soon found they could earn more by booking at several halls; since performances ran continuously from as early as 6.30 p.m. until past midnight, a turn could be worked at as many as five different places each night. Even after the system of twice-nightly shows was introduced stars could perform at many places in an evening. As the halls became larger and fewer in number after 1900, stars were often booked with exclusive engagements including a guarantee that they would perform at no other hall within the radius of so many miles. Contracts of this sort involved even higher salaries than usual.

In the 1890s a working man's club paid 3s.6d. to 5s. a turn, consisting of two or three songs plus encores; they had only ten, as opposed to the more usual fifteen to twenty, turns for an evening. A small music hall paid about £1 per week for the less popular turns, and £3 to £7 for the best. A West End hall paid £4 per week for less popular, and as much as £25 for the best, with a few exceptional stars receiving more. If a star worked three or four houses every night he earned a weekly income of £50 to £100. The yearly income of an artiste has been estimated at £150 to £400 for the third rate; £400 to £700 for the second rate; and £1000 to £3000 for the first rate. Earnings were higher than for the equivalent actors, but expenses were greater. Most established artistes had agents, whose standard fee was 5 per cent of the gross earnings. The better-off kept a full-time cabby waiting at the stage door to take them from hall to hall; a servant was necessary to prepare the quick clothing and make-up changes. Poorer artistes advertised in *The Era* (1838–1939) and usually received very short runs. The very poorest hung out around 'Poverty Corner' waiting to be picked up by the managers of small halls for a week's engagement.[26] When steadily employed even the worst artistes could earn substantially more than a skilled labourer. Whatever fantasies a music-hall attender might have about gaining wealth could be fulfilled — with luck and talent — by joining those who sang about the pleasures of money. The success of Morton and other London entrepreneurs had a pervasive effect upon working-class entertainment. The lure of London had always been present for any ambitious working man anxious to prove himself in journalism and entertainment. A few, such as Gerald Massey, succeeded and are now often remembered as natives. Others, such as the dialect writers, preferred the surer success and admiration of their own locale. But the situation was different for music-hall artistes. Not only was fame and money concentrated in London; the system of booking agents, mass transportation and communication made it possible for a single entertainer to visit all major working-class centres in a matter of months. Whatever song was a hit in London quickly became one in the provinces. Regional performers were expected to imitate the more magnificent Londoners or take a lesser position when they passed through town. George Leybourne, The Great Vance and Jenny Hill were able to break into the London circuit, but by the 1880s and '90s most performers were native Londoners or came from professional families. Successful local stars usually had to settle for lower wages and billings. Often they could only succeed by exploiting their regional differences — the canny Scotsman, the comic Lancashire lad or the sentimental Irishman. Perhaps in revenge provincial audiences frequently booed Londoners they disliked. But the dominant movement in the music halls was away from the particular and toward the general. National fads and national stars could not help but alter the nature of a class culture which had received its life and vitality from the concrete, the familiar and the local.

During the early stages of the halls, from approximately 1850 to 1875, programmes included songs from many different sources. Traditional folk elements and folk songs, borrowed from an oral culture and the broadsides, were very much part of an evening's repertoire. In turn, broadside sellers hawked music-hall hits, giving credence to their claims of keeping up with the times. Often these broadsides used wood-cuts from an earlier age (see Plate 26).[27] George Leybourne, who is better known for his drinking songs, also sang such pieces as 'Rock the Cradle, John', about old farmer Hodge who married a young servant girl:

> Now Humphrey Hodge walks round the farm,
> And his hair is silver grey,

With his wife before, and the child on his arm.
The fruits of December and May.
And people smile at the silly old man,
Being wed to a wife so young . . .[28]

'Vilikins and His Dinah' is about the traditional dastardly father who
attempts to marry his daughter off for money; she and Vilikins foil his
plot through suicide. Light opera, glees and such parlour favourites as
Tennyson's 'Come into the Garden, Maud' were all on early programmes. These songs had been popular in the pleasure gardens and
harmonic meetings of an earlier time, where they rather incongruously
blended with the voices of prostitutes. Northern audiences liked to hear
sentimental songs about pit disasters or factory fires, similar to
Robson's recitation piece (see p. 82). Music-hall historians have
over-emphasized the love of simple-minded drinking songs among early
audiences, neglecting the varied sources of songs.

In London two types of artistes were enormously popular from the
mid-'sixties: the cheeky and cheerful female serio-comic who guys the
young men in the audience, loving them in spite of, or because of, their
weaknesses, and the lion comique, an aristocrat in the pink of fashion
who drinks with the boys any night, and is always seen the next
morning on Rotten Row, tipping his hat to the ladies. This figure (see
Plate 27) is an interesting combination of admiration for and parody of
the idle. The female singer praised the average music-hall attender's life,
and the lion comique acted out his fantasies should a mysterious
inheritance arrive (this myth was one of the most common in music-hall
songs, accompanied by an equally large number showing a realistic
assessment of money). Both types sang about such popular subjects as
the seaside holiday, beer, patriotism, marriage, hard work, the lodger
and mothers-in-law. Class differences were exaggerated and enjoyed as a
source of fun and pride. Everyone in the audience could enjoy the
songs, despite obvious class divisions (the price of tickets revealed
subtle distinctions).

The lion comique had roots in eighteenth-century drinking songs and
Pierce Egan's Tom and Jerry escapades, but his popularity during the
years 1860–90 can best be explained as a reaction against restraint.
Lion comiques appealed primarily to a masculine audience, though
women did attend the halls at this time, who could join in the simple
choruses, roaring out such braggadocio as:

Champagne Charlie is my name!
Champagne Charlie is my name!
Good for any game at night, my boys!
Good for any game at night, my boys!
Champagne Charlie is my name!
Champagne Charlie is my name!
Good for any game at night, my boys!
Who'll come and join me in a spree?[29]

In songs such as this a working-class audience could join Champagne Charlie as 'one of the boys', deriving the pleasures of a total, if temporary, escape from the hardships of the day. By looking and acting like a swell on a night out, a young man could participate vicariously in the life of the wealthy. Critics of lions, however, believed that they encouraged an unhealthy adulation and the wasting of money. Such entertainment caused a permanent 'thirst for excitement', which drove men away from steady habits, temperance, religion and other virtues necessary for getting ahead.[30]

The lion comiques and not their imitators, however, paid the price of popularity. Leybourne lived the role of Champagne Charlie on and off stage, to the delight of his admirers. He wore suits of vivid puce, violet and green, shocking Victorian London. As an advertisement for the Canterbury Hall he rode in a carriage with four white horses, which was ridiculed by a rival who drove a cart and four donkeys. It was a hectic and exciting life for an ex-factory worker from Birmingham. Leybourne remained one of the boys, willingly paying for round after round of drinks, and generously helping the poor who came to his attention. Yet Oswald Stoll, later manager of a chain of halls, spoke of a time when as a boy he went to fetch the Great Leybourne from his lodgings: 'Your friends in front are waiting for you.' 'My friends? I have no friends', was the reply. That night at the hall he collapsed, but dragged himself on stage to sing the teashop romance 'Ting! Ting! That's how the Bell Goes!'[31] He struggled through a few more performances on champagne and whelks, to die at 44. The Great Vance, his rival, was dead at 49; Bessie Bellwood at 39; Jenny Hill at 46.

Music hall audiences delighted in parodies of their favourite swells almost as much as in the originals. The cart and donkeys might mock Leybourne's pretensions, but they also pointed up his obvious superiority. Almost every lion comique sang not only his drinking songs, but also verses exhorting the listeners to cheerful loyalty and hard work. Among the best remembered were 'Be Happy-go-lucky;

Never say die', 'Work, Boys, Work, And Be Contented', 'Try to be
Happy and Gay, My Boys', and 'Act on the Square, Boys, Act on the
Square'. Parodies of these songs were directed at the performer's
sanctimony, and not at the audience, who after all did believe in such
sentiments, even if they enjoyed seeing them attacked from time to
time. Frequently women comedians dressed as Cockneys would
realistically assess the 'work and be contented' suggestions with acid
humour, such as 'I'm All Right Up to Now'.

  Some satires showed how easy it was to live on nothing and imitate a
swell quite successfully. The man who came out in tattered evening
dress to declare himself 'One of the Upper Ten' mocked the lion and
those in the audience who might imitate him – and the wealthy. The
down-and-out who enjoys the privileges of the rich was a frequent and
popular figure:

> Don't try to force an acquaintance, or locks of my hair to grab,
> At present I'm travelling 'incog', it's cheaper than travelling in cab;
> I've just rushed away from the Carlton, For clubs to me get quite a
>   bore,
> A policeman he told me to 'move on', 'Cos I happened to stand near
>   the door.
> I'm one of the upper ten, Up at ten every morning.
> The Cecil Hotel is so common of late,
> I sleep in Hyde Park, the third seat from the gate;
> Don't look on me with envy, It's better far to be
> A poor man with a contented mind,
> Than a millionaire like me.
> The match-making mothers with daughters, All think I'm a very big
>   catch,
> Round Mayfair, yes, Bryant and May-fair, they tell me I'll make a
>   good match
> I always remove in the season, With the 'smart set' I have to
>   compete,
> So my house-party, and all my servants rusticate on an Embankment
>   seat.
> My pa was a man of great letters – A postman for nigh twenty years;
> Was called to the bar when a youngster, & soon became judge of
>   good beers.
> My footman is really annoying, my valet and he don't agree,
> So I've made up my mind to discharge them, For the seats in Hyde
>   park won't hold three.

Spoken during ad lib: I've just received a letter from the citizens
of London asking me to buy the City, I really intended doing so, but
I've spent the money on 'woodbines', I'm a devil for sport – I'd go
salmon fishing, only it's such a nuisance opening the tins. Eh, what?
(LOOKING AT RENTS AND HOLES IN CLOTHES) I wish they'd
spread a little more camphor in the wardrobe. I told my valet the
moths would be at it again, and instead of buying camphor, the idiot
brought home rat poison. (SPEAKING TO IMAGINARY PERSON)
John, bring the carriage round. I think I'll use the greys this
morning. If it turnsout foggy, harness the black ones, they'll match
it better. Lay out my ping-pong suit for to-morrow, my physician
has ordered exercise. I must be home early to-night. The Park
Keeper is grumbling at the late hours I keep, even the gate's got the
spike.[32]

The final three lines of the chorus best sum up the ambiguity of
response to the lion comique. The satire cuts two ways: against the
cliché 'poor but contented', and against the pretensions of real
millionaires. Having money really matters, but being yourself matters
more.

A further refinement on the lion comique was the male
impersonator. Early impersonators wore briefs and tights, carrying a
cane and top hat to indicate masculine apparel. Only after the
popularity of the lion had waned did such stars as Vesta Tilley
(1864–1952) come into their own, wearing immaculate male attire.
Tilley's impersonations were not so much of the lion himself as of the
young swells who imitated him. Burlington Bertie and Algy, 'the
Piccadilly Johnny with the little glass eye', were her most famous. An
even more direct satire was her poor clerk who saves his money to buy
a swell's outfit for his holiday at the seashore, and is recognized by
everybody as a one-week wonder:

Sidney's holidays are in September,
He's been saving up since last November,
His get-up is a sight you must remember. Naughty boy!
He sits upon the pier and hears the band out,
Upon my word he ought to hold his hand out,
    For he tells the girls such whoppers,
    As he's counting out his coppers,
My word, he is a naughty boy.[33]

Vesta Tilley appeared primarily in the West End where the gallerys were more likely to be filled with clerks than coalheavers. Her coy 'naughty boy' portrait was more suitable for such an audience, who would see Sidney in their employees or their distant youth. A more knockabout version would appeal to working-class audiences, many of whom had a relative who had raised himself to a clerkship and put on airs among those who still worked with their hands. Whatever the type, however, music-hall songs reflected a tolerance and good humour about the upper classes. Putting on airs was the greatest sin anyone could commit, and even that was forgiven a 'naughty boy' on holiday.

Whatever dreams the lion comique might conjure up in his audience, a serio-comic reminded the audience that if 'Arry acted like a swell on Saturday night, he deserved such an occasion because,

> 'Arry likes a jolly good joke;
>   Quite right, 'Arry.
> 'Arry won't mind the fun that I spoke;
>   What say, 'Arry?
> The 'Upper Ten' may jeer and say,
>   What 'cads' the 'Arries are,
> But the 'Arries *work* and *pay their way*
>   While doing the La-di-da.[34]

The aim of the lion comique was a deliberate distortion of social reality to fit a need for escapism and pleasure. The female serio-comic reminded her audience of this reality, but softened by humour. Women made up a small percentage of artistes, and their roles were quite limited. During the life of the halls, women came to be seen as good bad girls with whom the audience could sympathize. They personified not only the outward glories of music-hall life in their chic clothing, but also the potential for freedom and joy amidst a narrow life.

The early serio-comic was considered disreputable, and often both on and off stage encouraged this reputation. Bessie Bellwood was famous not only for her slanging matches with the audience, but also for her uninhibited behaviour off stage, where she was known to knock down male friends who offended her. She started out as a rabbit-skinner in the New Cut, near Bermondsey, singing Irish ballads at night in obscure free-and-easies; later she became best known as a singer of comic Cockney songs. Throughout her life she was known for her generosity to the poor, giving away all she had, caring for the sick and paying for masses to be sung for them.[35] Everything about her encouraged boisterous familiarity and jollity; her best songs were humorous mockeries of herself, the audience and those who had pretensions to gentility, however temporary. Her most famous song, 'Wot Cher, Ria' embodies these qualities:

> I am a gal what's doing very well
> In the vegitible line
> And as I've saved a bob or two
> I thought I'd cut a shine.
> So I goes into a music 'all
> Where I'd often been afore;
> I didn't go in the galler-y
> But on the bottom floor.
> I sit me down quite comfy like
> An' calls for a pot of stout.
> My pals in the gallery spotted me
> An' all commenced to shout:
>
> What cher, Ria!
>   Ria's on the job,
> What cher Ria!
>   Did she speculate a bob?
> Now Ria she's a toff
> And she looks immensikoff,
> So it's what cher, Ria, Ria,
>   Hi! Hi! Hi![36]

The audience would join in this chorus with the same enthusiasm as in 'Champagne Charlie', but here the toff is put in her place. Indeed, the music-hall nowhere reveals itself more as a working-class phenomenon than in songs such as these – like so many of the dialect pieces, the working class is reminded to keep its place, to enjoy what it has, and to stop others from stepping out of line.

The most famous serio-comic was Marie Lloyd (1870–1922) (Plate 28). So much has been written and said about her that it is difficult to separate legend from fact. Two anecdotes must suffice to show her spontaneous warmth and good humour. Unlike many music-hall artistes, Marie did not like to play in the Christmas pantomimes traditionally given year after year at legitimate theatres. They were meant to be highly moral family entertainment, and rather cramped her style. However, in 1891 and 1892 she agreed to play the principal girl

in two productions at the Drury Lane Theatre under the direction of
Augustus Harris. One night in *Little Red Riding Hood*, following
Harris's direction, she knelt by her bedside in her grandmother's home,
praying. As she got up Dan Leno off stage whispered, 'Marie, look
under the bed!' Marie, of course, found nothing there, but carrying the
joke to its logical conclusion, proceeded to look for what should
have – in every Victorian bedroom – been there. The audience was
delighted, but Harris nearly threw her out.[37] Marie's reputation for
risqué humour was equalled by her reputation for kindness. Unlike such
stars as Vesta Tilley and Albert Chevalier, she was unfailingly helpful in
giving advice and money to needy artistes or newcomers. On one
occasion, at the Cardiff Empire, she found the young Emerald Sisters
crying bitterly in a small dressing room; the manager had summarily
dismissed them after the first show because their dresses were so
shabby. Marie promptly insisted that they be kept not only for the
second show, but also for the rest of the week in which she wasbooked,
or she would quit. She then provided them with dresses from hr own
wardrobe, along with suggestions on how to improve their routine. To
rub in her triumph, she got them a better place on the programme, and
on the last night presented them with a bouquet of flowers.[38] It was
gestures such as these that made Marie beloved.

    Whatever else she may have been, Marie embodied for the Cockney
working class all they could ever aspire to achieve: she never forgot her
own kind or was ever impressed with her 'betters'. She remained herself
while recognizing and enjoying the benefits her money brought her. In
her person Marie became a living guarantee of the superiority of
working-class forms. She died after variety and the revue had come to
replace the music hall, but her own genius continued a tradition begun
by Jenny Hill and ''Arry'. She played two basic roles: the short-skirted,
pinafored ingenué who had somehow been led astray, and when she was
older, character parts, which defined and thereby lightened many
characteristic working-class problems. Whatever she sang, and most of
her songs were silly inanities, her timing and audience rapport were
flawless; indeed, those few times she got the bird have been lovingly
recorded because of their rarity. It is in Marie Lloyd that we find
stereotypes of the music hall, worn thin through years of repetition,
raised to a level of artistry that defies categorization. However much
she was a part of a mass entertainment, and however much she
participated in a world that had become popular among all classes, she
remained intrinsically apart through her genius, embodying not simply
a star's individuality, but also the measure and temper of her class.

Marie Lloyd's continuation of a class tradition is best exemplified by one of her late hits, 'My Old Man Said, "Follow the Van" ', sometimes known as 'The Cock Linnet Song'.

> We had to move away
> 'Cos the rent we couldn't pay,
> The moving van came round just after dark;
> There was me and my old man
> Shoving things inside the van,
> Which we'd often done before, let me remark . . .
>
> My old man said, 'Follow the van,
> And don't dilly-dally on the way!'
> Off went the cart with the home packed in it,
> I walked behind with my old cock linnet.
> But I dillied and dallied, dallied and dillied,
> Lost the van and don't know where to roam.
> I stopped on the way to have the old half-quartern,
> And I can't find my way home.[39]

The precariousness of working-class life had usually been portrayed melodramatically. 'Our Marie' captures an experience which many in her audience would know, but instead of anxiety and fear, it is all boozy good humour. 'Follow the Van' was so popular that even respectable working people who never dreamed of going to the music hall sang it. They may have derived a moral lesson from it – a disreputable midnight flit was a condition for which an individual and not society was responsible. Whatever the moral, the forthright music hall did not have to present idealized pictures, but could treat subjects with a candour that cannot be found in other forms of working-class art.

Marie Lloyd raised the level of popular entertainment through her individual genius, yet her songs in and of themselves show little worth remembering, with the exception of 'Follow the Van'. 'Saturday to Monday', to take one example among many, is indistinguishable from 'Champagne Charlie' or 'Wot Cher, Ria'.

> Oh, will you come with me
> To Brighton-by-the-Sea,
> And will you go upon my yacht on Sunday?

> If you'll only say the word,
> I'll take you like a bird,
> And bring you safely back to town on Monday.[40]

The major weakness of the music hall arose from its greatest strength — an art so dependent upon the performer, rather than the composer or lyricist, would die when audiences no longer supported performances. Music-hall songs had a transient relationship with everyday life, and were expendable pleasures. After the function of the music hall had been used up — when it no longer provided recreation, escape from daily cares, and a self-definition for individuals — it could not survive. Marie Lloyd's artistry could only endure through memories; her songs died with her. The atmosphere or mood of the halls is vainly sought by historians and fans; the essential art is irrevocably lost.

III
The Portrayal of the Working Man

Character parts were always a popular feature of every programme. Early music-hall sketches were often from a general class perspective, recounting a happy courtship, neighbourhood foibles or a marital tiff with which any working man or woman could identify. Artistes were fully representative of their class because they drew upon a culture which they shared with their audience. Later sketches were much more polished and detailed in their characterization, but also more stereotyped. The great care Vesta Tilley took in dressing like a young man was repeated by other characteractors determined to be correct in their costuming, gestures and language. While this may seem a contradiction to the overall movement of the music-hall from the particular to the general, it is not. A class perspective involves the use of characters and characterizations built upon details which speak for the condition and beliefs of an entire class. A mass perspective involves the use of stereotypes in which thebehaviour of a particular group or class is portrayed, but the emotions are generalized and acceptable to all classes. An artiste who performed for a mass audience almost without exception imitated particular class characteristics for the enjoyment of all classes, in contrast to the artiste who remained a part of his class. Vesta Tilley was not a young man, nor was Albert Chevalier a costermonger. They acted out characters which appealed to their entire audience, though obviously the responses of particular individuals might differ according to their class backgrounds.

Part of the shift from a distinctively class-based entertainment to a mass entertainment came as a natural development in the process of urbanization. People living in the cities were losing some of the characteristics that set them apart from other new emigrants – their own dialect soon changed if they had a job requiring a 'proper' accent or if they lived in an area with a distinctive accent, such as the East End. As John Trafford Clegg had pointed out, the dialect spoken in the cities contained a mixture of new words and accents picked up in conversation with others from different partsof the country. Moreover, aside from the most stable industries, more and more working men found themselves moving from job to job during their lifetimes so that loyalties to particular skills and people were broken down, although class loyalty might grow stronger. In the early years of the music hall singers particularly made much of local industries – cotton operatives in Lancashire or miners and keelmen in Northumbria were sure hits. Later songs about the working class centre on working people who can be found within that class in every part of the country, such as the green grocer, costermonger or pawnshop keeper. This section will examine a variety of music-hall portraits of working men between the years 1860 and 1900 in order to trace the changes in images and attitudes.

The homely working man found his place on the provincial stage. An all-time favourite amongst Tynesiders was Joe Wilson (1841–75) (see Plate 29). According to his autobiography, 'Me fether was a joiner an' cabinet myeker, an' me muther a straw bonnit myeker, – an' byeth natives o' the 'canny aud toon o' Newcassil.'[41] All of his life Wilson felt a part of this heritage – a Newcastle working man turned entertainer. He was apprenticed to a printer at fourteen, and through his kindness, he published a chapbook of his own songs at seventeen. By twenty-one Wilson had his own small shop, but like Corvan, he inherited tuberculosis, and did not have the stamina to run a business. He then took up the equally arduous career of music hall artiste, where he achieved rapid success. He disliked travelling, and tried at various times running a public house, managing a temperance hotel, and editing an almanac. While successful at all of these occupations, the financial pull of the halls brought him back into the circuit until his premature death. A very modest man, Wilsoninsisted when praise for his work came from all parts of England, 'I don't call myself a poet, I call myself a song-writer.'[42]

A contemporary reviewer complimented Wilson for being an
entertainer who 'never brings a blush to the cheek of maiden
modesty.'[43] He was able, nevertheless, to bring freshness to the
overworked subject of the family because he was willing to write about
its failures and difficulties. Typical songs were 'The Row upon the
Stairs', about two women arguing over who will clean the communal
stairs of a tenement (see Appendix), 'Dinnet Clash the Door', asking a
young girl to be quieter while her mother is ill, and 'Be Kind to me
Dowter', advice given by a father to a prospective son-in-law.

Wilson's originality as an entertainer can be seen in 'Geordy, Haud
the Bairn'. Unlike other artistes, Wilson seldom dressed in costume,
preferring the ordinary dress of a working man, as shown in Plate 29.
His appearance combined with his songs about the ordinary problems
of working men made him popular as an interpreter and reinforcer of a
familiar and established way of life.

> 'Cum, Geordy, haud the bairn,
>   Aw's sure aw'll not stop lang;
> Aw'd tyek the jewel mysel,
>   But really aw's not strang,
> Thor's floor and coals te get,
>   The hoose-turns thor not deun*:
> Sohaud the bairn for fairs+,
>   Ye've often deund for fun!'
>
> Then Geordy held the bairn,
>   But sair agyen his will;
> The poor bit thing wes gud,
>   But Geordy had ne skill:
> He haddint its muther's ways,
>   He sat both stiff an' num;
> Before five minutes wes past
>   He wish'd its muther wad cum.
>
>   . . . . . .
>
> 'Men seldum give a thowt
>   Te what thor wives indure:
> Aw thowt she'd nowt te de
>   But clean the hoose, aw's sure;

*hoose-turns thor not deun: the daily house cleaning is not done
+fairs: in earnest

Or myek me dinner an' tea —
(It's startin' te chow its thumb:
The poor thing wants its tit —
Aw wish yor muther wad cum!)

'What a selfish world is this!
Thor's nowt mair se than man:
He laffs at wummin's toil,
And winnet nurse his awn —
(It's startin' te cry agyen:
Aw see tuts* throo its gum;
Maw little bit pet, dinnet fret —
Aw wish yor muther wad cum!)

'But kindness dis a vast;
It's ne use getting vext:
It winnet please the bairn,
Or ease a mind perplext.
At last, it's gyen te sleep,
Me wife 'll not say aw's num;
She'll think aw's a real gud nurse —
Aw wish yor muther wad cum!'[44]

The strength of this song lies in the interplay between the father's humorous fears about his child and his musing over the way of the world. The comedy serves to point up the moral of appreciating the wife without degrading the husband. The straightforward conversational style and tone, giving an appearance of artlessness, is characteristic of Wilson. Because of the simple rhymes and metre many of his songs were easy to parody; there are almost as many variations to 'Geordy, Haud the Bairn' as 'Com Whoam to thy Childer an' Me'. Yet his songs endured among the Tyneside people. Fifteen years after Wilson's death a School Board Inspector heard the refrain 'Aw wish yor muther wad cum' while climbing the stairs of a tenement.[45]

Wilson never left the North-east. Had he done so it is questionable whether his specifically local material would have appealed to the 'fast' audiences of London. Wilson imitated so closely the idiosyncrasies and desires of his fellow workers as to be nearly inseparable from them; almost all of his songs were based on actual events ('Geordy' was

*tuts: tooths

written after watching his brother-in-law hold his new son). By the late 'eighties, however, London entertainers began to draw upon the resources of dialect; the new Cockney singers portrayed ordinary working-class life with wry humour and affection, though few achieved the ease and simplicity of Wilson.

The costermonger, or street vendor of fresh fish, fruits and vegetables, was the most frequent role played by Cockney singers. The coster remained throughout the nineteenth century the most intensely individualistic member of London's working population; he had capital invested in a cart and goods, kept his own hours and was part of a brotherhood of loyal fellow costers. He even had his own distinctive dress long after the miners had given up their posey jackets — the pearly suit, with pearl buttons running up and down the seams (see Plate 30). In no way could he be said to belong to the same dull routine as servants, factory workers or skilled labourers whose lives were at the command of their masters and who stole hours from sleep to attend the halls. The lion comique offered pleasures which could be enjoyed only as a holiday indulgence, but the coster lived every day in sweet independence. He embodied the romance of working-class life. The roving young blade of so many broadside songs has been divided and tamed: he is either the remote swell or the happy-go-lucky costermonger.

Albert Vance, 'The Great Vance', was the first to popularize the costermonger. Vance's background is obscure, but he appears to have come from a poorer middle-class family who managed to apprentice him to a solicitor; after three years he fled to the theatre. His theatrical experience stood him in good stead when he turned to the halls for a more lucrative living. Lacking Leybourne's aplomb and good looks, his greater acting skill enabled him to play a wider variety of roles — he was equally well known as Leybourne's rival lion as he was a coster. His most famous hits were 'Costermonger Joe', 'Going to the Derby', and 'The Chickaleery Cove', all sung in thick Cockney. 'Costermonger Joe' (Plate 26) probably catches best the combination of raffishness and gaiety that epitomized both the coster's life and the halls:

> I'm Costermonger Joe, and as my round I go,
>   For many miles the girls will smile at Costermonger Joe,
> With mind devoid of care and spirits light as air,
>   I whistle and sing and cabbages from Covent Garden, oh!
> I started young in trade, and a nice connection made,
>   Around the streets and terraces and squares,

And all I have to do, is to call a thing or two,
    While Ned, my little pony, draws my wares—draws my wares.
    While Ned, my little pony, draws my wares.

I'm Costermonger Joe, no money do I owe,
    For nôt a crust is had on trust by Costermonger Joe;
But yes to barely live, why I must credit give.
    Or none would deal or grease the wheel with Costermonger Joe.
I'm Costermonger Joe, and tho' I'm rather slow,
    I find the fast don't longer last than Costermonger Joe.
The steady going pace just suits the human race,
    It's better to stop than gallop and drop, says Costermonger Joe.

Your tradesmen in their shops, who live on mutton chops,
    Are often more unhappy I'll be bound,
Than I with bread and cheese, and a drive out at my ease,
    And the wholesale 20 shillings in the pound, in the pound and
    the wholesale 20 shillings in the pound.
It's not the likes of me, that you in the paper see.
    Petitioning in the court for a divorce.
But those who can almost, College education boast,
    So morality with learning loses force.[46]

This song is a direct descendent of such songs as 'Vilikins and his Dinah'
and 'The Ratcather's Daughter', but ironic mock-pastoralism has been
transformed into urban self-sufficiency. Unlike the lion comique songs,
which rarely portrayed the texture of the city, the coster songs
rendered the city streets with loving detail. Verse after verse describes
Joe's daily round, emphasizing his good fortune in comparison with his
more constrained 'betters', such as shopkeepers and City men.

The most authentic coster singer, according to contemporary
commentators, was Gus Elen (1863–1940), who became popular
during the 1890s at theheight of the costermonger craze. His best
known songs are ' 'E dunno where 'E Are', about an uppity coster,
'Never Introduce Your Donah to a Pal' (see Appendix), with obvious
results, and 'If It Wasn't for the 'Ouses in Between' (see Plate 31). Elen
was loved for his old-fashioned accent, said to belong to the time of Sam
Weller, and costume, combined with his portrayal of the familiar virtues
of solidarity, loyalty and warmth. The villain of ' 'E Dunno Where 'E
Are' has come into an inheritance and now drinks whisky and smokes
cigars instead of treating his mates to beer and cigarettes. The wry

humour, mixed with nostalgia and realism, which characterizes the best
music-hall songs, can be seen in 'The 'Ouses in Between':

> If you saw my little backyard, 'Wot a pretty spot!' you'd cry—
>   It's a picture on a summer day;
> Wiv the turnip tops and cabbages wot people don't buy
>   I makes it on a Sunday look all gay.
> The neighbours fink I grows 'em, and you'd fancy you're in Kent,
>   Or at Epsom, if you gaze into the mews;
> It's a wonder as the landlord doesn't want to raise the rent,
>   Because we've got such nobby distant views.
>
>   Oh! it really is a werry pretty garden,
>   And Chingford to the easrward could be seen;
>   Wiv a ladder and some glasses,
>   You could see to 'Ackney Marshes,
>   If it wasn't for the 'ouses in between.
>
> We're as countrified as can be wiv a clothes-prop for a tree,
>   The tub-school makes a rustic little stile;
> Every time the blooming clock strikes there's a cuckoo sings to me,
>   And I've apinted up 'To Leather Lane, a mile'.
> Wiv tom-ar-toes and wiv radishes wot 'adn't any sale,
>   The backyard looks a puffick mass o' bloom;
> And I've made a little beehive wiv some beetles in a pail,
>   And a pitchfork wiv the 'andle o' the broom.
>
>   Oh! it really is a werry pretty garden,
>   An' the Rye 'Ouse from the cockloft could be seen,
>   Where the chickweed man undresses,
>   To bathe among the watercresses,
>   If it wasn't for the 'ouses in between.
>
> . . . .
>
> Though the gas-works isn't wiolets, they improve the rural scene —
>   For mountains they would werry nicely pass;
> There's the mushrooms in the dust-hole, with the cowcumbers so
>   green —
>   It only wants a bit o' 'ot-'ouse glass.
> I wears this milkman's nightshire, and I sits outside all day,
>   Like the plough-boy cove what mizzled o'er the Lea;

And when I goes indoors at night they dunno what I say,
'Cause my language gets as yokel as can be.

Oh! it really is a werry pretty garden,
And the soap works from the 'ouse-tops could be seen;
   If I got a rope and pulley,
   I'd enjoy the breeze more fully,
If it wasn't for the 'ouses in between.[47]

The self-awareness and humour of this song mark a high point in the
music hall. Its sophisticated treatment of the rural myth is worth any
number of working-class Nature poems. As Chapters 4 and 5 showed,
nothing was so pervasive among working-class writers as the pastoral
myth. Whether a writer wished to escape into nature for moral lessons
or return to simple peasant ways, he never admitted any faults in rural
life. Elen, on the other hand, revels in the comic notion of a coster
preferring a smock and yokel's accent to the joys of street life. But, of
course, everything in his garden comes from the city, and costs him
nothing in labour. As one verse says, the landlord was likely to raise the
rent if any improvements were made. A coster, the most urbanized of
workers, was the perfect stage persona to satirize the pastoral myth.

The Cockney coster was too popular a figure to remain static. One
of Elen's contemporaries, Albert Chevalier (1862–1923), came to be
known among journalists as 'The Coster's Laureate', for his accurate
dramatizations of coster life (see Plate 30). Chevalier, born into a
respectable theatre family, was one of the most successful actors to
leave the legitimate stage for a major career in the halls. He prepared his
entry with immense care, learning a variety of music-hall techniques
and completing his coster imitation by visiting Covent Garden. His first
night at the London Pavilion on 2 February 1891 was an instant
success. 'Down at the Welsh 'Arp, Which is 'Endon Way' created a new
type – the quieter, more sentimental coster who loved his family and
looked for peace with his friends.

Chevalier can be usefully compared with Edwin Waugh, another
performer who achieved widespread popularity among the middle and
upper classes for his respectable portraits of working-class life. Both
Chevalier and Waugh put a premium on outward realism. Chevalier's
accent and costume were perfect; Waugh's dialect and geography
faultless. What was altered was the inner life; both not only idealized
their characters, as did most dialect and music-hall performers, but they
also sentimentalized them with great popular success. Joe Wilson's

working men came home drunk occasionally, quarrelled with their
neighbours and struck their wives; and they still hoped to do better by
themselves and their families. Waugh could never admit to anything less
than marital bliss, and Chevalier could admit to less only by including a
final vow of love curing all.

From Chevalier's first turn critics were divided between those who
believed he brought out the best in his audiences and those who believed
he pandered to the most sickly sentimentality. One of his most
saccharine — and popular — songs was 'My Old Dutch':

> I've got a pal,
>> A reg'lar out an' outer,
> She's a dear good old gal,
>> I'll tell yer all about 'er.
> It's many years since fust we met,
>> 'Er 'air was then as black as jet,
> It's whiter now, but she don't fret,
>> Not my old gal!
>
> We've been together now for forty years,
>> An' it don't seem a day too much;
> There ain't a lady livin' in the land
>> As I'd 'swop' for my dear old Dutch!
>
> I calls 'er Sal,
>> 'Er proper name is Sairer,
> An' yer may find a gal
>> As you'd consider fairer.
> She ain't a angel — she can start
>> A jawin' till it make yer smart;
> She's just a *woman*, bless 'er 'eart,
>> Is my old gal![48]

'No! There ain't' was repeated after each chorus with intense emotion,
drums rolling — and sobs rising from the audience. The wallowing in
bathos which characterized such dialect writing as 'Johnny's Clogs' was
equally evident at times in the halls; the new entertainers of the 1890s
did not want controversy. Chevalier did not offer relief from the
dominant belief in happy marriages, but instead exaggerated it. Elen's
gentle mockery of the Englishman's proverbial love of nature was the
opposite of Chevalier's tactics.

'My Old Dutch' began with a pantomime act: the curtain would open showing the front of a workhouse with its entrances marked 'Men' and 'Women'. Chevalier would enter arm in arm with 'my old Dutch', and the guardian would separate the two, gesturing to theappropriate doors. With a look of horror, Chevalier would say 'You can't do this to us – we've been together for forty years', and break into song.[49] Perhaps the workhouse was intrinsically a sentimental topic; certainly Nicholson and Story had done no better fifty years earlier. Yet it is difficult not to feel that Chevalier's emotional scene pandered to his audience's expectations in a way that made rigid, and ultimately false, the emotions he expressed. He exploited the most important myths of his day – something that most mass art does – but he also drew from his audience a stereotyped response. They could only respond to 'My Old Dutch' with tears or laughter, drawing totally apart or sinking completely into sentimentality. Those who accepted his portrayal of aged loyalty had their emotional responses defined for them; they learned not to trust their own unique feelings, and their vocabulary for these feelings, but depend upon outside sources.

There were those who believed that working people had no vocabulary for their finer feelings, and would recognize these feelings only if someone like Chevalier gave them the words. Indeed they might not even have such feelings at all were it not for Chevalier. The following praise was given at a private fund-raising party after the singing of 'My Old Dutch':

– 'Mrs. Ormiston Chant, when the applause which greeted her had ceased, asked those present to think of what they owed to men like Mr. Chevalier for making songs like that which had just been sung, that expressed the finest sentiments in the human heart; who had voiced themes that had been there, but before were not voiced, and had done so in a language understood of the people. Think of "Mrs. 'Enery 'Awkins", "Knocked 'em in the Old Kent Road", and others which had taken the place of the boozy, fighting, hateful songs which too often in former years were the songs supposed to belong to music halls. She had sat in a music hall in the poorest part of London where "My Old Dutch" was being sung, and where the whole audience took up the chorus, and again and again repeated it until one could not listen without the tears coming into one's eyes, and the feeling arising that music like that taking hold of the public heart might be the means of introducing into lives a tenderness and a sentiment not hitherto displayed (applause).'[50]

Chevalier's biographer goes on to complain that the song had been sung without written permission (Chevalier jealously guarded his songs and did not permit their singing even outside music halls), and that the public's greatest praise was *not* joining in the chorus. But such inaccuracies are less important than the approval gained. Although the new entertainers were clearly not the sole cause for this onslaught of gentility, they benefited from larger — and more affluent — audiences. Moreover, increasingly artistes brought forward anecdotes to prove the positive moral benefits of the halls.[51] Respectability had arrived, and those who did not fit, such as Marie Lloyd, were widely condemned inside and outside the profession.[52]

One comedian of the 1890s rose above any easy label — Dan Leno (1860—1904) (Plate 32). Born into a music-hall family, by the time he could walk and talk he was part of a routine, but times were hard for many years. He was to say, 'I've earned a good deal of butter to my bread — but I wish it had been spread more evenly.'[53] Leno's genius lay, like Corvan's, in his routine rather than n his songs. From the moment he walked on stage his enormous eyes riveted the audience, forcing them to see the seriousness of his problem. He would go into a patter of wild nonsense, picking up bits and pieces from current advertisements, fads and his own personal whimsy. It all appeared spontaneous, yet was carefully prepared from the details of costume to the minutest gestures; his best performances were the result of long interaction with his audiences, whereby he altered and trimmed his routine to suit them. Leno played a wide variety of roles — grocer's assistant, railway guard, waiter, fireman, one of the unemployed, Highland chieftain, professor of anatomy and pantomime dame, to nameonly the most famous. But the overall impression was always Leno's unique pathos. His comic genius lay in endowing a simple inanimate object with an almost uncontrollable life of its own. He spoke of a cake, 'It looks as ifit's got an extremely obstinate nature, but I think you'll enjoy that speck of jam in the middle', or of an egg, 'Do you know there's something awfully artful about an egg?' In a world where so many objects were out of control, Leno's personification of commonplace objects gone suddenly awry was symbolic of larger social forces which could not be understood. These forces are defined by the concrete objects absorbing one's attention; his art is a metaphor for social impotence.

A supreme effort is made to hold on to facts in 'The Midnight March', where 'one of the unemployed' warns his listeners:

> Plain it is to you that I am tired,
>   Nearly worn away to skin and bone;
>   Not the sort o' man to be admired,
>   Even by the Mrs. all alone.
> Here have I been spouting to the working classes,
> Tellin' them as 'ow as they are downright asses;
> Tryin' to improve 'em such a bootless farce is,
> I haven't got a Blucher fit to own.

Spoken: — It is my intention to hold a meeting here to-day and say a few speaks. Working men of England, you must rally round me. Working men, you don't seem to understand yourselves. You must rouse yourselves, get behind yourselves, and push yourself forward. Don't stand about the place and stand about just for the sake of standing. No! Now is the time and the only time. When time is time you can't get away from facts. What did Mr. Gladstone say the other day? I again ask you, working men of England, what did he say? You know some people see things when they look at 'em; you can't eat soap and wash with it. Well, that proves what I have just said, that the working men of England at the present day are nothing more or less than, than — than working men! You can't get away from facts! Again, is the working man going to be scrunched into the earth? No; why should he be scrunched? No more scrunching, and down with the scruncher! Now, working men, look at me. I love the working man; and I love to see him work. Work never killed any man yet; and it shall never kill me! Why have I organised myself here to-day? Simply to ask one question. What are you going to do with your money! Now I ask you working men, what are you going to do with your money and your children? I'll tell you what to do with it. Simply bring it to me! and what will I do with it? Do you think I'd give it to a lot of people what are nothing more nor less than a lot of people? No! I'd keep it myself! My dear people, what I've suffered for the working man no-one knows. I've had black eyes, broken noses, smashed heads and torn clothes.

> And all through joining in the midnight march.
>   With the pals of order and friends of Arch;
> You've read it through in Lloyd's,
>   The so-called unemployeds.
> Hard rare hard work to do the midnight march.[54]

Leno takes familiar phrases from politics which have been overworked, and denudes them of the remnants of their meaning. He reverses the more familiar function of art, and creates in his patter a disordered, half-coherent world. His satire of agitators is based upon their absurdity. The men addressed, by implication theaudience, are caught in events beyond their control or the control of the speaker. The humour comes from the comic meaninglessness of the agitator's message, summed up in the phrase 'the working men of England at the present day are nothing more or less than working men.' Leno creates a vision of . personal survival, rather than of class struggle or class divisions. He does not reflect class values, as did Marie Lloyd, but gives voice to working-class fears.

Commentators have spoken of Leno's comic act concealing a tragic view of life. He himself said, 'The Leno System of Philosophy regards the world as a football, kicked about by higher powers with me somewhere hanging on to the stitching with my teeth and toe-nails.'[5 5] Underneath Leno's comedy was horror; his humour did not exorcize those working-class fears he embodied, but transferred them to concrete objects. By fastening on to 'the facts' a man could survive – just. Leno himself, however, did not survive. He became obsessed with making more and more people laugh, on and off stage. Toward the end of the century he began to have breakdowns; he tried to come back, but died suddenly in 1904 at the age of forty-three. Leno raised a form of mass entertainment to art through his personal genius, but such art had a fragility beyond the weaknesses of the performer. He was not representative of the working-class or of working-class culture, but was a man alone, sustained by a private vision that illuminated the fears and needs of not only his working-class audience, but also of nearly everyone who heard him.

Artistes were frequently condescending in their portrayals of working people. At the beginning of the nineteenth century pitmen had hooted Billy Purvis off the stage when he mocked them; by the end of the century such mockery was considered theheight of music-hall humour. Part of the enjoyment came from self-confidence; individuals who respect themselves can enjoy a joke at their own expense. But the patronizing also implied the superiority of the artiste who had escaped the muck andphysical labour his audience faced daily because of his skill in manipulating them. Songs such as 'My Old Dutch' were popular because Chevalier successfully associated himself with important beliefs, and then used them for his own ends – the control of his listeners. Art, audience and experience were held together through the artiste's skill, rather than through a shared, communal art. The artistes and managers saw their working-class audiences as consumers from whom they could make a profit. The audiences accepted this relationship as a necessary basis for the freedom to choose their favourite stars. In such a position they had nothing to defend, unlike thepitmen who attacked Purvis. Until the development of mass entertainment, working-class literature had expressed a faith in the power of art to change people. But art as a commodity can only be consumed; it acts to prevent change. In the Palladiums, Odeons and other halls of the late nineteenth century working people participated in a mass entertainment based on class differences – money mattered more than ever – while denying that anyone had the power to change these divisions.

The circumstances in which working men wrote literature in the nineteenth century were difficult. Those anxious to further the written culture of the people were strongly influenced by the middle class, who largely controlled access to publication. The aims and values of working-class writers frequently coincided with those of the dominant middle class, particularly in regard to the uses of literature. With the possible exception of Joseph Skipsey, these men avoided separating themselves from generally accepted beliefs. Even those who wished to develop a class-based literature were often uncertain how this should be done; an obvious example is Thomas Cooper's insistence that his learned *Purgatory of Suicides* was for the working class. The possibilities of dialect remained largely unfulfilled, despite its wide popularity and its strong working-class ties. Working men of very different backgrounds and expectations agreed that literature should console, amuse and educate. Songs, dialogues and patter were often richer and more meaningful for working people, but they had the limitations of transitory popularity. Areas of emotional life are implied in Dan Leno's work which are rarely found in working-class writing, but he was unique, rather then characteristic of the music hall. Moreover, his artistic definition of the disturbing qualities of life negated much the working class valued in its own life and literature.

Although nineteenth-century working-class literature was undeniably impoverished by circumstances, it was nonetheless a strong and varied body of writings that has not been duplicated in the twentieth century. The songs, poems and sketches written throughout England by working men gave greater force and meaning to the lives of countless writers and readers. Since World War I far more potent forms of mass entertainment than the London music hall have accelerated the consumer relationship to art. In the twentieth century it is no longer possible to speak of a separate working-class literature. Social, economic and educational changes have radically altered the conditions under which an individual writer or performer pursues a career. The bitter fears and confined expectations of the past have been left, only to be replaced by equally potent limitations. Technology may undermine class differences, but it cannot bring creativity, solidarity and fulfilment any closer. The new media are producing more and more effectively a prepackaged culture that can only be accepted or rejected. The attractions of these forms of mass entertainment destroyed the developing working-class literary culture of the nineteenth century. But the literature that came out of that culture, despite all hardships, is a remarkable achievement of individual and class development.

Notes

1. There is, however, ample evidence that theatres in working-class districts broke these regulations. See Clive Barker, 'The Chartists, Theatre, Reform and Research', *Theatre Quarterly*, I, 4 (December, 1971), pp.3–10.

2. For a recent survey of the music hall, see Laurence Senelick, 'A Brief Life and Times of the Victorian Music-Hall', *Harvard Library Bulletin*, 19 (1971), pp.375–398.

3. W. Cooke Taylor, *Notes on a Tour in Manufacturing Districts of Lancashire* (London, 1842), quoted in Reginald Nettel, *Seven Centuries of Popular Song: A Social History of Urban Ditties* (London: Phoenix House, 1956), p.205.

4. Frank Leary, 'Low Singing Rooms', unpub. MS. (*c.* 1892), Manchester Central Reference Library.

5. David Price Miller, *The Life of a Showman: To which is added Managerial Struggles* (London and Leeds 1849), pp.79–80, quoted in David Mayer, 'Billy Purvis: Travelling Showman', *Theatre Quarterly*, I, 4 (December, 1971), p.34.

6. Anonymous account identified as 'Extract from *Chater's Illustrated Annual, 1881*', Arthur J. Fenwick Collection, quoted in David Mayer, 'Billy Purvis', p.33.

7. *The Life and Adventures of Billy Purvis containing many Humorous Incidents and Anecdotes, Not Hitherto Published* (Newcastle: D. Bowman, 1875), pp.152–4; 'Billy Purvis', *Monthly Chronicle of North-Country Lore and Legend*, 5 (July, 1891), pp.316–7; and Joseph B. Robson, *The Life and Adventures of Billy Purvis, Continued to the time of his death* (Newcastle: John Cristie, 1854). In 1849 Purvis paid Robson £20 to write his biography in order to help his faltering career; it was originally published in 1849, and in 1854 reprinted with some additions. The legend of Billy Purvis was profitable enough to generate several biographies and essays, including the 1875 Bowman edition, which Mayer considers to be by Bowman himself.

8. 'Ned Corvan', *Monthly Chronicle of North-Country Lore and Legend*, 5 (November, 1891), pp.522–3; *Allan's Illustrated Edition of Tyneside Songs and Readings*, rev. ed. (Newcastle: T. and G. Allan, 1891), pp.387–390. Henceforth cited as *Allan's Tyneside Songs*.

9. 'The Stage Struck Keelman' (Newcastle: W. Stewart, n.d.), Broadside Collection, University of Newcastle Library. To be sung to the air 'Bob and Joan'.

10. Very little work has been done to date on working-class theatre. See Clive Barker, 'The Chartists, Theatre, Reform and Research', and 'A Theatre for the People', *Nineteenth Century British Theatre*, eds. K. Richards and P. Thomson (London: Methuen, 1971), pp.3–24.

11. H. Chance Newton and W. H. Morton, *Sixty Years of Stage Service, Being The Record of the Life of Charles Morton, The Father of the*

Music Halls (London: Gale and Polder, 1905), pp.18–24.

12. H. Chance Newton and W. H. Morton, *Sixty Years of Stage Service*, pp.11–15. Morton opened the Canterbury Arms public house in 1848. C. D. Stuart and A. J. Parkin the first history of the music hall, *The Variety Stage: A History of the Music Halls from the Earliest Period to the Present Time* (London: T. Fisher Unwin, 1895), give the date 1849 for the opening of the Canterbury Hall. See pp.50–5 for an account of the Canterbury. It is unclear why Morton is considered the first to open a music hall since he so clearly was not. Dr. Louis James has suggested to me that he may have been the first to charge an admission that could not be redeemed for drink.

13. [Thomas Anstey Guthrie], *Harper's New Monthly Magazine*, 82 (December, 1892), pp.192–202.

14. *Tempted London: Young Men* (London: Hodder and Stoughton, 1888), p.184. For a more positive estimate of the music hall, see Robert Machray, *The Night Side of London* (London: John MacQueen, 1902), pp.112–24. For a critical account of a provincial hall, see James Burnley, *Phrases of Bradford Life* (Bradford: T. Brear, 1875), pp.54–63. All writers condemn the low intellectual and artistic level of the entertainment, and lament the lack of suitable alternatives.

15. *Allan's Tyneside Songs*, p.391.

16. Quoted from an article by Jerome K. Jerome, *The Idler Magazine* (March, 1892), in M. Willson Disher, *Winkles and Champagne: Comedies and Tragedies of the Music Hall* (London: B. T. Batsford, 1938), p.22.

17. J. B. Booth, *Seventy Years of Song* (London: Hutchinson, 1943), p.36.

18. Harold Scott, *The Early Doors: Origins of the Music Hall* (London: Nicholson and Watson, 1946), p.150.

19. Don Ross, personal letter to the author, 14 March 1972.

20. Christopher Pulling, *They were Singing, and What They Sang About* (London: George G. Harrap, 1952), pp.236–7.

21. Pulling, p.237; and Don Ross, letter, 14 March 1972.

22. W. N. B. 'Music-Hall Songs', undated newspaper cutting, Manchester Central Reference Library. See also A. T. Camden Pratt, 'Poverty Corner', *Unknown London: Its Romance and Tragedy* (London: Neville Beeman, n.d. [1900?]), pp.56–60.

23. *Before I Forget: The Autobiography of a Chevalier d'Industrie* (London: T. Fisher Unwin, 1902), pp.143–52.

24. M. Willson Disher, pp.17–19. A variety of figures are quoted by other historians of the music hall, but all are within the range of £20 to £30 per week and £100 to £150 per week figures. The variation, however, gives some indication of the difficulty of finding accurate information about the halls.

25. Naomi Jacob, *'Our Marie' (Marie Lloyd): A Biography* (London: Hutchinson, n.d. [1936]), pp.233–4.

26. Figures are quoted from Charles Booth, *Life and Labour of the*

People of London (London, 1903), as quoted in *Theatre Quarterly*, I, 4 (December, 1971), p.46. See also J. B. Booth, *Pink Parade* (New York: Dutton, 1933), pp.124–5.
27. Broadside sellers throughout the century were not slow in responding to their 'competitors'. See J. W. Robinson, *Theatrical Street Ballads* (London: Society for Theatre Research, 1971) for a discussion of the responses of nineteenth-century ballad writers to important or newsworthy theatre events.
28. 'Geo. Leybourne's "Rock the Cradle, John" ' (London: W. S. Fortey, n.d.) Broadside Collection, British Museum.
29. 'Champagne Charlie', words by George Leybourne, music by Alfred Lee (London: C. Sherard, 1867).
30. Henry Manton, editor of *The Nonconformist and Independent*, in *Letters on Theatres and Music Halls, Especially Intended for Sunday School Teachers and Senior Scholars* (Birmingham: C. Caswell, n.d. [1888]), spoke of how he found 'six youths guilty of thievery because their pocket money was not great enough for their thirst for excitement at the theatre' and how the greatest cause for the neglect of Sunday School was a love of the theatre and the music hall. He also adds that the music halls were always violating their license and showing actual plays. See pp.3–7. See also J. Ewing Ritchie, *Days and Nights in London; or Studies in Black and Gray* (London: Tinsley Brothers, 1880), pp.38–89 and *The Night Side of London* (London: William Tweedie, 1857); Frederick M. Charrington, *The Battle of the Music Halls* (London: Dyer Brothers, n.d. [1885?]); Elizabeth Pennell, 'The Pedigree of the Music Hall', *Contemporary Review*, 63 (April, 1893), pp.575–83; and *Tempted London: Young Men*.
31. M. Willson Disher, p.23.
32. Tom E. Hughes, 'One of the Upper Ten', (n.p., n.d.), Broadside Collection, British Museum.
33. 'Sidney's Holidays', Lady de Frece, *Recollections of Vesta Tilley* (London: Hutchinson, 1934), p.136.
34. Sung by Jenny Hill, words by E. V. Page. Quoted in Samuel McKechnie, *Popular Entertainments Through the Ages* (London: Sampson Low, Marston, n.d. [1931]), p.146.
35. Harold Scott, p.208; M. Willson Disher, p.21.
36. Words by Bessie Bellwood. Quoted in M. Willson Disher, pp.22–3.
37. Naomi Jacob, pp.82–3.
38. S. Theodore Felstead, *Stars Who Made the Halls* (London: T. Werner Laurie, 1946), pp.93–4.
39. Words by Fred W. Leigh, music by Charles Collins. Quoted in Colin MacInnis, *Sweet Saturday Night* (London: MacGibbon and Kee, 1967), pp.57–8.
40. Cutting from an American paper, Marie Lloyd, Enthoven Collection, Victoria and Albert Museum.
41. Joe Wilson, *Tyneside Songs and Drolleries, Readings and Temperance Songs* (Newcastle: T. and G. Allan, n.d. [1890?]), p.xvii. Henceforth cited as Joe Wilson.

42. Joe Wilson, p.xxxvi.
43. W. H. Dawson, 'Life of Joe Wilson', *Jarrow Chronicle*, 4 September 1869, quoted in *Joe Wilson's Tyneside Songs, Ballads and Drolleries* (Newcastle: T. Allan, n.d. [1872]), p.4.
44. Joe Wilson, pp.2–4; *Allan's Tyneside Songs*, pp.497–8.
45. Joe Wilson, p.xli.
46. 'Costermonger Joe', (n.p., n.d.) Broadside Collection, British Museum.
47. Words by Edgar Bateman, music by George Le Brunn (London: Francis, Day and Hunter, 1894).
48. Albert Chevalier, p.138. Words by Albert Chevalier, music by Charles Ingle (Chevalier's brother).
49. Colin MacInnis, pp.130–1.
50. Quoted from the *Western Daily Mail*, 28 January 1895, in Albert Chevalier with Brian Daly, *A Record of Myself* (London: John MacQueen, 1895), p.135. See also the review of the *Daily Telegraph*, 23 September 1893, quoted on pp.152 and 155. Mrs. Ormiston Chant was the leading opponent of music halls, who led the campaign in 1892 of the 'Prudes on the Prowl', as they were dubbed, against prostitutes found at the halls. She forced the LCC Licensing Committee to put up a partition separating the promenade bar and the auditorium of the Empire; it was torn down by a group of young men, including Winston Churchill, but this did not stop her campaigning against immorality.
51. In addition to Chevalier's two autobiographies which recount several tales of morality, see also H. Chance Newton, *Idols of the Halls: Being My Music Hall Memories* (London: Heath Cranton, 1928), pp.26–8 on Albert Vance; and 'Jolly' John Nash, *The Merriest Man Alive: Stories, Anecdotes, Adventures, etc.* (London: General Publishing, n.d. [1891]), pp.2–11, plus countless anecdotes to be found in every reminiscence or account of the halls.
52. Marie Lloyd had been warned by the management of the Pavilion about her indecency, and she was the only major star not invited to perform at the famous 1912 Command Performance in front of the king and queen. Yet her defenders argued from the same moral premise as her critics, claiming her 'a woman with a mission in life. . . . She blasted false sentiment. . . . She was a social reformer, in her way, as courageous as Ibsen.' (McKechnie, p.171). If our Marie could not be put into the prevalent mould of moral-uplift-through-entertainment, she was made to fit into the healthy-social-reform mould.
53. Colin MacInnis, p.66. An interesting sidenote to Leno's childhood is that his father was active in the Chartist movement.
54. *The Music Hall Songster, Containing a Selection of the Latest and Most Popular Songs now being sung with the Greatest Success by Leo Dryden, Little Tich, Dan Leno, H. Campbell, etc.* (London: W. Fortey, n.d. [1892]), p.24.
55. Dan Leno, *Hys Book: A Volume of Frivolities, Autobiographical, Historical, Philosophical, Anecdotal and Nonsensical* (London:

Greening, 1899), p.133. See also J. Hickory Wood, *Dan Leno: His Infinite Variety* (London: Methuen, 1905).

APPENDIX

Since the majority of the works discussed in this book are virtually unavailable, the following songs and poems are offered as a brief supplement. Selections are given to accompany every chapter except Chapter 4. All have been quoted in full. I have emphasized examples that reflect the changes working people underwent as a result of industrialization and urbanization. For reasons of space it has not been possible to quote any prose works. For additional examples of working-class songs and poems, see *The Common Muse*, eds. V. de Sola Pinto and A. E. Rodway (Harmondsworth: Penguin Books, 1965).

1
THE NEW TIMES

You lads and lasses give ear to my song,
You'll find it is true, and I'll not keep you long
Farmer's servants did well about twenty years since,
But now I do declare they are all ruined at once.

Chorus

O shame of the farmers O pity poor servants,
For master's ambition has been their downfall.

In my old mother's days as I understand
There were twenty pounds wages and a guinea in hand
But now the poor servants they are so brought down,
They scarcely can get ten pounds and a crown.

When they formerly went to a statute or fair,
They could spend half-a-guinea and a plenty to spare,
With plenty of roast beef liquor to spill,
But now they can hardly pay a shoemaker's bill.

The farmers to market did once use to walk,
Amusing each other with old fashioned talk,
But now on fine geldings are mounted so gay,
To ride over poor folks if they stand in the way.

Then the young farmer's daughters as I understand,
With young woman servants would walk hand in hand
But now near to them they scarcely will venture,
For fear their fine clothes should catch some distemper.

There is one thing more which I have not mentioned yet
Toast and ale for their breakfast they used for to get,
But instead now of getting suchold fashioned cheer,
Its black bread and skim dick and a drop of sour beer.

Each farmer he once wore a linsey great coat,
You would think by its looks was scarce worth a groat,
But now with broad cloth they are scarcely content,
Which occasions their landlord to double their rent.

So now to conclude and to finish my song,
I hope the times may mend before long,
The wages may rise and rent may come down,
So each jolly fellow can spend half-a-crown.

2
THE HAND-LOOM WEAVERS' LAMENT
(John Grimshaw)

You gentlemen and tradesmen, that ride about at will,
Look down on these poor people; it's enough to make you crill*;
Look down on these poor people, as you ride up and down,
I think there is a God above will bring your pride quite down.

> Chorus. — You tyrants of England, your race may soon be run,
> You may be brought unto account for what you've sorely done.

You pull down our wages, shamefully to tell;
You go into the markets, and say you cannot sell;
And when that we do ask you when these bad times will mend,
You quickly give an answer, 'When the wars are at an end.'

*Chilly, goose-fleshy.

When we look on our poor children, it grieves our hearts full sore,
Their clothing it is worn to rags, while we can get no more,
With little in their bellies, they to their work must go,
Whilst yours do dress as manky as monkeys in a show.

You go to church on Sundays, I'm sure it's nought but pride,
There can be no religion where humanity's thrown aside;
If there be a place in heaven, as there is in the Exchange,
Our poor souls must not come near there; like lost sheep they must
    range.

With the choicest of strong dainties your tables overspread,
With good ale and strong brandy, to make your faces red;
You call'd a set of visitors — it is your whole delight —
And you lay your heads together to make our faces white.

You say that Bonyparty he's been the spoil of all,
And that we have got reason to pray for his downfall;
Now Bonyparty's dead and gone, and it is plainly shown
That we have bigger tyrants in Boneys of our own.

And now, my lads, for to conclude, it's time to make an end;
Let's see if we canform a plan that these bad times may mend;
Then give us our old prices, as we have had before,
And we can live in happiness, and rub off the old score.

This ballad was sung to the favouriteair of 'A hunting we will go',
but better known in and near Manchester by a song of the time, of
which one verse runs —

> With Henry Hunt we'll go, we'll go,
> With Henry Hunt we'll go;
> We'll raise the cap of liberty,
> In spite of Nadin Joe.

Joseph Nadin was deputy-constable of Manchester for more than
twenty years. He resigned in March 1821, and was succeeded by
Mr. Stephen Lavender, from London.

3
STEAM LOOM WEAVER

One morning in summer I did ramble,
In the pleasant month of June,
The birds did sing the lambkins play,
Two lovers walking in theirbloom,
The lassie was a steam loom weaver,
The lad an engine driver keen,
All their discourse was about weaving.
And the getting up of steam.

She said my loom is out of fettle,
Can you right it yes or no,
You say you are an engine driver,
Which makes the steam so rapid flow;
My lambs and jacks are out of order,
My laith in motion has not been,
So work away without delay,
And quickly muster up the steam.

I said fair maid you seem determined,
No longer for to idle be,
Your healds and laith I'll put in motion,
Then work you can without delay,
She said young man a pair of pickers,
A shuttle too I want you ween,
Without these three I cannot weave,
So useless would be the steam.

Dear lass these things I will provide,
But when to labour will you begin,
As soon my lad as things are ready
My loom shop you can enter in,
A shuttle true and pickers too,
This young man did provide amain.
And soon her loom was put in tune
So well it was supplied with steam.

Her loom worked well the shuttle flew,
His nickers play'd the tune nick-nack,
Her laith did move with rapid motion,
Her temples, healds, long-lambs and jacks,
Her cloth beam rolled the cloth up tight,
The yarn beam emptied soon it's seam,
The young man cried your loom works, light
And quickly then off shot the steam.

She said young man another web,
Upon the beam let's get don't strike,
But work away while yet it's day,
This steam loom weaving well I like,
He said good lass I cannot stay,
But if a fresh warp you will beam
If ready when I come this way,
I'd strive for to get up the steam.

4

THE JOLLY GRINDER!

There was a jolly Grinder once,
    Lived by the river Don,
He work'd and sang from morn to night,
    And sometimes he'd work none;
But still the burden of his song
    For ever used tobe —
' 'Tis never worth while to work too long,
    For it doesn't agree with me!'

He seldom on a Monday work'd,
    Except near Christmas Day;
It was not the labour that he'd shun,
    For it was easier far than play;
But still the burden of his song
    For ever used to be —
' 'Tis never worth while to work too long,
    For it doesn't agree with me!'

A pale teetotaller chanc'd to meet
    Our grinder one fine day,
As he sat at the door with his pipe and his glass.
    And thus to our friend did say:
'You destroy your health and senses too;'
    Says the grinder 'you're muchtoo free,
Attend to your work, if you've ought to do,
    And don't interfere with me.

There's a many like you go sneaking about,
    Persuading beer drinkers to turn!
'Tis easier far on our failings to spout,
    Than by labour yourliving to earn;
I work when I like, and I play when I can,
    And I envy no man I see;
Such chaps as you won't alter my plan,
    For I know what agrees with me!'

5
THE WORKING MAN
Tune — 'The Englishman'

There's a class that bears the stamp of the great,
    Yet boasts not rank or line, —
The battle-field orpomp of state,
    Call forth no song of mine:
There's a nobler title far on earth,
    Than Lord, or Duke, or King,
And brave hearts have sprung from lowly birth,
    Of which I proudly sing;
For the impress of greatness, deny it who can,
Is stamp'd on the brow of the working man.

There's a hand that is hard with honest toil,
    For ever first to aid,
That breaks up the yielding mine and soil,
    From which all wealth is made:
There is not a mark but what's a gem,
    Upon that hard hand set,

And brighter far than the pearly stream,
    Are cheeks bedewed with sweat;
For the wealth of the earth, deny it who can,
Is raised by the sweat of the working man.

And the proud ship that rides from isle to isle,
    Proclaims the working man's skill,
If you asked who reared you stately pile,
    The cry is the labourer still.
England is proud of her lofty name,
    That sounds from shore to shore,
And what is the source of her wealth and fame,
    But labour evermore:
They are truth-telling foot-prints, deny it who can,
That are left on the earth by the working man.

Then glory be the manly brow,
    By labour dignified,
Hurrah! for the forge, the loom, and the plough,
    Our country's wealth and pride.
There's a brighter age for the toiling ones,
    Now struggling into birth,
When the world shall own its noblest sons,
    In every nook of the earth;
For the world-stirring lever, deny it who can,
Is the pen of the patriot working man.

6
THE DEVIL'S IN THE GIRL

It's of a lusty gentlemen, returning from the play,
He knock'd at his true love's door that night with her to lay,
She quickly let this young man in and called him her delight,
Saying, roll me in your arms love and lay till morning light.

This fair one was a crafty jade, and unto him did say,
What did please you most love when you was at the play?
He said my dear I've learnt a tune forget it I ne'er shall,
It called a very merry tune 'the devil's in the girl.'

O kind sir let me hear that tune if you your fife can play,
I'll listen with attention so now play up I pray,
Oh, the sound it is so beautiful, and pleases me so well,
All night I'll lay if you will play the devil's in the girl.

But the sound awoke her mother all on the second floor,
Who ran down in her bed gown and like a bull did roar,
She spoilt the young man's music she pummeled him so well,
Then said the jade he only played the devil's in the girl.

Now this young man quickly left them his journey to pursue,
But mark what follcwed after this young girl poorly grew,
Her mother said one morning why what's the matter Sal?
You mope about just like a goose the devil's in the girl.

Six months were soon passed over her gown it would'nt meet
Her mother finding out the same, she said it was treat,
O daughter said the mother the music's made you swell,
Why it's never good to play the tune, the devil's in the girl.

Twelve months being over this young man out of fun,
He went that way and met the maid who had a lovely son,
She said kind sir come marry me for you can please me well
He shook his head and smiling said, the devil's in the girl.

Oh, if I played the music it pleased you no doubt,
You ought to pay the piper if he the tune played out,
So you go your way maid I cannot be your pal,
You may get some other one to play the devil's in the girl.

So all you pretty fair maids pray be advised by me,
For you see that I'm rewarded with a baby on my knee,
There is a tune will please you and ruin you as well,
So maids beware don't get too near the devil's in the girl.

7
THE DODGER

Fare-ye-vell, my Vitechapel boys, fare-ye-well for a-while,
For you see the bobbies and the beaks has tumbled to my style
But it's all wery vell when you're in luck, your friends will stand a
    cup,
But vhen you're down they keeps you down acause they turns you
    up.
So fare-ye-vell, my Vitechapel boys, and you vot keeps a fence,
I'm going avay to Australia, but not at my own expense.

I've got an out an out good name for being a roving blade.
I'm fly to every downy dodge, and a stunner at my trade;
But the best of all the flyest coves am werry much to blame,
Because they makes the bobbies fly to tumble to their game.

I nailed this yellow vipe from a swell, whilst going up Drurylane;
And this bandanna from a bloke whilst drinking his champagne
This from a foreigner I took vhilst valking Leicester-square,
And this vone from another chap as grand as a Lord Mayor.

There's von or two more lately you see taken folks in quite unavares,
I should like to know the difference betvixt these vipes and the
    railway shares;
The Crystal Palace 'cotched it too, but they had themselves to
    thank,
But the biggest swindle of 'em all, was the Royal British Bank.

When Mr. Dickens wrote his vork, he drew my character so vell
Betvixt the artful dodger and me none could the difference tell.
Mr. Cruckedshanks vot drink no gin — in his picture you may see
The very dodger vhat I mean — all of a tvist like me.

I never injured any one, and vorked hard for what I got
For nothing comes amiss me, except the vile garotte,
For every finger dodge there is, I'se got a happy knack,
And never like a coward struck any man behind his back.

Now fare ye vell, my Vitechapel boys, to part with you I grieve
But I'll return to you vonce more, vhen I've vorked the ticket of
   leave.
Here's one dodge that keeps up my pluck, and does my spirits cheer,
That is ven I return again, you'll welcome the dodger here.

8
MANCHESTER'S IMPROVING DAILY

This Manchester's a rare fine place,
   For trade and other such like movements;
What town can keep up such a race,
   As ours has done for prime improvements
For of late what sights of alterations,
Both streets and buildings changing stations,
That country folks, as they observe us,
Cry out, 'Laws! pickle and presarve us!'
   Sing hey, sing ho, sing hey down, gaily,
   Manchester's improving daily.

Once Oldham Jone, in his smock frock,
   I'th' town stop'd late one afternoon, sir,
And staring at th' infirmary clock,
   Said, Wounds, that must be th' harvest moon, sir;
And ecod, it's fix'd fast up i'th' place there,
And stands behind that nice clock-face there:
Well, this caps aw, for I'll be bound, sir,
They mak' it shine there aw th' year round, sir.
   Sing hey, etc.

Our fine town hall, that cost such cash,
   Is to all buildings quite a sample;
And they say, sir, that, to make a dash,
   'Twas copied from Grecan temple:
But sure in Greece none e'er could view, sir,
Such a place built slanting on a brow, sir!
But Cross-Street, when there brass to spare is,
Must be rais'd and called the Town-Hall Terrace.
   Sing hey, etc.

Once Market-Street was called a lane,
   Old Toad-Lane too, a pretty pair, sir;
While Dangerous-Corner did remain,
   There was hardly room for a sedan chair, sir:
But now they both are open'd wide, sir,
And dashing shops plac'd on each side, sir:
And to keep up making old things new, sir,
They talk of levelling th' Mill-Brew, sir.
   Sing hey, etc.

Steam coaches soon will run from here
   To Liverpool and other place;
And their quicker rate and cheaper fare
   Will make some folks pull curious faces:
But though steam-dealers may be winners,
'Twill blow up all the whip-cord spinners;
And stable boys may grieve and weep, sir,
For horse-flesh soon will be dog cheap, sir.
   Sing hey, etc.

With bumping stones our streets wur paved,
   From earth like large peck-loaves up rising:
All jolts and shakings now are saved
   The town they're now Mc.Adamizing:
And so smooth and soft is Cannon-Street, sir,
It suits the corns ontender feet sir:
And hookers-in, when times a'n't good there,
May fish about for eels i'th' mud there.
   Sing hey, etc.

But though these roads are all the go,
   The rail-ways beat 'em, I've a notion;
For carts beawt horses there will show
   We've found the true perpetual motion.
And none can say but we may try, sir,
To steer large ship-balloons i'th' sky, sir;
That folks may mount sky-larking there in,
And grow sea-sick by going an airing.
   Sing hey, etc.

Th' owd Stony-Knolls must be renew'd,
   And feel, in turn, improvement's power;
From there to Bury they'll mak' good
   A great hee-road by cutting lower:
The view from hence wur quite a show, sir,
And none but foot-folks o'er must go, sir,
Yet in Whitsun-week, as thick as grass is,
The Knolls wur fill'd wi' creawds of asses.
   Sing hey, etc.

A powerful large steam-engine's bought,
   And plac'd beneath a'r owd church steeple,
To warm up th' church, and soon it's thought
   'Twill play the deuce wi' single people:
For a clever chap's fun eawt a scheme, sir,
To tie the marriage-knot by steam, sir;
And there's no doubt, when they begin it,
They'll wed above a score a minute.
   Sing hey, etc.

The spinning-jennies whirl along,
   Performing strange things, I've been told, sir,
For twisting fresh and making young
   All maids who own they're grown too old, sir.'
The power-loom factories, of late, sir,
Have wrought such wonders, when agate, sir,
That we can weave, in time, who knows, sir,
Neat patent stays for dandy beaux, sir.
   Sing hey, etc.

Thus at improvements on we go,
   We're ever trying at invention;
New objects starting up to view,
   And catching all our spare attention:
Then the ship canal, and all such schemes, sir,
Tho' some may call themfancy's dreams, sir,
They'll all succeed, you need not fret, sir,
As soon as John Bull's out of debt, sir.
   Sing hey, etc.

9
COLLIER LASS

My name's Polly Parker, I'm come o'er from Worsley,
   My father and mother work in a coal mine:
Our family's large, we have got seven children,
   So I too am obliged to work in a mine.
And as this is my fortune, I know you'll feel sorry,
   That in such employment my days theyshould pass;
But I keep up my spirits, I sing and look merry,
   Although I am nought but a collier lass.

By the greatest of dangers, each day I'm surrounded,
   I hang in the air by a rope or a chain,
The mine may fall in, I may be killed or wounded,
   May perish by damp, or the fire of a train.

And what would you do, were it not for our labour?
   In wretched starvation, our days they would pass
While we can provide you with life's greatest blessing,
   O do not despise a poor collier lass.

All the long day you may see we are buried,
   Deprived of the light and the warmth of the sun,
And often at night from our beds we are hurried,
   The water is in, and barefooted we run.
Although we go ragged, and black are our faces,
   As kind and as free as the best we are found;
And our hearts are as white as your lords in fine places,
   Although we're poor colliers that work under ground.

I am growing up fast, and somehow or other,
   There's a collier lad strangely runs into my mind,
And in spite of the talking of father and mother,
   I think I should marry if he was inclin'd;
But should he prove surly and will not befriend me,
   Perhaps a better chance will come to pass,
And my heart I know, will to him recommend me,
   And I will no longer be a collier lass.

10
THE BONNIE PIT LADS

As I walked forth one summers morn all in the month of June.
The flowers they were springing and the birds were in full tune.
I overheard a lovely maid and this was all her theme.
Success attend the Pit Lads, for they are lads of fame.

I stepped up to her and bending on my knee,
I asked her pardon for making with her so free,
Your pardon is granted young Pit Lad she replies
Pray do you belong to the brave Union boys.

You may see I'm a Pitman as black as a sloe.
And all the night long I am working down below;
O I do love a Pitman as I do love my life
My father was a pitman all the days of his life.

Come now my young Pitman and rest here awhile,
And when I am done milking I'll give you a smile;
He kissed her sweet lips while milking her cow,
And the lambs they were sporting all in the morning dew.

Come all you noble gentlemen wherever that you be,
Do not pull down their wages nor break their unity
You see they hold like brothers like sailors on the sea
They do their best endeavours for their wives and family.

Then she clapt her arms around him like Venus round the vine,
You are my jolly Pit Lad you've won this heart of mine,
And if that you do win the day as you have won my heart.
I'll crown you with honour and for ever take your part.

The Pit Lads are the best of boys their work lies under ground
And when they to the Ale-house go they value not a crown.
They spend their money freely and pay before they go.
They work under ground while the storm winds do blow.

So come all you pretty maidens wherever you may be,
A pit Lad do not despise in any degree.
Forif that you do use them well they'll do the same to thee,
There is none in this world like a pit-boy for me.

11
HOW TO BE A GREAT LORD

Would you be a Great Lord? Let me shew you the way;
Too proud to be honest, a debt never pay;
Your fame and your fortune on prostitutes squander,
With a pimp in your coach, at your table a pander.
Or mount your own box, 'tis by far the less evil,
That pimp and that pander drive post to the devil.
Roast a child for your sport, set the hamlet on fire,
Then cut down with your sword both the sun and the fire:
A terrible Colonel now bully and swagger,
And plant in the heart of your country − a dagger.

When sharpers have done you, regard my advice,
Repair with a bribe what you lost by the dice.
Think little − drink much − your best principles barter,
And instead of a rope be preferred with a garter.
Or a mime on the stage, and becoming your part,
In character act, and be still what thou art.
Does indigence ask? shut your purse and your door; −
Distress is so shocking! God d − − n all the poor!
Now job for a borough, now truck for a place,
Or stoop to a pension, and rise by disgrace;
And last to your friend let your kindness be shewn; −
Be true to his wife − and be chaste to your own.

Now if thou art not a Great Lord, by St. Peter
Thou art a great rascal, in prose or in metre.

12
PAUPER'S DRIVE

There's a grim horse hearse at a jolly round trot.
To the churchyard a pauper is going, I wot,
The road it is rough, the hearse has no springs,
And hark to the dirge the sad driver sings,
Rattle his bones over the stones,
He's only a pauper whom nobody owns.

Oh! where are the mourners? alas there are none,
He has left not a gap in the world now he's gone.
Not a tear in the eye of child, woman, or man,
To the grave with his carcase as fast as you can.
Rattle his bones, over the stones,
He's only a pauper whom nobody owns.

What a jolting and cracking and splashing and din,
The whip how it cracks, the wheels how they spin!
How the dirt right and left o'er the hedges is hurl'd
The pauper at length makes a noise in the world.
Rattle his bones over the stones,
He's only a pauper whom nobody owns.

But a truce to this strain, for my soul it is sad,
To think that a heart in humanity clad,
Should make, like the brute, such a desolate end
And depart from the world without leaving a friend.
Bear softly his bones over the stones,
Though a pauper, he's one whom his Maker yet owns.

13
THE LION OF FREEDOM

The lion of freedom comes from his den,
We'll rally around him again and again,
We'll crown him with laurels our champion to be,
O'Connor, the patriot of sweet liberty.

The pride of the nation, he's noble and brave
He's the terror of tyrants, the friend of the slave,
The bright star of freedom, the noblest of men,
We'll rally around him again and again.

Though proud daring tyrants his body confined,
They never could alter his generous mind;
We'll hail our caged lion, now freed from his den,
And we'll rally around him again and again.

Who strove for the patriots? was up night and day?
And save them from falling to tyrants a prey?
It was Feargus O'Connor was diligent then!
We'll rally around him again and again.

14
A HYMN
(John Henry Bramwich)

BRITANNIA'S sons, though slaves ye be,
God your Creator made you free;
He, life to all, and being, gave —
But never, never made a slave!

His works are wonderful to see —
All, all proclaim the Deity; —
He made the earth, and formed the wave —
But never, never made a slave!

He made the sky, with spangles bright —
The moon to shine by silent night —
The sun, — and spread the vast concave —
But never, never made a slave!

The verdant earth on which we tread
Was, by His hand, all carpeted;
Enough for all He freely gave —
But never, never made the slave!

All men are equal in His sight —
The bond, the free, the black, the white; —
He made them all, — them freedom gave —
He made the man, — Man made the Slave!

15
THE DULE'S I' THIS BONNET O' MINE
(Edwin Waugh)

The dule's i' this bonnet o' mine;
    My ribbins'll never be reet;
Here, Mally, aw'm like to be fine,
    For Jamie'll be comin' to-neet;
He met me i'th lone○ t'other day, —
    Aw're gooin' for wayter to th' well, —
An' he begged that aw'd wed him May; —
Bi th' mass,△ iv he'll let me, aw will.

When he took my honds into his,
    God Lord, heaw they trembled between;
An' aw durstn't look up in his face,
    Becose† on him seein' my e'en;
My cheek went as red as a rose; —
    There's never a mortal can tell
Heaw happy aw felt; for, thae knows,
    Aw couldn't ha' axed⊕ him mysel'.

But th' tale wur at th' end o' my tung, —
    To let it eawt wouldn't be reet —
For aw thought to seem forrud□ wur wrong,
    So aw towd him aw'd tell him to-neet;
But, Mally, thae knows very weel, —
    Though it isn't a thing one should own, —
If aw'd th' pikein'☆ o'th world to mysel',
    Aw'd oather■ ha' Jamie or noan.

Neaw, Mally, aw've towd tho my mind;
    What wouldto do iv 'twur thee?
'Aw'd tak him just while he're inclined,
    An' a farrantly bargain● he'd be;
For Jamie's as gradely▲ a lad
    As ever stept eawt into th' sun; —

So jump at thy chance, an' get wed,
    An' do th' best tho con, when it's done!'

Eh, dear, but it's time to be gwon, —
    Aw shouldn't like Jamie to wait, —
Aw connot for shame be too soon,
    An' aw wouldn't for th' world be too late;
Aw'm o' ov a tremble to th' heel, —
    Dost think at my bonnet'll do?
'Be off, lass, — thae looks very weel; —
    He wants noan o'th bonnet, thae foo★!'

○ lone, lane   ⊕ Bi th' mass: by the mass; an expression brought down from Catholic times   □ Becose: because   ☆ axed: asked   ■ forrud, forward   ● pikein', picking, choosing   ▲ oather: either   ★ a farrantly bargain: a decent bargain, a good bargain   ◖ gradely: proper, right   ◆ foo: fool

16
AH NIVVER CAN CALL HER MY WIFE
(Ben Preston)

Ah'm a weyver, ye knaw, an' awf deead,
    So ah due all'at ivver ah can
To put away aht o' my eead
    The thowts an' the aims of a man.
Eight shillin' i' t'wick's○ what ah arn
When ah've varry gooid wark an' full time,
An' ah thinks it's a sorry consarn
    For a fellah at's just in his prime.

Bud ahr maister says things is as well
    As they have been or ivver can be
An' ah happen sud think so mysel'
    If he'd nobbud swop places wi' me.
Bud he's welcome to all he can get,
    Ah begrudge him o'noan ov his brass,
An, ah'm nowt bud a maddlin⊕ to fret,
    Ur to think o' yond bewtiful lass.

Ah nivver can call her my wife,
    My love ah sal nivver mak' knawn,
Yit the sorra that darkens her life
    Thraws its shadda across o' my awn.
When ah knaw 'at her heart is at eease,
    Theer is sunshine a' singing' i' mine;
An' misfortunes may come as they please,
    Yit they seldom can mak' ma repine.

Bud that Chartist wor nowt bud a sloap □ –
    Ah wor fooild by his speeches an' rhymes,
For his promises wottered my hoap,
    An' ah leng'd for his sunshiny times;
Bud I feel 'at my dearest desire
    Within ma al wither away,
Like an ivy-stem trailin' i' t'mire
    It's deein for t'want of a stay.

When ah laid i' my bed day an' neet,
    An' wor geen up by t'doctors for deead,
God bless her! shoo'd com' wi' a leet
    An' a basin o' grewil an' breead,
An' ah once thowt ah'd aht☆wi' it all,
    Bud soa kindly shoo chatted an' smiled,
Ah wor fain to turn ovver to t'wall,
    An' to bluther an' roar like a child.

An' ah said, as I thowt of her een,
    Each breeter for t'tear 'at wor in't,
It's a sin to be nivver forgeen,
    To yoke her to famine an' stint;
So ah'll een travel forrad throo life,
    Like a man throo a desert unknawn;
Ah mun neer hev a hoam nur a wife,
    Bud my sorras al all be my awn.

Soa ah trudge on aloan as ah owt,
    An' whotivver my troubles may be,
They'll be sweetened, poor lass, wi' the thowt
    'At I've nivver browt trouble to thee.

Yit a burd hes its young uns to guard,
A wild beast a mate in his den,
An' ah cannot bud think 'at it's hard –
Nay, deng it, ah'm roarin' agen.

○ wick: week   ⊕ madlin: confused, foolish person   □ sloap: liar
☆ aht: out

17
BITE BIGGER
(John Hartley)

As aw hurried throo th' taan to mi wark,
(Aw wur lat, for all th' whistles had gooan,)
Aw happen'd to hear a remark,
At ud fotch tears throo th' heart ov a stooan. –
It wor raanin, an snawin, an cowd
An th' flagstoans wor covered wi muck,
An th' east wind booath whistled an howl'd,
It saanded like nowt but ill luck;
When two little lads, donn'd i' rags,
    Baght○ stockins or shoes o' ther feet,
Coom trapesin away ower th' flags,
    Booath on em sodden'd wi th' weet. –
Th' owdest mud happen be ten,
        Th' young en be hauf on't, – noa moore;
As aw luk'd on, aw sed to misen,
        God help fowk this weather at's poor!
Th' big en sam'd⊕ summat off th' graand,
    An aw luk'd just to see what't could be;
'Twur a few wizened flaars□ he'd faand,
    An they seem'd to ha fill'd him wi glee:
An he sed, 'Come on, Billy, may be
    We shall find summat else by and by,
An if net, tha mun share thease wi me
    When we get to some spot where its dry.'
Leet-hearted they trotted away,
    An aw follow'd, coss 'twur i' mi rooad;
But aw thowt awd ne'er seen sich a day –
    It worn't fit to be aght for a tooad.

Sooin th' big en agean slipt away,
An sam'd summat else aght o'th' muck,
An he cried aght, 'Luk here, Bill! to-day
Arn't we blest wi a seet o' gooid luck?
Here's a apple! an' th' mooast on it's saand:
What's rotten aw'll throw into th' street —
Worn't it gooid to ligg☆ thear to be faand?
Nah booath on us con have a treat.'
Soa he wiped it, an rubb'd it, an then
Sed, 'Billy, thee bite off a bit;
If tha hasn't been lucky thisen
Tha shall share wi me sich as aw get.'

Soa th' little en bate off a touch,
T'other's face beemed wi pleasur all throo,
An he sed, 'Nay, tha hasn't taen much,
Bite agean, an bite bigger; nah do!'

Aw waited to hear nowt noa moor, —
Thinks aw, thear's a lesson for me!
Tha's a heart i' thi breast, if tha'rt poor:
Th' world wur richer wi moor sich as thee!
Tuppince wur all th' brass aw had,
An awd ment it for ale when coom nooin,
But aw thowt aw'll give it yond lad,
He desarves it for what he's been dooin.
Soa aw sed, 'Lad, here's tuppince for thee,
For thi sen,' -- an they stared like two geese;
But he sed, woll th' tear stood in his e'e,
'Nay, it'll just be a penny a piece.'
'God bless thi! do just as tha will,
An many better days speedily come;
Tho clam'd,■ an hauf donn'd,●mi lad, still
Thairt a deal nearer Heaven nur some.'

○ Baght: ·without   ⊕ sam'd: sighted   □ flaars: flowers   ☆ ligg: lie
■ clam'd: starved   ● donn'd: drowned

18
TH' SHURAT WEAVER'S SONG
(Samuel Laycock)

Confound it! aw ne'er wur so woven afore,
Mi back's welly brocken, mi fingers are sore;
Aw've bin starin' an' rootin' among this Shurat
Till aw'm very near getten as bloint as a bat.

Every toime aw go in wi mi cuts⊕to owd Joe,
He gies mi a cursin', an' bates□mi an' o;
Aw've a warp i' one loom wi' booath selvedges marr'd,
An' th' other's as bad for he's dress'd it to hard.

Aw wish aw wur tur enuff off, eawt o' th road,
For o' weavin' this rubbitch aw'm getting' reet stow'd☆;
Aw've nowt i' this world to lie deawn on but straw,
For aw've only eight shillin' this fortni't to draw.

Neaw aw haven't mi family under mi hat,
Aw've a woife an' six childer to keep cawt o' that;
So aw'm rayther among it at present yo see,
Iv ever a fellow wur puzzled, it's me!

Iv one turns eawt to steal, folk'll co me a thief,
An' aw conno' put th' cheek on to ax for relief;
As aw said i' eawr heawse t' other neet to mi woife,
Aw never did nowt o' this sort i' mi loife.

One doesn't like everyone t' know heaw they are,
But we'n suffered so long thro' this 'Merica war;
'At there's lot's o' poor factory folk getten t' fur end,
An' they'll soon be knocked o'er iv th' toimes don't mend.

Oh, dear! iv yon Yankees could only just see
Heaw they're clemmin' an' starvin' poor weavers loike me,
Aw think they'd soon settle their bother, an' strive
To send us some cotton to keep us alive.

There's theawsands o' folk just i'th' best o' their days,
Wi' traces o' want plainly seen i' their face;
An' a future afore 'em as dreary an' dark,
For when th' cotton gets done we shall o be beawt wark.

We'n bin patient an' quiet as long as we con;
Th' bits o' things we had by us are welly o gone;
Aw've bin trampin' so long, mi owd shoon are worn eawt,
An' mi halliday clooas are o on 'em 'up th' speawt'■.

It wur nobbut last Monday aw sowd a good bed —
Nay, very near gan it — to get us some bread;
Afore these bad times cum aw used to be fat,
But neaw, bless yo'r loife, aw'm as thin as a lat!

Mony a toime i' mi loife aw've seen things lookin' feaw,
But never as awk'ard as what they are neaw;
Iv there isn't some help for us factory folk soon,
Aw'm sure we shall o be knocked reet eawt o' tune.

Come give us a lift, yo' 'at han owt to give,
An' help yo're poor brothers an' sisters to live;
Be kind, an' be tender to th' needy an' poor,
An' we'll promise when th' times mend we'll ax yo no moor.

⊕ cuts: cuts of finished cloth   □ bates: fines   ☆ stow'd: hindered, stopped
■ 'up th' speawt': pawned

19
TH' ROW BETWEEN TH' CAIGES
(Tommy Armstrong)

One mornen wen aw went to wark,
　Th' seet wis most exsiten ○,
Ad ard a noise, en luckt eroond,
　En we de ye think wis fiten?
Aw stud amais'd en at thim gaisd,
　To see thim in such raiges;
For aw nivor seed e row like that
　Between th' Brockwil caiges.

Wor aud caig sais, 'Cum over th' gaits,
  Becaws it's mei intenshin
To let th' see wethor thoo or me
  Is th' best invenshin.'
Th' neuin⊕ been rais'd, teuk off his clais,
  Then at it thae went dabin;
Th' blud wis runen doon th' skeets,
  En past th' weimin's cabin.

Wor aud caige sais, 'Let's heh me clais,
  Thoo thwot thit thoo cud flae me;
But if aw'd been is young is thoo
  Aw's certain aw cud pae th'.'
Th' paitint □ nockt hees ankel off,
  En th' buaith ad cutten fuaices; ☆
Th' shifters rapt three for te ride,
  So th' buaith went to thor plaices.

Wen ganen up en doon th' shaft.
  Th' patint caige did threetin
For te tuaik wor audin's life
  If thae stopt it meeten;
Wor aud cage bauld oot is thae pas't;
  'Thoo nasty, dorty paitint,
Rub thee jes eguain th' skeets —
  Aw think thoo's ardly wakinit.'

Th' paitint te wor aud caige sais:
  'Altho' aw be e strangor,
Aw kin work me wark is weel is thoo.
  An free th' men freh daingor:
Noo, if th' rope shud brick we me,
  Aud skinny jaws, just watch us.
Thoo'l see me clag on te th' skeets,
  For aw's full e springs en catches.

○ exsiten: exciting   ⊕ neuin: new one   □ paitint: patent [lift]   ☆ en th'
buaith ad cutten fuaices: and they both had cut faces

Wor aud caige te th' paitint sais;
   'Aw warnd thoo think thoo's clivor,
Becaws thi'v polished thoo we paint,
   But thoo'l not last for ivor;
Th' paint on thoo 'ill weer awae,
   En then thoo's lost thei beuty;
Th' nivor painted me at awl,
   En still aw've deun me deuty.'

Th' braiksmin browt thim buaith te bank,
   Th' mischeef for te sattil;
Thae fit freh five o'clock te six,
   En th' paitint won th' battle.
It teuk th' braikemin half e shift
   To clag thim up we plaistors;
Wor aud caige sent hees noatece in,
   But just to vext th' maistors.

Spoken. — Thor matcht to fite eguain, but not under Queensbury Rools. Wor aud caige fancies fiten we th' bare fist. Aw'll let ye naw wen it comes off. It 'ill heh to be kept quiet; if the bobby gets to naw, thae'll be buaith teun, becaws th' winit aloo bare fist fiten noo. Keep on lucken in th' Christian Arald, en yil see wen it comes off, en ware. Thor's six to fower on the auden noo. Bet nowt te that dae, en aw'll see ye in the field; it's a cheet.

20

THE TOON IMPROVEMENT BILL
(OR, NE PLEYCE NOO TE PLAY.)
(Ned Corven)

Noo, O dear me, what mun aw de?
   Aw've ne place noo te play,
Wor canny Forth, an' Spital tee,
   Eh, man! they've tyuen away.

Ne place te bool wor peyste eggs○ noo,
   Te lowp the frog, or run:
They're elways beeldin' summick⊕ noo —
   They'll spoil Newcassel suen.

Spoken. – Thor's ne pleyce te play the wag noo; the grun's a' tuen up wi' High Levels, Central Stations, an' dear knaws what else. Aw used te play the wag doon the Kee thonder. Aw've seen me fish for days tegither. The lads ca'd me the fisherwoman's boy. Aw was a stunner. Aw've mony a time browt up three French apples at a time; but wor aud wife said if aw fell in an' gat drooned she'd skin me alive when aw com hyem; so aw played the wag doon the Burn efter that. But, noo to myek improvemints, they've filled it up wi' cairt loads o' muck to beeld hooses on. Sum o' wor lads an' me petitioned the magistrates for a new play grund, an' they tell'd us te gan te bordin' skuels. What an idea! Wor and wife hes sair tues□ to raise the penny for Monday mornin's: the maister seldom gets it tho': aw buy claggum☆ wid: then the maister hes to tyek't oot in flaps.■ But aw's broken hearted when aw think aboot wor canny Forth, wiv its aud brick wall. What curious days aw've spent there! Man, aw've seen me play the wag for hyel● days tetither, wi' maw mooth a' covvered wi' claggum an' clarts▲. What a chep aw was for one-hole-teazer then! mony a time aw've fowt an oor for a farden bullocker★. Aw used to skin thor knuckles, when aw won mee beeks. Aw used te fullock◆ – man, what a fullocker aw was! But what's the use o' jawin' noo? the gams are a' gyen. Thor's widdy-widdy-way-the-morrow's-the-market-day-slyater-cummin-away and King-Henry's-boys-go-round – what a gam that was! – aw used te be King Henry! But aw'd better drop off, or maw feelin's will set me on a bubblin' – for

                    Chorus
              Oh dear! what mun aw de
              Aw've ne pleyce noo te play,
              Wor canny Forth, an' Spital tee,
              Eh, man! they tyuen away.

              The Toon Improvemint's myed greet noise,
                  But aw heard me fethur say,
              Thor was summick mair than little boys
                  Kept wor wise heed at play;

○ te bool wor peyste eggs: to bowl our pace eggs   ⊕ beeldin' summick: building something   □ sair tues: poor time   ☆ claggum: treacle candy   ■ flaps: blows, strikes   ● hyel: whole   ▲ clarts: dirt, smudges   ★ farden bullocker: farthing marble   ◆ fullock: to jerk the hand when playing marbles

Thor's bonny wark amang thorsels,
But aw mun haud mee jaw;
But still thor's folks 'boot here that smells
The cash buik wiv its flaw.

Spoken. — Aw heard my fethur tell my muther yen neet all aboot the toon concerns. They thowt aw was asleep, but aw's a cute lad. Aw's elways waken when the tripe's fryin' for fethur's supper. Aw heard him say thor was a vast o' rates — sic as poor rates, leet rates, sewer rates, an' watch rates; but aw think, at ony rate, thor's ne first-rate rates amang them. Noo, thor's the watch-rate — that's the pollis. Noo, we cannit de wivoot pollis, but it's not fair te tyek a chep up for playin' at holes; but the migistrators isn't dein' fair wiv us at nowt. Aw's lossin' a' maw learnin' noo. What a heedpiece aw had yen time! Aw'd te use a shoe-horn te put my Sunday hat on, my heed gat swelled wiv knowledge se. Noo, a' thor days is gyen, so aw'll lairn te chow backy.

For, O dear me, etc.

Bedstocks — that canny gam's noo duen,
An' three hole teazer, tee;
They've duen away wor best o' fun,
So, lads, what mun aw de?
Aw'll bubble tiv aw dee, begox!
Or tyek sum arsynack,
Then corporation men may funk,
When aw's laid on maw back.

For, O dear me, etc.

Noo, a' ye canny folks that's ere,
Just thnk on what aw say,
And reckolect yor youthful days,
When ye were fond o' play.
Ye say yor skuel days was the best,
So help me in maw cawse,
An' cheer poor Bobby Snivvelnose
By gi'en him yor applause.

For, O dear me, etc.

21
BLAYDON RACES
(George Ridley)
Tune – 'Brighton'

Aw went to Blaydon Races, 'twas on the ninth of Joon;
Eiteen hundred an' sixty-two, on a summer's efternoon;
Aw tyuk the 'bus frae Balmbra's, an' she wis heavy laden,
Away we went alang Collingwood Street, that's on the road to
  Blaydon.

Chorus
O lads, ye shud only seen us gannin',
We pass'd the foaks upon the road just as they wor stannin';
Thor wes lots o' lads an' lasses there, all wi' smiling faces,
Gawn alang the Scotswood Road, to see the Blaydon Races.

We flew past Armstrong's factory, and up to the 'Robin Adair',
Just gannin doon te the railway bridge, the 'bus wheel flew off there.
The lasses lost their crinolines off, an' the veils that hide their faces,
An' aw got two black eyes an' a broken nose in gan te Blaydon
  Races.

Chorus – O lads, ye shud only seen us gannin', etc.

When we gat the wheel put on away we went agyen,
But them that had their noses broke, they cam back ower hyem;
Sum went to the dispensary, an' uthers to Doctor Gibbs,
An' sum sought out the Infirmary to mend their broken ribs.

Chorus – O lads, you shud only seen us gannin', etc.

Noo when we gat to Paradise those wes bonny gam begun;
Thor wes fower-and-twenty on the 'bus, man, hoo they danced an'
  sung;
They called on me to sing a sang, them 'Paddy Fagan',
Aw danced a jig an' swung my twig that day aw went to Blaydon.

Chorus – O lads, ye shud only seen us gannin', etc.

We flew across the Chain Bridge reet into Blaydon toon,
The bellman he was callin' there — they call him Jackey Brown;
Aw saw him talkin' to sum cheps, an' them he was pursuadin'
To gan an' see Geordy Ridley's concert in the Mechanics' Hall at
  Blaydon.

Chorus — O lads, ye shud only seen us gannin', etc.

The rain it poor'd aw the day, an' myed the groons ○ quite muddy,
Coffy Johnny had a white hat on — they war shootin' 'Whe stole the
  cuddy'⊕.
There was spice stalls an' munkey shows, an' aud wives selling ciders,
An' a chep wiv a happeny roond aboot shootin' 'Now me boys, for
  riders.'

Chorus — O lads, ye shud only seen us gannin', etc.

22
THE ROW UPON THE STAIRS
(Joe Wilson)
Tune — 'Uncle Sam'

Says Mistress Bell te Mistress Todd,
    'Ye'd better clean the stairs!
Ye've missed yor turn for monny a week,
    The neybors a' did theirs!'
Says Mistress Todd to Mistress Bell,
    'Aw tell ye Mistress Bell,
Ye'd better mind yor awn affairs,
    An clean the stairs yor-sel.'

    Korus
Oh what tungs i' the row upon the stairs,
Clitterin, clatterin, scandal, an' clash,
I' the row upon the stairs.

Says Mistress Todd — 'When it suits me
    Te think that it's me turn;
Ye've a vast o' cheek te order me,
    Thor's not a wummin born

That keeps a cleaner hoose than me;
   An' mark ye, Mistress Bell,
Ef ye'd oney de the syem as me,
   Ye'd gan an' clean — yor-sel!'

Says Mistress Bell — 'Ye clarty fah,○
   We was't that stole the beef?'
'What de ye say?' cries Mistress Todd,
   'De ye mean that aw'm a thief?
Let's heh the sixpence that aw lent
   Te treat Meg Smith wi' gin!
An where's the blanket that ye gat
   The last time ye lay in?'

Says Mistress Bell — 'Ye knaw yor-sel
   The sixpence's lang been paid,
An' the raggy blanket that ye lent
   Wes ne use then ye said!'
'A raggy blanket! Mistress Bell,'
   Cries Mistress Todd — 'What cheek!
Yor dorty stockin had two holes
   Full twice the size last week!'

'Maw holey stockins, Mistress Todd,
   Luks better i' the street
Than yor gud man's awd blucher beuts ⊕
   Ye weer te hide yor feet!
The eer-rings ye gat frae the Jew
   On tick the tuthor day,
'Ill be like the fine manadge man's shawl
   The syem as gien away!'

Says Mistress Todd — 'Ye greet sk'yet gob □
Ye'd bettor had yor jaw,
The varry shift upon yor back
   Belangs the wife belaw!'

○ clarty fah: dirty fool   ⊕ blucher beuts: rubber boots   □ sk'yet gob: slant mouth

'Ye lazy wretch!' — shoots Mistress Bell,
   'It's true, thor is ne doot,
Last neet ye fuddled wi' Bob the Snob,
   The time yor man wes oot!'

'Oh, Mistress Bell!' — says Mistress Todd,
   'Ye brazind-luckin slut,
Ye may tawk away — te clean the stairs
   Aw'll nivor stir a fut!
Afore aw'd lift a skoorin cloot
   The mucky stairs te clean,
Aw'd see them turn as black as ye,
   Ye pawnship-luckin queen!'

23
TA-RA-RA BOOM-DE-AY
(Sung by Miss Lottie Collins)

A smart and stylish girl you see,
Belle of good society;
Not too strict, but rather free,
Yet as right as right can be!
Never forward, never bold —
Not too hot, and not too cold,
But the very thing I'm told,
That in your arms you'd like to hold.

   Chorus — Ta-ra-ra Boom-de-ay.

I'm not extravagantly shy,
And when a nice young man is nigh,
For his heart I have a try —
And faint away with tearful cry.
When the good young man in haste,
Will support me round the waist,
I don't come to, while thus embraced,
Till of my lips he steals a taste.

   Chorus — Ta-ra-ra Boom-de-ay.

I'm a timid flower of innocence –
Pa says that I have no sense,
I'm one eternal big expense;
But men say that I'm just immense
Ere my verse I conclude,
I'd like it known and understood,
Though free as air, I'm never rude,
I'm not too bad, and not too good.

        Chorus – Ta-ra-ra Boom-de-ay.

You should see me out with pa,
Prim and most particular;
The young men say, 'ah, there you are!'
And pa says, 'that's peculiar!'
'It's like their cheek' I say, and so
Off again with pa I go –
He's quite satisfied – although,
When his back's turned – well, you know –

        Chorus – Ta-ra-ra Boom-de-ay

24
NEVER INTRODUCE YOUR DONAH TO A PAL
(Sung by Gus Elen)

I've lost my gal through a pal o' mine as was,
Always wi' me nar, I'll tell yer why becos,
Me and 'im was partners in a donkey cart.
That's what made me introdooce him to the tart.
One day I sez, 'Bill, I wants the cart today,'
'E sez, 'me too,' in a aggrawatin' way;
As I did not want to go and needle 'im,
I takes my gal along o' me to wheedle 'im.

    Chorus
    Never introduce yer donah to a pal,
    'Cos the odds is 10 to 1 he sneaks yer gal;
    He'll stand her whelks and porter,
    And upon the sly 'e'll court her,

Never introdooce yer donah to a pal,
Take my tip,
Always keep yer blinkers on yer gal.

Once I spotted Bill and Sal a-making eyes,
Then he goes and lushes 'er, to my surprise,
I sez, 'look 'ere, this is far beyond a joke,'
He sez, 'chuck it, else I'll land yer on the boke;'
I spars up, but though yer won't believe the fact,
In one short round I gits both my peepers black'd,
From the cart Sal shouted, 'gar'n, it sarves yer right,'
In jumped Bill, and then the pair druv out o' sight.

Bill and Sal got spliced a month ago today,
For their 'oneymoon, at Bow they went to stay,
Just to rile me, and to finish up the fake,
They sends me a pound and 'alf 'o wedding cake.
They're in business, and a nobby start they've made,
As for me. I'm gettin' broke and losin' trade.
Things, in fact, is now a-lookin' precious blue,
For I'm seedy, sad and broken-'earted too.

25
OUR LODGER'S SUCH A NICE YOUNG MAN
(Sung by Vesta Victoria)

At our house not long ago a lodger came to stay,
At first I felt as if I'd like to drive him right away;
But soon he prov'd himself to be so very good and kind,
That, like my dear mamma, I quite made up my little mind,

Chorus – Our lodger's such a nice young man, such a good young
    man is he;
So good, so kind to all our family!
He's never going to leave us – Oh dear, oh dear, no!
He's such a good – goody – goody man, mamma told me so.

He made himself at home before he'd been with us a day –
He kissed mamma and all of us, 'cos papa was away;
Before he goes to work he lights the fires and scrubs the floor,
And puts a nice strong cup of tea outside   ma's bedroom door.

Chorus — Our lodger's such a nice young man.

At night he makes the beds and does the other little jobs,
And if the baby hurts itself he really cries and sobs;
On Sunday when ma's cooking and papa is at the club,
He takes the kids and baths us all inside the washing tub.

Chorus — Our lodger's such a nice young man.

We usually go to Margate, in the sea to have a splash,
This year pa said, 'I'm busy!' but I think he had no cash;
The lodger took us down instead — mamma and baby too,
And never charged pa anything,— now there's a pal for you!

Chorus — Our lodger's such a nice young man.

Notes

1. 'The New Times' (London: J. Catnach, n.d. [*c.* 1820]).
2. John Grimshaw, 'The Hand-loom Weavers' Lament', in John Harland and T. T. Wilkinson, *Ancient Ballads and Songs of Lancashire*, 3rd ed. (Manchester: John Heywood, 1882), pp.193–5. Grimshaw was a village broadside song writer and seller in Gorton, near Manchester.
3. 'Steam Loom Weaver' (*c.* 1830). Broadside Collection, British Museum.
4. 'The Jolly Grinder' (Sheffield: Joseph Ford, n.d. [*c.* 1835]). Sheffield Central Reference Library.
5. 'The Working Man' (London: H. Such, n.d. [*c.* 1850]). 'Tune – "The Englishman" '. The Crampton Collection, British Museum.
6. 'The Devils in the Girl' (*c.* 1825). Harris Public Library, Preston.
7. 'The Dodger' (London: H. Disley, n.d. [after 1840]). The Crampton Collection, British Museum. Street literature was very sensitive to political changes, but rarely includes any reactions to the literary currents of the day. This work is an interesting exception. Tennyson's 'Come into the garden, Maud' was reprinted as a broadside after it became a hit song.
8. 'Manchester's Improving Daily' (Manchester: Swindells, n.d. [*c.* 1830]). Broadside Collection, Manchester Central Reference Library. There are two versions of this song. The one printed here comments more directly upon the differences between the town and country. Verses 6–10 were written by Alexander Wilson, and appear in both versions. The other version, according to a handwritten note on the broadside, was written by one W. B. Oldfield.
9. 'Collier Lass' (Manchester: J. Swindells, n.d. (*ca.* 1835]). Harris Public Library, Preston.
10. 'The Bonnie Pit Lads (Newcastle: T. Dodds, n.d. [*ca.* 1842–44]). 'Pitmen's Strike, 1844,' Wigan Central Library.
11. 'How to be a Great Lord,' quoted in 'The Beauties of the Press,' *Northern Star*, 12 September 1840. A typical example of Chartist satire.
12. 'The Pauper's Drive.' This version comes from a broadside in the John Johnson collection, Bodleian Library, Oxford, in which the publisher's name and address have been cut out. 'William Tell' and 'Let Fame Sound the Trumpet' accompany it. It is one of the few Chartist songs to be found on a popular broadside (as opposed to the broadsides the Chartists themselves published). It originally appeared in the *Northern Star*, 5 February 1842. According to Mary Russell Mitford the author was 'a secluded country gentleman,' Thomas Noel (*Recollections of a Literary Life*) [London: Richard Bentley, 1852], I, pp.39–56. It appears anonymously in all popular sources.
13. 'The Lion of Freedom,' quoted in the *Northern Star*, 11 September 1841. A slightly different version is published by Thomas Cooper

in his *Life* (London: Hodder and Stoughton, 1872), pp.175—176. This song is often incorrectly attributed to Cooper. It was written by a Welsh woman in honor of Feargus O'Connor's release from prison, and was sung wherever he went for the next decade.

14. John Henry Bramwich, 'A Hymn,' quoted in the *Northern Star*, 4 April 1846. Bramwich attended Cooper's Shakespearean Chartist meetings, and under his encouragement wrote a number of Chartist hymns. This was his most famous. It was widely sung at the close of Chartist meetings and other solemn occasions, such as Chartist funerals.

15. Edwin Waugh, 'The Dule's i' this Bonnet o' Mine' (*ca.* 1860). Edwin Waugh, *Poems and Songs*, VIII of *Collected Works*, ed. George Milner (Manchester: John Heywod, n.d. [1892]), pp.23—24. This is one of Waugh's most popular recitation pieces.

16. Ben Preston, 'Ah Nivver Can Call her my Wife' (1856). Ben Preston, *Dialect and Other Poems* (Bradford: T. Brear, 1881), pp.17—18.

17. John Hartley, 'Bite Bigger' (*ca.* 1862). John Hartley, *Yorkshire Lyrics* (London: W. Nicholson, n.d. [1898]), pp.30—32. At 23 Hartley read Waugh's 'Come Whoam to thy Childer an' Me,' and it influenced his entire future career. He wrote 'Bite Bigger,' his first poem, under the influence of Waugh, for the Beacon Club, a social and educational club for young working men. Like Waugh's poem, it was immensely successful as a penny broadside, and helped to insure Hartley's career as a dialect reader.

18. Samuel Laycock, 'Th' Shurat Weaver's Song' (1861—62). Samuel Laycock, *Warblin's fro' an Owd Songster* (Oldham: W. E. Clegg n.d. [1893]), pp.51—52. During the American Civil War the only cotton available in Lancashire came from Egypt and India. It was of very low quality, and involved much cleaning and combing before the power looms could be set up, and then the fibers often broke. Since the workers were paid on a piece rate, their wages could be as low as 5/- to 7/- a week for sixty hours of work. Even the fully employed suffered during the Cotton Famine. This poor quality cotton was called 'shurat' after the Indian port of Surat. Note the echo of 'Jone o' Grinfilt, Jr.' in this song.

19. Tommy Armstrong, 'The Row between the Cages' (*c.* 1880). *Tommy Armstrong Sings*, intro. by Tom Gilfellon (Newcastle: Frank Graham, 1971), pp.43—4. 'To the tune Robin Thomson's Smiddy, O.' The installation of a new patented safety lift alongside the older lift set Tommy thinking about the changes he had seen in mining. See A. L. Lloyd, *Folk Song in England* (London: Lawrence and Wishart, 1967), pp.382—4.

20. Ned Corvan, 'The Toon Improvement Bill' (*c.* 1850). *Allan's Illustrated Edition of Tyneside Songs and Readings*, rev. ed. (Newcastle: T. & G. Allan, 1891), pp.395—7. One of Corvan's earliest music-hall hits.

21. George Ridley, 'Blaydon Races' (1862). *Allan's Tyneside Songs*, pp.451—2. George Ridley (1835—64), along with Wilson

and Corvan, was one of the three most popular music-hall singers of the early 1860s in the Newcastle area. After being crushed in a wagon accident, he became a singer, but died after less than five years on stage, from the effects of the accident. 'Blaydon Races' is sung by Newcastle United football fans at every game, so it remains one of the most famous nineteenth-century Newcastle songs.

22. Joe Wilson, 'The Row upon the Stairs' (*c.* 1860). Joseph Wilson, *Tyneside Songs and Drolleries, Readings and Temperance Songs* (Newcastle: T. & G. Allan, n.d. [1890]), pp.33–4. 'Tune – "Uncle Sam" '.

23. 'Ta-ra-ra Boom-de-ay' (1891). Music by C. Sheard. *The Music Hall Songster* (London: W. Fortey, n.d. [1892]), p.2. One of the most popular songs of its day, greatly admired for its daring. Lottie Collins performed a high-kicking dance as she sang the chorus with the audience.

24. 'Never Introduce Your Donah to a Pal' (1890), written by A. Ellis, music by Augustus Durandeau. *The Music Hall Songster,* p.2.

25. 'Our Lodger's Such a Nice Young Man' (1897), written and composed by Fred Murray and Lawrence Barclay (London: Francis, Day & Hunter, 1897).

BIBLIOGRAPHY

The ephemeral nature of the material studied has made it impossible to list all the works of each writer. A great deal of evidence is available in the form of newspaper cuttings, book reviews and personal memorabilia, none of which has been listed separately. Important periodicals and newspapers have been listed, but not individual articles within them. The major broadside collections examined are listed separately, but in addition, nearly every public library has at least a handful of interesting local broadside publications.

I. Primary Sources
Upublished Material

Bamford, Samuel. 'Diary: 28 February 1858 – 26 December 1861.' MS. Manchester Central Reference Library.

The Bell Collection. Broadsides, accounts, cuttings, personal memorabilia. The Newcastle-Upon-Tyne University Library.

The Bell Collection. Misc. unpub. material and broadsides. Newcastle Central Reference Library.

Burland, John. 'Annals of Barnsley and its Environs'. 4 vols. MS. Barnsley Publi Library.

'Coal Trade: Pitmen's Strike, 1844'. Letters, cuttings and broadsides. Newcastle Central Reference Library.

Dun, Matthias. Unpub. diary. Newcastle Central Reference Library.

Falkner, George and Alexander. 'Private Journal and Weekly Balance Sheet, 1843–47' George Falkner and Sons, Ltd, Mancherster.

Harlan, John. MSS., cuttings, transcripts and notes. Manchester Central Reference Library.

Hartley, John. Unpub. correspondence. Bradford Central Reference Library.

Leary Fred. MSS. and scrapbooks. Manchester Central Reference Library.

'Pitmen's Strike, 1844'. Letters, cuttings and broadsides. Wigan Central Library.

Prince, John Critchley. 'The Olio'. Unpub. commonplace book. Manchester Central Reference Library.

——————Unpub. correspondence. Manchester Central Reference Library.

Procter, John. Account books, correspondence and printing samples. Private collection, Robert Wood, West Hartlepool.

Ridings, Elijah. Commonplace book. Untitled MS. Manchester Central Reference Library.

Scruton, William. Personal papers. MSS., letters, cuttings, broadsides. Bradford Central Reference Library.

Skipsey, Joseph. Letters to Thomas Dixon. The Stone Gallery, Newcastle-upon-Tyne.
Waugh, Edwin. Commonplace book, notebooks and memorabilia. Untitled MSS. Manchester Central Reference Library.
_____'Diary: 21 July 1847 – 10 February 1851'. MS. Manchester Central Reference Library.

Broadside and Music Hall Collections
Baring-Gould, Sabine. *Broadside Collection.* 9 vols. London, 1800–70. British Museum.
Broadside Collection. 3 vols. Manchester Central Reference Library.
Broadside Collection. Harris Public Library, Preston.
Crampon, Thomas. *A Collection of Broadside Ballads Printed in London.* 7 vols. London, n.d. [1860?].
Enthoven Music Hall Collection. The Victoria and Albert Museum.
Holder, Reuben. Broadsides. Bradford Central Reference Library.
The John Johnson Collection. Bodleian Library, Oxford.
Oastler and the Factory Movement. Broadside Collection. 3 vols. Goldsmiths' Library, University of London.
Old Street Ballads. Broadside Collection. 2 vols. Brown, Picton and Hornby Libraries, Liverpool.
Ten Hours Movement. Broadside Collection. Bradford Central Reference Library.
The Robert White Collection of Chapbooks, Garlands and Broadsides. Newcastle-upon-Tyne University Library.

Government Documents
Great Britain. *Report of the Commission for Inquirying into the Employment and Condition of Children in Mines and Manufactures.* 1842.
Great Britain.*Report of the Select Committee on Factory Children's Labour.* vol.XV. 1831–32.

Newspapers
Barnsley Chronicle. Obituary notices and cuttings.
The British Labourer's Protector and Factory Child's Friend. Leeds, 1832–3.
The Chartist Circular. Glasgow, 1839–41.
Durham Chronicle. 1843–5.
The English Chartist Circular London, 1841–42.
The Friend of the People. London, 1850–51.
Halifax Courier. Obituary notices and cuttings.
Illustrated London News. 1844, 1862–4.
Manchester City News. Obituary notices and cuttings.
Manchester Guardian. Obituary notices and cuttings.
Manchester Weekly Times. Obituary notices and cuttings.
Miners' Advocate. Newcastle, 1843–6.
Oldham Weekly Chronicle. Obituary notices and cuttings.
The National Instructor. London, 1850.

Newcastle Advertiser. 1843–5.
Newcastle Journal. 1843–5.
Northern Star. Leeds and London, 1838–52.
Notes to the People. London, 1851–2.
The Red Republican. London, 1850.
Reynolds's Weekly Political Instructor. London, 1849–50.
Sunderland Echo. Cuttings.
Ten Hours Advocae and Journal of Literature. Manchester, 1846–7.
Yorkshire Observer. Bradford. Obituary notices and cuttings.
Yorkshire Weekly Post. Bradford, Obituary notices and cuttings.

Periodicals and Almanacs

Ab-o'-th-Yate's Christmas Annual. ed. Ben Brierley. Manchester, 1876–80.
Bairnsla Foaks Annual, an Pogmoor Olmenack. ed. Tom Treddlehoyle [Charles Rogers]. Barnsley, 1838–75. ed. Isaac Binns. Batley, 1876–83.
Th' Beacon Almanack. ed. William Bickerdike. Halifax, 1873–6.
Ben Brierley's Journal. ed. Ben Brierley. Manchester, 1869–85.
Bill o' Jack's Monthly. ed. William Baron. Blackburn, 1897.
The Bowton Loominary, Tumfowt Telegraph, un Lankishire Lookin-Glass. ed. James T. Staton. Bolton, 1852–62.
The Bradfordian. ed. Abraham Holroyd. Bradfod, 1860–62
Bradsaw's Jornal ed. Georgé Falkner. Manchester, 1841–3.
The Call Boy Journal of the British Music Hall. London, 1964.
The City Jackdaw. ed. John Heywood. Manchester, 1875–78.
Comus. Manchester, 1877–78.
Cooper's Journal, or Unfettered Thinker and Plain Speaker for Truth, Freedom and Progress. ed. Thomas Cooper. London, 1850.
Country Words. ed. Charles Hardwick. Manchester, 1866.
Country Words of the West Riding. vol.I, ed. Isaac Binns, vol.II, ed. William Andrews. Leeds, 1870–71.
The Democratic Review. ed. G. Julian Harney. London, 1849–50.
Dewsbre Back at Mooin Olmenac. [later: *The Back at Moin Olmenac an' t' West Ridin' Historical Calendar.*] ed. W. Bentley. Dewsbury, 1864–72, 1875–9, 1881.
Eliza Cook's Journal. ed. Eliza Cook. London, 1849–51.
The English Republic. ed. W. J. Linton. London, 1851.
The Frogland Olmenac an Leeds Loiners Annual. ed. Henry Frogland, Hisquire. [John Cooke?]. Leeds, 1852–63.
Illustrated Comic Tyneside Almanac. ed. J. W. Chater. Newcastle, 1862–9, 1872 and 1875.
Holroyd's Bradford Historical Almanack. ed. Abraham Holroyd. Bradford, 1860–65.
Journal of the English Folk Song and Dance Society. London, 1899–1930.
The Lankishire Loominary un Wickly Lookin-Glass. ed. James T. Staton. Manchester, 1864–65.

The Labourer. eds. Feargus O'Connor and Ernest Jones. Nottingham, 1847–48.

T' Leeds Loiners' Comic Olmenac. ed. J. H. Eccles. Leeds, 1873–81.

The Leicestershire Movement; or Voices from the Frame, and the Factory, the Field and the Railway. Leicester, 1850.

The Magazine of Temperance Poetry. ed. Benjamin Glover. London, 1852.

Manchester Notes and Queries. Manchester, 1878–91.

Manchester Quarterly. ed. Manchester Literary Club. Manchester, 1875–1914.

Miners' Journal. ed. R. Beasley. Newcastle, 1843–5.

The Miners' Monthly Magazine. ed. W. P. Roberts. Newcastle, 1844–5.

Monthly Chronicle of North Country Lore and Legend. 5 vols. Newcastle, 1887–91.

The National: A Library for the People. ed. W. J. Linton. London, 1839.

T' Nidderdill Olminac an' Ivvery Body's Kalinder. [later: *T'Nidderdill Comic Casket, Comic Annual and Almanac*.] ed. Nattie Nydds [Thomas Blackah] Pateley Bridge, 1864–80.

Northern Tribune. ed. Joseph Cowen. Newcastle, 1854–5.

The Original Halifax Illuminated Clock Almenack. ed. John Hartley. 1868–1956.

Howitt's Journal of Literature. ed. William Howitt. London, 1849–51.

The Phoenix. eds. John Boton Rogerson and John Hewitt. Manchester, 1828.

The Saunterer's Satchel and West Riding Almanac. [later: *The Yorkshireman's Comic Annual*.] ed. James Burnley. Bradford, 1875–81.

The Shevvild Chap's Annual. ed. Abel Bywater. Sheffield, 1840- 3, 1853, 1855.

South Yorkshire Notes and Queries. Sheffield, 1899–1902.

The Sphinx. ed. J. H. Nodal. Manchester, 1868–71.

The Temperance Advocate and Journal Douglas, 1839.

Tommy's Toddles Comic Almenack for all t' foaks e Leeds*. ed. Tommy Toddles [J. Hamer, later J. Eccles]. Leeds, 1862–75.

Transactions of the Yorkshire Dialect Society. 1898–1910

Tweddell's Yorkshire Miscellany ᵗᵈ Englishman's Magazine*. ed. George Tweddell. Stokesley, ₁844–6.

Yorkshire Notes and Queries. ed. Charles Forshaw. Bradford, 1885–90, 1904–7.

Yorkshire Tribune. ed. William Mitchell. Leeds, 1855–56.

The Yorkshireman: A Monthly Literary Miscellany. Bradford, 1875–8.

Writers and Anthologies

Allan's Illustrated Edition of Tyneside Songs and Readings. rev. ed. Newcastle, 1891.

Anderson, Alexander. *A Song of Labour*. London, 1873.

——————— *Songs of the Rail*. London, 1878.

Anderson, James. *A Collection of Blyth and Tyneside Poems and Songs*. Blyth, n.d. [1891].

Anderton, Henry. *The Temperance and other Poems*. Preston, 1863.

Andrews, William, ed.*Modern Yorkshire Poets*. London, 1885.

_____ *North Country Poets*. 2 vols. London, 1888.

Armstrong, Thomas. *Song Book*. ed. W. H. Armstrong. 2nd. ed. Chester-le-Street, 1930.

_____ *Tommy Armstrong Sings*. intro. by Tom Gilfellon. Newcastle, 1971.

Ashton, John, ed. *Modern Street Ballads*. London, 1888.

Bailey, Philip, J. *Festus*. 2nd ed. London, 1845.

Bamford, Samuel. *The Autobiography of Samuel Bamford*. 2 vols. ed. W. H. Chaloner. London, 1968 [1848–9].

_____ *The Dialect of South Lancashire, or Tim Bobbin's Tummus and Meary, with his Rhymes*. 2nd ed. London, 1854.

_____ *Homely Rhymes, Poems and Reminiscences*. rev. ed. Manchester, 1864.

_____ *Hours in the Bowers*. Manchester, 1834.

_____ *Walks in South Lancashire and on its Borders*. Manchester, 1844.

Band of Hope Union, ed. *Temperance Rhymes and Melodies*. London, 1855.

Barrass, Alexander. *Pitman's Social Neet*. Consett, 1897.

Bealey, Richard Rome. *After Business Jottings*. Manchester, 1865.

_____ *Field Flowers and City Chimes*. Manchester, 1866.

_____ *Later Life Jottings in Verse and Prose*. Manchester, 1884.

Bell, John, ed. *Rhymes of Northern Bards*. Newcastle, 1971 [1812].

Bennett, James, ed. *A Lancashire Miscellany of Dialect Verse*. Oldham, 1960.

Billington, William. *Lancashire Songs, Poems and Sketches*. Blackburn, 1883.

_____ *Sheen and Shade: Lyrical Poems*. Blackburn, 1861.

The Bishoprick Garland. London, 1834.

Blackah, Thomas. *Dialect Poems*. Pateley Bridge, 1867.

_____ *Dialect Poems and Prose*. ed. H. J. L. Bruff. York, 1937.

Blackburn Independent Order of Mechanics. *Flowers of Many Hues*. Blackburn, 1847.

Bloomfield, Robert. *The Poems of Robert Bloomfield*. 3 vols. London, 1827.

Bobbin, Tim. [John Collier]. *The Works of Tim Bobbin in Prose and Verse*. Rochdale, 1819.

Bobbinwinder, Sally. [Joseph Crabtree]. *A Conversation between Peter Pickenpeg, Jack Shuttle and Harry Emptybobbin*. Barnsley, 1838.

Book of the Words to Songs in Roylance's 'Vamping to Songs Made Easy', together with 63 other favourites. London, n.d.

Bourne, Hugh, ed. *A Collection of Hymns for Camp Meetings, Revivals, etc. for the Use of Primitive Methodists*. 6th ed London, 1848.

Brierley, Ben. *Ab-o'-th'-Yate Sketches and Other Short Stories*. James

Dronsfield, 3 vols. Oldham, 1896. *Collected Works*
─────── *Collected Works.* 9 vols. Manchester, 1882–86.
─────── *Failsworth: My Native Village. With Incidents of the Struggles of its Early Reformers.* Oldham, n.d. [1895].
─────── *Home Memories and Recollections.* Manchester, 1886.
─────── *Humorous Rhymes.* Manchester, 1889.
─────── *The Lancashire Weaver: A Domestic Drama.* Manchester, n.d.
─────── *Nights with Ben Brierley; being a selection of Lancashire Readings and Recitations from the Works of Ben Brierley.* 4 pts. Manchester, 1885.
─────── *Personal Recollections of the Late Edwin Waugh.* Manchester, n.d. [1890].
─────── *Popular Edition of Tales and Sketches of Lancashire Life.* 5 vols. Manchester, 1882–86.
Brierley, Thomas. *Nonsense and Tomfoolery in Prose.* Manchester, 1870.
─────── *The Silk Weaver's Fust Bearin' Whoam and Other Tales.* Manchester, 1864.
Bruce, John Collingwood and John Stokoe, eds. *Northumbrian Minstrelsy.* Newcastle, 1882.
Burgess, Joseph. *A Potential Poet? His Autobiography and Verse.* Ilford, n.d. [1927].
Burland, John Hugh. *Poems on Various Subjects.* Barnsley, 1865.
Burnley, James. *Idonia and other Poems.* Bradford, 1869.
Bywater, Abel, *The Sheffield Dialect.* Sheffield, 1839.
─────── *The Shevvild Chap's Song Book.* Sheffield, n.d.
The Canterbury Mogul Songster: A Collection of Favourite Songs. London, n.d. [1892].
Carnie, Ethel. *Rhymes from the Factory.* 2nd ed. Blackburn, 1908.
Chevalier, Albert (with Brian Daly). *A Record of Myself.* London, 1895.
─────── *Before I Forget: The Autobiography of a Chevalier d'Industrie.* London, 1902.
Chicken, Edward. *The Collier's Wedding.* Newcastle, 1829.
Chirgwin, G. H., *Chirgwin's Chirrup. Being the Life and Reminiscences of George Chirgwin, the 'White Eyed Musical Kaffir'.* London, 1912.
Clegg, John Trafford. *Stories, Sketches and Rhymes, Chiefly in the Rochdale Dialect.* Rochdale, 1898.
Close, John. *Poet Close's Lectures and Orations.* Kirkby-Stephens, Westmorland, 1865.
─────── *Political Works with a Biographical Sketch by Delta.* Kirkby-Stephens, Westmorland, 1860.
A Collection of Songs, Comic Satirical and Descriptive. Newcastle, 1827.
Collins, Samuel. *Miscellaneous Poems and Songs.* Manchester, n.d. [1859].
Cook, George. *A Poem on the Page Bank Pit Calamity.* Newcastle, n.d.

[1858].
Cooper, Thomas. *Life*. London, 1872.
_____ *Old Fashioned Stories*. London, 1874.
_____ *Poetical Works*. 2nd. ed. London, 1886.
_____ *Purgatory of Suicides*. London, 1847.
_____ *Wise Saws and Modern Instances*. 2 vols. London, 1845.
Corvan, Edward. *Corvan's Song Book*. Newcastle, n.d.
Crawhall, Joseph, ed. *A Beuk o Newcasel Songs*. Newcastle, 1888.
Cresswell, Marshall. *Local Songs, Recitations, etc.* 2nd ed. Newcastle, 1883.
Crossley, Thomas. *Flowers of Ebor*. London, 1837.
_____ *Poems Lyrical, Moral and Humorous*. London, 1828.
Cum All Yo Cutlin' Heroes: Songs from Sheffield and District. eds. Paul S. Smith, David A. E. Spalding and Frank Sutton. Sheffield, 1967.
Davlin, Charles. *The Democrat, or a Cursory Picture of the Present Crisis*. Bolton, n.d. [1839].
_____ *Gilbart, A Poem Illustrative of the Evils of Intemperance*. Preston, 1838.
Dearden, William. *The Vale of Caldene, or the Past and Present*. Halifax, 1844.
Dickens, Charles. *Hard Times*. London, 1853.
Disraeli, Benjamin. *Sybil*. London, 1845.
Eccles, Joseph H. *Deein be Inches and Workin Foaks*. Manchester, 1870
_____ *Yorkshire Songs*. London, 1870.
Egan, Pierce. *Life in London*. London, 1821.
Eliot, George. *Felix Holt*. London, 1866.
Elliott, Ebenezer. 'Autobiographical Memoir', *The Atheneum*. (12 Jan 1850), pp.46–9.
_____ *Poetical Works*. ed. Edwin Elliott. 2 vols. rev. ed. London, 1876.
Everett, James. *Gatherings from the pit-heaps, or the Allens of Shiny Row*. London, 1861.
_____ *The Wall's End Miner, or a Brief Memoir of the Life of William Cristie*. 2nd ed. London, 1838.
A Factory Girl. *The Cotton Famine and the Lancashire Operatives: A Poem*. Preston, 1862.
Fawcett, Stephen. *Bradford Legends*. Bradford, 1872.
_____ *Edwy and Elgiva*. Bradford, 1843.
_____ *Wharfedale Lays*. Bradford, 1837.
Forshaw, Charles, ed. *Holroyd's Collection of Yorkshire Ballads*. Bradford, 1892.
_____ *The Poets of Keighley, Bingley, Haworth and District*. Bradford, 1891.
_____ *The Poets of the Spen Valley*. Bradford, 1892.
_____ *Yorkshire Poets, Past and Present*. 4 vols. Bradford, 1888–91.
Frost, Thomas. *Forty Years' Recollections, Literary and Political*. London, 1880.

_____ *Reminiscences of a Country Journalist* London, 1886.

Furness, Richard. *The Poetical Works of the Late Richard Furness.* London, 1858.

Gaskell, Elizabeth. *Mary Barton.* London, 1848.

_____ *North and South.* London, 1854.

Gaspey, William. *Poor Law Melodies.* London, 1841.

Gilchrist, Robert. *A Collection of Original Local Songs.* 2nd ed. Newcastle, 1824.

_____ *A Collection of Original Songs, Local and Sentimental.* Newcastle, 1836.

Goodwin, Ralph [James Waddington]. *Flowers from the Glen.* ed. Eliza Craven Green. Bradford, 1862.

Grainge, William, ed. *Poets and Poetry of Yorkshire.* 2 vols. Wakefield, 1868.

Hall, Spencer T. *The Forester's Offering.* London, 1841.

_____ *Lays from the Lakes and other Poems.* London, 1875.

_____ *The Upland Hamlet and other Poems.* London, 1847.

Hallam, William. *Pleasley Vale, or the Wanderer's Sketch of Home.* Nottingham, 1852.

Halliday, W. J. and Arthur S. Umpleby, eds. *The White Rose Garland of Yorkshire: Dialect Verse and Local Folk Lore Rhymes.* London, 1949.

Halstead, David, ed. *A Lancashire Garland of Dialect Prose and Verse.* Staleybridge, 1936.

Hanby, George. *Autobiography of a Colliery Weighman.* Barnsley, 1874.

_____ *England's Commerce, or a Word to the South Yorkshire Miners.* Barnsley, 1867.

_____ *A Visit to Newgate and Holloway Prisons.* Barnsley, 1875.

Hardacre, Ben. *Miscellanies in Prose and Verse.* Bradford, 1874.

Hardaker, Joseph. *The Aeropteron or Steam Carriage.* Keighley, 1830.

_____ *The Bridal of Tomar.* Keighley, 1831.

_____ *Poems Lyrical and Moral.* Bradford, 1822.

Harland, John and T. T. Wilkinson, eds. *Ballads and Songs of Lancashire, Ancient and Modern.* 3rd ed. Manchester, 1882.

Harper, William. *Cain and Abel.* Manchester, 1844.

_____ *The Genius.* Manchester, 1840.

Hartley, John. *Grimes's Trip to America.* Bradford, n.d. [1877].

_____ *Seets i' Lundun.* London, n.d. [1874].

_____ *Pensive Poem and Startling Stories.* London, 1876.

_____ *Yorksher Puddin': A Collection of the Most Popular Dialect Stories from the pen of John Hartley.* London, 1877.

_____ *Yorkshire Ditties.* 1st ser. London, n.d. [1890?].

_____ *Yorkshire Ditties.* 2nd ser. London, n.d. [1900?].

_____ *Yorkshire Lyrics.* London, 1915.

_____ *Yorkshire Tales.* London, 1890.

Heaton, William. *The Flowers of Calderdale.* Halifax, 1847.

_____ *The Old Soldier, the Wandering Lover, and other Poems.* Halifax, 1857.

Hemans, Felicia, *Poetical Works*. London, n.d. [1879].

Henderson, William, ed. *Victorian Street Ballads*. London, 1937.

Hindley, Charles, ed. *Curiosities of Street Literature*. London, 1871.

Hird, James. *A Voice from the Muses*. Bradford, 1866.

Holroyd, Abraham, ed. *A Garland of Poetry by Yorkshire Authors Relating to Yorkshire*. Saltaire, 1873.

Horsfield, Louisa. *The Cottage Lyre*. 2nd ed. Leeds, 1862.

Hull, George, ed. *Poets and Poetry of Blackburn*. Blackburn, 1902.

Ingledew, C. J. D., ed. *The Ballads and Songs of Yorkshire*. London, 1860.

Jones, Ebenezer. *Studies in Sensation and Event*. London, 1843.

Jones, Ernest. *Ernest Jones: Chartist. Selections from the Writings and Speeches of Ernest Jones*. ed. John Saville. London, 1952.

Jones, John. *The Cotton Mill, a poem*. Manchester, 1821.

Jones, William, *Poems, Descriptive, Progressive and Humorous*. Leicester, n.d. [1853].

————— *The Spirit; or a Dream in the Woodlands*. Leicester, 1849.

Kenworthy, Charles. *Original Poems on Miscellaneous Subjects*. Manchester, 1847.

Kershaw, Thomas Bentley. *Buds of Poetry*. Manchester, 1845.

Kingsley, Charles. *Alton Locke*. London, 1849.

Kovalev, Y. V., ed. *The Literature of Chartism*. Moscow, 1957.

Lancashire Poems, Sketches and Stories. Manchester, n.d. [1902].

Langton, Millicent. *Musings of the Workroom*. Leicester, 1865.

Law, John [Margaret Harkness]. *A City Girl*. London, 1887.

————— *In Darkest London*. London, 1890.

————— *Out of Work*. London, 1888.

Laycock, Samuel. *Collected Writings*. ed. George Milner. 2nd ed. Oldham, 1908.

————— *Warblin's Fro' an Owd Songster*. Oldham, n.d. [1893].

Leatherland, J. A. *Essays and Poems*. Leicester, 1862.

Leno, Dan. *Hys Book: Written by Himself*. 6th ed. London, 1899.

Linton, W. J. *Memories*. London, 1894.

————— *Poems and Translations*. London, 1889.

Lister, Thomas. *Rhymes of Progress*. Leeds, 1862.

————— *The Rustic Wreath: Poems, Moral, Descriptive and Miscellaneous*. Leeds, 1834.

Lloyd, A. L., ed. *Come All Ye Bold Miners: Ballads and Songs of the Coal Fields*. London, 1952.

The Lyric Songster. London, n.d. [1892?].

MacColl, Ewen, ed. *The Shuttle and Cage: Industrial Folk Ballads*. London, 1954.

Marshall, John, ed. *A Collection of Songs, Comic, Satirical and DDescriptive, Chiefly in Newcastle Dialect*. Newcastle, 1819.

————— *The Northern Minstrel, or Gateshead Songster*. 4 vols. I and II, Gateshead, 1806. vols. III and IV, n.d.

Massey, Gerald, *My Lyrical Life*. 2 vols. London, 1889.

————— *Poems and Ballads*. 3rd. ed. New York, 1854.

————— *Poetical Works*. London, 1861.

_____ *Voices of Freedom and Lyris of Love* London 1851.
Mather, Joseph. *Songs of Joseph Mather*. ed. John Wilson. Sheffield, 1862.
Maudslay, Amos. *Poetry of a Day*. Barnsley, 1853.
_____ *Roland, a Masque*. Barnsley, 1853.
_____ *Workshop Musings*. Barnsley, 1851.
Middleton, Thomas. *Poets, Poems and Rhymes of East Cheshire*. Hyde, 1908.
Millhouse, Robert. *The Destinies of Man*. Nottingham, 1832–34.
_____ *Songs of the Patriot*. Nottingham, 1828.
_____ *Sonnets and Songs of Robert Millhouse*. Nottingham, 1881.
_____ *Vicissitude*. Nottingham, 1821.
Montgomery, James. *Sacred Poems and Hymns*. ed. John Holland. London, 1854.
Moorman, F. W., ed. *Yorkshire Dialect Poems (1673–1915) and Traditional Poems*. London, 1917.
The Music Hall Songster: Containing a Selection of the Latest and Most Popular Songs now being sung. London, n.d. [1892?].
Nash, 'Jolly' John. *The Merriest Man Alive: Stories, Anecdotes, Adventures, etc.* London, n.d. [1891].
The National Paragon Songster. London, n.d.
The Newcastle Song Book or Tyneside Songster. Newcastle, 1842.
Newsam, William Cartwright, ed. *The Poets of Yorkshire*. Completed by John Holland. Sheffield, 1845.
Nicholson, John. *Airedale in Ancient Times and other Poems*. London, 1825.
_____ *The Airedale Poet's Walk*. Bradford, 1826.
_____ *Lines on the Present State of the Country*. Bradford, 1826.
_____ *Poems, with a sketch of his life by John James*. ed. W. Dearden. 4th ed. London, 1859.
_____ *Poetical Works*. ed. W. G. Hird. Bradford, 1876.
An Odd Collection of Odd Songs, Original, Local, and Miscellaneous, as sung by Odd Fellows in the Newcastle Lodges and Principally Written by Odd Members of that Odd Fraternity. Newcastle, 1825.
An Operative of Keighley. *The Weaver's Complaint, or a bundle of Plain Facts, a novel Poem*. Keighley, 1834.
Overs, John. *Evenings of a Working Man*. London, 1844.
The Oxford Songster. London n.d. [1893].
Pinto, V. de Sola, and A. E. Rodway, eds. *The Common Muse: Popular British Ballad Poetry from the 15th to the 20th Century*. Harmondsworth, 1965.
Plummer, John. *Songs of Labour*. London, 1861.
Preston, Benjamin. *Dialect and other Poems*. Bradford, 1881.
_____ *Dialect Poems*. Saltaire, 1872.
Prince, John Critchley. *Autumn Leaves*. Hyde, 1856.
_____ *Dreams and Realities*. London, 1847.
_____ *Hours with the Muses*. Manchester, 1841.

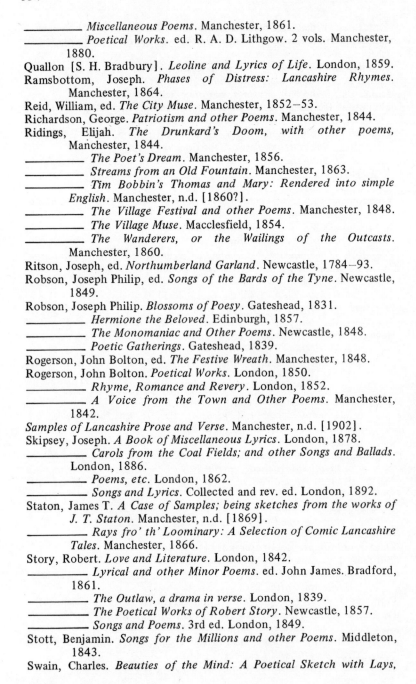

_____ *Miscellaneous Poems.* Manchester, 1861.
_____ *Poetical Works.* ed. R. A. D. Lithgow. 2 vols. Manchester, 1880.
Quallon [S. H. Bradbury]. *Leoline and Lyrics of Life.* London, 1859.
Ramsbottom, Joseph. *Phases of Distress: Lancashire Rhymes.* Manchester, 1864.
Reid, William, ed. *The City Muse.* Manchester, 1852–53.
Richardson, George. *Patriotism and other Poems.* Manchester, 1844.
Ridings, Elijah. *The Drunkard's Doom, with other poems,* Manchester, 1844.
_____ *The Poet's Dream.* Manchester, 1856.
_____ *Streams from an Old Fountain.* Manchester, 1863.
_____ *Tim Bobbin's Thomas and Mary: Rendered into simple English.* Manchester, n.d. [1860?].
_____ *The Village Festival and other Poems.* Manchester, 1848.
_____ *The Village Muse.* Macclesfield, 1854.
_____ *The Wanderers, or the Wailings of the Outcasts.* Manchester, 1860.
Ritson, Joseph, ed. *Northumberland Garland.* Newcastle, 1784–93.
Robson, Joseph Philip, ed. *Songs of the Bards of the Tyne.* Newcastle, 1849.
Robson, Joseph Philip. *Blossoms of Poesy.* Gateshead, 1831.
_____ *Hermione the Beloved.* Edinburgh, 1857.
_____ *The Monomaniac and Other Poems.* Newcastle, 1848.
_____ *Poetic Gatherings.* Gateshead, 1839.
Rogerson, John Bolton, ed. *The Festive Wreath.* Manchester, 1848.
Rogerson, John Bolton. *Poetical Works.* London, 1850.
_____ *Rhyme, Romance and Revery.* London, 1852.
_____ *A Voice from the Town and Other Poems.* Manchester, 1842.
Samples of Lancashire Prose and Verse. Manchester, n.d. [1902].
Skipsey, Joseph. *A Book of Miscellaneous Lyrics.* London, 1878.
_____ *Carols from the Coal Fields; and other Songs and Ballads.* London, 1886.
_____ *Poems, etc.* London, 1862.
_____ *Songs and Lyrics.* Collected and rev. ed. London, 1892.
Staton, James T. *A Case of Samples; being sketches from the works of J. T. Staton.* Manchester, n.d. [1869].
_____ *Rays fro' th' Loominary: A Selection of Comic Lancashire Tales.* Manchester, 1866.
Story, Robert. *Love and Literature.* London, 1842.
_____ *Lyrical and other Minor Poems.* ed. John James. Bradford, 1861.
_____ *The Outlaw, a drama in verse.* London, 1839.
_____ *The Poetical Works of Robert Story.* Newcastle, 1857.
_____ *Songs and Poems.* 3rd ed. London, 1849.
Stott, Benjamin. *Songs for the Millions and other Poems.* Middleton, 1843.
Swain, Charles. *Beauties of the Mind: A Poetical Sketch with Lays,*

Historical and Romantic. London, 1831.
——————— *Dramatic CChapters, Poems and Songs.* Manchester, 1847.
Ta-Ra-Ra-Boom De-e Songster. London, n.d.
Thom, William. *Rhymes and Recollections of a Handloom Weaver.* London, 1844.
Thompson, Robert. *Poems.* rev. and enlarged ed. Blyth, 1879.
Thompson, Thomas. et. al. *A Collection of Songs, Comic, Satirical, and Descriptive, chiefly in the Newcastle Dialect.* Newcastle, 1827.
Tirebuck, W. E. *Miss Grace of All Souls.* London, 1895.
Trussell, Robert. [Robert Noonan]. *The Ragged Trousered Philanthropists.* London, 1955.
Trollope, Francis. *The Life and Adventures of Michael Armstrong, the Factory Boy.* London, 1840.
Turner, J. Horsfall, ed. *Yorkshire Anthology.* Bingley, 1901.
The Universal Songster or Museum of Mirth. 3 vols. London, 1834.
Varley, Isabella [Mrs. G. Linnaeus Banks]. *Ivy Leaves.* London, 1844.
——————— *The Manchester Man.* London, 1876.
Walker, J. Bradshaw. *Spring Leaves of Prose and Poetry.* London, 1845.
——————— *Wayside Flowers or Poems Lyrical and Descriptive.* Leeds, 1840.
Warburg, Jeremy, ed. *The Industrial Muse.* London, 1958.
Waugh, Edwin. *Collected Works.* 11 vols. Manchester, 1881.
——————— *Collected Works.* ed. George Milner. 8 vols. Manchester, n.d. [1892].
——————— *Home Life of the Lancashire Factory Folk during the Cotton Famine.* Manchester, 1867.
Wildon, Robert Carrick. *Tong on a Summer's Day; the Forbidden Union and other Poems.* Leeds, 1850.
Wilson, Alexander and M. T. *Songs of the Wilsons.* ed. John Harland. Manchester, n.d. [1842].
Wilson, Joseph. *Joe Wilson's Tyneside Songs, Ballads and Drolleries.* Newcastle, n.d. [1873].
——————— *Tyneside Songs and Drolleries, Readings and Temperance Songs.* Collected ed. Newcastle, n.d. [1890?].
Wilson, Robert. *Poems.* rev. ed. Blyth, 1879.
Wilson, Thomas. *The Pitman's Pay and Other Poems.* London, 1872.
Wheeler, James, ed. *Manchester Poetry.* Manchester, 1838.
White, Henry Kirke. *The Remains of Henry Kirke White . . . with an account of his life by Robert Southey.* 2 vols. 5th ed. corrected. London, 1811.
Whitmore, William. *Firstlings.* London, 1852.
——————— *Gilbert Marlowe and other Poems.* London, 1859.
Wrigley, Ammon. *Lancashire Idylls.* London, 1942.
Yates, May. *A Lancashire Anthology.* Liverpool, 1923.

Contemporary Books and Pamphlets
Abram, William Alexander. *Blackburn Characters of a Past Generation.* Blackburn, 1894.
Adams, E. *Memoirs of a Social Atom.* 2 vols. London, 1903.

Alfred, [Samuel Kydd]. *History of the Factory Movement.* 2 vols. London, 1857.

An Address to the Public by the Delegates from the Coal Mines of Northumberland and Durham, now in London. London, n.d. [1844].

Axon, W. E. A. *Folk Song and Folk Speech in Lancashire.* Manchester, n.d. [1871].

—————— *Lancashire Gleanings.* Manchester, 1883.

—————— *The Literature of the Lancashire Dialect. A Bibliographical Essay.* London, 1870.

Baines, Edward. *History of Cotton Manufacture in Great Britain.* London, 1835.

—————— *History of the County Palatinate and Duchy of Lancashire.* 2 vols. London, 1836.

Bartlett, D. V. G. *London by Day and Night.* London, 1852.

Baynes, John. *The Cotton Trade.* Blackburn, 1857.

Brief Observations in Reply to 'A Voice from the Coal Mines'. Newcastle, 1825.

Bischoff, J. *A Comprehensive History of the Woollen and Worsted Manufacture.* London, 1842.

Booth, Charles. *Life and Labour of the People in London.* 2nd ser. vol.IV. London, 1902–4.

Boyd, R. Nelson. *Coal Pits, and Pitmen, A Short History of the Coal Trade and the Legislation Affecting it.* London, 1895.

Brown. Cornelius. *Lives of Nottinghamshire Worthies.* London, 1882.

Burnley, James. *History of Wool and Woolcombing.* London, 1889.

—————— *Phases of Bradford Life.* Bradford, 1875.

—————— *West Riding Sketches.* Bradford, 1875.

Burton, Alfred. *Rush-bearing.* Manchester, 1891.

A Candid Appeal to the Coal Owners and Viewers of Collieries on the Tyne and Wear. Newcastle, 1826.

Canterbury Theatre of Varieties, Souvenir, 1200–1907. (55th anniversary commemoration of the Canterbury, 5 December 1907.) London, 1907.

Carpenter, J. E., ed. *Penny Readings.* 3 vols. London, 1869.

Chappell, William. *The Ballad Literature and Popular Music.* London, 1859.

—————— *Popular Music of the Olden Time.* 2 vols. London, 1859.

Charrington, Frederick Michaels. *The Battle of the Music Halls.* London, n.d. [1885?].

Christophers, S. W. *The New Methodist Hymn Book and its Writers.* London, n.d.

—————— *The Poets of Methodism.* London, 1875.

Collinson, Edward. *The History of the Worsted Trade, and historic sketch of Bradford.* Bradford, 1854.

Costley, Thomas. *Lancashire Poets and other Literary Sketches.* Manchester, 1897.

Cudworth, William. *Roundabout Bradford: A Series of Sketches.* Bradford, 1876.

A Defence of 'A Voice from the Coal Mines'. Newcastle, 1825.
The Dialect of Leeds and Its Neighbourhod. London, 1862.
Distress in Lancashire, a sermon preached October 12, 1862. London, 1862.
Dixon, J. H. *Chronicles and Stories of the Craven Dales*. intro. Robert Collyer. Skipton. n.d. [1881].
Dunn, Matthias. *An Historical, Geological, and Descriptive View of the Coal Trade of the North of England*. Newcastle, 1844.
Dyer, Samuel. *Dialect of the West Riding of Yorkshire: A Short History of Leeds and other Towns*. Leeds, 1891.
Engels, Frederick. *The Condition of the Working Class in 1844*, trans. W. O. Henderson and W. H. Chaloner. New York, 1958.
Espinasse, Francis. *Lancashire Worthies*. London, 1874, 1877.
——————— *Literary Recollections and Sketches*. London, 1893.
Evans, John. *Lancashire Authors*. Manchester, 1850.
A Few Brief Observations, Illustrations and Anecdotes Respecting Pitmen in a Northern Colliery Village. Newcastle, 1862.
Fielden, John. *Curse of the Factory System*. Halifax, n.d. [1836].
Flower, B. G. *Gerald Massey: Poet, Prophet, and Mystic*. New York, 1895.
Fordyce, William. *Coal and Iron: A History of Coal, Coke, Coal Fields, Iron, its Ores, and Processes of Manufacture*. Newcastle, 1860.
——————— *The History and Antiquities of the County Palatinate of Durham*. 2 vols. Newcastle, 1855–57.
Forshaw, Charles F. *John Hartley: poet, and author. An Appreciation*. Bradford, 1909.
Fynes, Richard. *The Miners of Northumberland and Durham*. Sunderland, 1923 [1873].
Galloway, Robert. *A History of Coal Mining in Great Britain*. London, 1882.
Gammage, R. G. *A History of the Chartist Movement*. 2nd rev. ed. London, 1894.
Gaskell, Peter. *The Manufacturing Population of England*. London, 1833.
Gaskell, William. *Two Lectures on the Lancashire Dialect*. London, 1854.
[Gibson, James]. *The Bibliography of Robert Burns with biographical and bibliographical notes*. Kilmarnock, 1881.
Grainge, William. *Nidderdale: An Historical, Topographical and Descriptive Sketch of the Valley of the Nidd*. Pateley Bridge, 1863.
Hall, Spencer T. *Biographical Sketches of Remarkable People*. London, 1873.
Hardwich, Charles. *Traditions, Superstitions and Folklore*. Manchester, 1872.
Harland, John and T. T. Wilkinson. *Lancashire Folk Lore*. London, 1867.
——————— *Lancashire Legends, traditions, pageants, sports, etc.* London, 1873.

Haweis, H. R. *Music and Morals*. 6th ed. London, 1875.

Henderson, William. *Notes on the Folk-lore of the Northern Counties of England and the Borders*. London, 1866.

Heywood, Thomas. *On the South Lancashire Dialect with Biographical Notices of John Collier, author of 'Tim Bobbin'*. Manchester : Chetham Society, vol. 57 (1861).

Hill, Samuel. *Old Lancashire Songs and their Singers*. Manchester, 1906.

Hindley, Charles. *The Catnach Press*. London, 1869.

_____ *History of the Catnach Press*. London, 1887.

_____ *Life and Times of James Catnach*. London, 1878.

Holland, John. *The History and Description of Fossil Fuel, the Collieries, and Coal Trade of Great Britain*. 2nd ed. London, 1841.

_____ and James Everett. *Memoirs of the Life and Writings of James Montgomery*. 7 vols. London, 1854–56.

Hollingshead, John. *My Lifetime*. 2 vols. London, 1895.

Holroyd, Abraham. *Collectanea Bradfordiana: A Collection of Papers on the History of Bradford and the Neighbourhood*. Saltaire, 1873.

Howitt, William. *Homes and Haunts of the Most Eminent British Poets*. 3rd ed. London, 1874.

An Incumbent in the diocese of Durham. *A Few Brief Observations, Illustrations and Anecdotes respecting pitmen in a Northern Colliery Village*. Sunderland, 1862.

James, John. *History and Topography of Bradford*. rev. ed. London, 1867.

_____ *History of Worsted Manufacture in England*. London, 1857.

Kay-Shuttleworth, James P. *Moral and Physical Condition of the Operatives employed in the Cotton Manufacture in Manchester*. London, 1832.

Lawson, William D. *Lawson's Tyneside Celebrities*. Newcastle, 1873.

The Life and Adventures of Billy Purvis, containing many humorous Incidents and Anecdotes. Newcastle, 1875.

Lithgow, R. A. D. *Life of John Critchley Prince*. Manchester, 1880.

Losh, James. *The Diaries and Correspondence of James Losh*. ed. Edward Hughes. Newcastle: Surtees Society, vols. 171 (1956) and 174 (1959).

Lovett, William. *Life and Struggles*. 2 vols. London, 1920.

Machray, Robert. *The Night Side of London*. London, 1902.

Mackay, Charles. *Forty Years' Recollections*. London, 1877.

Manton, Henry. *Letters on Theatres and Music Halls, Especially Intended for Sunday School Teachers and Senior Scholars*. Birmingham, n.d. [1888].

Mayhew, Henry. *London Labour and the London Poor*. 4 vols. New York, 1968 [1861–62].

[Millhouse, Robert]. *Sketches of Obscure Poets*. London, 1833.

Mitchell, William. *The Question Answered: "What do the Pitmen Want?"*. 3rd ed. Bishopwearmouth, 1844.

Newbigging, Thomas. *Speeches and Addresses: Political, Social and Literary*. Manchester, 1887.

Newton, H. Chance. *Idols of the Halls: Being My Music Hall Memories*. London, 1928.

——— and W. H. Morton, *Sixty Years of Stage Service, being a Record of the Life of Charles Morton, the Father of the Music Halls*. London, 1905.

Peel, Frank. *The Risings of the Luddites, Chartists and Plug-drawers*. 4th ed. London, 1968.

Petty, John. *History of Primitive Methodism*. new ed. London, 1864.

Pratt, A.T. Camden. *Unknown London: Its Romance and Tragedy*. London, n.d. [1900?].

Proceedings of the Manchester Literary Club. Manchester, 1873–4.

Procter, R. W. *Literary Reminiscences and Gleanings*. Manchester, 1860.

——— *Memorials of Bygone Manchester*. Manchester, 1880.

——— *Memorials of Manchester Streets*. Manchester, 1874.

Radcliffe, William. *Origin of the New System of Manufacture, commonly called 'Power Loom Weaving' and the Purpose for which this System was invented and brought into use, fully explained in a narrative, containing William Radcliffe's struggles through life to remove the cause which has brought this country to its present crisis*. Stockport, 1828.

Ritchie, J. Ewing. *Days and Nights in London; or Studies in Black and Gray*. London, 1880.

——— *The Night Side of London*. London, 1857.

Robson, Joseph P. *The Life and Adventures of Billy Purvis, Continued to the time of his death*. Newcastle, 1854.

Rules of the Barnsley Franklin Club. Barnsley, 1845.

Ruskin, John. *Time and Tide, by Weare* [sic] *and Tyne*. 2nd ed. London, 1868.

Schofield, Sim. *Short Stories about Failsworth Folk*. Blackpool, 1905.

Scholes, James C. *Bolton Bibliography and Jottings of Book-lore*. Manchester, 1886.

Scott, W. *An Earnest Address and Urgent Appeal to the People of England, in behalf of the Oppressed and Suffering Pitmen, of the Counties of Northumberland and Durham, with a glance at a few of the grievances of the laborious and useful body of men, and hints to the means of ameliorating their conditions*. Newcastle, 1831.

Scruton, William. *Pen and Pencil Sketches of Old Bradford*. Bradford, 1889.

Searle, January [George Searle Phillips]. *Memoirs of Ebenezer Elliot*. London, 1852.

[Shimmin, Hugh]. *Liverpool Life: Its pleasures, practices and pastimes*. Liverpool, 1857.

Slugg, J. T. *Reminiscences of Manchester Fifty Years Ago*. Manchester, 1881.

Smiles, Samuel. *Self-Help*. rev. ed. New York, n.d.

Smith,Wiliam, ed. *Old Yorkshire*. 5 vols. London, 1881–84.

Southey, Robert. *The Lives and Works of the Uneducated Poets*. ed. J. S. Childers. London, 1925.

Stevens, William. *A Memoir of Thomas Martin Wheeler*. London, 1862.

Stuart, C. D. and A. J. Park. *The Variety Stage: A History of the Music Halls from the Earliest Period to the Present time*. London, 1895.

Sutton, C. W. *A List of Lancashire Authors*. Manchester, 1876.

Swann, John. *Lancashire Authors: A Series of Biographical Sketches*. St-Anne's-on-the-Sea, 1924.

——————— *Manchester Literary Club: Some Notes on its History 1862–1908*. Manchester, 1908.

Swindells, Thomas. *Manchester Streets and Manchester Men*. Manchester, 1906.

Taylor, W. Cooke. *Notes on a Tour in the Manufacturing Districts of Lancashire*. 2nd ed. London, 1842.

Tempted London: Young Men. London, 1888.

Thackrah, C. T. *The Effects of the Principal Arts, Trades and Professions on Health and Longevity*. London, 1831.

A Traveller Underground. [J. R. Leifchild]. *Our Coal and Our Coal-Pits*. London, 1856.

Turner, J. Horsfall. *Halifax Books and Authors*. Brighouse, 1906.

Ure, Andrew. *The Cotton Manufacture of Great Britain investigated and illustrated*. supp. P. L. Simmonds. 2 vols. London, 1861.

——————— *The Philosophy of Manufactures*. London, 1835.

A Voice from the Coal Mines. Newcastle, 1825.

Ward, John. 'Diary of John Ward of Clitheroe, Weaver, 181860–1864.' ed. R. Sharpe-France. *Transactions of the Historic Society of Lancashire and Cheshire*. CV (1953), pp.137–85.

Warne, Frederick. *The State of the London Theatre and Music Hall*. London, 1887.

Watkins, John. *Life, Poetry and Letters of Ebenezer Elliot, with an abstract of his politics*. London, 1850.

Watson, Robert S. *Joseph Skipsey – His Life and Work*. London 1909.

Watts, John. *The Facts of the Cotton Famine*. Manchester, 1866.

Welford, Richard. *Men of Mark 'twixt Tyne and Tweed*. 3 vols. London, 1895.

A Well Wisher to Society. *The Collier's Friend: being a Comprehensive View of the State of Society and Manners in the Minery Districts on the Tyne and Wear, also an enumeration of various Evils under which they Labour, with Hints for their Removal*. North Shields, n.d. [1825].

Wilson, Benjamin. *Struggles of an Old Chartist*. Halifax, 1887.

Wilson, John. *The History of the Durham Miners' Association*. Durham, 1907.

Winskill, P. T. *The Temperance Movement and its Workers*. 4 vols. London, 1892.

Wood, J. Hickory [Owen Hall]. *Dan Leno: His Infinite Variety*.

London, 1905.
Young Manchester [D. Buxton]. *Neglect of Literary Men: John Critchley Prince*. Ashton-under-Lyne, n.d. [1846].

Contemporary Articles
Anstey, F. [Thomas Anstey Guthrie]. 'London Music Halls', *Harper's New Monthly Magazine*, 82 (1890), pp.190–202.
Axon, W. E. A. 'Charles Davelin [sic], the Weaver Poet', *The Temperance Spectator*, VIII (1866), pp.124–6.
[Carlyle, Thomas]. 'Corn Law Rhymes', *Edinburgh Review*, LV (1832), pp.338–61.
Chasles, Philarète. 'De la poésie chartiste en angleterre', *Revue des deux mondes*, 2me. ser. XXVI (1856), pp.370–400.
Etienne, L. 'Les poètes des pauvres en Angleterre', *Revue des deux monde]*, 2me. ser. XXVI (1856), pp.370–400.
[Fox, W. J.]. 'The Poetry of the Poor', *London Review*, I (1835), pp.187–201.
'How to Teach and Preach to Colliers', *Tait's Edinburgh Magazine*, n.s., XIX (1852), pp.86–92.
Jerrold, Douglas. 'New Books', *Douglas Jerrold's Shilling Magazine*, III (1846), pp.95–6.
[Kingsley, Charles]. 'Burns and His School', *North British Review*, XVI (1851–52), pp.149–83.
'Life, Enterprise and Peril in Coal Mines', *Quarterly Review*, CX (1861), pp.329–67.
[Lister, T. H.]. 'Review of *Attempts at Verse, by John Jones, an old servant; with some account of the Writer, written by himself; and an Introductory Essay on the Lives and Works of Uneducated, Poets, by Robert Southey*', *Edinburgh Review*, 54 (1831), pp.69–84.
'Machinery and the Passions', *Cornhill Magazine*, XI (1865), pp.541–7.
'Manners of Coal Miners', *Penny Magazine*, V (1836), pp.242–4.
'Mischievous Literature', *The Bookseller* (July, 1868), pp.445–9.
Pennell, Elizabeth. 'The Pedigree of the Music Hall', *Contemporary Review*, 63 (April, 1893), pp.575–83.
'The Poetry of Seven Dials', *Quarterly Review*, CXXII (1867), pp.200–10.
'The Radical Poets', *Tait's Edinburgh Magazine*, I (1832), pp.137–60.
'Street Ballads', *National Review*, XIII (1861), pp.397–419.
Veritas [Ebenezer Elliott]. 'Poetry of the Loom, by one of the Victims of the Spy System', *Tait's Edinburgh Magazine* n.s., II (1835), pp.223–6.

II. Secondary Sources
Unpublished Material

Hair, P.E.H. 'The Social History of British Coal Miners, 1800–1845', unpub. D.Phil. thesis, Oxford University, 1955.
Ramage, Ethel. 'Chartism in English Literature, 1838–1876', unpub. Ph.D. dissertation, University of Wisconsin, 1939.

Ross, Dan. Personal correspondence with the author.
Trawick, Buckner. 'The Works of Gerald Masey', unpub. Ph.D. dissertation, Harvard University, 1942.

Modern Boks and Pamphlets

Altick, Richard D. *The English Common Reader: A Social History of the Mass Reading Public, 1800–1900*. Chiago, 1957.
Ashton, T. S and J. Sykes. *The Coal Industry in the 18th Century*. Manchester, 1929.
Barker, Felix. *The House that Stoll Built: The Story of the Coliseum Theatre*. London, 1957.
Bett, Henry. *The Hymns of Methodism*. enlarged ed. London, 1920.
Booth, J. B. *Old Pink 'Un Days*. London, 1924.
——— *Pink Parade*. New York, 1933.
——— *Seventy Years of Song*. London, 1943.
Briggs, Asa. *The Age of Improvement*. London, 1959.
——— ed. *Chartist Studies*. London, 1959.
——— *Victorian Cities*. London, 1963.
Brown, Simon. *Ebenezer Elliott: The Corn Law Rhymer, A Bibliography and List of Letters*. Leicester, 1971.
Bythell, Duncan. *The Handloom Weavers: A Study in the English Cotton Industry during the Industrial Revolution*. Cambridge, 1969.
Challinor, Raymond and Brian Ripley. *The Miners' Association: A Trade Union in the Age of the Chartists*. London, 1968.
Chapman, S. J. *The Lancashire Cotton Industry*. Manchester, 1904.
Coleman, Terry. *The Railway Navvies*. London, 1965.
Collier, Frances. *The Family Economy of the Working Classes in the Cotton Industry, 1784–1853*. ed. R. S. Fitton. Manchester, 1964.
Collinson, Robert. *The Story of Street Literature: Forerunner of the Popular Press*. London, 1973.
Conklin, R. J. *Thomas Cooper, the Chartist*. Manila, 1935.
Corbridge, Sylvia. *It's an Old Lancashire Custom*. London, 1952.
Craig, David. *Scottish Literature and the Scottish People, 1680–1830*. London, 1961.
Cruse, Amy. *The Englishman and his Books in the Early Nineteenth Century*. London, 1930.
——— *The Victorians and Their Books*. London, 1935.
Cuthbertson, David. *Alexander Anderson* (('*Surfaceman*')). Roseville, Midlothian, 1929.
Dalziel, Margaret. *Popular Fiction of a Hundred Years Ago*. London, 1957.
Daniels, George William. *Early English Cotton Industry*. Manchester, 1920.
Davies, David. *An Enquiry into the Reading of the Lower Classes*. Pasadena, 1970.
Disher, M. Willson. *Music Hall Memories*. London, 1935.
——— *Winkles and Champagne: Comedies and Tragedies of the*

Music Hall. London, 1938.

Dolleans, Etienne. *Le chartisme*. 2 vols. Paris, 1912–13.

Donovan, F. P. *The Railroad in Literature: A Brief Survey of Railroad Fiction, Poetry, Songs, Biography, Essays, Travel, and Drama in the English Language*. Boston, 1940.

Driver, Cecil Herbert. *Tory Radical, the Life of Richard Oastler*. New York, 1946.

Empson, William. *Some Versions of Pastoral*. London, 1935.

Evans, Ifor. *English Poetry in the Later 19th Century*. 2nd rev. ed. London, 1966.

Felstead, S. Theodore. *Stars who made the Halls*. London, 1946.

Fergusson, Louis. *Old Time Music Hall Comedians*. Leicester, 1949.

Fitton, R. S. and A. P. Wadsworth. *The Strutts and Arkwrights, 1785–1830*. Manchester, 1958.

Fitton, Sam. *Gradely Lancashire*. Manchester, 1929.

Fowler, David. *A Literary History of the Popular Ballad*. Durham, North Carolina, 1968.

de Frece, Lady. *Recollections of Vesta Tilley*. London, 1934.

Gerould, Gordan Hall. *The Ballad of Tradition*. Oxford, 1932.

Grant, E. M. *French Poetry and Modern Industry, 1830–1870*. Cambridge, Mass., 1927.

Greenway, John. *American Folksongs of Protest*. Philadelphia, 1953.

Haddon, Archibald. *The Story of the Music Hall*. London, 1935.

Hall, Stuart and Paddy Whannel. *The Popular Arts: A Critical Guide to the Mass Media*. London, 1964.

Hammond, J. L. and Barbara Hammond. *The Skilled Labourer, 1760–1832*. London, 1919.

———————— *The Town Labourer, 1760–1832*. rev. ed. London, 1949.

———————— *The Village Labourer, 1760–1832*. 4th ed. London, 1927.

Harrison, Brian. *Drink and the Victorians*. London, 1971.

Harrison, J. F. C. *The Early Victorians, 1832–1851*. London, 1971.

———————— *Learning and Living: 1790–1960*. London, 1961.

Hobsbawm, Eric and George Rudé. *Captain Swing*. London, 1968.

Hodgart, M. J. C. *The Ballads*. 2nd ed. London, 1962.

Hoggart, Richard. *The Use of Literacy*. Harmondsworth, 1958.

Hollis, Patricia. *The Pauper Press: A Study of Working Class Radicalism in the 1830s*. London, 1970.

Hovell, Mark. *The Chartist Movement*. 2nd ed. Manchester, 1925.

Howard, Diane. *London Theatres and Music Halls, 1850–1950*. London, 1970.

Jacob, Naomi. *'Our Mari' (Marie Lloyd): A Biography*. London, n.d. [1936].

James, Louis. *Fiction for the Working Man, 1830–1850*. London, 1963.

Johnson, Edgar. *Charles Dickens: A Biography*. 2 vols. New York, 1952.

Heating, P. J. *The Working Classes in Victorian Fiction*. London, 1971.

King, Robert. *North Shields Theatres*. Gateshead, 1948.

Korson, George. *Coal Dust on the Fiddle: Songs and Stories of the*

Bituminous Industry. Hartboro, Pa., 1965.

Minstrels of the Mine Patch. Philadelphia, 1938.

Leavis, Q. D. *Fiction and the Reading Public*. London, 1932.

Lipson, E. *The History of the English Woollen and Worsted Industries*. 3rd ed. London, 1921.

———— *A Short History of Wool and its Manufacture*. London, 1953.

Lloyd, A. L. *Folk Song in England*. London, 1967.

Lockwood, H. O. *Tools and the Man: French Working Men and English Chartists*. New York, 1927.

Machin, Frank. *The Yorkshire Miners*. London, 1958.

MacInnis, Colin. *Sweet Saturday Night*. London, 1967.

Mackerness, E. D. *A Social History of English Music*. London, 1964.

MacQueen-Pope, W. *The Melody Lingers On*. London, 1950.

Mander, Raymond and Joe Mitchenson. *British Music Hall: A Story in Pictures*. London, 1965.

Mantoux, Paul. *The Industrial Revolution in the 18th Century*. trans. Marjorie Vernon. rev. ed. New York, 1961.

McKechnie, Samuel. *Popular Entertainments through the Ages*. London, n.d. [1931].

Mellor, G. J. *The Northern Music Hall*. Newcastle, 1970.

Muir, Willa. *Living with Ballads*. London, 1965.

Nettel, Reginald. *Seven Centuries of Popular Song, A Social History of Urban Ditties*. London, 1956.

———— *A Social History of Popular Song*. London, 1954.

Odom, William. *Two Sheffield Poets: James Montgomery and Ebenezer Elliott*. London, 1929.

Opie, Iona and Peter. *The Lore and Language of Children*. London, 1959.

Pinchbeck, Ivy. *Women Workers and the Industrial Revolution, 1750–1850*. London, 1950.

Pulling, Christopher. *They Were Singing, and What They Sang About*. London, 1952.

Read, Donald and Eric Glasgow. *Feargus O'Connor: Irishman and Chartist*. London, 1961.

Reisman, David. *The Oral Tradition, the Written Word and the Screen Image*. Yellow Springs, Ohio, 1955.

Robinson, J. W. *Theatrical Street Ballads*. London, 1971.

Schoyan, A. R. *The Chartist Challenge: A Portrait of George Julian Harney*. London, 1958.

Scott, Harold. *The Early Doors: Origins of the Music Hall*. London, 1946.

Sharp, Cecil. *English Folk Songs: Some Conclusions*. 4th rev. ed. prepared by Maud Karpeles. Belmont, California, 1965.

Shepard, Leslie. *The Broadside Ballad*. London, 1962.

———— *The History of Street Literature*. Newton Abbot, 1973.

———— *John Pitts, Ballad Printer of Seven Dials, 1765–1844*. London, 1969.

Sigal, Clancy. *Weekend in Dinlock*. London, 1960.

Smelser, Neil J. *Social Change in the Industrial Revolution: An Application of Theory to the British Cotton Industry*. Chicago, 1969.

Smith, F. B. *Radical Artisan: William James Linton 1812–97*. Manchester, 1973.

Smith, H. P. *Literature and Adult Education a Century Ago: Pantopragmatics and Penny Readings*. Documentary 3. Oxford, 1960.

Thompson, E. P. *The Making of the English Working Class*. London, 1963.

Thomson, Frances M. *Newcastle Chapbooks in the Newcastle-upon-Tyne University Library*. Newcastle, 1969.

Tynmouth, W. *Blaydon Races*. Newcastle, 1962.

Unwin, Rayner. *The Rural Muse: Studies in the Peasant Poetry of England*. London, 1954.

Waddington, J. H. *John Hartley: the most famous Yorkshire Dialect Writer*. Halifax, 1939.

Wadsworth, A. P. and J. de Lacy-Mann. *The Cotton Trade and Industrial Lancashire, 1600–1780*. Manchester, 1931.

Ward, J. T. *The Factory Movement: 1830–1855*. London, 1962.

Wearmouth, R. F. *Methodism and the Working-Class Movements of England, 1800–1850*. London, 1957.

——————— *Some Working Class Movements of the 19th Century*. London, 1948.

Welbourne, E. *The Miners' Unions of Northumberland and Durham*. Cambridge, 1923.

Webb, R. K. *The British Working Class Reader: 1790–1848*. London, 1955.

Webb, Sidney. *The History of the Durham Miners, 1662–1921*. London 1921.

——————— and Beatrice Webb. *The History of Trade Unionism*. new ed. London, 1921.

Whittaker, G. H. *The Reedmaker Poet: John Critchley Prince*. Stalybridge, 1936.

Williams, Raymond. *Culture and Society: 1780–1950*. Harmondsworth, 1958.

——————— *The Long Revolution*. New York, 1961.

Williamson, G. C. *Curious Survivals, Habits and Customs of the Past that Still live in the Present*. London, 1923.

Young, Michael. *The Rise of the Meritocracy, 1870–2033*. Harmondsworth, 1961.

Modern Articles

Armitage, W. H. G. 'Joseph Mather: Poet of the Filesmiths', *Notes and Queries*, 195 (22 July 1950), pp.320–2.

Aydellotte, William. 'The England of Marx and Mill as Reflected in Fiction', *The Making of English History*, eds. R.,L. Schuyler and H. Ausubel. New York, 1952, pp.511–21.

Barker, Clive. 'The Chartists, Theatre, Reform and Research', *Theatre*

346 The Industrial Muse

Quarterly, I, 4 (1971), pp.3–10.
_____ 'A Theatre for the People', *Nineteenth Century British Theatre*. eds. K. Richards and P. Thomson. London, 1971, pp.3–24.

Briggs, Asa. 'Ebenezer Elliott, the Corn Law Rhymer', *Cambridge Journal*, III (1950), pp.686–95.
_____ 'The Language of "Class" in Early Nineteenth Century England', *Essays in Labour History*, eds. Asa Briggs and John Saville. London, 1960, pp.43–73.

Clark, G. Kitson. 'The Romantic Element, 1830–1850', *Studies in Social History*. ed. J. H. Plumb. London, 1955, pp.211–39.

Goody, Jack and Ian Watt. 'The Consequences of Literacy', *Literacy in Traditional Societies*. ed. Jack Goody. Cambridge, 1968, pp;27–68.

Gray, Donald J. 'The Uses of Victorian Laughter', *Victorian Studies*, vol. 10 (1966–67), p.145–76.

Groves, Reg. 'English Songs of Revolt', *Folk: Review of People's Music*, vol. 11 (1945), pp.10–12.

Handle, Johnny [John Pandrich]. 'Industrial Folk Music', *English Dance and Song*, 37 (1958), pp.106–8, 138–41, and 38 (1959), pp.6–9.

Haworth, Peter. 'A Lancashire Classic', *English Hymns and Ballads and other Studies in Popular Literature*. Oxford, 1927, pp.58–70.

Henderson, W. P. 'The Cotton Famine in Lancashire', *Transactions of the Historic Society of Lancashire and Cheshire*, 84 (1932), pp.37–62.

Herford, C. H. 'A Sketch of the History of Literature, Drama and Music in Manchester', *Anglica*, II (1925), pp.386–99.

Higson, Charles. ' "Jone o' Grinfilt, Jr." and "Oldham Rushbearing" '. *Oldham Standard*. 1 May 1926.

Hobsbawm, Eric. 'Methodism and the Threat of Revolution', *Labouring Men: Studies in the History of Labour*. London, 1964, pp.23–33.

Holloway, John. 'Cherry Girls and Crafty Maidens', 'Broadside Verse Traditions', and 'The Irish Ballads', *The Listener*, 83 (21 May, 28 May, 4 June, 1970), pp.680–5, 710–14, 744–8.

Hume, William Elliott. 'The Geordie Tradition: From Music Hall to Folk Song in Northumbria', *Poetry Review*, 54 (1963), pp.148–53.

Lloyd, A. L. 'Folk Songs of the Coalfields', *Coal*, May 1951, pp.26–7.
_____ 'Miners' Folk Song Competition', *Coal*, October, 1951, pp.22-3.

McCready, H. W. 'The Cotton Famine in Lancashire, 1863', *Transactions of the Historic Society of Lancashire and Cheshire*, 106 (1954), pp.127–33.

Mayer, David. 'Billy Purvis: Travelling Showman', *Theatre Quarterly*, I, 4 (1971), pp.27–34.

McKelvie, Donald. 'Aspects of Oral Tradition and Belief in an Industrial Region', *Folk Life*, I (1963), pp.77–94.

Miller, John. 'Songs of the British Radical and Labour Movement', *Marxism Today*, VII (1963), pp.180–6.

———— 'Songs of the Labour Movement', *Our History*, 30 (Summer, 1963).

Nettel, Reginald. 'The Influence of the Industrial Revolution on English Music', *Proceedings of the Royal Music Association*, 72 (1946), pp.23–40.

Neuberg, Victor. 'The Literature of the Street', *The Victorian City*. eds. H. J. Dyos and Michael Wolff. London, 1973, I, pp.191–209.

Read, Donald. 'John Harland: "Father of Provincial Reporting" ', *Manchester Review*, vol. VIII (1958), pp.205–12.

Rollins, Hyder E. 'The Black-Letter Broadside Ballad', *PMLA*, 34 (1919), pp.258–339.

Rutherford, Frank. 'The Collecting and Publishing of Northumbrian Folk-Song', *Archaelogia Aeliana*, 4th ser. 42 (1964), pp.261–78.

Sanderson, Michael. 'Literacy and Social Mobility in the Industrial Revolution', *Past and Present*, 56 (1972), pp.75–104.

Seeger, Charles. 'Folk Music as a Source of Social History', *The Cultural Approach to History*. ed. Caroline Ware. New York, 1940, pp.316–24.

Seary, E. R. 'Robert Southey and Ebenezer Elliott: Some New Southey Letters', *RES*, 15 (1939), pp.1–10.

Senelick, Lawrence. 'A Brief Life and. Times of the Victorian Music-Hall', *Harvard Library Bulletin*, 19 (1971), pp.375–98.

Soffer, R. N. 'Attitudes and Allegiances of the Unskilled North, 1830–1850', *International Review of Social History*, 10 (1965), pp.429–54.

Spencer, J. H. 'A Preston Chapbook and Its Printer', Preston *Herald*, 2 January 1948.

Stone, Lawrence. 'Literacy and Education in England, 1640–1900', *Past and Present*, 42 (1969), p.69–139.

Taylor, A. J. 'The Miners' Association of Great Britain and Ireland, 1842–1848: A Study in the Problem of 'Integration', *Economica*, n.s. 22 (1955), pp.45–60.

Tholfsen, Trygve. 'The Intellectual Origins of Mid-Victorian Stability', *Political Science Quarterly*, 86 (1971), pp.57–91.

Vicinus, Martha. 'The Literary Voices of an Industrial Town: 1810–1870', *The Victorian City*, eds. H. J. Dyos and Michael Wolff. London, 1973, II, pp.739–61.

———— 'The Study of Nineteenth-Century Working-Class Poetry', *The Politics of Literature*. eds. Louis Kampf and Paul Lauter. New York, pp.322–55.

Waller, Ross. 'Letters Addressed to Mrs. Gaskell by Celebrated Contemporaries, now in the possession of the John Rylands Library', *Bulletin of the John Rylands Library*, 19 (1935), pp.102–69.

Warburg, Jeremy. 'Poetry and Industrialism: Some Refractory Material in Nineteenth Century and Later English Verse', *MLR*, 53 (1958), pp.161–70.

Whittaker, W. G. 'The Folk-Music of Northern England'. *Collected Essays*, London, 1940, pp.1–64.

Webb, R. K. 'Literacy Among the Working Classes in Nineteenth Century Scotland', *Scottish Historical Review*, 33 (1954), 100–14.

——————— 'The Victorian Reading Public', *Universities Quarterly*, 12 (1957), pp.24–44.

——————— 'Working Class Readers in Early Victorian England', *English Historical Review*, 65 (1950), pp.333–57.

Woodcock, George. 'The English Hymn', *Folk: Review of People's Music*, I (1945), pp.2–9.

Records

Deep Lancashire. ed. A. L. Lloyd. Sung by Harry Boardman, Mike Harding, et. al. Topic 12T188.

The Iron Muse: A Panorama of Industrial Folk Music. Arranged by A. L. Lloyd, Topic 12T86.

Jack Elliott of Birtley: Songs and Stories of a Durham Miner. ed. Bill Leader. Sung by Jack Elliott. Leader LEA4001.

Steam Whistle Ballads: Industrial Songs Old and New. Sung by Ewen McColl. Topic 12T104.

Tommy Armstrong of Tyneside. ed. A. L. Lloyd. Sung by Lou Killen and Johnny Handle. Topic 12T189.

INDEX

Ab-o'-th-Yate, 193, 200-1, 202-3, 212
Ab-o'-th-Yate in Yankeeland, 200
Ab-o'-th-Yate insures his Life, 202-3
Ackroyd, George, 161
Advertising, 196, 197
Ainsworth, Harriet, 111
Airedale in Ancient Times, 151-2, 162-3, 164
Alcohol, see Drink
Almanacs, 193, 195, 196-201, 203, 207
American Civil War, 49, 222, 322n
Anderton, Henry, 183n
Anstey, F., 249
Antiquarianism, 186-7, 203
Antiquities of the Common People, 186
Appeal on Behalf of the Uneducated, 176-7
Aristocracy, 98, 126, 128, 247-8
Armstrong, Tommy, pl.22, 25, 83, 191, 192, 220-1, 309-11, 322n
Armstrong, William, 80
Art and Song, 237n
Ashton, Teddy, 234n
Athenaeum Club, 159
Australia, 37
Autobiography of Timothy Twinckle, 120-1
Aw Nivver can call Her my Wife, 218, 304-6
Aw'll Ne'er be Fuddled Agen, 212
Aw'm Lonely, an' Weary, an' Sad, 212
Axon, W.E.A., 204

Bain, W., 253
Bairnsla Foaks' Annual, 196, 197
Ballad of Sam Hall, 246
Bamford, Samuel, 11, 149, 160, 181-2n, 194, 204, 232n, 234n, 235n
Bang, Great Jack, 250-1
'Bards of the Tyne', 33-36, 82
Baring-Gould, S., 161
Barnes, William, 232n
Barnsley, 25, 107, 141, 171
Baron, John T., 192, 230-1, 237n

Bealey, R.R., 204
Beauty, 104-5, 106-7, 147, 151-5
Beesley, William, 80
Bell, John, 187
Bellwood, Bessie, pl.25, 252-3, 259, 262
Ben Brierley's Journal, 201-2
Bermondsey Star, 252
Besom Ben, 193, 194
Bewick, Thomas, 14
Billington, William, 141, 167, 212, 227
Binns, Isaac, 196
Birkbeck, George, 170
Bite Bigger, 306-7, 322n
Blackah, Thomas, 192, 196
Blackburn, 141
Blackburn Times, 230
Blacklegs, 66-8, 70, 71, 72-3, 83-4, 88n
Blacklisting, 71
Blackpool, 220, 233n
Blaize, Bishop, 12
Blaydon Races, 314-5, 323n
Blind Willie, see Purvis, Blind Willie
Bob Cranky, 33-4, 60, 72, 75, 187
Bob Cranky's 'Size Sunday, 34
Bobbin, Tim, 188, 232n
Bobbinwinder, Sally, 188-9, 196
Bolton, 201
Bolton Mechanics Institute, 201
Bonaparte, Louis, 204
Bonnie Pit Lads, 72, 299-300
Bourne, Henry, 186
Bowker, James, 222-5, 229
Bowton Loominary, 201, 234n
Bradford, 24, 141, 152, 155, 162, 169, 171, 199
Bradford Observer, 192
Bradfordian, 161-2
Bradshaw's Journal, pl.14, 160, 161, 197
Bramwich, John H., 302-3, 322n
Brierley, Ben, pl.16, 53, 190, 192-3, 194, 195, 196, 198, 200-3, 204, 205-7, 212, 215, 227, 228, 229, 231, 233n, 234n, 245

349